Teacher's Guide

Revised Framework Edition

Jeannie McNeill • Steve Williams

www.pearsonschools.co.uk

✓ Free online support
✓ Useful weblinks
✓ 24 hour online ordering

0845 630 33 33

9.2012

Part of Pearson

Heinemann is an imprint of Pearson Education Limited, a company incorporated in England and Wales, having its registered office at Edinburgh Gate, Harlow, Essex, CM20 2JE. Registered company number: 872828

www.pearsonschoolsandfecolleges.co.uk

Heinemann is a registered trademark of Pearson Education Limited.

First published 2010

14 13 12
10 9 8 7 6 5 4 3

British Library Cataloguing in Publication Data is available from the British Library on request.

ISBN 978 0 435041 229

Edited by Melanie Birdsall
Designed by Artistix
Typeset by Saxon Graphics Ltd, Artistix and TechType
Cover design by The Wooden Ark Studio
Cover photo © Powerstock
Printed in the UK by Ashford Colour Press Ltd

We would like to thank Julie Green and Jenny Gwynne for their contributions to this new edition.

Acknowledgements
Every effort has been made to contact copyright holders of material reproduced in this book. Any omissions will be rectified in subsequent printings if notice is given to the publishers.

CD-ROM
Important notice
This software is suitable for use on PCs only. It will not run on a Mac.

If the CD is loaded into a CD drive on a PC it should autorun automatically. If it does not, please click on RB32.exe (D:Echo1TGRFSoW.exe).

Active content
Your browser security may initially try to block elements of this product. If this problem occurs, please refer to the Troubleshooting document which can be found in the root of this CD (D:Echo1TGRFSoW/Troubleshooting.doc).

Installation instructions
This product may be installed to your local hard drive or to the network. Further instructions on how to do this are available from the main menu.

VLE Pack
The root of this CD contains the content from this product as a zipped SCORM 1.2 Content Pack to allow for convenient uploading to your VLE.

Please follow the usual instructions specific to your VLE system to upload this content pack.

Contents

Introduction

Echo is the tried, tested and successful 11–14 course for pupils starting German in Year 7. This New Edition has been updated in line with the Key Stage 3 Programme of Study for Modern Foreign Languages (2007) and the MFL Framework (2009). References to the Key Stage 3 Framework are also provided throughout. Echo is designed for pupils of a wide range of ability, providing differentiated activities throughout the course, with parallel books in Year 9.

Teaching Foundation Subjects MFL and the MFL Framework (2009) using *Echo*

Framework objectives

All the ***framework objectives*** for Year 7 are covered in Echo 1. At least two opportunities for each objective are identified.

Details of where the objectives are covered are given:

a in the Framework Overview grid on page 5 of this Teacher's Guide to help you with your **long-term planning;**

b in the Teacher's Guide in the overview grids at the beginning of each chapter (e.g. page 16) to help you with your **medium-term planning:**

c in the Teacher's Guide in the overview boxes at the start of each teaching unit to help with your **short-term i.e. lesson planning.**

In addition, all activities in the Pupil's Book are cross-referenced to the MFL Framework, to allow you to visit the teaching objectives at different points in the course if you wish. The references are given in the Teacher's Guide at the start of each activity.

The CD-ROM which accompanies this Teacher's Guide provides a customisable scheme of work that includes coverage of the 2009 Framework.

Lesson starters

Two starters are provided for each unit of the Pupil's Book in the Teacher's Guide, the first at the beginning of every unit, the second approximately half-way through the unit at the point when a second lesson is likely to begin. Most of them are simple ideas designed to focus pupils' attention and to promote engagement and challenge. They allow you to recap on previous knowledge or prepare the pupils for new language to be learnt in the unit. Some of the activities have an accompanying worksheet in the Resource & Assessment File.

Plenaries

Every unit in the Pupil's Book ends with a plenary session. Again, these are simple ideas described in the Teacher's Guide. They aim to draw out the key learning points. Pupils are actively involved and are expected to demonstrate and explain what they have learnt in the unit. They identify links with what the pupils have learnt so far and what they will learn later in the course.

Skills development

Throughout the Pupil's Book, Resource & Assessment File, and Workbooks, there are **learning skills** tip boxes as well as activities and worksheets specifically designed to challenge the pupils to think about the language they are learning, the skills required to learn and how to improve those skills.

Thinking skills

In addition, the Pupil's Book, Teacher's Guide, Workbooks and Resource & Assessment File contain specific activities and ideas to develop **thinking skills,** encouraging pupils to engage with language and use their brains in ways that are not traditionally associated with language learning, for example through categorising, lateral thinking and deduction.

Assessment for Learning

Pupils can be assessed formally at the end of every chapter using the *Kontrollen* in the Resource & Assessment File. There is also an end-of-year *Kontrolle 7.* All the tests are matched to the National Curriculum Attainment Target levels. Pupils have the opportunity to reach National Curriculum Level 5 by the end of *Echo 1.* Lower-ability pupils who do not progress beyond Levels 1 and 2 can still be formally assessed throughout the whole year. The pattern of assessment is as follows:

Kapitel 1	Levels 1 – 2
Kapitel 2	Levels 1 – 3
Kapitel 3	Levels 1 – 3
Kapitel 4	Levels 1 – 4
Kapitel 5	Levels 1 – 4
Kapitel 6	Levels 1 – 5
End-of-year	Levels 1 – 5

Opportunities for Assessment for Learning:

- At the end of every third unit in each chapter there is a *Mini-Test,* a checklist of what the pupils have learnt so far in the chapter.
- The *Lernzieltest* at the end of each chapter provides the longer checklist of "I can do"

statements. These appear in the Resource & Assessment File so that pupils can keep a handy record of their progress.

- *Mein Fortschritt* pages in the Workbooks and the Resource & Assessment File allow pupils to record their National Curriculum level in each Attainment Target and set themselves improvement targets for the next chapter.
- The Workbooks and the Resource & Assessment File both contain the National Curriculum level descriptors in pupil-friendly language to help pupils with their target-setting.
- The plenary sessions focus on what the pupils have learnt in the units and invite pupils to identify key learning points and links with previous learning.

Echo 1 Framework Objectives (Year 7) long-term plan

Framework objective		
1.1/Y7 Listening – gist and detail	Chapter 3, Unit 2	Chapter 3, Unit 4
1.2/Y7 Listening – unfamiliar language	Chapter 5, Unit 6	Chapter 6, Unit 6
1.3/Y7 Listening – (a) interpreting intonation and tone 1.3/Y7 Speaking – (b) using intonation and tone	Chapter 2, Unit 2 Chapter 2, Unit 2	Chapter 5, Unit 1 Chapter 5, Unit 1
1.4/Y7 Speaking – (a) social and classroom language 1.4/Y7 Speaking – (b) using prompts	Chapter 1, Unit 3 Chapter 5, Unit 1	Chapter 3, Unit 1 Chapter 6, Unit 3
1.5/Y7 Speaking – (a) presenting 1.5/Y7 Speaking – (b) expression/non-verbal techniques	Chapter 3 *Mehr* Chapter 3 *Mehr*	Chapter 5, Unit 2 Chapter 5, Unit 2
2.1/Y7 Reading – main points and detail	Chapter 4, Unit 5	Chapter 5, Unit 5
2.2/Y7 Reading – (a) unfamiliar language 2.2/Y7 Reading – (b) text selection	Chapter 3, Unit 5 Chapter 5 *Mehr* or teachers can provide alternative texts	Chapter 5 *Mehr* Chapter 4 *Mehr*
2.3/Y7 Reading – text features	Chapter 1 *Mehr*	Chapter 4, Unit 4
2.4/Y7 Writing – (a) sentences and texts as models 2.4/Y7 Writing – (b) building text	Chapter 3, Unit 3 Chapter 2, Unit 5	Chapter 4, Unit 4 Chapter 4, Unit 1
2.5/Y7 Writing – different text types	Chapter 5 *Mehr*	Chapter 6, Unit 6
3.1/Y7 Culture – aspects of everyday life	Chapter 1 *Mehr*	Chapter 4 *Mehr*
3.2/Y7 Culture – (a) young people: interests/opinions 3.2/Y7 Culture – (b) challenging stereotypes	Chapter 2, Unit 3 Chapter 3, Unit 6	Chapter 3, Unit 6 Chapter 6, Unit 5
4.1/Y7 Language – letters and sounds	Chapter 1, Unit 1	Chapter 1, Unit 4
4.2/Y7 Language – high frequency words	Chapter 1, Unit 1	Chapter 1, Unit 2
4.3/Y7 Language – gender and plurals	Chapter 1, Unit 4 Chapter 3, Unit 2	Chapter 2, Unit 5 Chapter 6, Unit 2
4.4/Y7 Language – sentence formation	Chapter 1, Unit 5	Chapter 2 *Mehr*
4.5/Y7 Language – (a) present tense verbs 4.7/Y7 Language – (a) future using present tense 4.5/Y7 Language – (a) set phrases about the past 4.5/Y7 Language – (b) modal verbs	Chapter 2, Unit 4 Chapter 4 *Mehr* Chapter 5, Unit 6 Chapter 4, Unit 6	Chapter 5, Unit 3 Chapter 6, Unit 6 Chapter 6, Unit 1
4.6/Y7 Language – (a) questions 4.6/Y7 Language – (b) negatives	Chapter 1, Unit 6 Chapter 2, Unit 6	Chapter 4, Unit 2 Chapter 5, Unit 2
5.1 Strategies – patterns	Chapter 1, Unit 5	Chapter 5, Unit 4
5.2 Strategies – memorising	Chapter 1, Unit 2	Chapter 6, Unit 2
5.3 Strategies – English/other languages	Chapter 2, Unit 1	Chapter 6, Unit 5
5.4 Strategies – working out meaning	Chapter 2, Unit 1	Chapter 3, Unit 6
5.5 Strategies – reference materials	Chapter 4, Unit 2	Chapter 5 *Mehr*
5.6 Strategies – reading aloud	Chapter 2, Unit 6	Chapter 6, Unit 4
5.7 Strategies – planning and preparing	Chapter 2, Unit 6	Chapter 3 *Mehr*
5.8 Strategies – evaluating and improving	Chapter 4, Unit 3	Chapter 6, Unit 3

Differentiation

Echo 1 and *Echo 2* each provide one book for the whole ability range. The range is catered for in the following ways:

- Differentiated activities at a range of AT levels throughout the Pupil's Book.
- Ideas in the Teacher's Guide for simplifying and extending the Pupil's Book activities.
- A *Mehr* unit at the end of every chapter contains longer reading and listening passages to provide opportunities for extension work.
- The *Lesen/Schreiben* section at the back of the book provides extra reading and writing activities at reinforcement and extension levels.
- The Workbooks are differentiated at two levels: reinforcement (*Übungsheft A*) and extension (*Übungsheft B*).

Echo 1 takes pupils up to Level 5 of the National Curriculum and *Echo 2* takes pupils up to Level 6. *Echo 3* is differentiated by means of parallel books. *Echo 3 Grün* covers National Curriculum Levels 1–5. *Echo 3 Rot* covers National Curriculum Levels 4–7.

Grammar

Grammar is fully integrated into the teaching sequence in *Echo* to ensure that pupils have the opportunity to learn thoroughly the underlying structures of the German language. The key grammar points are presented in the *Echo-Detektiv* boxes in the Pupil's Book, with short explanations. Fuller explanations and practice activities are provided in the *Grammatik* section at the back of the Pupil's Book. In addition, there are worksheets in the Resource & Assessment File which specifically focus on grammar.

Grammar points explained and practised in Echo 1:

1 Nouns
Gender
Singular/Plural

2 Articles and cases
The definite article
The indefinite article
The nominative
The accusative
The dative
The negative article (*kein*)
Possessive adjectives

3 Adjectives

4 Pronouns
Nominative pronouns
It
Man
Du and *Sie*

5 Verbs
The infinitive
Regular verbs (present)
Irregular verbs (present)
Sein and *haben* (present)
Present tense for future plans
Talking about the past (*war*)

6 Word order
Normal word order
Verb as second idea
Word order with infinitives

7 Questions
Without question words
With question words

8 *Es gibt*

9 *Gern*

10 Negatives with *nicht*

11 Extras
Numbers
Days
Dates
Times

List of grammar worksheets (Grammatik) *in the Resource & Assessment File*

Resource & Assessment File	Grammar	Teacher's Guide
Ch. 1 Arbeitsblatt 1.4	Saying 'the' and 'a'	p.30
Ch. 1 Arbeitsblatt 1.5	*Haben* and *sein*	p.31
Ch. 2 Arbeitsblatt 2.4	Regular verbs	p.58
Ch. 2 Arbeitsblatt 2.5	Accusative: *eine / eine / ein*	p.61
Ch. 2 Arbeitsblatt 3.2	Plural forms	p.83
Ch. 3 Arbeitsblatt 3.4	*Haben* and *sein*	p.88
Ch. 3 Arbeitsblatt 3.5	Adjectives	p.91
Ch. 4 Arbeitsblatt 4.2	Regular and irregular verbs	p.114
Ch. 4 Arbeitsblatt 4.4	Questions	p.114
Ch. 5 Arbeitsblatt 5.2	*Kein* (accusative)	p.143
Ch. 5 Arbeitsblatt 5.4	Word order (verb second)	p.146
Ch. 5 Arbeitsblatt 5.6	Talking about the past	p.153
Ch. 6 Arbeitsblatt 6.6	Talking about the future	p.183

The components

- Pupil's Book
- Audio CDs
- Workbooks
- Resource & Assessment File
- Teacher's Guide
- Flashcards
- Echo Elektro 1 Teacher Presentation Package
- Echo Elektro 1 Pupil Activity Package

Pupil's Book

The Pupil's Book consists of six chapters, sub-divided as follows:

- Six double-page core units. These units contain the core material in all four skills that must be taught to ensure that all the key language and grammar is covered in Year 7.
- *Lernzieltest* – a checklist of "I can do" statements allowing the pupils to keep a check on their progress as part of assessment for learning (see "Teaching Foundation Subjects MFL" above).
- *Wiederholung* – optional revision activities that can be used preceding the end-of-chapter *Lernzieltest* in the Resource & Assessment File.
- One optional two-page extension unit, *Mehr*.
- *Wörter* – two pages of chapter word lists for vocabulary learning and revision plus a *Strategie* tip box to help pupils acquire the skills they need to learn vocabulary more effectively.

At the back of the Pupil's Book there are three further sections:

- *Lesen/Schreiben* – self-access differentiated reading and writing activities. *Lesen/Schreiben A* contains reinforcement activities for lower-ability and *Lesen/Schreiben B* extension activities for higher-ability pupils. These are ideal for use as homework.
- *Grammatik* – the grammar reference and practice section.
- *Wortschatz* – a comprehensive German–English word list, a shorter English–German word list and a list of instructions covered in the Pupil's Book.

Audio CDs

There are three audio CDs for *Echo 1*. The material includes dialogues, interviews and songs recorded by native speakers, as well as activities designed for pronunciation practice.

Workbooks (New Edition)

There are two parallel Workbooks to accompany *Echo 1*, one for reinforcement (*Übungsheft A*) and one for extension (*Übungsheft B*). The Workbooks fulfil a number of functions:

- They provide enjoyable self-access reading and writing activities to consolidate the language learnt in each unit.
- They give extra practice in grammar and thinking skills with integrated activities throughout the Workbooks.
- Revision pages at the end of each chapter (*Wiederholung*) help pupils revise what they have learnt during the chapter.
- Chapter word lists (*Wörter*) with English translations are invaluable for language-learning homeworks.
- *Mein Fortschritt* pages at the end of each chapter allow pupils to record their National Curriculum level in each Attainment Target and set themselves improvement targets.
- National Curriculum level descriptors in pupil-friendly language allow pupils to see what they must do to progress up through the National Curriculum levels.

Resource & Assessment File

The Resource & Assessment File is organised into chapters for ease of use. It comes with an audio CD and worksheets on a customisable CD-ROM.

Worksheets (*Arbeitsblätter*) include:

- Lesson Starter sheets to accompany some of the lesson starter suggestions in the Teacher's Notes.
- Learning Skills sheets designed to help pupils become effective and independent language learners.
- Thinking Skills sheets.
- Grammar sheets (*Grammatik*). Page 6 of this Teacher's Guide shows where these sheets fit into the scheme of work.
- Chapter word lists (*Wörter*) in a photocopiable format.

Assessment pages:

- *Lernzieltest*: "I can do" checklist for self-assessment and/or peer-assessment.
- *Kontrollen*: end-of-chapter (and end-of-year) tests for formal assessment.
- *Mein Fortschritt*: target-setting sheets to allow pupils to record their National Curriculum level in each Attainment Target and set themselves improvement targets for the next chapter.
- National Curriculum levels: National Curriculum level descriptors in pupil-friendly language.
- The listening test material is provided on an audio CD with the file.

Teacher's Guide (New Edition)

The Teacher's Guide contains:

- A customisable scheme of work on CD-ROM.
- A long-term plan grid for the teaching objectives of the new MFL Framework (2009).
- Overview grids for each chapter to help with medium-term planning.
- Mapping of activities to the 2007 National Curriculum Programmes of Study.
- Clear teaching notes for short-term planning together with full audio transcript.
- Suggestions for extra activities for reinforcement and extension.
- Indications of how the course offers cross-curricular opportunities (Citizenship, English, ICT, Mathematics).
- Ideas for using the flashcards and other games in the classroom.

Flashcards

There are 96 full-colour single-sided flashcards with the name of the object on the reverse. They can be used for presentation of new language or practice. A full list of the *Echo 1* flashcards can be found on page 11. Here are some imaginative methods of using the flashcards to help pupils learn and memorise new vocabulary more effectively.

Method 1
Show one card, say the word or phrase and pupils repeat in fun and varied ways (loud/soft, high/low etc.)

Use four cards. Show one that you've just used and give a choice of two words. Pupils say the correct word. Keep going until they know about eight.

Method 2
Once you've been through about 6–9 cards and they've heard the words a few times, stick a selection on the board, numbered. Say one in German; a pupil gives you the number. Then say the number; a pupil gives you the word. This can then be done from pupil to pupil.

You could then read out an easy sum, but use words instead of the numbers (e.g. *ein Hund und eine Katze, macht …?*) The pupils calculate the answers and give a third word, instead of a number.

Method 3
Put nine cards on the board, in rows of three, divide the class into two teams and play noughts and crosses. Pupils choose a card and say the German, the aim being to get three in a row.

Method 4
Stick a series of cards on the board. Two pupils stand by the board. You or another pupil say a word. The two pupils race to be the first to point to the correct card.

Method 5
Guess the card. You conceal a card behind your back (look at it quickly first). The pupils have to guess which one it is by saying the words.

Method 6
After term 1 use the cards to elicit phrases, negatives, opinions. Aim for longer sentences incorporating the word.

Echo Elektro 1 Teacher Presentation Package

The Teacher Presentation Package is designed for use with the interactive whiteboard or data-projector and screen. It offers:

- presentations of new language
- grammar sections
- whole-class games
- video activities
- audio activities
- texts ready to read and adapt on screen.

It is divided into ready-made lesson sequences that are aligned with the units in the Pupil's Book, cutting preparation time to a minimum.

Echo Elektro 1 Pupil Activity Package

The Pupil Activity Package provides differentiated practice of the language taught, in all four skills. It is ideal for independent use in the computer suite. Scores can be recorded and tracked so that both pupils and teachers have a clear idea of progress being made.

Each sequence consists of the following activity types:

- Listening
- Vocabulary learning
- Listening and speaking
- Word and sentence work, e.g. phonetic practice, sentence building
- Grammar
- Reading and writing.

Integrating ICT

Suggestions for ICT activities have been included in the Teacher's Guide. The following grid shows the location and nature of these activities.

Unit reference	Activity type
Chapter 1, Unit 3	Powerpoint presentation
Chapter 1, Unit 6	Using a spreadsheet to write up survey results
Chapter 2, Unit 1	Using a spreadsheet to write up survey results
Chapter 2, Unit 4	Creating a tuck shop price list with clip art
Chapter 2, Unit 6	Planning and writing a mini webpage
Chapter 3, Unit 2	Creating a poster about pets
Chapter 3, Unit 6	Word-processing, writing an email
Chapter 3, *Mehr*	Powerpoint presentation or poster about a celebrity
Chapter 4, Unit 3	Importing graphics to illustrate a text
Chapter 4, Unit 4	Word-processing a letter and importing graphics to illustrate it
Chapter 5, Unit 2	Creating the plan of an ideal house
Chapter 5, Unit 2	Using a spreadsheet to write up survey results
Chapter 6, Unit 2	Word-processing
Chapter 6, Unit 6	Word-processing texts and importing graphics

Games and other teaching suggestions

Reading aloud

1 Set a challenge – 'I bet no-one can read this without making a single mistake' – or ask a volunteer pupil to predict how many mistakes they will make before having a go. See if they can do better than their prediction.
2 Texts could be read round the class with pupils simply reading up to a full-stop and then passing it on to someone else in the room.
3 You can also read texts, pause and the pupils have to say the next word.

Reading follow-up

1 You read aloud and stop for pupils to complete the word or sentence.
2 You read aloud and insert the word 'beep' for pupils to complete.
3 You read aloud and make a mistake (either in pronunciation or saying the wrong word). Pupils put up their hands as soon as they spot a mistake.
4 *Hot-potato:* pupils read a bit and pass it on quickly to someone who may not be expecting it.
5 *Marathon:* one pupil reads aloud until (s)he makes a mistake. Pupils have to put up their hand as soon as they hear a mistake. The second pupil then takes over, reading *from the beginning* and trying to get further than the previous one.
6 *Random reading:* you read a phrase at random and the pupils have to say the next bit.

Mime activities

Mimes are a motivating way to help pupils to learn words.

1 You say a word and the pupils mime. This could be done as a knockout, starting with six volunteers at the front who mime to the class as you say each word. The ones who do the wrong mime or who are slow to react are knocked out. Impose a 2-minute time limit.
2 A pupil says a word or phrase and you mime it – but only if the pupil says it correctly.
3 You mime and pupils say the word or phrase.
4 One person goes out of the room. The rest of the class all mime one characteristic. The volunteer comes back into the room and has to guess the adjective that the class are miming.
5 *(Class knock-down)* As above but this time everyone in the class can choose different qualities to mime. The volunteer returns to the room with everyone doing their own mime. The volunteer points to each pupil and says the word or phrase. If correct, the pupil sits down. This works well as a timed or team activity. The aim is to sit your team down as quickly as possible.
6 A version of charades. This is a good activity at the end of the lesson. Organise two teams, A and B. Have words or phrases on separate cards. Put the cards in a pile at the front. A volunteer from Team A comes to the front, picks up the first card and mimes it. Anyone from Team A can put up their hand and say the word. If correct, the volunteer picks up the next card and mimes it. The aim is to get through the whole list as quickly as possible. Note down the time for Team A. Then Team B tries to beat their time.

Exploiting the songs

1 Pupils sing along. You fade out certain parts whilst they continue. When most of them know the song quite well, you can pause the recording whilst they give you the next line from memory. Then try the chorus by heart. Then try a few verses completely from memory.
2 You could try the 'pick up song' game – you fade the song after a few lines, the pupils continue singing and then you fade the song in again towards the end.

Writing follow-up (Text dissection)

1 Display some anagrams of key words from the text and ask pupils to write them correctly. You will need to prepare these in advance and check carefully. Award points for correct answers.

2 Display some jumbled phrases from a text (words in the wrong order), e.g. *ich am spiele Montag Computer am.* Pupils rewrite the phrase correctly in their books or on the board.
3 Display a word or phrase in German. See if pupils can spot a mistake and correct it. This can also be done as 'spot the missing word' or 'spot the word that is in the wrong place'.
4 *Mini dictation.* Read four or five short sentences in German for pupils to write out. Again, this could be a group exercise.
5 If the group is good, give them phrases in English to write down in German.

Vocabulary treasure hunt

1 Find the word for … .
2 Find (3) opinions.

Grammar treasure hunt

1 Find (3) adjectives.
2 Find (2) feminine adjectives.
3 Find a verb in the *wir* form.
4 Find a plural noun.
5 Find a negative.

Other games

Wounded soldier

This game can be used to consolidate asking and answering questions on any topic. Draw a soldier on the board and ask pupils to stand in a circle or horseshoe. You ask a question and throw a ball or soft toy to each pupil in turn. He/She must answer as quickly as possible and throw it back to you. (More able pupils could ask the next question themselves, before throwing.) This can be played against the clock. If a pupil does not answer the question correctly, then the soldier loses a leg, an arm or an eye (rub these out on the board) until a correct answer is given.

Wer hat was?

This activity is useful for practising closed questions. Send one pupil out of the room and distribute objects or pictures to some members of the class. The whole class then hide their hands under the desk. The pupil returns and has one minute to find as many objects or pictures as possible by asking a specific question to individual pupils, e.g. *Hast du ein Lineal?* Pupils respond with a full sentence.

Pupils must only hand over the card if the question has been asked accurately and if the answer is yes. The pupil guessing can only continue when his/her question has been answered.

Get your own back

This can be used to practise items of vocabulary or whole phrases. Ask pupils to write or draw (on a piece of paper) a correct sentence using, for example, a particular high-frequency word, such as *mein.* Pupils then pair up with someone else, exchange information and pieces of paper. They then find a new partner and exchange the new information with them. This continues until the pupils get their original papers back.

Sounds hangman

This can be played to practise spelling words with particular sounds in them. Say the word and write up a dash for each letter. Pupils then isolate the sounds in the word and tell you which letters make that sound and where they go (e.g. for *Schwester*: the sound *sch* is spelled s-c-h and that's the first three letters of the word).

Pass the bomb

This can be played to practise items of high-frequency language. Divide the class into two teams. A soft toy or sponge ball is used as the bomb. Write a phrase on the board (e.g. *ich habe*); the pupil holding the toy or ball must make a sentence using that verb. He/She then throws the bomb to someone on the other team, who must make a different sentence using the same phrase. This continues until the bomb goes off. The team holding the bomb when it goes off is given a penalty point. You should allocate a certain amount of time for each verb ranging from 30 to 60 seconds before the bomb goes off. To show when the time has run out, make a noise or set a watch alarm.

Symbols used in the teaching notes

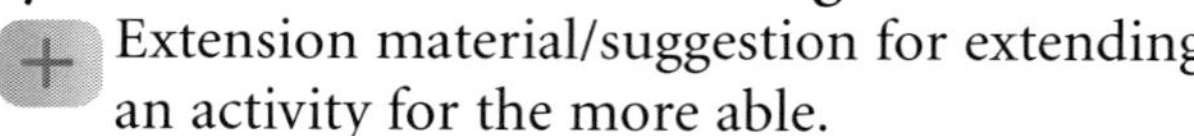

+ Extension material/suggestion for extending an activity for the more able.

R Reinforcement material/suggestion for simplifying an activity for the less able

Thinking skills activities in the *Übungsheft A/B*, and *Arbeitsblätter* in the Resource & Assessment File, as well as against activities in the teaching notes.

ICT ICT activity

List of flashcards

1 Deutschland	26 Mathe	51 laut	76 der Dachboden
2 England	27 Naturwissenschaften	52 unpünktlich	77 der Keller
3 Schottland	28 Werken	53 launisch	78 der Balkon
4 Wales	29 Kunst	54 musikalisch	79 der Garten
5 Irland	30 Musik	55 schüchtern	80 die Garage
6 Frankreich	31 Theater	56 lustig	81 mit dem Auto
7 Österreich	32 Erdkunde	57 faul	82 mit dem Zug
8 die Schweiz	33 Geschichte	58 Tennis	83 mit dem Bus
9 der Bleistift	34 Sport	59 Fußball	84 mit dem Taxi
10 das Buch	35 der Orangensaft	60 Basketball	85 mit der U-Bahn
11 die Diskette	36 die Cola	61 Volleyball	86 mit der Straßenbahn
12 das Etui	37 das Wasser	62 Federball	87 mit dem Flugzeug
13 das Heft	38 das Brötchen	63 Tischtennis	88 zu Fuß
14 der Klebstift	39 der Apfel	64 Rugby	89 Hamburger
15 der Kuli	40 die Orange	65 reiten	90 Bratwurst
16 das Lineal	41 die Banane	66 schwimmen	91 Pizza
17 die Schere	42 Chips	67 angeln	92 Schaschlik
18 die Schultasche	43 Kuchen	68 wandern	93 Pommes
19 der Taschenrechner	44 Kekse	69 Snowboard fahren	94 Limonade
20 das Wörterbuch	45 Schokolade	70 das Wohnzimmer	95 Kaffee
21 Deutsch	46 Bonbons	71 das Esszimmer	96 Tee mit Zitrone / mit Milch
22 Englisch	47 freundlich	72 die Küche	
23 Französisch	48 intelligent	73 das Schlafzimmer	
24 Religion	49 sportlich	74 das Badezimmer	
25 Informatik	50 kreativ	75 die Toilette	

Personal Learning and Thinking Skills

The activities and contexts provided throughout the course offer a range of opportunities for pupils to apply skills from the six groups of the Personal Learning and Thinking Skills framework.

Personal Learning and Thinking skills	Examples in Echo 1
1 Independent enquirers	Pupil's Book activities throughout the course (e.g. Ch2 U6 ex 6 p35, Ch4 U4 ex 9 p67); ICT-based activities (e.g. ICT suggestions in the TG p9)
2 Creative thinkers	Regular activities developing skills strategies (how to improve listening/reading, etc.) (e.g. Ch3 U6 p53 tip box); Starters and Plenaries requiring pupils to apply logic and make connections (e.g. Ch3 U4 Starter 1 TG p87)
3 Reflective learners	Ongoing opportunities to assess work and identify areas for improvement (all *Mini-Tests* e.g. p47 PBk), all Plenaries (e.g. Ch5 U4 Plenary TG p149)
4 Team workers	Regular pair work activities (Ch2 U4 ex 3 & 6 pp30-31), and groupwork activities (Ch3 U3 ex 3 p101) including many Starters; regular peer assessment, including *Lernzieltest* pages at the end of each chapter (e.g. p18)
5 Self-managers	Ongoing advice on managing learning (e.g. *Strategie* p95 and all other *Strategie* boxes on the *Wörter* pages), including strategies to improve learning (e.g. Plenary Ch2 U1 TG p53)
6 Effective participators	Opportunities throughout the course for pupils to contribute (e.g. Ch3 U5 ex 8 p51), including presentations (e.g. Ch5 U2 ex 4 p81) and all Starters and Plenaries (e.g. Ch3 U1 Starter 2 TG p79 and Ch4 U1 Plenary TG p111)

Covering the Programmes of Study

1. Key concepts

There are a number of key concepts outlined in the **QCA Programmes of Study**, which underpin the study of languages. Pupils need to understand these concepts in order to deepen and broaden their knowledge, skills and understanding. These are addressed in all chapters of *Echo 1*, so are not included in the tables below, but are listed here for reference.

1.1 Linguistic competence
a developing the skills of listening, speaking, reading and writing in a range of situations and contexts
b applying linguistic knowledge and skills to understand and communicate effectively
1.2 Knowledge about language
a understanding how a language works and how to manipulate it
b recognising that languages differ but may share common grammatical, syntactical or lexical features
1.3 Creativity
a using familiar language for new purposes and in new contexts
b using imagination to express thoughts, ideas, experiences and feelings
1.4 Intercultural understanding
a appreciating the richness and diversity of other cultures
b recognising that there are different ways of seeing the world, and developing an international outlook

The tables below indicate where, in *Echo 1*, pupils have the opportunity to progress in the **Key processes**, **Range and content**, and **Curriculum opportunities** prescribed in the QCA Programmes of Study. For each area we have indicated where these appear in the core units of the Pupil's Book. There are further opportunities both in the Pupil's Book and the supplementary components. More detail is provided in the grids at the beginning of each chapter in this Teacher's Guide.

2. Key processes

These are the essential skills and processes in languages that pupils need to learn to make progress.

2.1 Developing language-learning strategies – pupils should be able to:	
a identify patterns in the target language	Chapter 1 Unit 3, Chapter 1 Unit 5, Chapter 1 Unit 6, Chapter 2 Unit 2, Chapter 4 Unit 5, Chapter 4 Unit 6, Chapter 6 Unit 6
b develop techniques for memorising words, phrases and spellings	Chapter 1 Unit 6, Chapter 2 Unit 1, Chapter 3 Unit 2
c use their knowledge of English or another language when learning the target language	Chapter 2 Unit 1, Chapter 4 Unit 1, Chapter 6 Unit 2
d use previous knowledge, context and other clues to work out the meaning of what they hear or read	Chapter 2 Unit 6, Chapter 3 Unit 6, Chapter 4 Unit 4
e use reference materials such as dictionaries appropriately and effectively	Chapter 4 Unit 2, Chapter 6 Unit 2
2.2 Developing language skills – pupils should be able to:	
a listen for gist or detail	Chapter 2 Unit 4, Chapter 3 Unit 1, Chapter 5 Unit 6
b skim and scan written texts for the main points or details	Chapter 2 Unit 4, Chapter 3 Unit 6, Chapter 5 Unit 6
c respond appropriately to spoken and written language	Chapter 2 Unit 6, Chapter 3 Unit 6, Chapter 5 Unit 4
d use correct pronunciation and intonation	Chapter 2 Unit 2, Chapter 3 Unit 3, Chapter 4 Unit 2, Chapter 4 Unit 3
e ask and answer questions	Chapter 1 Unit 6, Chapter 4 Unit 2, Chapter 5 Unit 1
f initiate and sustain conversations	Chapter 2 Unit 4, Chapter 5 Unit 1
g write clearly and coherently, including an appropriate level of detail	Chapter 2 Unit 6, Chapter 3 Unit 2, Chapter 4 Unit 4, Chapter 5 Unit 5, Chapter 6 Unit 2, Chapter 6 Unit 5, Chapter 6 Unit 6
h redraft their writing to improve accuracy and quality	Chapter 6 Unit 6

i re-use language that they have heard or read in their own speaking and writing	Chapter 2 Unit 2, Chapter 2 Unit 5, Chapter 3 Unit 3, Chapter 6 Unit 4, Chapter 6 Unit 6
j adapt language they already know in new contexts for different purposes	Chapter 4 Unit 3, Chapter 6 Unit 4, Chapter 6 Unit 6
k deal with unfamiliar language, unexpected responses and unpredictable situations	Chapter 2 Unit 1

3. Range and content

This section outlines the breadth of the subject on which teachers should draw when teaching the key concepts and key processes. The study of languages should include:

a the spoken and written form of the target language	All chapters
b the interrelationship between sounds and writing in the target language	Chapter 1 Unit 1, Chapter 1 Unit 4, Chapter 2 Unit 1, Chapter 4 Unit 4
c the grammar of the target language and how to apply it	Chapter 1 Unit 5, Chapter 2 Unit 4, Chapter 3 Unit 2, Chapter 3 Unit 4, Chapter 5 Unit 5
d a range of vocabulary and structures	Chapter 3 Unit 5, Chapter 4 Unit 3, Chapter 5 Unit 2
e learning about different countries and cultures	Chapter 5 Unit 1, Chapter 5 Unit 6, Chapter 6 Unit 1
f comparing pupils' own experiences and perspectives with those of people in countries and communities where the target language is spoken	Chapter 2 Unit 6, Chapter 5 Unit 2, Chapter 6 Unit 5

4. Curriculum opportunities

During the key stage pupils should be offered the following opportunities that are integral to their learning and enhance their engagement with the concepts, processes and content of the subject. The curriculum should provide opportunities for pupils to:

a hear, speak, read and write in the target language regularly and frequently within the classroom and beyond	All chapters
b communicate in the target language individually, in pairs, in groups and with speakers of the target language, including native speakers, where possible, for a variety of purposes	Chapter 1 Unit 6, Chapter 3 Unit 1, Chapter 4 Unit 1, Chapter 3 Unit 6
c use an increasing range of more complex language	Chapter 6 Unit 6
d make links with English at word, sentence and text level	Chapter 2 Unit 1, Chapter 4 Unit 1, Chapter 6 Unit 2
e use a range of resources, including ICT, for accessing and communicating information	Chapter 2 Unit 6, Chapter 3 *Mehr*
f listen to, read or view a range of materials, including authentic materials in the target language, both to support learning and for personal interest and enjoyment	Chapter 3 *Mehr*, Chapter 4 Unit 4
g use the target language in connection with topics and issues that are engaging and may be related to other areas of the curriculum	Chapter 2 Unit 4, Chapter 3 Unit 1, Chapter 3 Unit 6, Chapter 3 *Mehr*, Chapter 5 Unit 1

Solutions to *Grammatik* exercises (Pupil's Book pp. 124–135)

1
1 Garten – masculine (der), garden 2 Hemd – neuter (das), shirt 3 Jeans – feminine plural (die), jeans 4 Kaninchen – neuter (das), rabbit 5 Keks – masculine (der), biscuit 6 Küche – feminine (die), kitchen 7 Lineal – neuter (das), ruler 8 Schere – feminine (die), (pair of) scissors 9 Schlange – feminine (die), snake 10 Wasser – neuter (das), water

2
1 Äpfel 2 Bleistifte 3 Brüder 4 Disketten 5 Katzen 6 Hunde 7 Kaninchen 8 Kekse 9 Autos 10 Stühle

3
1 das Bett 2 das Brötchen 3 der Bruder 4 das Lineal 5 die Orange 6 der Saft

4
1 eine Schlange 2 eine Tante 3 ein Klebstift 4 ein Etui 5 eine Hose 6 ein Goldfisch

5
1 *Ich* finde Mathe langweilig. 2 *Marcus* hat kurze, lockige Haare. 3 *Mein Cousin* spielt Gitarre. 4 *Tanja* isst einen Apfel. 5 Hast *du* einen Bleistift für mich? 6 *Religion* beginnt um elf Uhr.

6
1 Der Kuli ist blau. 2 Sind die Jeans blau? 3 Die Schuhe sind lila. 4 Das Pferd ist groß und braun. 5 Die Schuluniform ist schwarz und rot. 6 Das Kaninchen ist weiß.

7
1 Sie isst *ein Brötchen.* 2 Ich habe *einen Bleistift.* 3 Hast du *eine Diskette*? 4 Ich trage *eine Jacke.* 5 Susi hat *ein Pferd.* 6 Ich habe *keine Haustiere.*

8
1 Ich habe einen Bleistift. 2 Hast du eine Diskette? 3 Ich trage einen Rock und ein Hemd. 4 Ich esse ein Brötchen. 5 Hast du einen Kuli für mich? 6 Ich habe einen Wellensittich.

9
1 because of 'auf' 3 because of 'zwischen' 6 because of 'in'

10
1 Beate hat keinen Computer. 2 Beate hat keine Gitarre. 3 Beate hat keinen Fernseher. 4 Beate hat keine Freunde. 5 Beate hat keine Jacke. 6 Beate hat keine Katzen.

11
1 your 2 my 3 his 4 your 5 her 6 my 7 his 8 your

12
1 Mein 2 Ihr 3 deine 4 Meine 5 ihr 6 dein 7 Mein 8 Sein

13
1 braune 2 bunt 3 schicke 4 intelligent 5 blaue 6 graue 7 intelligente 8 kräftig 9 schwierig 10 graue

14
1 Wir 2 Er 3 Sie 4 du 5 Ich

15
1 You can cycle. 2 Where can you play football? 3 You can go to the town hall. 4 Can you go to the cinema? 5 You can go by tram/take the tram.

16
1 du 2 Sie 3 du 4 du 5 Sie 6 Sie

17
essen, hören, gehen, haben, schwimmen, lesen, sein, trinken, wohnen, heißen

18
1 spiele 2 faulenzt 3 wohnt 4 gehen 5 Wohnen 6 Spielst 7 gehen 8 wohnen 9 hört 10 kochen

19
1 ich nehme 2 du schläfst 3 du siehst 4 er sieht 5 sie liest 6 du fährst 7 ich esse 8 er isst 9 sie schläft 10 ich schlafe

20
1 habe 2 Hast 3 Hat 4 haben 5 hast 6 hat

21
1 ist 2 bin 3 ist 4 sind 5 bist 6 sind

22
1 Ich fahre in zwei Wochen nach Irland. – I'm going to Ireland in two weeks.
2 Ich spiele am Wochenende Tischtennis. – I'm playing table tennis at the weekend.
3 Er geht morgen angeln. – He's going fishing tomorrow.
4 Wir kaufen nächste Woche einen Hund. – We're buying a dog next week.
5 Er fährt nächstes Jahr nach Amerika. – He's going to America next year.
6 Ich bleibe in den Sommerferien zu Hause. – I'm staying at home in the summer holidays.

23

1 I, yesterday, at the cinema 2 he, last week, in town 3 Simon, last year, in Austria 4 my cat, yesterday, in my room 5 My grandpa, last Monday, in the garden 6 Sarah, yesterday, in school

24

1 Ich habe zwei Schwestern. 2 Petra ist fünfzehn Jahre alt. 3 Meine Mutter hat blonde Haare. 4 Wir wohnen in einem Reihenhaus. 5 Geschichte ist mein Lieblingsfach *or* Mein Lieblingsfach ist Geschichte. 6 Mein Hund heißt Wuffi. 7 Ich sehe gern fern. 8 Meine Adresse ist Ludwigstraße achtzehn.

25

1 In meinem Zimmer habe ich einen Computer. 2 Deutsch ist mein Lieblingsfach. 3 Am Montag habe ich Geschichte. 4 Mathe finde ich schwierig. 5 In der Schule trage ich eine Jeans. 6 In ihrer Schultasche hat sie einen Apfel.

26

1 Man kann ins Kino gehen. 2 Man kann Tennis spielen. 3 Man kann mit dem Zug fahren. 4 Ich möchte Pommes essen. 5 Man kann Cola trinken. 6 Man kann in die Disko gehen.

27

1 Spielst du gern am Computer? 2 Ist Deutsch ihr Lieblingsfach? 3 Ist sie dreizehn Jahre alt? 4 Wohnt er in Leipzig? 5 Kann man mit der U-Bahn fahren? 6 Beginnt Kunst um elf Uhr? 7 Isst du gern Pommes? 8 Ist er groß und kräftig?

28

1 Who are you? *b* 2 Where are you? *e* 3 What are you like? *d* 4 How old are you? *c* 5 What's your favourite subject? *g* 6 When's your birthday? *a* 7 What's your address? *f* 8 When does break begin? *h*

29

1 Es gibt ein Kino. 2 Es gibt eine Kirche. 3 Es gibt einen Supermarkt. 4 Es gibt ein Verkehrsamt. 5 Es gibt einen Markt. 6 Es gibt einen Bahnhof.

30

1 Ich trinke gern Cola. 2 Wir sehen gern fern. 3 Ingo spielt gern Gitarre. 4 Chris fährt gern mit dem Bus. 5 Anke hört gern Musik. 6 Ich spiele gern Tischtennis. 7 Gehst du gern schwimmen? 8 Fährt sie gern Rad? 9 Gehst du gern in den Jugendklub? 10 Mein Freund Alex trägt gern Sportschuhe.

31

1 Wir spielen nicht gern Tennis. 2 Man kann nicht mit dem Bus fahren. 3 Deutsch ist nicht mein Lieblingsfach. 4 Mein Bruder ist nicht sehr intelligent. 5 Ich trinke nicht gern Wasser. 6 Sie wohnt nicht in Birmingham. 7 Ich kann nicht Snowboard fahren. 8 Petra und Susi faulenzen nicht gern.

32

1 am zehnten September 2 am ersten Dezember 3 am dreiundzwanzigsten April 4 am achten Mai 5 am neunzehnten Februar 6 am dritten November 7 am fünfzehnten März 8 am neunundzwanzigsten Oktober 9 am vierten Juni 10 am einundzwanzigsten Juli

33

1 Es ist sieben Uhr zehn. 2 Es ist neun Uhr. 3 Um elf Uhr fünfzig. 4 Um ein Uhr fünfzehn. 5 Es ist zwei Uhr dreiundzwanzig. 6 Um vier Uhr fünfundfünfzig. 7 Um acht Uhr fünf. 8 Es ist drei Uhr neunundreißig. 9 Um neun Uhr zwanzig. 10 Es ist zwölf Uhr sechs.

1 Hallo!

Unit Learning targets	Key framework objectives	NC levels and PoS coverage	Grammar and key language	Skills
1 Wie heißt du? (pp. 6–7) • Introducing yourself • Learning how to use some everyday expressions	4.1/Y7 Language – letters and sounds 4.2/Y7 Language – high frequency words	NC levels 1–3 2.1b memorising 2.2a listen for gist 2.2d pronunciation and intonation 2.2e ask and answer questions 2.2i re-use language they have met 3b sounds and writing 4b communicate in pairs, etc.	*Wie heißt du?* *Ich heiße … . Und du?* *Hallo!* *Guten Tag!* *Tschüs!* *Auf Wiedersehen!* *Wie geht's?* *Gut, danke.* *Nicht schlecht, danke.* *Nicht so gut.* *Und dir?*	Pronunciation: *ß* and *w* Social conventions
2 Eins, zwei, drei … (pp. 8–9) • Counting to 19 • Understanding what your teacher says in class	4.2/Y7 Language – high frequency words 5.2 Strategies – memorising	NC levels 1–2 2.1b memorising 2.2a listen for gist 2.2e ask and answer questions 3b sounds and writing 3c apply grammar 4b communicate in pairs, etc.	Irregular verb *sein: ich bin, du bist* Cardinal numbers 0–19 *Wie alt bist du?* *Ich bin … Jahre alt.* *Ruhe, bitte!* *Hört zu!* *Macht das Heft auf!* *Macht das Buch auf! Seite …* *Macht das Buch zu!* *Steht auf!* *Setzt euch!* *Alles einpacken!* *Jetzt Partnerarbeit!* *Schreibt es auf!*	Responding to instructions
3 Ich wohne in Deutschland (pp. 10–11) • Saying where you live • Using verbs with *ich* and *du*	1.4/Y7 Speaking – (a) social and classroom language	NC levels 1–3 2.1a identify patterns 2.2a listen for gist 2.2b skim and scan 2.2d pronunciation and intonation 2.2e ask and answer questions 2.2g write clearly and coherently 2.2i re-use language they have met 3b sounds and writing 3c apply grammar	Regular verb *wohnen: ich wohne, du wohnst* *Wo wohnst du?* *Ich wohne in England, Schottland, Wales, Irland, Deutschland, Österreich, der Schweiz.*	Pronunciation: *sch/ch* Reviewing progress
4 Das Alphabet (pp. 12–13) • Spelling in German • Using the definite article (*der, die, das*) to say 'the'	4.1/Y7 Language – letters and sounds 4.3/Y7 Language – gender	NC levels 1–3 2.2d pronunciation and intonation 2.2e ask and answer questions 3b sounds and writing 3c apply grammar 4b communicate in pairs, etc.	Noun gender Definite article in nominative Capital letters for nouns Letters of the alphabet *der Apfel, die Banane, der Computer, der Detektiv, das Eis, der Fußball, die Gitarre, das Haus, die Idee, der Joghurt, die Kamera, die Lampe, die Milch, die Nummer, die Orange, die Party, das Quiz, die Ratte, die Schule, das T-Shirt, die Uniform, der Vater, die Wespe, das Xylophon, die Yacht, der Zoo* *Wie schreibt man … ?* *Das Buch ist rot, blau, gelb, braun, grün, orange, schwarz, weiß, grau.*	Spelling Asking for help

Unit Learning targets	Key framework objectives	NC levels and PoS coverage	Grammar and key language	Skills
5 Hast du einen Bleistift? (pp. 14–15) • Describing what you have in your school bag • Using the indefinite article (*ein, eine*) to say 'a'	**4.4/Y7** Language – sentence formation **5.1** Strategies – patterns	NC levels 1–3 **2.1a** identify patterns **2.1b** memorising **2.2a** listen for gist **2.2b** skim and scan **2.2e** ask and answer questions **2.2i** re-use language they have met **3b** sounds and writing **3c** apply grammar **4b** communicate in pairs, etc.	Indefinite article in nominative and accusative *der Bleistift, das Buch, die Diskette, das Etui, das Heft, der Klebstift, der Kuli, das Lineal, die Schere, die Schultasche, der Taschenrechner, das Wörterbuch* *Das ist ein / eine / ein …* *Hast du einen / eine / ein … für mich?* *Ja, ich habe einen / eine / ein … .* *Nein.*	
6 Wann hast du Geburtstag? (pp. 16–17) • Learning the numbers from 20 to 69 • Saying when your birthday is	**4.6/Y7** Language – (a) questions	NC levels 1–3 **2.1a** identify patterns **2.1b** memorising **2.2a** listen for gist **2.2e** ask and answer questions **2.2g** write clearly and coherently **2.2i** re-use language they have met **3b** sounds and writing **3c** apply grammar **4b** communicate in pairs, etc.	Question words: *wie, wo, wann, was* Irregular verb *haben: ich habe, du hast* Cardinal numbers 20–69 *Wann hast du Geburtstag?* *Ich habe am … … Geburtstag.* *ersten, zweiten, dritten … einunddreißigsten* *Januar, Februar, März, April, Mai, Juni, Juli, August, September, Oktober, November, Dezember*	
Lernzieltest und Wiederholung (pp. 18–19) • Pupils' checklist and practice test		NC levels 1–3 **2.2b** skim and scan **3c** apply grammar **3d** use a range of vocab/structures **4b** communicate in pairs, etc.		
Mehr (pp. 20–21) • Extension material	**2.3/Y7** Reading – text features **3.1/Y7** Culture – aspects of everyday life	NC levels 3–4 **2.1d** previous knowledge **2.2a** listen for gist **2.2b** skim and scan **2.2e** ask and answer questions **2.2j** adapt previously-learned language **3c** apply grammar **3d** use a range of vocab/structures	Revision of question formation Regular verb *kaufen: du kaufst* *die Schere, der Klebstift, das Wörterbuch, die CD* *… Euro* *Kaufst du einen Bleistift / eine Diskette / ein Wörterbuch? Ja. Nein.* *Wann hast du Geburtstag?* *Ich habe am … … Geburtstag.* *Wo wohnst du?* *Ich wohne in …* *Wie alt bist du?* *Ich bin … Jahre alt.* *Wie heißt du?* *Ich heiße …*	Reading a longer text for gist
Extra (pp. 112–113) • Self-access reading and writing at two levels		NC levels 1–4 **2.2e** ask and answer questions **3c** apply grammar **3d** use a range of vocab/structures		

1 Wie heißt du?

Learning targets

- Introducing yourself
- Learning how to use some everyday expressions

Key framework objectives

4.1/Y7 Language – letters and sounds
4.2/Y7 Language – high frequency words

Grammar

ich heiße, du heißt

Key language

Wie heißt du?
Ich heiße .... Und du?
Hallo!
Guten Tag!
Tschüs!
Auf Wiedersehen!
Wie geht's?
Gut, danke.
Nicht schlecht, danke.
Nicht so gut.
Und dir?

High-frequency words

wie
ich, du
gut
und
danke
nicht
schlecht
so

Pronunciation

w and *ß*

Resources

CD 1, tracks 2–4
Workbooks A and B, p.2
Echo Elektro 1 TPP, Mod 1 1.1–1.5

Starter 1 4.2/Y7

Aims

To learn some first expressions in German.
To develop confidence in speaking.
To learn the social conventions of greetings.

Say *Guten Tag! Ich heiße ....* Write this language on the board and clarify its meaning. Choose a pupil, greet him/her as above and encourage him/her to respond in kind. (You could also shake hands to introduce this typical German custom.) Perform the exchange with a few more pupils. Finally, ask pupils to mingle and perform the exchange amongst themselves.

1 Hör zu. Wer spricht? (1–3) (AT 1/1) 1.1/Y7 4.2/Y7

Listening. Pupils listen to the recording and decide who is speaking in each dialogue, taking the names from the boxes next to the rubric. After checking the answers, play the recording again and elicit the meanings of *Ich heiße ...* , *Wie heißt du?* and *Und du?*.

1 – *Wie heißt du?*
– *Ich heiße Niklas. Und du?*
– *Ich heiße Marie.*
– *Hallo, Marie!*
– *Hallo, Niklas!*

2 – *Wie heißt du?*
– *Ich heiße Alexander. Und du?*
– *Ich heiße Lea.*
– *Hallo, Lea!*
– *Hallo, Alexander!*

3 – *Wie heißt du?*
– *Ich heiße Valentina. Und du?*
– *Ich heiße Hamit.*
– *Hallo, Hamit!*
– *Hallo, Valentina!*

Answers

1 Marie + Niklas
2 Alexander + Lea
3 Valentina + Hamit

Aussprache: *w und ß* 4.1/Y7

This box explains the pronunciation of *w* and *ß*. Make sure that pupils understand that *ß* is equivalent to *ss* in some words, and do not confuse it with capital B! (If asked for a rule, explain that it is only used after a long vowel.)

2 Hör zu und wiederhole. 4.1/Y7

Listening. Pupils listen to the chant and repeat it, to practise the pronunciation of *w* and *ß*. You could get the class to repeat the chant several times in time with the recording, increasing in loudness as you turn down the volume of the recording.

3

Wie wie wie
Wie heißt du?
Heiße heiße heiße
Ich heiße Sue!

3 Partnerarbeit. (AT 2/2) 1.4a/Y7

Speaking. Pupils work in pairs to create greeting dialogues based on those in exercise 1. They use the greetings as introduced in exercise 1, but replace the names with their own.

Encourage pupils to shake hands (as a German custom) while introducing themselves. Draw their attention to how the voice rises at the end of *Und du?* to signal that it is a question.

Starter 2 5.5

Aim

To introduce the **Echo 1** Pupil's Book.

Run through the main features of the Pupil's Book, then do a quiz about where in the book to find various things. For example:

1 What is the title of Chapter 1?
2 What are the objectives of Unit 1?
3 Where can you look up the meaning of a word you don't know?
4 What page is the first Mini-Test on?
5 Where can you look up the meanings of 'noun', 'adjective' and 'verb'?

4 Hör zu und lies. (1–5) 2.1/Y7 4.2/Y7

Listening. Pupils listen to the recording and follow the photostory in their books. Before playing the recording, ask pupils to scan the story and explain what they think is happening in each picture, and what is being said. After listening to the recording a number of times, pupils could practise the dialogue in pairs.

R Take a soft ball. Ask *Wie geht's?* and throw the ball to a pupil. He/She must respond in a suitable way, e.g. *Gut, danke. Und dir?* and then throw the ball back. Continue round the class.

The *Sie* form of address is introduced in Chapter 6.

4

1 – *Tschüs, Mutti!*
– *Tschüs, Julia!*

2 – *Guten Tag, Frau Fischer!*
– *Guten Tag, Julia!*

3 – *Auf Wiedersehen!*
– *Auf Wiedersehen!*

4 – *Hallo, Peter!*
– *Hallo, Julia! Wie geht's?*
– *Gut, danke. Und dir?*
– *Nicht schlecht, danke.*

5 – *Hallo, Stefanie!*
– *Hallo, Julia! Wie geht's?*
– *Gut, danke. Und dir?*
– *Nicht so gut.*

5 Partnerarbeit. (AT 2/3) 1.4a/Y7

Speaking. Pupils work in pairs to create dialogues, using the model dialogue and the picture cues. Pupils could then also move around the class creating further dialogues with others. You could prepare by running through the model with the class, then looking at the cartoon characters to elicit how each of them might respond to the question *Wie geht's?*.

6 Schreib einen Dialog. (AT 4/3) 2.4a/Y7

Writing. Pupils write their own dialogues, using the language they practised in exercise 5. You could prepare by looking again at exercise 5 with the class and discussing which parts will stay the same and which parts might change.

Plenary 5.8

Aim

To encourage pupils to review their own learning.

Pupils work together in pairs or small groups to draw up a list of five things they have learned in this unit. You may wish to give them headings, e.g.

1 meeting new people
2 talking about yourself
3 being polite
4 pronunciation
5 useful little words.

Gather ideas from the class and summarise them on the board in groups.

Gather ideas for recording things they have learned, and making sure that they remember them.

2 Eins, zwei, drei ...

Learning targets

- Counting to 19
- Understanding what your teacher says in class

Key framework objectives

4.2/Y7 Language – high frequency words
5.2 Strategies – memorising

Grammar

- Present tense of *sein: ich bin, du bist*

Key language

Cardinal numbers 0–19
Wie alt bist du?
Ich bin … Jahre alt.
Ruhe, bitte!
Hört zu!
Macht das Heft auf!
Macht das Buch auf! Seite …
Macht das Buch zu!
Steht auf!
Setzt euch!
Alles einpacken!
Jetzt Partnerarbeit!
Schreibt es auf!

High-frequency words

ich bin, du bist
wie?
jetzt
bitte
alles
zu
auf

Mathematics

Basic arithmetic

Resources

CD 1, tracks 5–9
Workbooks A and B, p.3
Arbeitsblatt 1.6, p.9
Echo Elektro 1 TPP, Mod 1 2.1–2.8

Starter 1 4.2/Y7

Aims

To revise greetings.

To improve confidence and fluency.

Display on an OHT the key language from page 7 in the Pupil's Book. Pupils choose one of the sentences they like, and write it on a piece of paper. They then circulate in the class and greet another pupil in German. They must use the sentence on their piece of paper in their exchange. Once the exchange is complete, they swap paper with their partner, and move on to a new person.

1 Hör zu und wiederhole. 4.2/Y7

Listening. Pupils listen to the recording and repeat the numbers 0 to 12. After pupils have listened and repeated a number of times, stop the recording while the class continues chanting. Finally, the class could count down from 12 to 0. Make sure that pupils can pronounce the sounds *ei*, *ie* and *eu*.

null, eins, zwei, drei, vier, fünf, sechs, sieben, acht, neun, zehn, elf, zwölf

Suggestion

Ask the class to think of all the situations in which they need numbers in English, e.g. buying things, giving telephone numbers, counting pocket money. Can they see that this makes numbers a very important and useful thing to learn in German too?

2 Hör zu. Welche Zahl ist das? (AT 1/1) 1.1/Y7

Listening. Pupils listen to the recording and write down the numbers.

neun, zwei, sieben, eins, null, drei, elf, zwölf

Answers
9, 2, 7, 1, 0, 3, 11, 12

Ask pupils to try to make a link between each German word and its English equivalent, either in spelling or sound, e.g. *elf* begins with *el* like 'eleven'; *zehn* sounds like 'ten'. If it helps, they can use lateral thinking, e.g. for 'eleven' think of an elf with the number 11 on its hat; think of 'three' as being 'dry'; think of 'four' as being 'scary' (for 'fear'). This could be a group exercise, with one pupil noting the ideas on a sheet of paper. Each group then describes its best idea(s) to the class. Note the ideas for use in the plenary.

3 Schreib die Wörter auf. (AT 4/1)

4.1/Y7

Writing. Pupils write out the numbers as words. Remind pupils that they can refer back to exercise 1 to find out how to spell the numbers.

Answers
eins, neun, zwölf, acht, sieben, sechs, drei, elf, vier, zwei, fünf, zehn

4 Was passt zusammen? (AT 3/1)

4.2/Y7

Reading. Pupils match the words to the numbers. This requires them to use their knowledge of the numbers 1–10 to work out the numbers 13–19. (You will probably need to guide a lower-ability class through this exercise step by step, or simply present the numbers on the board or an OHT.)

Answers
13 dreizehn; **14** vierzehn; **15** fünfzehn; **16** sechzehn; **17** siebzehn; **18** achtzehn; **19** neunzehn

5 Hör zu und überprüfe es. (AT 1/1)

4.2/Y7

Listening. Pupils listen to the recording to check their answers to exercise 4.

dreizehn, vierzehn, fünfzehn, sechzehn, siebzehn, achtzehn, neunzehn

7

6 Lös die Rechenaufgaben. (AT 3/1)

4.2/Y7

Reading. Pupils solve the sums and write them out as words. Give pupils the German words *plus*, *minus* and *gleich* (equals) so that they can read out their answers.

Answers
1. elf + drei = vierzehn
2. sieben + zehn = siebzehn
3. neun + sechs = fünfzehn
4. sechs + dreizehn = neunzehn
5. neun + sieben = sechzehn
6. zehn + acht = achtzehn
7. zwölf – elf = eins
8. dreizehn – zehn = drei

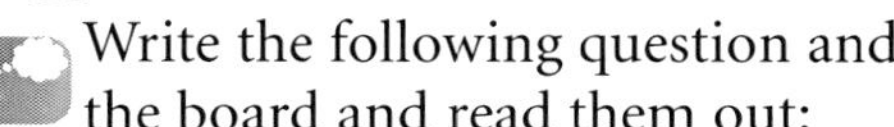

Starter 2

4.2/Y7

Aim

To consolidate the numbers 0 to19.

Do some basic arithmetic with the numbers 0 to 19. Write the sums on the board as you say them, e.g.

Teacher: *Zwei plus sieben macht ...*
Pupil: *Neun.*

After a few examples, divide the class into two teams. The teams set sums for each other, using only addition and subtraction, and answers in the range 0 to 19. Correct answers score one point; invalid sums and incorrect answers are penalised with one minus point. Team members can confer before answering, but each team member can only answer once. With a lower-ability class, continue to write the sums on the board as pupils say them.

Suggestion

Write the following question and answer on the board and read them out:

Wie alt bist du?
Ich bin zwölf Jahre alt.

Ask for volunteers to guess what the question and answer mean. Ask pupils who guess correctly how they worked it out.

7 Hör zu. Wie alt sind sie? (1–6) (AT 1/1)

1.1/Y7

Listening. Pupils listen to the dialogues and write down the ages of the speakers. After checking answers, play the recording again to focus on the structure of the question and the answer, in preparation for exercise 8.

8

1 – *Wie alt bist du, Ralf?*
– *Ich bin dreizehn Jahre alt.*

2 – *Und du, Emma? Wie alt bist du?*
– *Ich bin elf Jahre alt.*

3 – *Und du, Hasan? Wie alt bist du?*
– *Ich bin neunzehn Jahre alt.*

4 – *Hallo, Hanna! Wie alt bist du?*
– *Ich bin zehn Jahre alt.*

5 – *Hi, Erik! Sag mal, wie alt bist du?*
– *Ich bin fünfzehn Jahre alt.*

6 – *Hallo, Jasmin! Wie alt bist du?*
– *Ich bin zwölf Jahre alt.*

Answers
1 13 **2** 11 **3** 19 **4** 10 **5** 15 **6** 12

8 Partnerarbeit. (AT 2/2) 1.4A/Y7

Speaking. Pupils work together in pairs to ask each other their ages. In preparation, focus on the formulation of the question and the answer, especially the forms of *sein*. Drill the question and answer with the whole class.

\+ To achieve more variety in the answers and to practise more numbers, ask pupils to choose an age between 2 and 19. They could circulate in the class asking the question of several classmates. Alternatively, ask pupils to write their chosen age on a piece of paper, then race to find another pupil with the same age. When they find their 'twin', they sit down together. For further exploitation of this activity, use Other games on page 10.

ECHO-Detektiv 4.5a/Y7

This panel introduces pupils to the conjugation of the verb *sein* in the *ich* and *du* forms. You may wish to take this opportunity to introduce the class to the **Grammatik** section at the back of the Pupil's Book. (Only exceptionally able pupils should attempt exercise 20 on *sein* at this point.)

9 Hör zu. Was passt zusammen? (1–10) (AT 1/2) 1.1/Y7

Listening. Pupils listen to the recording and match the spoken instructions to the ones in their books.

R To consolidate the instructions, you could play a game of *Simon sagt* with the instructions and silent/mimed responses.

\+ As above, but pupils take turns at being the 'teacher' and giving the instructions in *Simon sagt.*

9

1 *Macht das Buch auf! Seite zehn.*
2 *Steht auf!*
3 *Macht das Buch zu!*
4 *Hört zu!*
5 *Setzt euch!*
6 *Alles einpacken!*
7 *Jetzt Partnerarbeit!*
8 *Ruhe, bitte!*
9 *Macht das Heft auf!*
10 *Schreibt es auf!*

Answers
1 d **2** f **3** e **4** b **5** g **6** h **7** i **8** a
9 c **10** j

Plenary 5.2

Aim
To develop learning strategies.

Pupils work in groups to brainstorm ideas for learning numbers. After a set time limit has expired, ask each group for its best idea. List the ideas on the board or an OHT. Also make the link back to the mnemonics pupils suggested for learning the numbers 0 to12. Further ideas could include:

– Whenever you see a number in the street (e.g. house number, bus number), try to think of the German number.
– Chant the numbers in groups of three.
– Sing the numbers to a well-known tune such as 'Twinkle, twinkle little star'.

Set the class the target of learning the numbers 0 to 19 by the next lesson.

Further practice of learning new words can be found on **Arbeitsblatt 1.6.**

3 Ich wohne in Deutschland

Learning targets

- Saying where you live
- Using verbs with *ich* and *du*

Key framework objectives

1.4/Y7 Speaking – (a) social and classroom language

Grammar

- Present tense of the verb *wohnen*: *ich* and *du* forms

Key language

Wo wohnst du?
Ich wohne in …
England
Wales
Schottland
Irland
Frankreich
Deutschland
Österreich
der Schweiz
Wie heißt du?
Wie alt bist du?
Ich heiße …
Ich bin …

High-frequency words

wo
in
ich bin
ich heiße
ich wohne
wie
wie alt?

Pronunciation

sch and *ch*

ICT

Powerpoint presentation

Citizenship

European countries and their geographical location

Resources

CD 1, tracks 10–13
Workbooks A and B, p.4
Arbeitsblatt 1.1, p.4
Flashcards 1–8
Echo Elektro 1 TPP, Mod 1 3.1–3.6

Starter 1

4.2/Y7

Aim

To revise the numbers 0 to 19.

Bingo: ask pupils to note down any five numbers between 0 and 19 on a mini-whiteboard or a sheet of paper. They must not write the same number twice. Call out numbers at random, repeating each twice. Pupils cross off their numbers when they hear them. The first pupil to cross off all his/her numbers calls out *Lotto!* and holds up his/her board or paper for you to check. The winner could receive a small reward.

Suggestion

To assess the level of geographical knowledge in the class, ask pupils to name European countries in English. Do they know the three countries where German is the main language?

1 Rate mal: Wie heißt das Land? (AT 3/1) 5.3

Reading. Pupils study the map and work out which of the German names goes with each country. They complete exercise 2 to check their own answers.

Answers

1 Irland
2 Wales
3 Schottland
4 England
5 Frankreich
6 Deutschland
7 Österreich
8 die Schweiz

2 Hör zu und überprüfe es. (1–8) (AT 1/1) 5.3

Listening. Pupils listen to the recording to check their answers to exercise 1.

Suggestion

Ask pupils who had the right answers how they worked them out. Was it prior knowledge, similarity to English, a process of elimination or a lucky guess? Tell them that all of these things are important in 'decoding' German.

10

1 Das ist Irland.
2 Das ist Wales.
3 Das ist Schottland.
4 Das ist England.
5 Das ist Frankreich.
6 Das ist Deutschland.
7 Das ist Österreich.
8 Das ist die Schweiz.

3 Hör zu. Wo wohnen sie? (1–8) (AT 1/2) 1.1/Y7

Listening. Pupils listen to the recording and note which country the speakers live in. You could use this opportunity to point out that this is an exercise in listening for key information: pupils should listen for country names and not be distracted by other parts of the dialogue they may not understand.

1 – Wo wohnst du, Rikki?
– Ich wohne in Deutschland.

2 – Anke, hallo! Wo wohnst du?
– Ich wohne in der Schweiz.

3 – Wo wohnst du, Tom?
– Ich wohne in England.

4 – Delphine! Hi! Wo wohnst du?
– Ich wohne in Frankreich.

5 – Wo wohnst du, Diarmuid?
– Ich wohne in Irland.

6 – Wo wohnst du, Elke?
– Ich wohne in Österreich.

7 – Und du, Harry? Wo wohnst du?
– Ich wohne in Schottland.

8 – Wo wohnst du, Rhiannon?
– Ich wohne in Wales.

Answers

1 Deutschland	5 Irland
2 die Schweiz	6 Österreich
3 England	7 Schottland
4 Frankreich	8 Wales

Aussprache: sch/ch 4.1/Y7

This panel explains the difference between the pronunciation of *sch* and *ch.*

4 Hör zu. Sagt man „sch“ oder „ch“? (1–6) 4.1/Y7

Listening. Pupils listen to the recording and distinguish whether the word contains *sch* or *ch.* Go through the **Aussprache** panel with the class before playing the recording.

12

1 Schottland
2 Frankreich
3 Schule
4 acht
5 Deutschland
6 Schweiz

Answers
1 sch 2 ch 3 sch 4 ch 5 sch 6 sch

5 Partnerarbeit: Wer ist das? (AT 2/2) 1.4a/Y7

Speaking. Pupils create dialogues based on the picture cues. The partner asking the question decides which character is speaking, then the roles are reversed.

ECHO-Detektiv 4.5a/Y7

This panel shows the conjugation of the regular verb *wohnen* in the *ich* and *du* forms. Explain to the class that most other verb endings are like those of *wohnen*. You could also introduce the concept of regular verbs at this point. Elicit from the class what the regular endings for *ich* and *du* verb forms are.

Starter 2 4.4/Y7

Aims
To revise giving personal information.
To develop confidence and proficiency in building basic sentences.

Make enough paper copies of **Arbeitsblatt 1.1** to give one copy to each group of three or four pupils. Pupils draw lines to join the ‘word islands’ to make as many sentences as possible. Pupils can make up questions and answers using the available words. Set a time limit of about four minutes. Collect answers around the class.

6 Hör zu. Wie ist es richtig? (1–3) (AT 1/3) 1.1/Y7

Listening. Pupils listen to the recording and choose the correct answers for each of the three dialogues.

13

1 – *Wie heißt du?*
– *Ich heiße Peter.*
– *Wo wohnst du, Peter?*
– *Ich wohne in Deutschland.*
– *Und wie alt bist du?*
– *Ich bin dreizehn Jahre alt.*

2 – *Wie heißt du?*
– *Ich heiße Laura.*
– *Also Laura, wo wohnst du?*
– *Ich wohne in der Schweiz.*
– *In der Schweiz. Und wie alt bist du?*
– *Ich bin vierzehn Jahre alt.*

3 – *Wie heißt du?*
– *Ich heiße Alex.*
– *Und wo wohnst du, Alex?*
– *Ich wohne in Österreich.*
– *In Österreich, sehr gut. Und wie alt bist du?*
– *Ich bin zwölf Jahre alt.*

Answers
1 a, d, h
2 c, f, i
3 b, e, g

Lies die Texte und füll die Tabelle aus. (AT 3/3) 2.1/Y7

Reading. Pupils read the texts and complete the table with the personal details of the three teenagers.

Answers

Heißt …	… Jahre alt	Wohnt in …
1 Birgit	12	Leipzig, Deutschland
2 Michel	14	Lille, Frankreich
3 Sam	10	Liverpool, England

8 Schreib über dich. (AT 4/3) 2.4a/Y7

Writing. Pupils write short texts about themselves, based on those in exercise 7. Focus pupils on accuracy, including capital letters, spelling and punctuation. You could assist lower-ability pupils by providing a writing frame or showing them how they can adapt one of the texts from exercise 7. For example, show an OHT of Birgit's text, with all the items to be changed highlighted.

+ Quick finishers can check each other's work when they have completed the exercise.

ICT Pupils could present the text as a mini Powerpoint slideshow, using photos, their own drawings or clipart to illustrate the text.

Plenary: Mini-Test 5.8

Aim

To review language learned to date and identify areas for improvement.

Pupils work in pairs to check the language they have learned so far, using the **Mini-Test** checklist. Ask pupils which points their partners found most difficult. Give them the task of helping their partner to improve those points by the next lesson.

4 Das Alphabet

Learning targets

- Spelling in German
- Using the definite article (*der, die, das*) to say 'the'

Key framework objectives

4.1/Y7 Language – letters and sounds
4.3/Y7 Language – gender

Grammar

- Noun gender
- Definite article: *der, die, das*

Key language

Letters of the alphabet
der Apfel
die Banane
der Computer
der Detektiv
das Eis
der Fußball
die Gitarre
das Haus
die Idee
der Joghurt
die Kamera
die Lampe
die Milch
die Nummer
die Orange
die Party
das Quiz
die Ratte
die Schule
das T-Shirt
die Uniform
der Vater
die Wespe
das Xylophon
die Yacht
der Zoo
Wie schreibt man … ?
Das T-Shirt ist rot / blau / gelb / braun / grün / orange / schwarz / weiß / grau.

High-frequency words

wie?
der, die, das
man
schreiben
ist

English

The alphabet, accurate spelling
Definite and indefinite articles with nouns

Resources

CD 1, tracks 14–16
Workbooks A and B, p.5
Arbeitsblatt 1.2, p.5
Flashcards 9–20
Echo Elektro 1 TPP, Mod 1 4.1–4.9

Starter 1 4.2/Y7

Aim
To revise country names in German.

Make an OHT of **Arbeitsblatt 1.2.** (You may also wish to photocopy the worksheet for each pupil to fill in and then stick in their exercise books as a reference.) Pupils work in pairs to write down the country names. With a higher-ability class, you may wish to remove the support from the bottom of the sheet.

Suggestion
Spell out the name of a pupil in the class, using the German alphabet, writing the letters on the board as you do so. Ask the pupil to put his/her hand up. Spell out further names of class members, without writing them. Pupils put up their hands when they hear their name spelled. Other pupils can prompt them.

1 Hör zu und lies. 4.1/Y7

Listening. Pupils listen to the recording and follow the alphabet in their books. Draw their attention to the sounds of E and I, which are easily confused. You may wish to use this recording as a 'listen and repeat' exercise, instead of the alphabet song in exercise 2.

+ As a follow-up activity, pupils work in pairs. Partner A reads out the German pronunciation of each letter (as in the Pupil's Book). Partner B writes the letter in one of two columns: letters that sound similar in German and English, and those that do not (e.g. G, H, J, V, W, Y).

R Pupils stand up in pairs. When you call out letters, pairs work together to make the shape of those letters, using just their arms or their whole bodies. Alternatively, pupils 'write' letters on their partner's back with a finger. The partner tries to say the correct letter in German.

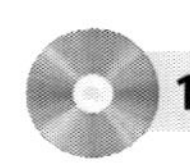

A, B, C
D, E, F, G
H, I, J,

K, L, M
N, O, P, Q
R, S, T, U
V, W, X
Y, Z

ECHO-Tipp 4.1/Y7

This panel introduces pupils to the Umlaut and reminds them about the letter *ß*. These pronunciation points are treated in greater detail later in the course. At this point, you may just want to say that the Umlaut is a special accent to change the way you say certain letters – and that pupils will be finding out more later in the year. You could ask pupils to look for words they have met with these letters in them (*grün, tschüs, hör zu*).

2 Hör zu und sing den Alphabet-Rap mit. 4.1/Y7

Listening. Pupils listen to the alphabet song and sing along. You could divide the class into two groups, singing alternate lines. To focus on spelling and meaning, draw attention to the fact that all nouns in German start with a capital letter. Elicit from the class that all the words are very close to English. You could also introduce the concept of cognates at this point. What do pupils think the words *der, die* and *das* mean? (The definite article is dealt with in detail in the **ECHO-Detektiv** panel.)

See also the ideas for using songs in Exploiting the songs on p.9.

\+ Pupils work in pairs to discover ways in which German spelling/pronunciation of cognates differs from English (e.g. -e is not silent, k = c, au = ou, j = y). Collect ideas around the class and discuss.

15

A ist der Apfel.
B ist die Banane.
C ist der Computer.
D ist der Detektiv.
E ist das Eis.
F ist der Fußball.
G ist die Gitarre.
H ist das Haus.
I ist die Idee.
J ist der Joghurt.
K ist die Kamera.
L ist die Lampe.
M ist die Milch.
N ist die Nummer.
O ist die Orange.
P ist die Party.
Q ist das Quiz.
R ist die Ratte.
S ist die Schule.
T ist das T-Shirt.
U ist die Uniform.
V ist der Vater.
W ist die Wespe.
X ist das Xylophon.
Y ist die Yacht.
Z ist der Zoo.

3 Partnerarbeit: Wie schreibt man ... ? (AT 2/2) 1.4a/Y7

Speaking. Pupils work in pairs, asking each other in German how to spell words from exercise 2. Demonstrate with volunteers from the class before pupils work by themselves. Encourage pupils to monitor the accuracy of their partner's pronunciation of the German letters. Higher-ability pupils could attempt to spell the words with their books closed, while their partners monitor their accuracy in the book.

Starter 2 4.1/Y7 4.2/Y7

Aims
To consolidate everyday words.
To practise pronunciation of the alphabet in German.

Play a game of hangman with the class, using words from exercise 2 on page 12. The winner of each round comes up to the board and provides the next word (confirm the word in a whisper before the pupil writes in the spaces on the board).

4 Hör zu. Was passt zusammen? (1–9) (AT 1/1) 4.2/Y7

Listening. Pupils listen to the recording and match the spoken colours to those in their books. You could use this exercise to focus on the correct pronunciation of *au*.

R To practise the colours, make colour swatches from sheets of coloured paper/card, cut up. Each pupil or pair receives one colour. When pupils hear their colour, they must stand up or hold up their swatch. Pupils holding up the wrong colour are 'out'. Increase the speed of the game until only one pupil or pair remains 'in'.

16

1 *blau* **4** *schwarz* **7** *braun*
2 *grau* **5** *grün* **8** *orange*
3 *gelb* **6** *rot* **9** *weiß*

Answers
1 b **2** i **3** c **4** g **5** e **6** a **7** d
8 f **9** h

5 Sieh dir die Bilder auf Seite 12 an. Richtig oder falsch? (AT 3/2)

4.3/Y7

Reading. Pupils read the sentences and compare them with the pictures from exercise 2. They decide whether the sentences are true or false. Higher-ability pupils can then supply correct sentences for numbers 2 and 5. They could also do the exercise with their books closed. After checking the answers, you could focus pupils' attention on the definite articles, referring to the **ECHO-Detektiv** panel.

Answers

1 richtig	**2** falsch	**3** richtig
4 falsch	**5** falsch	**6** richtig

ECHO-Detektiv 4.3/Y7

This panel explains that there are three words for 'the' in German, *der*, *die* and *das*, corresponding to the three noun genders masculine, feminine and neuter. Check comprehension by asking pupils to identify masculine, feminine and neuter nouns in exercise 2 on page 12. After going through the panel with the class, you could refer them to the relevant section of the **Grammatik** at the back of their books (page 124).

6 Schreib Sätze. Teste deinen Partner / deine Partnerin. (AT 4/3)

4.3/Y7

Writing. Pupils write true or false sentences about the pictures from exercise 2 in their exercise books and use them to test their partners. Their partners write *richtig* or *falsch* next to their sentences. Encourage pupils to focus on accuracy in spelling and in use of the correct article, as well as on neat presentation.

Plenary 4.3/Y7

Aim

To consolidate the gender of nouns.

Briefly elicit from the class the main points about gender and the definite article, then divide the class into four teams. Each team appoints a team captain. Read out nouns from exercise 2 on page 12, without the article. (Pupils can play with books open.) The first team to supply the correct article wins a point. Team members can confer, but only the team captain's answer counts. Incorrect answers score minus points. With a higher-ability class, award bonus points for using the noun correctly in a sentence. The team with the most points at the end of the game wins.

If you wish, you can move on to use some words from the **Wortschatz** at the back of the Pupil's Book.

5 Hast du einen Bleistift?

Learning targets

- Describing what you have in your school bag
- Using the indefinite article (*ein, eine*) to say 'a'

Key framework objectives

4.4/Y7 Language – sentence formation
5.1 Strategies – patterns

Grammar

- Using the indefinite article: *ein / eine / ein* and *einen / ein / ein*
- Present tense of the verb *haben* in the *ich* and *du* forms

Key language

der Bleistift
das Buch
die Diskette
das Etui
das Heft
der Klebstift
der Kuli
das Lineal
die Schere
die Schultasche
der Taschenrechner
das Wörterbuch
Das ist ein / eine / ein …
Hast du einen / eine / ein … für mich?
Ja, ich habe einen / eine / ein … .
Nein.

High-frequency words

Was ist das?
das ist ein / eine / ein …
hast du … ?
ich habe einen / eine / ein …
ja, nein
für
mich
danke

Resources

CD 1, tracks 17–18
Workbooks A and B, p.6
Arbeitsblatt 1.3, p.6
Arbeitsblatt 1.4, p.7
Arbeitsblatt 1.5, p.8
Echo Elektro 1 TPP, Mod 1 5.1–5.7

Starter 1

4.2/Y7

Aim

To revise colours.

Brainstorm colours in German to revise those which pupils have met so far (*blau, grau, gelb, schwarz, grün, rot, braun, orange* and *weiß*). Then call out the following pairs of colours in German:

Blau plus Gelb!	*Schwarz plus Weiß!*
Rot plus Gelb!	*Orange plus Schwarz!*

If you introduce the new colour *lila*, you can also use *Blau plus Rot!* For more practice, repeat combinations with the colours reversed. Pupils, working individually or in pairs, write down the colour that is made by mixing the two colours.

Suggestion

Assemble the objects featured in exercise 1. Introduce them one at a time, with the class repeating the name of each object. Then hold up the objects at random (or place them on the OHP, so that their silhouettes can be seen), asking, e.g. *Ist das die Schere?*. Pupils respond with *Ja* or *Nein*. More able groups can add *das ist …*

1 Hör zu. Was passt zusammen? (1–12) (AT 1/1) 4.2/Y7

Listening. Pupils listen to the recording and find the corresponding items in their books.

CD 17

1 *das Buch*	**7** *die Diskette*
2 *das Heft*	**8** *der Bleistift*
3 *das Etui*	**9** *der Taschenrechner*
4 *das Lineal*	**10** *das Wörterbuch*
5 *die Schere*	**11** *der Klebstift*
6 *die Schultasche*	**12** *der Kuli*

Answers
1 b **2** e **3** d **4** h **5** i **6** j **7** c **8** a
9 k **10** l **11** f **12** g

2 Schreib die Sätze ab und füll die Lücken aus. Welches Bild ist das? (AT 3/2) 5.1

Reading. Pupils complete the sentences with *ein* or *eine* and then find the matching pictures. Prepare for this exercise by going through the **ECHO-Detektiv** panel with the class.

Answers

1 Das ist eine Schere. – b
2 Das ist ein Kuli. – f
3 Das ist ein Lineal. – c
4 Das ist ein Klebstift. – d
5 Das ist ein Wörterbuch. – e
6 Das ist ein Etui. – a

ECHO-Detektiv 5.1

This panel shows the correspondence between noun gender and the form of the indefinite article (nominative). To check pupils' understanding, supply the nouns with the definite articles and elicit the correct indefinite article in each case. Refer pupils to the relevant section of the **Grammatik** at the back of their books (page 125). There is further practice on **Arbeitsblatt 1.4**.

3 Partnerarbeit: Was ist das? (AT 2/2–3) 4.2/Y7

Speaking. Pupils work together in pairs. They ask each other to identify the pictures from exercise 2, using *Das ist ein / eine ... .* Run through the form of the question and the answer with the class first, in preparation.

Starter 2 5.1

Aims

To develop thinking skills, e.g. pattern recognition, logic, lateral thinking.
To revise the meaning and gender of everyday words.

Make **Arbeitsblatt 1.3** into an OHT or photocopy it for pupils to use as individual worksheets. Pupils work through the three tasks in pairs.

4 Hör zu und lies. Was braucht Peter? (1–3) (AT 3/3) 2.1/Y7

Listening/Reading. Pupils listen to the recording and follow the dialogue in their books. They then write down in English what Peter needs. Before playing the recording, ask pupils to scan the text and look at the photo. What do they think is going on? Ask for evidence to support their answers. After checking answers, you could point out or elicit high-frequency words from the dialogue, e.g. *danke, für, ich, du* and *mich.*

18

– Julia, hast du einen Bleistift für mich?
– Ja, ich habe einen Bleistift.
– Danke ... Hast du eine Schere für mich?
– Ja, ich habe eine Schere.
– Danke ... Hast du ein Lineal für mich?
– Nein!

Answers

Pencil, pair of scissors, ruler

ECHO-Detektiv 5.1

This panel introduces the indefinite article in the accusative case. Elicit what the difference is from the nominative case, on page 14. Refer higher-ability pupils to the relevant section in the **Grammatik** at the back of their books (page 126).

5 Partnerarbeit. (AT 2/2–3) 1.4a/Y7 4.4/Y7

Speaking. Pupils work in pairs. They ask each other for various items of school equipment, using the key language panel. When replying, if practical, they could produce the item itself. Encourage pupils to be accurate in their use of *einen, eine* and *ein* (although less able pupils may not manage this) and on the word order of questions.

\+ Pupils can extend the exercise with other nouns they know, e.g. *Hast du einen Apfel für mich?* This could be played as a group game, with pupils throwing a ball to each other. The pupil catching the ball must answer the question and pose a question of his/her own.

For further exploitation of this activity, see Other games on page 10.

Lies den Text. Was ist nicht im Bild? (AT 3/3) 2.1/Y7

Reading. Pupils read the text and compare it with the picture. They identify the items in the text that are not in the picture.

Answers
Exercise book (*ein Heft*), pair of scissors (*eine Schere*), football (*einen Fußball*)

7 Was hast du in der Schultasche? (AT 4/3) 2.4a/Y7 4.4/Y7

Writing. Pupils write a short text about what they have in their schoolbags. (This does not have to reflect reality exactly!) Remind pupils to think about the gender of each noun and select *einen, eine* or *ein* as appropriate.

+ Encourage higher-ability pupils to include items from the previous unit and to add extra information, e.g. *Ich habe ein T-Shirt. Das T-Shirt ist rot.* Further practice of *haben* and *sein* can be found on **Arbeitsblatt 1.5.**

Plenary 5.8

Aims
To consolidate the vocabulary of school objects.
To focus on accuracy in written work.

Pupils close their books. Give them two minutes to write down as many German nouns as they can for things in a schoolbag. Higher-ability pupils should write *der, die* or *das* as appropriate before each noun. Their partners then check their work using the Pupil's Book. They should check for:

1 logic (e.g. *das Haus* is incorrect!)
2 the correct spelling
3 the correct article, if relevant.

If in doubt, they should consult you. Each word scores a maximum of three points; the winner is the pupil with the most points.

6 Wann hast du Geburtstag?

Learning targets

- Learning the numbers from 20 to 69
- Saying when your birthday is

Key framework objectives

4.6/Y7 Language – (a) questions

Grammar

- Forming questions with question words
- The present tense of the verb *haben* in the *ich* and *du* forms

Key language

Cardinal numbers 20–69
Ordinal numbers 1st to 31st
Wann hast du Geburtstag?
Ich habe am … … Geburtstag.
ersten, zweiten, dritten …
einunddreißigsten
Januar
Februar
März
April
Mai
Juni
Juli
August
September
Oktober
November
Dezember

High-frequency words

wie? wo? wann? was?
ich habe, du hast
am

Pronunciation

z

ICT

Using a spreadsheet application to show survey results

Mathematics

Using cardinal numbers and ordinal numbers (dates)
Gathering and analysing statistics

Resources

CD 1, tracks 19–23
Workbooks A and B, p.7
Echo Elektro 1 TPP, Mod 1 6.1–6.10

Starter 1 4.2/Y7

Aim

To revise numbers 0–19.

Write out a selection of numbers between 0 and 19 in words on an OHT. Place the OHT back-to-front on the projector, making sure the numbers are covered to start with. Display the numbers one at a time. Pairs of pupils decipher the number and write it in figures on a mini-whiteboard or on paper. Elicit how to say the number from pupils as you go along.

1 Hör zu und wiederhole. 5.1

Listening. Pupils listen to the recording and repeat the numbers. Elicit from the class what 31 etc. will be, helping pupils as necessary so that they see the pattern, i.e. that Germans write the number as one word, and say 'one-and-twenty' etc. instead of 'twenty-one'.

R Practise numbers up to 69, chorusing or counting round the class.

+ With a higher-ability class, practise counting up or down in threes. As pupils' confidence and fluency increases, move on to further variations, e.g. with a ball or soft toy: the pupil who catches the ball must give the number above or below.

CD 19

zwanzig, einundzwanzig, zweiundzwanzig, dreiundzwanzig, vierundzwanzig, fünfundzwanzig, sechsundzwanzig, siebenundzwanzig, achtundzwanzig, neunundzwanzig, dreißig, vierzig, fünfzig, sechzig

2 Hör zu. Welche Zahl ist das? (AT 1/1) 4.2/Y7

Listening. Pupils listen to the recording and identify which numbers they hear. After checking answers, ask the class which numbers they found most difficult. Discuss what this shows about points of difficulty concerning numbers (e.g. easy to mix up teens and tens – *dreizehn / dreißig*, etc.; easy to confuse tens and units – 34 instead of 43).

a einundzwanzig
b dreiundzwanzig
c vierunddreißig
d vierundvierzig
e fünfunddreißig
f neunundsechzig
g dreißig
h vierzehn
i fünfzig
j sechzig

20

Answers
a 21 **b** 23 **c** 34 **d** 44 **e** 35 **f** 69 **g** 30 **h** 14
i 50 **j** 60

Aussprache: *z* 5.1

This box explains the pronunciation of *z*. Make sure that pupils understand that *z* is similar in sound to *ts*.

3 Hör zu und wiederhole dreimal. 5.1

Listening. Pupils listen to the recording and repeat the phrase to practise the pronunciation of *z*. You could get the class to repeat the phrase several times in time with the recording, increasing in loudness as you turn down the volume of the recording.

Zehn Zebras im Zoo

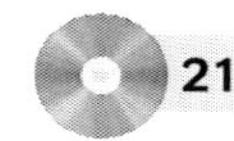

4 Partnerarbeit: Üb die Zahlen. (AT 2/2) 1.4b/Y7

Speaking. Pupils work together in pairs. They practise numbers between 20 and 69 using the picture cues in their books.

+ Higher-ability pupils can write numbers at random for their partners to read out, or write down the number that their partner says. Alternatively, pupils can write numbers in the air or with a finger on each other's back.

5 Schreib die Monate in der richtigen Reihenfolge auf. (AT 3/1) 4.2/Y7

Writing. Pupils write the months in the correct order, using cognates to help them. They check their own answers by doing exercise 6.

Answers
Januar, Februar, März, April, Mai, Juni, Juli, August, September, Oktober, November, Dezember

6 Hör zu und überprüfe es. (AT 1/1) 4.2/Y7

Listening. Pupils listen to the recording to check their answers to exercise 5. Focus their attention on the different pronunciation of the months in German, even when written identically to English. Chorus them with the class.

Januar, Februar, März, April
Mai, Juni, Juli, August
September, Oktober
November, Dezember

Starter 2 4.2/Y7

Aim

To consolidate numbers up to 69.

Divide the class into groups of equal size. Each group appoints a secretary, who must sit facing the back of the room. Display six numbers between 13 and 69 as words on the board or an OHT. The numbers should be in jumbled order. The groups dictate the numbers in German, in ascending order, to their secretary, who must write them on a mini-whiteboard or a sheet of paper as figures. As soon as he/she has finished, the secretary comes to the front of the class with the group's answers. The first group with correct answers wins.

7 Hör zu. Wann haben sie Geburtstag? (1–8) (AT 1/2) 1.1/Y7

Listening. Pupils listen to the recording and identify when the speakers' birthdays are. Before starting, introduce the context by asking pupils what they think this activity will be about – which should be evident from the visuals in their books. By identifying the months, pupils should be able to complete this exercise before the ordinal numbers have been systematically introduced.

After checking the answers, ask the class what they noticed about how to say dates in German. Replaying the recording as necessary, guide the class towards recognising that the rule is *am …ten* for numbers below 20, and *am …sten* for numbers 20 and above, but that there are a few irregular ones (*am ersten, dritten, siebten*). Draw pupils' attention to the little word *am* which will prove useful to say 'on' in other contexts as well.

+ With a higher-ability class, you may wish to draw attention to the convention for writing dates in German, i.e. with a full stop after the number.

1 – Ingo, wann hast du Geburtstag?
– Ich habe am dritten Dezember Geburtstag.

2 – Birgit, wann hast du Geburtstag?
– Ich habe am dreizehnten April Geburtstag.

3 – *Jonas, wann hast du Geburtstag?*
– *Ich habe am siebten Mai Geburtstag.*

4 – *Svenja, wann hast du Geburtstag?*
– *Ich habe am einundzwanzigsten Juni Geburtstag.*

5 – *Max, wann hast du Geburtstag?*
– *Ich habe am vierundzwanzigsten August Geburtstag.*

6 – *Heike, wann hast du Geburtstag?*
– *Ich habe am neunundzwanzigsten März Geburtstag.*

7 – *Kemal, wann hast du Geburtstag?*
– *Ich habe am dritten Februar Geburtstag.*

8 – *Ingrid, wann hast du Geburtstag?*
– *Ich habe am ersten Juli Geburtstag.*

Answers

1 am 3. Dezember
2 am 13. April
3 am 7. Mai
4 am 21. Juni
5 am 24. August
6 am 29. März
7 am 3. Februar
8 am 1. Juli

ECHO-Detektiv 4.6a/Y7

This panel reviews the question words which pupils have met so far in this chapter. Ask for volunteers to give an example of a question with each question word. Refer pupils to the relevant section of the **Grammatik** at the back of their books (page 133).

8 Umfrage. (AT 2/3) 4.6a/Y7

Speaking. Pupils circulate around the class, interviewing each other about their birthdays and ages. If results are to be recorded, pupils should start by writing a list of the months (or abbreviations) in their exercise books to note names, dates and ages next to. You could set pupils the task of finding at least one birthday for each month – is there a month with no class birthdays?

ICT Survey results could be recorded as described above and then represented in a spreadsheet application (or by hand) as a pie chart or bar chart, or in a DTP or drawing application by creative graphic ideas, e.g. slices of a birthday cake, or candles of different heights representing the number of pupils with birthdays in a particular month.

Note: You may wish to confer first with the Maths department about the types of charts/graphs which pupils have encountered so far.

9 Schreib über dich. (AT 4/3) 2.4a/Y7

Writing. Pupils write a short text about themselves, giving their name, age and birthday.

+ Higher-ability pupils should be encouraged to include other personal information, e.g. *Ich wohne in Birmingham, in England. Ich habe eine Gitarre und einen Computer.*

R Less able pupils could be provided with a simple writing frame.

Plenary 5.8

Aims

To consolidate dates.
To learn to work in a collaborative environment.

Ask for a volunteer to come to the board and explain to the class how to say dates in German. The volunteer can nominate two assistants to help him/her. The rest of the class can ask questions. The volunteer 'teacher' can then test the class's understanding by asking individual pupils *Wann hast du Geburtstag?*.

Lernzieltest und Wiederholung

Lernzieltest 5.8

This is a checklist of language covered in Chapter 1. Pupils can work in pairs with the checklist to check what they have learned. Points which directly address grammar and structures are marked with a G.

There is a **Lernzieltest** sheet in the Resource and Assessment File (page 12). Encourage pupils to look back at the chapter and to use the grammar section to revise what they are unclear about. You can also use the **Lernzieltest** as an end-of-chapter plenary.

Wiederholung

This is a revision page to prepare pupils for the **Kontrolle** at the end of the chapter.

Resources

CD 1, tracks 24–25

1 Hör zu. Wie alt sind sie? (1–10) (AT 1/1) 1.1/Y7

Listening. Pupils listen to the recording and write down the ages of the speakers.

24

1 – *Hallo! Wie alt bist du, Niels?*
– *Ich bin vierzehn Jahre alt.*

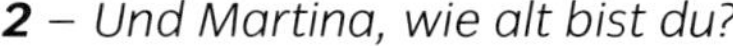

2 – *Und Martina, wie alt bist du?*
– *Ich bin zwölf Jahre alt.*

3 – *Wie alt bist du, Klaus?*
Ich bin siebenundzwanzig Jahre alt.

4 – *Tag, Jana, wie alt bist du?*
– *Ich bin dreißig Jahre alt.*

5 – *Paul, wie alt bist du?*
– *Ich bin vierundfünfzig Jahre alt.*

6 – *Hallo Barbara! Wie alt bist du?*
– *Ich bin dreizehn Jahre alt.*

7 – *Wie alt bist du, Gustav?*
– *Ich bin fünfundvierzig Jahre alt.*

8 – *Und du, Kerstin, wie alt bist du?*
– *Ich bin siebzehn Jahre alt.*

9 – *Wie alt bist du, Anton?*
– *Ich bin achtundzwanzig Jahre alt.*

10 – *Steffi? Wie alt bist du?*
– *Ich bin dreiunddreißig Jahre alt.*

Answers
1 14 **2** 12 **3** 27 **4** 30 **5** 54 **6** 13 **7** 45 **8** 17
9 28 **10** 33

2 Hör zu. Welches Bild ist das? (1–8) (AT 1/1) 1.1/Y7

Listening. Pupils listen to the recording and match the words to the pictures.

25

1 das Etui
2 der Kuli
3 das Wörterbuch
4 der Taschenrechner
5 der Klebstift
6 der Bleistift
7 das Heft
8 das Lineal

Answers
1 g **2** c **3** h **4** d **5** b **6** f **7** a **8** e

3 Partnerarbeit: Mach Interviews. (AT 2/3) 1.4a/Y7

Speaking. Pupils work together in pairs to interview each other, using the questions and ID cards provided.

4 Lies die E-Mail. Beantworte die Fragen auf Englisch. (AT 3/3) 2.1/Y7

Reading. Pupils read the email and answer the questions in English.

Answers
1 Switzerland
2 13
3 8 February
4 a rat

5 Lies die E-Mail noch mal. Schreib eine Antwort für eine Person aus Aufgabe 3. (AT 4/3) 2.4a/Y7

Writing. Pupils write their own emails, using the one in exercise 4 as a model. They need only change the coloured words.

Learning targets

- Learning about the euro
- Revising numbers and school items
- Revising personal information

Key framework objectives

2.3/Y7 Reading – text features
3.1/Y7 Culture – aspects of everyday life

Grammar

- Forming questions with question words
- *du kaufst*

Key language

die Schere
der Klebstift
das Wörterbuch
die CD
… Euro
Kaufst du einen Bleistift / eine Diskette / ein Wörterbuch?
Ja. Nein.
Wann hast du Geburtstag?
Ich habe am … … Geburtstag.
Wo wohnst du?
Ich wohne in …
Wie alt bist du?
Ich bin … Jahre alt.
Wie heißt du?
Ich heiße …

High-frequency words

ja, nein
wann? wo? wie?
ich bin, du bist

Mathematics

Prices in euros

Citizenship

Currencies in other European countries

Resources

CD 1, tracks 26–27
Workbooks A and B, p.8

Starter 1 3.1/Y7

Aim

To check knowledge of the euro.

Ask pupils what currency is used in Germany; establish that it is the euro (*der Euro*), divided into cents (*der Cent*). If possible, show the class real examples of the notes and coins. Ask whether any pupils have used euros abroad, and if so, in which country or countries they used them. Establish that the euro is used in Austria also, but not in Switzerland, whose currency is the Swiss franc (*der Franken*).

1 Hör zu und lies. (AT3/4) 2.3/Y7

Listening. Pupils listen to the recording and follow the story in their books. In preparation, ask the class to scan the story and decide what Valentina is doing. They should be prepared to justify their answers with reference to the text and pictures. Ask pupils how the word 'euro' is pronounced in German.

26

1 – *Ich habe dreißig Euro. Was brauche ich für die Schule? … Ich brauche eine Schere, einen Klebstift und ein Wörterbuch.*
2 – *Die Schere kostet sieben Euro. Der Klebstift kostet drei Euro. Das macht zehn Euro.*
3 – *Das Wörterbuch kostet achtzehn Euro. Das macht achtundzwanzig Euro. Ich habe dreißig Euro.*
4 – *Die neue CD von 'Rammstein'! Zwanzig Euro!*
5 – *Das Wörterbuch oder die CD? … Ich habe eine Idee!*
6 – *Vati, hast du zwanzig Euro für mich? Ich brauche ein Wörterbuch.*
– *Für die Schule? Ja, natürlich!*

2 Lies den Text noch mal. Was passt zusammen? (AT 3/4) 2.3/Y7

Reading. Pupils read the story again and match the items to the price tags. Pupils could check their answers in pairs: provide them with *Was kostet der/die/das … ?* and *Der/Die/Das … kostet … Euro* to enable them to go through the answers verbally.

For further exploitation of this activity, see Vocabulary treasure hunt on page 10.

Answers
1 b 2 a 3 d 4 c

3 Partnerarbeit: Was kaufst du? Wähle drei Sachen. Kann dein Partner / deine Partnerin sie erraten? (AT 2/3) 1.4b/Y7

Speaking. Pupils work in pairs to create dialogues. They take turns to guess which three things their partner has picked. Prepare by asking the class where they could find the necessary vocabulary if they have forgotten the names or genders of the items (in the relevant unit, in the wordlist at the end of the chapter, in the **Wortschatz** at the back of the Pupil's Book, in a dictionary). They should make sure that they can name all of the items in German before beginning the activity.

+ Very able pupils could invent prices for the items, and then act out shop dialogues, e.g.

- *Ich kaufe einen Taschenrechner.*
- *Das kostet dreißig Euro.*
- *Ich kaufe auch ein Wörterbuch. Was kostet das?*
- *Achtundzwanzig Euro. Das macht achtundfünfzig Euro …*

Starter 2 4.2/Y7

Aims

To consolidate dates.
To improve fluency and clarity of speech.

Pupils sit back-to-back. Write dates in number form on the board or an OHT, e.g. '10.9', '3.11', etc. The pupil facing the board dictates the dates in German to his/her partner, e.g. *am zehnten September, am dritten November*, etc. The partner writes them on a mini-whiteboard or a sheet of paper. As soon as he/she finishes the task, he/she holds the answers in the air. The first pair to write all of the dates correctly wins.

4 Hör zu. Wann haben sie Geburtstag? (AT 1/4) 1.1/Y7

Listening. Pupils listen to the recording and note down the birthdays of the four characters. Although they may use figures in their notes, pupils should then write out the dates as words.

27

- *Julia Döring.*
- *Hallo, Julia! Hier ist Nina.*
- *Nina! Wie geht's?*
- *Gut, danke. Und dir?*
- *Auch gut.*
- *Julia, wann hast du Geburtstag?*
- *Am ersten September.*
- *Und Peter? Wann hat Peter Geburtstag?*
- *Ähmm, Peter hat am 23. August Geburtstag.*
- *Und Viktor?*
- *Viktor hat … am 19. Mai Geburtstag.*
- *Und Stefanie?*
- *Stefanie hat am dritten März Geburtstag.*
- *Danke, Julia. Tschüs!*
- *Tschüs, Nina!*

Answers

1 Julia – am ersten September
2 Peter – am dreiundzwanzigsten August
3 Viktor – am neunzehnten Mai
4 Stefanie – am dritten März

5 Hier sind die Antworten. Schreib die Fragen auf. (AT 4/3) 4.6a/Y7

Writing. Pupils write questions to go with the answers.

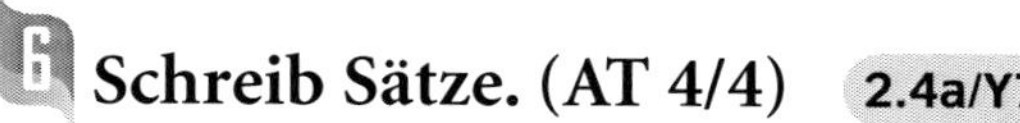

Answers

1 Wie alt bist du?
2 Wo wohnst du?
3 Wann hast du Geburtstag?
4 Wie heißt du?

6 Schreib Sätze. (AT 4/4) 2.4a/Y7

Writing. Pupils write short texts based on the two ID cards.

Answers

1 Ich heiße Jean-Luc Dupont. Ich wohne in Frankreich. Ich bin vierzehn Jahre alt. Ich habe am fünften Juni Geburtstag.
2 Ich heiße Lucy McDonald. Ich wohne in Schottland. Ich bin zwölf Jahre alt. Ich habe am achtzehnten Februar Geburtstag.

Plenary 1.4b/Y7

Aim

To develop fluency in spontaneous talk

Pairs of pupils try to keep a conversation going in German for one minute, using questions and answers learned in Chapter 1. After a minute, pupils find another partner and try again.

SELF-ACCESS READING AND WRITING AT TWO LEVELS

A Reinforcement

1 Wie alt sind sie? (AT4/2) 4.4/Y7

Writing. Pupils identify the correct age for each person, and write out the sentences.

Answers
1 Ich bin vier Jahre alt.
2 Ich bin zehn Jahre alt.
3 Ich bin sieben Jahre alt.
4 Ich bin zwölf Jahre alt.
5 Ich bin zwei Jahre alt.
6 Ich bin dreizehn Jahre alt.

2 Was passt zusammen? (AT3/2) 2.1/Y7

Reading. Pupils match pictures of classroom equipment to sentences.

Answers
1 a **2** e **3** c **4** b, d **5** f

3 Was passt zusammen? (AT3/2) 2.1/Y7

Reading. Pupils match each question to the correct answer. They could then copy both out.

Answers
1 d **2** b **3** f **4** a **5** e **6** c

B Extension

1 Ordne die Buchstaben. (AT4/1) 4.2/Y7

Writing. Pupils solve the anagrams and write out the expressions.

Answers
1 Hallo
2 Guten Tag
3 Wie geht's?
4 Gut, danke
5 Auf Wiedersehen
6 Tschüs

2 Welcher Satz ist anders? Warum? (AT3/2) 4.4/Y7

Reading. Pupils identify a sentence that they consider to be the odd-one-out, and explain why. There are various possibilities – you could tell them to find and list as many as they can.

Suggested Answers
1 a (it does not contain the word *Geburtstag* / it uses *sein* rather than *haben*)
c (it is a question / it does not start with *ich* / it does not contain the number *neun*)
2 b (it is a question / it uses *du* rather than *ich*)
c (a country rather than a city)
3 a (three words)
b (no *bitte*)
c (no movement required / noun rather than imperative verb ending in 't')
4 a (colour does not start with 'g' / noun is a cognate)
b (feminine noun)
c (colour does not rhyme with the others)

3 Was hat Viktor in seiner Schultasche? Zeichne es in dein Heft. (AT3/3) 2.1/Y7

Reading. Pupils read the text about Viktor's school bag, and show their comprehension of it by drawing and colouring in the contents in their book.

4 Was sagen sie? (AT4/4) 2.4b/Y7

Writing. Pupils write short texts about each of the pets, based on the illustrations.

Answers
1 Ich heiße Josef. Ich bin vierzehn Jahre alt. Ich habe am zweiten Mai Geburtstag. Ich wohne in Deutschland.
2 Ich heiße Bryn. Ich bin zwei Jahre alt. Ich habe am dreißigsten Oktober Geburtstag. Ich wohne in Wales.
3 Ich heiße Pierre. Ich bin dreiundzwanzig Jahre alt. Ich habe am sechzehnten Januar Geburtstag. Ich wohne in Frankreich.

Übungsheft A, Seite 2

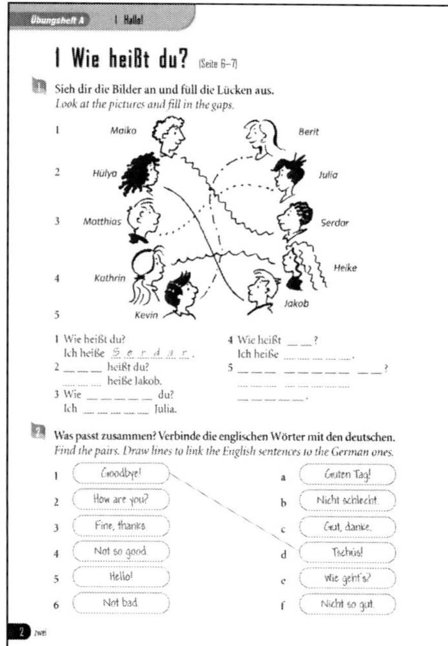
Übungsheft A 1 Hallo!

I Wie heißt du? (Seite 6–7)

1 Sieh dir die Bilder an und füll die Lücken aus.
Look at the pictures and fill in the gaps.

1 Maiko Berit
2 Hülya Julia
3 Matthias Serdar
4 Kathrin Heike
5 Kevin Jakob

1 Wie heißt du?
Ich heiße S e r d a r.
2 ___ heißt du?
___ heiße Jakob.
3 Wie ___ du?
Ich ___ Julia.
4 Wie heißt ___?
Ich heiße ___.
5 ___ ___ ___?
___ ___ ___.

2 Was passt zusammen? Verbinde die englischen Wörter mit den deutschen.
Find the pairs. Draw lines to link the English sentences to the German ones.

1 Goodbye! a Guten Tag!
2 How are you? b Nicht schlecht.
3 Fine, thanks c Gut, danke.
4 Not so good d Tschüs!
5 Hello! e Wie geht's?
6 Not bad f Nicht so gut.

2 zwei

1 (AT3 Level 2, AT4 Level 1–2) 2 Wie heißt du? – **Ich** heiße Jakob. **3** Wie **heißt** du? – Ich **heiße** Julia. **4** Wie heißt **du**? – Ich heiße **Heike**. **5 Wie heißt du? – Ich heiße Berit**.

2 (AT3 Level 1/2) 1 d **2** e **3** c **4** f **5** a **6** b

Übungsheft B, Seite 2

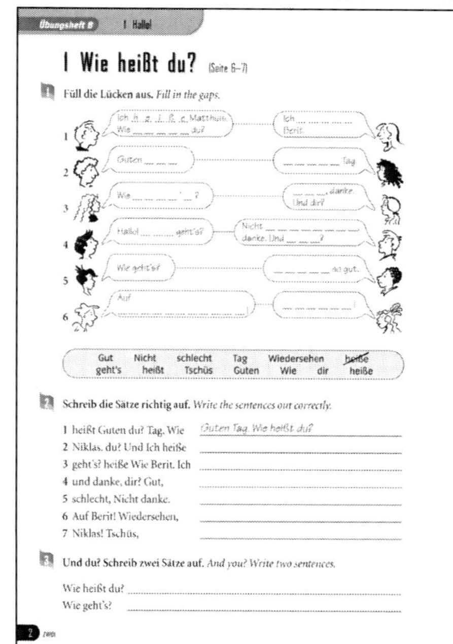
Übungsheft B 1 Hallo!

I Wie heißt du? (Seite 6–7)

1 Füll die Lücken aus. *Fill in the gaps.*

1 Ich h e i ß e Matthias. Wie ___ du? – Ich ___ Berit.
2 Guten ___ – ___ Tag.
3 Wie ___'___? – ___, danke. Und dir?
4 Hallo! ___ geht's? – Nicht ___ danke. Und ___?
5 Wie geht's? – ___ so gut.
6 Auf ___! – ___!

Gut Nicht schlecht Tag Wiedersehen ~~heiße~~ geht's heißt Tschüs Guten Wie dir heiße

2 Schreib die Sätze richtig auf. *Write the sentences out correctly.*

1 heißt Guten du? Tag. Wie — *Guten Tag. Wie heißt du?*
2 Niklas. du? Und Ich heiße
3 geht's? heiße Wie Berit. Ich
4 und danke, dir? Gut,
5 schlecht, Nicht danke.
6 Auf Berit! Wiedersehen,
7 Niklas! Tschüs,

3 Und du? Schreib zwei Sätze auf. *And you? Write two sentences.*

Wie heißt du?
Wie geht's?

2 zwei

1 (AT3 Level 2, AT4 Level 1) 1 Ich **heiße** Matthias. Wie **heißt** du? – Ich **heiße** Berit. **2** Guten **Tag**. – **Guten** Tag. **3** Wie **geht's**? – **Gut,** danke. Und dir? **4** Hallo! **Wie** geht's? – Nicht **schlecht**, danke. Und **dir**? **5** Wie geht's? – **Nicht** so gut. **6** Auf **Wiedersehen**! – **Tschüs**!

2 (AT4 Level 2) 1 Guten Tag. Wie heißt du? **2** Ich heiße Niklas. Und du? **3** Ich heiße Berit. Wie geht's? **4** Gut, danke, und dir? **5** Nicht schlecht, danke. **6** Auf Wiedersehen, Berit. **7** Tschüs, Niklas.

3 (AT4 Levels 2–3)

Übungsheft A, Seite 3

1 Hallo! Übungsheft A

2 Eins, zwei, drei ... (Seite 8–9)

1 Lös die Rechenaufgaben. Wähle die richtige Antwort.
Do the sums. Choose the correct answer.

1 2 × 6 = zwölf / drei
2 14 – 8 = zehn / sechs
3 4 + 9 = zwanzig / dreizehn
4 6 – 3 = sieben / drei
5 3 × 3 = neun / sechs
6 15 + 3 = achtzehn / acht
7 8 – 4 = vier / vierzehn
8 6 + 5 = eins / elf

2 Entziffere die Wörter. Schreib das Wort und die Zahl auf.
Unjumble the words. Write the word and the number.

1 zwölf (12) 3 ___ 5 ___
2 ___ 4 ___ 6 ___

zehn elf ~~zwölf~~ dreizehn vierzehn fünfzehn

drei 3

1 (AT3 Level 1) 1 zwölf **2** sechs **3** dreizehn **4** drei **5** neun **6** achtzehn **7** vier **8** elf

2 (AT3 Level 1/2, AT4 Level 1) 1 zwölf (12) **2** zehn (10) **3** elf (11) **4** dreizehn (13) **5** fünfzehn (15) **6** vierzehn (14)

Übungsheft B, Seite 3

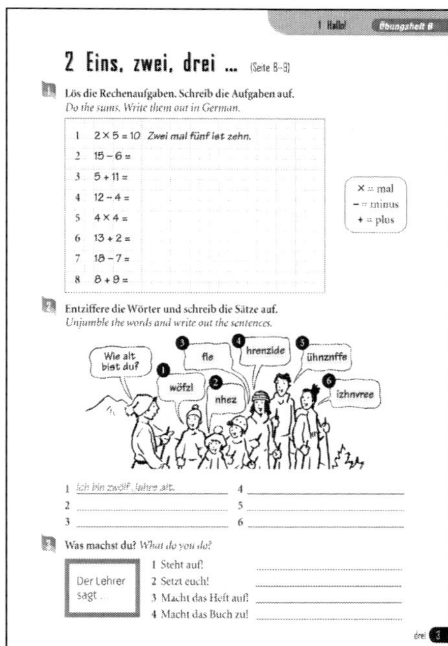
1 Hallo! Übungsheft B

2 Eins, zwei, drei ... (Seite 8–9)

1 Lös die Rechenaufgaben. Schreib die Aufgaben auf.
Do the sums. Write them out in German.

1 2 × 5 = 10 *Zwei mal fünf ist zehn.*
2 15 – 6 =
3 5 + 11 =
4 12 – 4 =
5 4 × 4 =
6 13 + 2 =
7 18 – 7 =
8 8 + 9 =

× = mal
– = minus
+ = plus

2 Entziffere die Wörter und schreib die Sätze auf.
Unjumble the words and write out the sentences.

1 *Ich bin zwölf Jahre alt.* 4 ___
2 ___ 5 ___
3 ___ 6 ___

3 Was machst du? *What do you do?*

Der Lehrer sagt ...
1 Steht auf!
2 Setzt euch!
3 Macht das Heft auf!
4 Macht das Buch zu!

drei 3

1 (AT4 Level 2) 1 Zwei mal fünf ist zehn. **2** Fünfzehn minus sechs ist neun. **3** Fünf plus elf ist sechzehn. **4** Zwölf minus vier ist acht. **5** Vier mal vier ist sechzehn. **6** Dreizehn plus zwei ist fünfzehn. **7** Achtzehn minus sieben ist elf. **8** Acht plus neun ist siebzehn.

2 (AT4 Level 2) 1 Ich bin zwölf Jahre alt. **2** Ich bin zehn Jahre alt. **3** Ich bin elf Jahre alt. **4** Ich bin dreizehn Jahre alt. **5** Ich bin fünfzehn Jahre alt. **6** Ich bin vierzehn Jahre alt.

3 (AT3 Level 2) 1 Stand up. **2** Sit down. **3** Open exercise book. **4** Shut book.

Übungsheft A, Seite 4

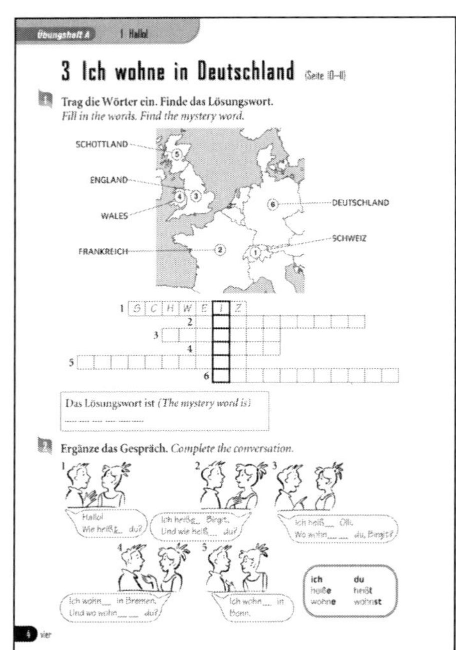
Übungsheft A 1 Hallo!

3 Ich wohne in Deutschland (Seite 10–11)

1 Trag die Wörter ein. Finde das Lösungswort.
Fill in the words. Find the mystery word.

Das Lösungswort ist *(The mystery word is)*

2 Ergänze das Gespräch. *Complete the conversation.*

4 vier

1 (AT3 Level 1, AT4 Level 1) 1 Schweiz **2** Frankreich **3** England **4** Wales **5** Schottland **6** Deutschland

Das Lösungswort ist Irland.

2 (AT3 Level 2) 1 Hallo! Wie hei**ßt** du? **2** Ich heiß**e** Birgit. Und wie hei**ßt** du? **3** Ich heiß**e** Olli. Wo wohn**st** du, Birgit? **4** Ich wohn**e** in Bremen. Und wo wohn**st** du? **5** Ich wohn**e** in Bonn.

Übungsheft B, Seite 4

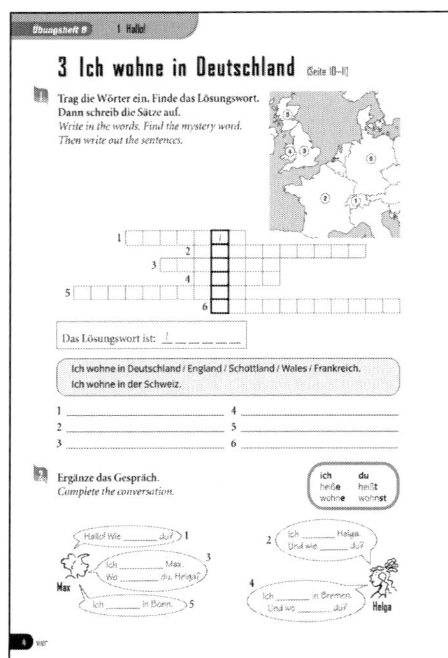
Übungsheft B 1 Hallo!

3 Ich wohne in Deutschland (Seite 10–11)

1 Trag die Wörter ein. Finde das Lösungswort. Dann schreib die Sätze auf.
Write in the words. Find the mystery word. Then write out the sentences.

Das Lösungswort ist: I _ _ _ _ _

2 Ergänze das Gespräch. *Complete the conversation.*

4 vier

1 (AT4 Level 1–2) 1 Schweiz **2** Frankreich **3** England **4** Wales **5** Schottland **6** Deutschland

Das Lösungswort ist Irland.

1 Ich wohne in der Schweiz. **2** Ich wohne in Frankreich. **3** Ich wohne in England. **4** Ich wohne in Wales. **5** Ich wohne in Schottland. **6** Ich wohne in Deutschland.

2 (AT3 Level 3, AT4 Level 1) 1 Hallo! Wie **heißt** du? **2** Ich **heiße** Helga. Und wie **heißt** du? **3** Ich **heiße** Max. Wo **wohnst** du, Helga? **4** Ich **wohne** in Bremen. Und wo **wohnst** du? **5** Ich **wohne** in Bonn.

3 (AT4 Level 3)

Übungsheft A, Seite 5

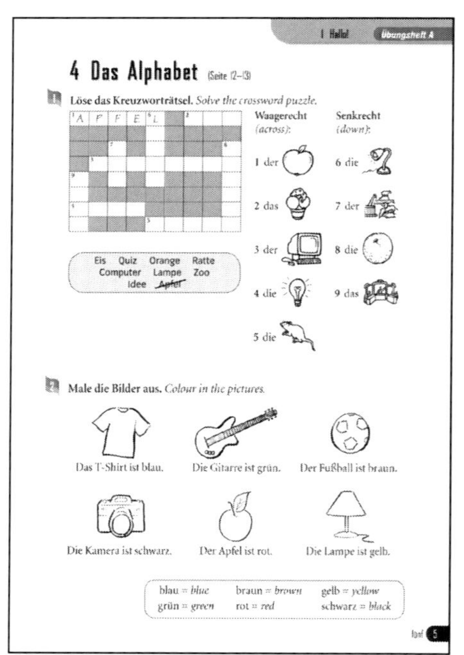
1 Hallo! Übungsheft A

4 Das Alphabet (Seite 12–13)

1 Löse das Kreuzworträtsel. *Solve the crossword puzzle.*

Waagerecht *(across)*: 1 der 2 das 3 der 4 die 5 die
Senkrecht *(down)*: 6 die 7 der 8 die 9 das

2 Male die Bilder aus. *Colour in the pictures.*

Das T-Shirt ist blau. Die Gitarre ist grün. Der Fußball ist braun.
Die Kamera ist schwarz. Der Apfel ist rot. Die Lampe ist gelb.

fünf 5

1 (AT3 Level 1, AT4 Level 1)

Answers

1 Apfel **2** Eis **3** Computer **4** Idee **5** Ratte **6** Lampe **7** Zoo **8** Orange **9** Quiz

2 (AT3 Level 2) blue T-shirt, green guitar, brown football, black camera, red apple, yellow lamp

Übungsheft B, Seite 5

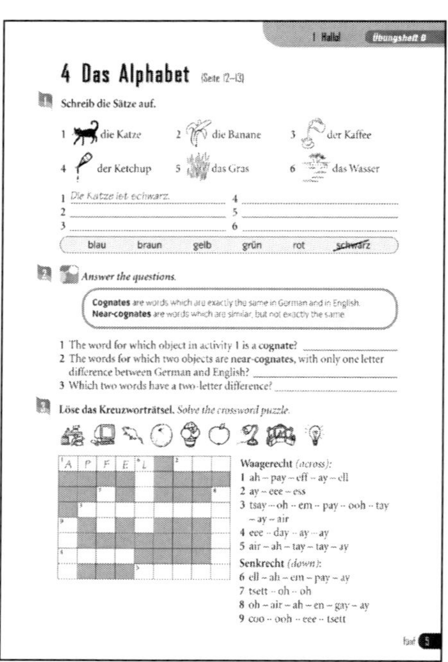
1 Hallo! Übungsheft B

4 Das Alphabet (Seite 12–13)

1 Schreib die Sätze auf.

1 die Katze 2 die Banane 3 der Kaffee
4 der Ketchup 5 das Gras 6 das Wasser

1 Die Katze ist schwarz.

2 *Answer the questions.*

Cognates are words which are exactly the same in German and in English.
Near-cognates are words which are similar, but not exactly the same.

1 The word for which object in activity 1 is a cognate?
2 The words for which two objects are near-cognates, with only one letter difference between German and English?
3 Which two words have a two-letter difference?

3 Löse das Kreuzworträtsel. *Solve the crossword puzzle.*

Waagerecht *(across)*:
1 ah – pay – eff – ay – ell
2 ay – eee – ess
3 tsay – oh – em – pay – ooh – tay – ay – air
4 eee – day – ay – ay
5 air – ah – tay – tay – ay
Senkrecht *(down)*:
6 ell – ah – em – pay – ay
7 tsett – oh – oh
8 oh – air – ah – en – gay – ay
9 coo – ooh – eee – tsett

fünf 5

1 (AT4 Level 2) 1 Die Katze ist schwarz. **2** Die Banane ist gelb. **3** Der Kaffee ist braun. **4** Der Ketchup ist rot. **5** Das Gras ist grün. **6** Das Wasser ist blau.

2 (AT4 Level 1) 1 Ketchup **2** Banane, Gras **3** Kaffee Wasser

3 (AT4 Level 1) 1 Apfel **2** Eis **3** Computer **4** Idee **5** Ratte **6** Lampe **7** Zoo **8** Orange **9** Quiz

Übungsheft A, Seite 6

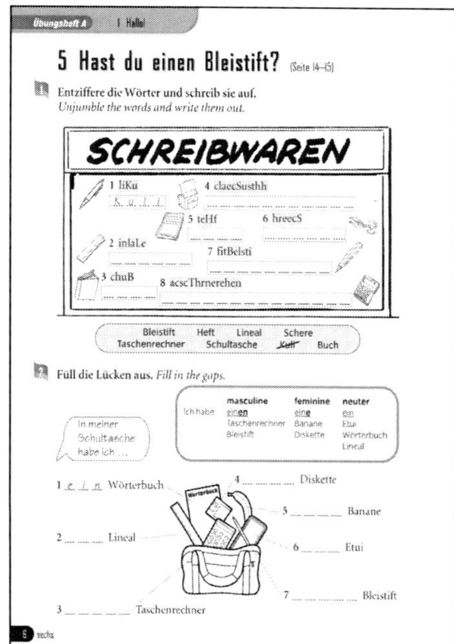
Übungsheft A | 1 Hallo!

5 Hast du einen Bleistift? (Seite 14–15)

1 Entziffere die Wörter und schreib sie auf. *Unjumble the words and write them out.*

SCHREIBWAREN

1 liKu 2 inlaLe 3 chuB 4 claecSusthh 5 teHf 6 hreecS 7 fitBelsti 8 acscThrnerehen

Bleistift Heft Lineal Schere Taschenrechner Schultasche Kuli Buch

2 Füll die Lücken aus. *Fill in the gaps.*

In meiner Schultasche habe ich ...

	masculine	feminine	neuter
Ich habe	einen	eine	ein
	Taschenrechner	Banane	Etui
	Bleistift	Diskette	Wörterbuch
			Lineal

1 e i n Wörterbuch 2 ___ Lineal 3 ___ Taschenrechner 4 ___ Diskette 5 ___ Banane 6 ___ Etui 7 ___ Bleistift

6 sechs

1 (AT3 Level 1, AT4 Level 1) 1 Kuli **2** Lineal **3** Buch **4** Schultasche **5** Heft **6** Schere **7** Bleistift **8** Taschenrechner

2 (AT3 Level 1/2, AT4 Level 1) In meiner Schultasche habe ich ... **1 ein** Wörterbuch, **2 ein** Lineal, **3 einen** Taschenrechner, **4 eine** Diskette, **5 eine** Banane, **6 ein** Etui und **7 einen** Bleistift.

Übungsheft B, Seite 6

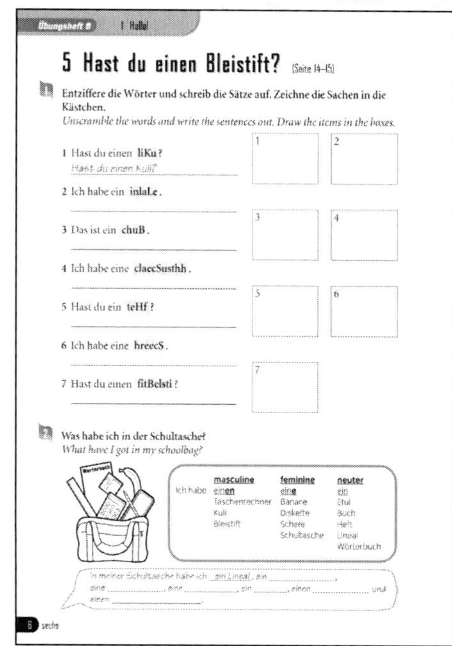
Übungsheft B | 1 Hallo!

5 Hast du einen Bleistift? (Seite 14–15)

1 Entziffere die Wörter und schreib die Sätze auf. Zeichne die Sachen in die Kästchen. *Unscramble the words and write the sentences out. Draw the items in the boxes.*

1 Hast du einen liKu? Hast du einen Kuli?
2 Ich habe ein inlaLe.
3 Das ist ein chuB.
4 Ich habe eine claecSusthh.
5 Hast du ein teHf?
6 Ich habe eine hreecS.
7 Hast du einen fitBelsti?

2 Was habe ich in der Schultasche? *What have I got in my schoolbag?*

	masculine	feminine	neuter
Ich habe	einen	eine	ein
	Taschenrechner	Banane	Etui
	Kuli	Diskette	Buch
	Bleistift	Schere	Heft
		Schultasche	Lineal
			Wörterbuch

In meiner Schultasche habe ich ein Lineal, ein ...

6 sechs

1 (AT3 Level 2, AT4 Level 2) 1 Hast du einen **Kuli**? **2** Ich habe ein **Lineal**. **3** Das ist ein **Buch**. **4** Ich habe eine **Schultasche**. **5** Hast du ein **Heft**? **6** Ich habe eine **Schere**. **7** Hast du einen **Bleistift**?

2 (AT3 Level 3, AT4 Level 2) In meiner Schultasche habe ich ein Lineal, ein Wörterbuch, eine Diskette, eine Banane, ein Etui, einen Bleistift und einen Taschenrechner.

Übungsheft A, Seite 7

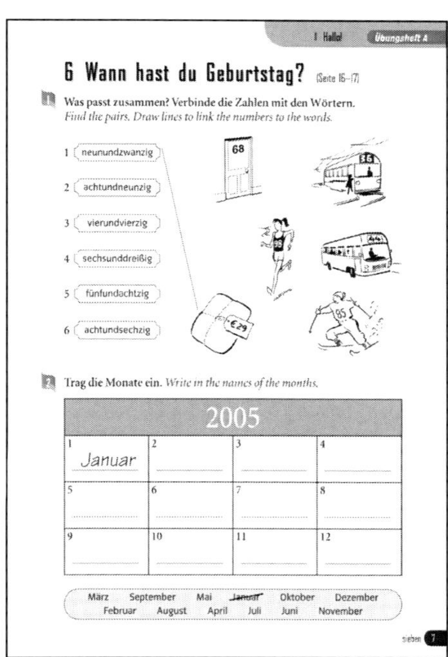
1 Hallo! Übungsheft A

6 Wann hast du Geburtstag? (Seite 16–17)

1 Was passt zusammen? Verbinde die Zahlen mit den Wörtern. *Find the pairs. Draw lines to link the numbers to the words.*

1 neunundzwanzig
2 achtundneunzig
3 vierundvierzig
4 sechsunddreißig
5 fünfundachtzig
6 achtundsechzig

2 Trag die Monate ein. *Write in the names of the months.*

2005			
1 Januar	2	3	4
5	6	7	8
9	10	11	12

März September Mai Januar Oktober Dezember Februar August April Juli Juni November

sieben 7

1 (AT3 Level 1) 1e **2** c **3** d **4** b **5** f **6** a

2 (AT3 Level 1, AT4 Level 1) 1 Januar **2** Februar **3** März **4** April **5** Mai **6** Juni **7** Juli **8** August **9** September **10** Oktober **11** November **12** Dezember

Übungsheft B, Seite 7

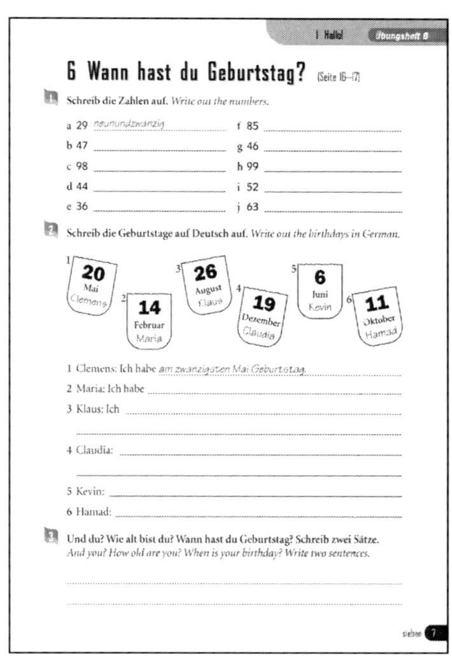
1 Hallo! Übungsheft B

6 Wann hast du Geburtstag? (Seite 16–17)

1 Schreib die Zahlen auf. *Write out the numbers.*

a 29 neunundzwanzig f 85
b 47 g 46
c 98 h 99
d 44 i 52
e 36 j 63

2 Schreib die Geburtstage auf Deutsch auf. *Write out the birthdays in German.*

1 20 Mai Clemens 2 14 Februar Maria 3 26 August Klaus 4 19 Dezember Claudia 5 6 Juni Kevin 6 11 Oktober Hamad

1 Clemens: Ich habe am zwanzigsten Mai Geburtstag.
2 Maria: Ich habe
3 Klaus: Ich
4 Claudia:
5 Kevin:
6 Hamad:

3 Und du? Wie alt bist du? Wann hast du Geburtstag? Schreib zwei Sätze. *And you? How old are you? When is your birthday? Write two sentences.*

sieben 7

1 (AT4 Level 1) a neunundzwanzig **b** siebenundvierzig **c** achtundneunzig **d** vierundvierzig **e** sechsunddreißig **f** fünfundachtzig **g** sechsundvierzig **h** neunundneunzig **i** zweiundfünfzig **j** dreiundsechzig

2 (AT3 Level 2, AT4 Level 2) 1 Clemens: Ich habe am zwanzigsten Mai Geburtstag. **2** Maria: Ich habe am vierzehnten Februar Geburtstag. **3** Klaus: Ich habe am sechsundzwanzigsten August Geburtstag. **4** Claudia: Ich habe am neunzehnten Dezember Geburtstag. **5** Kevin: Ich habe am sechsten Juni Geburtstag. **6** Hamad: Ich habe am elften Oktober Geburtstag.

3 (AT4 Level 3)

Übungsheft A, Seite 8

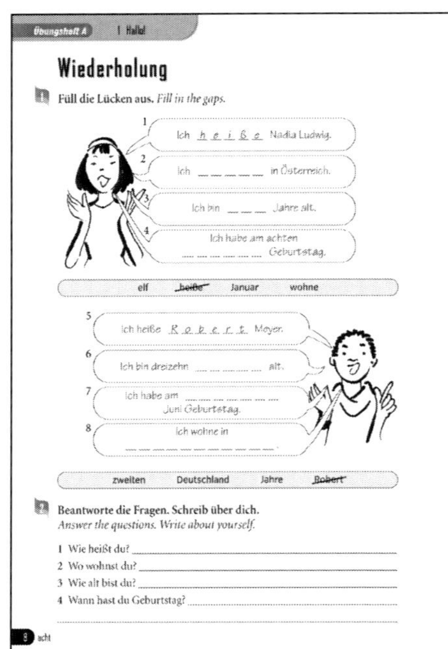
Übungsheft A 1 Hallo!

Wiederholung

1 Füll die Lücken aus. *Fill in the gaps.*

1 Ich h e i ß e Nadia Ludwig.
2 Ich ______ in Österreich.
3 Ich bin ____ Jahre alt.
4 Ich habe am achten ______ Geburtstag.

elf ~~heiße~~ Januar wohne

5 Ich heiße R o b e r t Meyer.
6 Ich bin dreizehn ______ alt.
7 Ich habe am ______ Juni Geburtstag.
8 Ich wohne in ______.

zweiten Deutschland Jahre ~~Robert~~

2 Beantworte die Fragen. Schreib über dich.
Answer the questions. Write about yourself.

1 Wie heißt du? ______
2 Wo wohnst du? ______
3 Wie alt bist du? ______
4 Wann hast du Geburtstag? ______

8 acht

1 (AT3 Level 2, AT4 Level 1) Ich **heiße** Nadia Ludwig. Ich **wohne** in Österreich. Ich bin **elf** Jahre alt. Ich habe am achten **Januar** Geburtstag.

Ich heiße **Robert** Meyer. Ich bin dreizehn **Jahre** alt: Ich habe am **zweiten** Juni Geburtstag. Ich wohne in **Deutschland**.

2 (AT3 Level 2, AT4 Level 2) 1 Ich heiße … **2** Ich wohne in … **3** Ich bin … Jahre alt. **4** Ich habe am … Geburtstag.

Übungsheft B, Seite 8

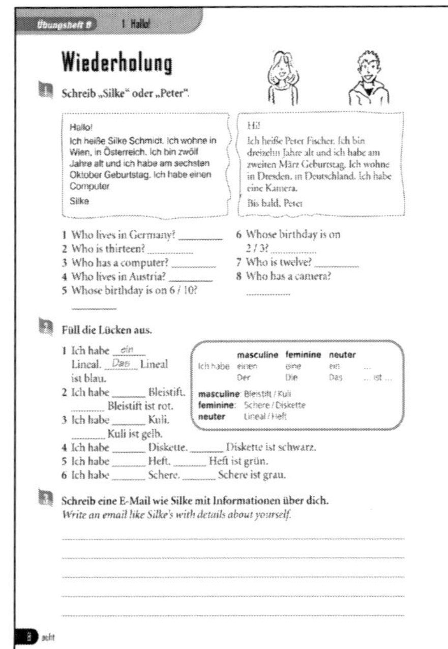
Übungsheft B 1 Hallo!

Wiederholung

1 Schreib „Silke“ oder „Peter“.

Hallo!
Ich heiße Silke Schmidt. Ich wohne in Wien, in Österreich. Ich bin zwölf Jahre alt und ich habe am sechsten Oktober Geburtstag. Ich habe einen Computer.
Silke

Hi!
Ich heiße Peter Fischer. Ich bin dreizehn Jahre alt und ich habe am zweiten März Geburtstag. Ich wohne in Dresden, in Deutschland. Ich habe eine Kamera.
Bis bald, Peter

1 Who lives in Germany? ______
2 Who is thirteen? ______
3 Who has a computer? ______
4 Who lives in Austria? ______
5 Whose birthday is on 6 / 10? ______
6 Whose birthday is on 2 / 3? ______
7 Who is twelve? ______
8 Who has a camera? ______

2 Füll die Lücken aus.

1 Ich habe ein Lineal. Das Lineal ist blau.
2 Ich habe ______ Bleistift. ______ Bleistift ist rot.
3 Ich habe ______ Kuli. ______ Kuli ist gelb.
4 Ich habe ______ Diskette. ______ Diskette ist schwarz.
5 Ich habe ______ Heft. ______ Heft ist grün.
6 Ich habe ______ Schere. ______ Schere ist grau.

	masculine	feminine	neuter	
Ich habe	einen	eine	ein	…
	Der	Die	Das	… ist …

masculine: Bleistift / Kuli
feminine: Schere / Diskette
neuter: Lineal / Heft

3 Schreib eine E-Mail wie Silke mit Informationen über dich.
Write an email like Silke's with details about yourself.

8 acht

1 (AT3 Level 3) 1 Peter **2** Peter **3** Silke **4** Silke **5** Silke **6** Peter **7** Silke **8** Peter

2 (AT 3 Level 2, AT 4 Level 1)

Answers
1 Ich habe **ein** Lineal. **Das** Lineal ist blau. **2** Ich habe **einen** Bleistift. **Der** Bleistift ist rot. **3** Ich habe **einen** Kuli. **Der** Kuli ist gelb. **4** Ich habe **eine** Diskette. **Die** Diskette ist schwarz. **5** Ich habe **ein** Heft. **Das** Heft ist grün. **6** Ich habe **eine** Schere. **Die** Schere ist grau.

3 (AT4 Level 3)

Arbeitsblatt 1.1

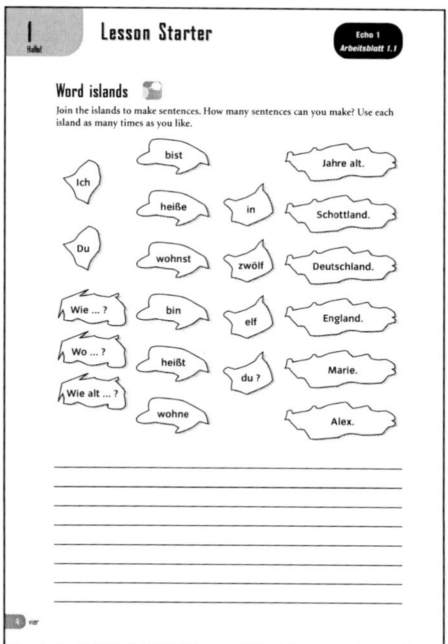
1 Hallo!

Lesson Starter

Echo 1 Arbeitsblatt 1.1

Word islands

Join the islands to make sentences. How many sentences can you make? Use each island as many times as you like.

4 vier

Possible answers

Ich bin zwölf Jahre alt. Ich bin elf Jahre alt. Du bist zwölf Jahre alt. Du bist elf Jahre alt. Ich heiße Marie. Ich heiße Alex. Du heißt Marie. Du heißt Alex. Ich wohne in Schottland. Ich wohne in Deutschland. Ich wohne in England. Du wohnst in Schottland. Du wohnst in Deutschland. Du wohnst in England.

Possible questions include

Wie heißt du? Wo wohnst du? Wie alt bist du?

Arbeitsblatt 1.2

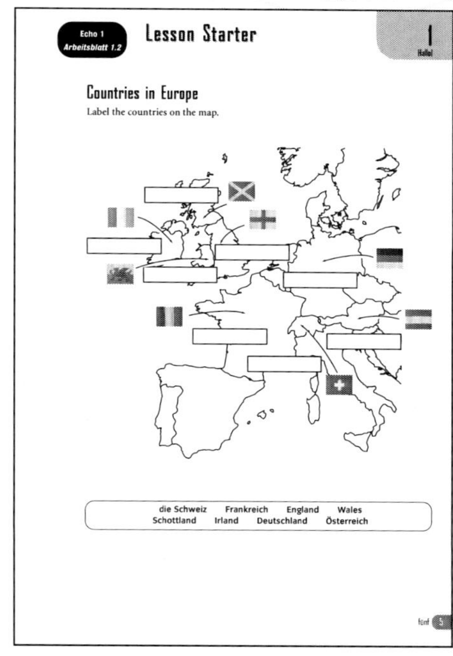
Echo 1 Arbeitsblatt 1.2

Lesson Starter

1 Hallo!

Countries in Europe

Label the countries on the map.

fünf 5

Irland; Wales; Schottland; England; Frankreich; Deutschland; Österreich; die Schweiz

Arbeitsblatt 1.3

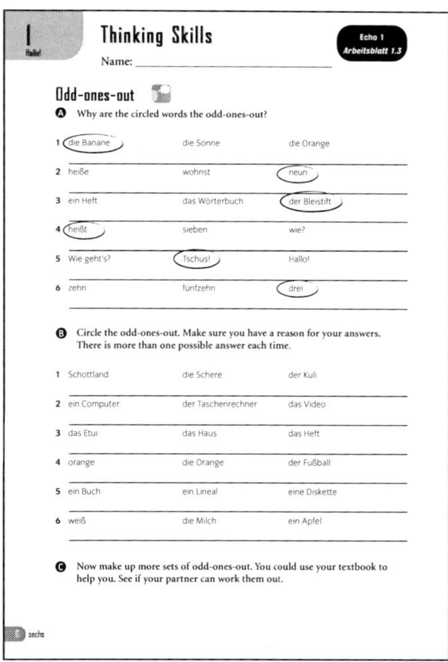
1 Hallo!

Thinking Skills

Name: ____________

Echo 1 Arbeitsblatt 1.3

Odd-ones-out

A Why are the circled words the odd-ones-out?

1 die Banane | die Sonne | die Orange
2 heiße | wohnst | neun
3 ein Heft | das Wörterbuch | der Bleistift
4 heißt | sieben | wie?
5 Wie geht's? | Tschüs! | Hallo!
6 zehn | fünfzehn | drei

B Circle the odd-ones-out. Make sure you have a reason for your answers. There is more than one possible answer each time.

1 Schottland | die Schere | der Kuli
2 ein Computer | der Taschenrechner | das Video
3 das Etui | das Haus | das Heft
4 orange | die Orange | der Fußball
5 ein Buch | ein Lineal | eine Diskette
6 weiß | die Milch | ein Apfel

C Now make up more sets of odd-ones-out. You could use your textbook to help you. See if your partner can work them out.

6 sechs

A
Accept any reasonable alternative explanations.

1 The others are round. **2** The others are verbs. **3** *Der Bleistift* is masculine; the others are neuter. The others are also books. **4** The others contain *ie*. **5** The others are greetings. **6** The others are multiples of five. The others also have *zehn* in them.

Arbeitsblatt 1.4

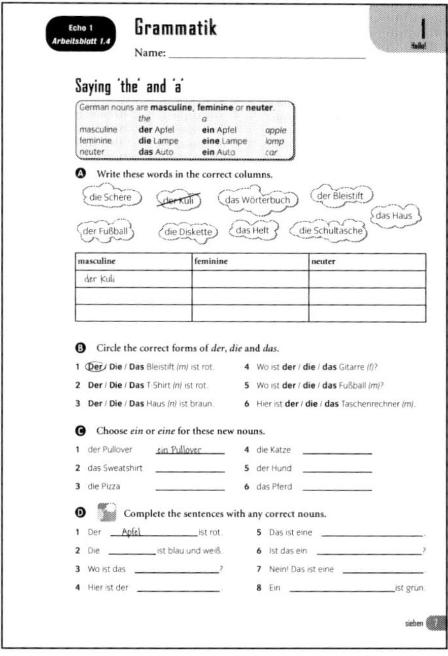
Echo 1 Arbeitsblatt 1.4

Grammatik

Name: ____________

1 Hallo!

Saying 'the' and 'a'

German nouns are **masculine**, **feminine** or **neuter**.

	the	*a*	
masculine	**der** Apfel	**ein** Apfel	*apple*
feminine	**die** Lampe	**eine** Lampe	*lamp*
neuter	**das** Auto	**ein** Auto	*car*

A Write these words in the correct columns.

die Schere, der Kuli, das Wörterbuch, der Bleistift, das Haus, der Fußball, die Diskette, das Heft, die Schultasche

masculine	feminine	neuter
der Kuli		

B Circle the correct forms of *der*, *die* and *das*.

1 **Der** / **Die** / **Das** Bleistift *(m)* ist rot.
2 **Der** / **Die** / **Das** T-Shirt *(n)* ist rot.
3 **Der** / **Die** / **Das** Haus *(n)* ist braun.
4 Wo ist **der** / **die** / **das** Gitarre *(f)*?
5 Wo ist **der** / **die** / **das** Fußball *(m)*?
6 Hier ist **der** / **die** / **das** Taschenrechner *(m)*.

C Choose *ein* or *eine* for these new nouns.

1 der Pullover ein Pullover
2 das Sweatshirt ______
3 die Pizza ______
4 die Katze ______
5 der Hund ______
6 das Pferd ______

D Complete the sentences with any correct nouns.

1 Der Apfel ist rot.
2 Die ______ ist blau und weiß.
3 Wo ist das ______?
4 Hier ist der ______.
5 Das ist eine ______.
6 Ist das ein ______?
7 Nein! Das ist eine ______.
8 Ein ______ ist grün.

sieben 7

A
Masculine: Kuli, Bleistift, Fußball; *Feminine:* Schere, Diskette, Schultasche; *Neuter:* Wörterbuch, Haus, Heft

B
1 der **2** das **3** das **4** die **5** der **6** der

C
1 ein Pullover **2** ein Sweatshirt **3** eine Pizza **4** eine Katze **5** ein Hund **6** ein Pferd

Arbeitsblatt 1.5

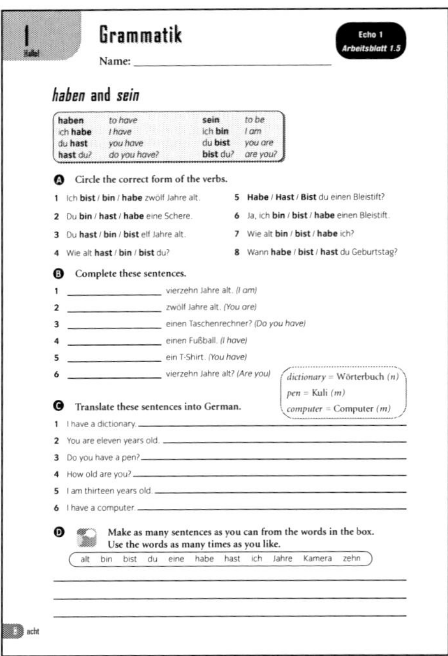

1 Hallo!

Grammatik

Echo 1 *Arbeitsblatt 1.5*

Name: ______________________

haben and *sein*

haben	*to have*	**sein**	*to be*
ich **habe**	*I have*	ich **bin**	*I am*
du **hast**	*you have*	du **bist**	*you are*
hast du?	*do you have?*	**bist** du?	*are you?*

A Circle the correct form of the verbs.

1 Ich **bist / bin / habe** zwölf Jahre alt.
2 Du **bin / hast / habe** eine Schere.
3 Du **hast / bin / bist** elf Jahre alt.
4 Wie alt **hast / bin / bist** du?
5 **Habe / Hast / Bist** du einen Bleistift?
6 Ja, ich **bin / bist / habe** einen Bleistift.
7 Wie alt **bin / bist / habe** ich?
8 Wann **habe / bist / hast** du Geburtstag?

B Complete these sentences.

1 ______________ vierzehn Jahre alt. *(I am)*
2 ______________ zwölf Jahre alt. *(You are)*
3 ______________ einen Taschenrechner? *(Do you have)*
4 ______________ einen Fußball. *(I have)*
5 ______________ ein T-Shirt. *(You have)*
6 ______________ vierzehn Jahre alt? *(Are you)*

dictionary = Wörterbuch *(n)*
pen = Kuli *(m)*
computer = Computer *(m)*

C Translate these sentences into German.

1 I have a dictionary. ______________
2 You are eleven years old. ______________
3 Do you have a pen? ______________
4 How old are you? ______________
5 I am thirteen years old. ______________
6 I have a computer. ______________

D Make as many sentences as you can from the words in the box. Use the words as many times as you like.

alt bin bist du eine habe hast ich Jahre Kamera zehn

8 acht

Arbeitsblatt 1.6

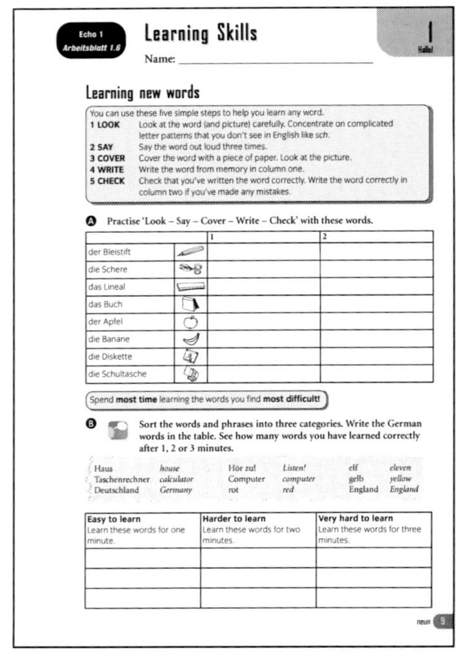

Echo 1 *Arbeitsblatt 1.6*

Learning Skills

1 Hallo!

Name: ______________________

Learning new words

You can use these five simple steps to help you learn any word.
1 LOOK Look at the word (and picture) carefully. Concentrate on complicated letter patterns that you don't see in English like *sch*.
2 SAY Say the word out loud three times.
3 COVER Cover the word with a piece of paper. Look at the picture.
4 WRITE Write the word from memory in column one.
5 CHECK Check that you've written the word correctly. Write the word correctly in column two if you've made any mistakes.

A Practise 'Look – Say – Cover – Write – Check' with these words.

		1	2
der Bleistift			
die Schere			
das Lineal			
das Buch			
der Apfel			
die Banane			
die Diskette			
die Schultasche			

Spend **most time** learning the words you find **most difficult!**

B Sort the words and phrases into three categories. Write the German words in the table. See how many words you have learned correctly after 1, 2 or 3 minutes.

Haus	*house*	Hör zu!	*Listen!*	elf	*eleven*
Taschenrechner	*calculator*	Computer	*computer*	gelb	*yellow*
Deutschland	*Germany*	rot	*red*	England	*England*

Easy to learn Learn these words for one minute.	**Harder to learn** Learn these words for two minutes.	**Very hard to learn** Learn these words for three minutes.

neun 9

A
1 bin **2** hast **3** bist **4** bist **5** Hast **6** habe **7** bin **8** hast

B
Ich bin **2** Du bist **3** Hast du **4** Ich habe **5** Du hast **6** Bist du

C
1 Ich habe ein Wörterbuch. **2** Du bist elf Jahre alt. **3** Hast du einen Kuli? **4** Wie alt bist du? **5** Ich bin dreizehn Jahre alt. **6** Ich habe einen Computer.

D
Possible answers

Ich habe eine Kamera. Du hast eine Kamera. Ich bin zehn Jahre alt. Du bist zehn Jahre alt. Habe ich eine Kamera? Hast du eine Kamera? Bin ich zehn Jahre alt? Bist du zehn Jahre alt?

2 Die Schule

Unit Learning targets	Key framework objectives	NC levels and PoS coverage	Grammar and key language	Skills
1 Was ist dein Lieblingsfach? (pp. 24–25) • Saying which is your favourite subject • Asking for help in class without using English	5.3 Strategies – English/other languages 5.4 Strategies – working out meaning	NC level 2 **2.1b** memorising **2.1c** knowledge of language **2.2a** listen for gist **2.2d** pronunciation and intonation **2.2e** ask and answer questions **2.2f** initiate / sustain conversations **2.2k** deal with unfamiliar language **3b** sounds and writing **3c** apply grammar **3d** use a range of vocab / structures **4b** communicate in pairs etc. **4d** make links with English	Irregular verb *sein: ist* Questions with question words *Was ist dein Lieblingsfach?* *Mein Lieblingsfach ist …* *Deutsch / Englisch / Französisch / Religion / Informatik / Mathe / Naturwissenschaften / Werken / Kunst / Musik / Theater / Erdkunde / Geschichte / Sport* *Entschuldigung! Ich habe ein Problem.* *Wie schreibt man das?* *Ich verstehe nicht.* *Wie bitte?* *Wie heißt … auf Englisch?* *Wie heißt … auf Deutsch?* *Wie spricht man das aus?* *Ich muss mal.*	Pronunciation: cognates
2 Wie findest du Deutsch? (pp. 26–27) • Saying which days you have different subjects • Giving your opinion	1.3/Y7 Listening – (a) interpreting intonation and tone 1.3/Y7 Speaking – (b) using intonation and tone	NC levels 1–4 **2.1a** identify patterns **2.1b** memorising **2.1d** previous knowledge **2.2a** listen for gist **2.2d** pronunciation and intonation **2.2e** ask and answer questions **2.2f** initiate / sustain conversations **2.2i** reuse language they have met **3b** sounds and writing **3c** apply grammar **3d** use a range of vocab / structures **4b** communicate in pairs etc.	Irregular verb *haben: ich habe, du hast* Regular verb *finden: ich finde, du findest* Questions with question words *Montag, Dienstag, Mittwoch, Donnerstag, Freitag, Samstag, Sonntag* *Was hast du am (Montag)?* *Ich habe am (Montag) (Deutsch).* *Wie findest du Deutsch (etc.)?* *Ich finde (Deutsch) gut / schlecht / interessant / langweilig / einfach / schwierig / toll / furchtbar.*	Pronunciation: *ei/ie* Expressing opinions
3 Wie viel Uhr ist es? (pp. 28–29) • Talking about the school timetable • Telling the time	3.2/Y7 Culture – (a) young people: interests/ opinions	NC levels 2–3 **2.1b** memorising **2.2a** listen for gist **2.2d** pronunciation and intonation **2.2e** ask and answer questions **3b** sounds and writing **3c** apply grammar **3f** compare experiences **4b** communicate in pairs etc.	Irregular verb *sein: es ist* Question formation with question words *Wie viel Uhr ist es?* *Es ist … Uhr …* *Wann beginnt/endet (Deutsch)?* *Um … Uhr …*	Telling the time Reviewing progress Pronunciation: *v/w*

Unit Learning targets	**Key framework objectives**	**NC levels and PoS coverage**	**Grammar and key language**	**Skills**
4 Pausenbrot (pp. 30–31) • Talking about what you eat and drink at break • Checking verb endings	**4.5/Y7** Language – (a) present tense verbs	**NC levels** 2–3 **2.1b** memorising **2.1c** knowledge of language **2.2a** listen for gist **2.2b** skim and scan **2.2e** ask and answer questions **2.2f** initiate / sustain conversations **3b** sounds and writing **3c** apply grammar **3d** use a range of vocab / structures **4b** communicate in pairs etc. **4d** make links with English **4g** language for a range of purposes	Review of regular and irregular verbs: *ich trinke, du trinkst* *ich wohne, du wohnst* *ich esse, du isst* *ich habe, du hast* *ich bin, du bist* *die Kekse (der Keks) / die Chips / der Apfel / die Orange / die Banane / die Schokolade / die Bonbons (das Bonbon) / das Brötchen / die Cola / der Orangensaft / das Wasser / der Kuchen* *Was isst/trinkst du in der Pause?* *Ich esse einen Apfel / einen Kuchen / eine Orange / eine Banane / ein Brötchen / Schokolade / Kekse / Chips / Bonbons / nichts.* *Ich trinke Cola / Orangensaft / Wasser/nichts.* *Ja, bitte?* *Ein Brötchen, bitte.* *Das macht fünfzig Cent.* *Bitte. Danke.*	Polite expressions
5 Was trägst du in der Schule? (pp. 32–33) • Describing what you wear to school • Revising *einen, eine, ein*	**4.3/Y7** Language – gender **2.4/Y7** Writing – (b) building text	**NC levels** 1–4 **2.1b** memorising **2.1c** knowledge of language **2.2a** listen for gist **2.2b** skim and scan **2.2e** ask and answer questions **2.2f** initiate / sustain conversations **2.2i** reuse language they have met **3b** sounds and writing **3c** apply grammar **3d** use a range of vocab / structures **4b** communicate in pairs etc. **4d** make links with English **4f** language of interest / enjoyment	Indefinite article, accusative Irregular verbs *sein* and *tragen:* *es ist / sie sind* *ich trage / du trägst* *die Jacke / die Hose / das Hemd / der Pullover / die Krawatte / die Schuhe (der Schuh) / der Rock / die Socken (die Socke) / das Sweatshirt / das T-Shirt / die Jeans / die Stiefel (der Stiefel)* *Der Rock (etc) ist …* *Die Schuhe (etc) sind …* *blau / braun / gelb / grau / grün / lila / orange / rot / schwarz / weiß.* *Was trägst du in der Schule?* *Ich trage einen Rock / Jeansrock / Pullover / Kleid, eine Hose / Bluse / Jacke, ein Hemd / T-Shirt / Sweatshirt, Jeans / Schuhe / Stiefel / Sportschuhe.* *Ich finde das cool, bequem, schick, gut.*	Expressing opinions

Unit Learning targets	Key framework objectives	NC levels and PoS coverage	Grammar and key language	Skills
6 Meine Schule (pp. 34–35) • Learning about school life in German-speaking countries • Understanding a longer text	**4.6/Y7** Language – (b) negatives **5.6** Strategies – reading aloud **5.7** Strategies – planning and preparing	**NC levels** 3–4 **2.1d** previous knowledge **2.2a** listen for gist **2.2b** skim and scan **2.2c** respond appropriately **2.2d** pronunciation and intonation **2.2g** write clearly and coherently **3b** sounds and writing **3c** apply grammar **3d** use a range of vocab / structures **3e** different countries' cultures **3f** compare experiences **4e** use a range of resources **4f** language of interest / enjoyment **4g** language for a range of purposes	Negative article, accusative Review of regular and irregular verbs, first person singular: *ich heiße* *ich wohne* *ich bin* *ich esse* *ich trinke* *ich finde* *ich trage* *ich habe* *Ich heiße … .* *Ich bin … Jahre alt.* *Ich wohne in …* *Ich bin in der Klasse … .* *Die Schule beginnt um … .* *In der Pause esse/trinke ich … .* *Mein Lieblingsfach ist …* *Ich finde … schwierig (etc.).* *Ich trage … in der Schule.* *Ich habe keine Schuluniform.*	Planning a longer text (webpage) Reading a text aloud
Lernzieltest und Wiederholung (pp. 36–37) • Pupils' checklist and practice test		**NC levels** 2–4 **2.2a** listen for gist **2.2b** skim and scan **2.2e** ask and answer questions **2.2f** initiate / sustain conversations **3b** sounds and writing **4b** communicate in pairs etc.		
Mehr: (pp. 36–37) • Extension material	**4.4/Y7** Language – sentence formation	**NC levels** 3–4 **2.1d** previous knowledge **2.1e** use reference materials **2.2b** skim and scan **2.2c** respond appropriately **2.2d** pronunciation and intonation **2.2j** adapt previously-learnt language **3b** sounds and writing **3c** apply grammar **3d** use a range of vocab / structures	*Die Schule beginnt um …* *In der Pause esse/trinke ich …* *Um … Uhr habe ich Englisch (etc.).*	Reading a longer text for gist Using reference materials
Extra (pp. 114–115) • Self-access reading and writing at two levels		**NC levels** 1–4 **2.2b** skim and scan **2.2e** ask and answer questions **3c** apply grammar **3d** use a range of vocab / structures		

1 Was ist dein Lieblingsfach?

Learning targets

- Saying which is your favourite subject
- Asking for help in class without using English

Key framework objectives

5.3 Strategies – English/other languages
5.4 Strategies – working out meaning

Grammar

- Third person singular of *sein*: *ist*
- Possessive adjectives: *mein* and *dein*
- Questions with *Was … ?* and *Wie … ?*

Key language

Was ist dein Lieblingsfach?
Mein Lieblingsfach ist …
Deutsch
Englisch
Französisch
Religion
Informatik
Mathe
Naturwissenschaften
Werken
Kunst
Musik
Theater
Erdkunde
Geschichte
Sport
Entschuldigung! Ich habe ein Problem.
Wie schreibt man das?
Ich verstehe nicht.
Wie bitte?
Wie heißt … auf Englisch?
Wie heißt … auf Deutsch?
Wie spricht man das aus?
Ich muss mal.

High-frequency words

mein
dein
was?
wie?
ist
nicht
ich habe
auf
das (that)

Pronunciation

Cognates

Mathematics

Quantifying survey results

ICT

Using a spreadsheet application to show survey results

Resources

CD 1, tracks 28–30
Workbooks A and B, p.12
Arbeitsblatt 2.1, p.20
Flashcards 21–34
Echo Elektro 1 TPP, Mod 2 1.1–1.6

Starter 1 5.4

Aims
To encourage recognition of cognates.
To develop strategies for finding out the meanings of unfamiliar words.

Use **Arbeitsblatt 2.1.** Collect ideas about what sort of words these might be (school subjects). Pupils work in pairs. They categorise the words into two groups: words whose meaning they can guess, and those they cannot. Follow up by choosing two which the class cannot guess, and ask for ideas about where to find the meanings. Pupils race to see who can find the meanings quickest in the word list or the **Wortschatz.**

1 Hör zu und wiederhole. 5.3

Listening. Pupils listen to and repeat the school subjects on the recording while reading them in the book.

28

Deutsch, Englisch, Französisch, Religion, Informatik, Mathe, Naturwissenschaften, Werken, Kunst, Musik, Theater, Erdkunde, Geschichte, Sport

Suggestion
Focus on the close cognates:

Englisch, Religion, Mathe, Musik, Sport, Theater

Ask pupils how they would say these words in English. Now play the recording again and ask pupils to listen to the differences when the words are said in German. Drill pronunciation of the cognates (or all the subjects, if you prefer) with the class.

2 Hör zu. Welches Fach ist das? (1–12) (AT 1/2) 1.1/Y7

Listening. Pupils listen to people talking about their favourite subjects, and write down the correct German word for each. Suggest to weaker pupils that they note the first two letters of the subject heard, and perhaps write out the complete word later or when listening again.

1 – *Hallo. Was ist dein Lieblingsfach?*
– *Mein Lieblingsfach ist Musik.*

2 – *Und du, was ist dein Lieblingsfach?*
– *Mein Lieblingsfach? Also ... mein Lieblingsfach ist Sport.*

3 – *Hast du ein Lieblingsfach?*
– *Ähm...mein Lieblingsfach ist Theater.*

4 – *Und was ist dein Lieblingsfach?*
– *Mein Lieblingsfach ist ... ähm... Erdkunde.*

5 – *Was ist dein Lieblingsfach?*
– *Mein Lieblingsfach ist Werken.*

6 – *Ist dein Lieblingsfach auch Werken?*
– *Nein. Mein Lieblingsfach ist Religion.*

7 – *Und du. Was ist dein Lieblingsfach?*
– *Ähm ...Mein Lieblingsfach ist Mathe.*

8 – *Hallo. Was ist dein Lieblingsfach?*
– *Englisch ist super. Mein Lieblingsfach ist Englisch.*

9 – *Und was ist dein Lieblingsfach?*
– *Ähm, mein Lieblingsfach ist Geschichte.*

10 – *Hast du ein Lieblingsfach?*
– *Ja. Mein Lieblingsfach ist Deutsch.*

11 – *Was ist dein Lieblingsfach?*
– *Mein Lieblingsfach ist Kunst.*

12 – *Und was ist dein Lieblingsfach?*
– *Mein Lieblingsfach ist Informatik.*

Answers

1 Musik **2** Sport **3** Theater **4** Erdkunde
5 Werken **6** Religion **7** Mathe **8** Englisch
9 Geschichte **10** Deutsch **11** Kunst
12 Informatik

3 Wer sagt das? (AT 3/2) 2.1/Y7

Reading. Pupils read the speech bubbles and look at the pictures. They match each speech bubble to the appropriate picture.

Answers

1 Hamit **2** Marie **3** Valentina
4 Niklas **5** Alexander **6** Lea

4 Umfrage. (AT 2/2) 1.4a/Y7

Speaking. Pupils move around the class asking each other what their favourite subject is and keeping a tally of how many people liked each subject. Before pupils start the exercise, you could demonstrate that they only need to change one word in the sentence to convey personally relevant information. Stress that adapting sentences is an important language-learning skill.

ICT Pupils could present their results as pie or bar charts using a spreadsheet application.

ECHO-Tipp 4.2/Y7

This draws pupils' attention to the importance of the high-frequency words *mein* and *dein*. (In Chapter 3, pupils will learn that these words are inflected when used in front of the noun.) You could discuss the concept of high-frequency words at this point. Ask pupils about different situations in which they would use the words 'my' and 'your' in English. Point out that this is just the same in German, which makes these words particularly useful to learn. Higher-ability groups may be able to pick out other German words that would be useful in lots of different situations. (Answers from this unit include *Was?* and *ist.*) You could contrast these with *Erdkunde*, which is only likely to come up in the context of school subjects.

Starter 2 5.2

Aims

To revise school subjects.
To explore ways of memorising words.

Write nine subjects on the board and ask pupils to write them down in three groups. They can choose the principles behind the groupings (e.g. subject areas (sciences, arts, humanities); personal feelings about the subject; whether they have the subject today; the way the subjects are spelled). They then explain the grouping to their partner. (The partner could try to guess the principle of the grouping first.) You could select some of the groupings for discussion with the whole class.

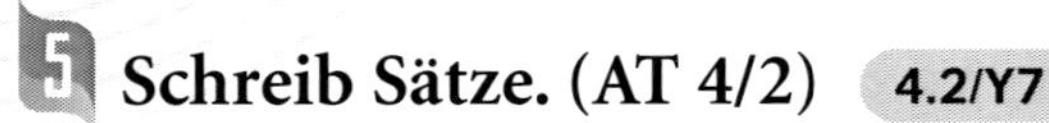

5 Schreib Sätze. (AT 4/2) 4.2/Y7

Writing. Pupils use the picture cues to write sentences.

Answers

1 Mein Lieblingsfach ist Erdkunde.
2 Mein Lieblingsfach ist Naturwissenschaften.
3 Mein Lieblingsfach ist Englisch.
4 Mein Lieblingsfach ist Geschichte.
5 Mein Lieblingsfach ist Mathe.
6 Mein Lieblingsfach ist Religion.

\+ More able pupils go on to check each other's work for spelling and punctuation issues and award a mark for accuracy.

6 Hör zu und lies. (1–8) 2.1/Y7

Listening. Pupils listen to the classroom language on the recording while reading the sentences in their books.

Suggestion

Ask pupils which sentences they would find most useful if (a) in class and (b) in Germany, and why. Accept all answers with an explanation as valid.

30

1 Entschuldigung! Ich habe ein Problem.
2 Wie bitte?
3 Ich verstehe nicht.
4 Wie schreibt man das?
5 Wie heißt „Lieblingsfach" auf Englisch?
6 Wie heßt „maths" auf Deutsch?
7 S-C-I-E-N-C-E. Wie spricht man das aus?
8 Ich muss mal.

7 Wie sagt man das auf Deutsch? (AT 3/2) 4.4/Y7

Writing. Pupils supply the German equivalents (from exercise 6) of the English sentences. For further exploitation of this activity, please see Writing follow-up on pages 9–10.

Answers

1 Wie schreibt man das?
2 Entschuldigung! Ich habe ein Problem.
3 Ich muss mal.
4 Ich verstehe nicht.
5 Wie bitte?
6 Wie spricht man das aus?
7 Wie heißt … auf Englisch?
8 Wie heißt … auf Deutsch?

ECHO-Tipp 1.4a/Y7

This tip suggests that pupils compile and learn their own lists of classroom language. Explain to the class how you want them to arrange these lists, e.g. on a separate page in their exercise books. You may want to gather ideas from the class about other useful classroom expressions they would like to be able to say in German, and encourage pupils to use these phrases with each other as well as with you.

Plenary 5.2

Aims

To reinforce names of school subjects.
To develop strategies for learning vocabulary.

Ask pupils to close their books. Divide the class into two or more teams. Do a quick-fire quiz on names of school subjects: pupils supply the German or the English as appropriate. Each team member is only allowed to score one correct answer for his/her team. To follow up, ask pupils to discuss in pairs which subjects they find most difficult to remember, and to work out ways in which they could learn them. Set a time limit for the discussion. Finally, gather learning strategies from the whole class.

Learning targets

- Saying which days you have different subjects
- Giving your opinion

Key framework objectives

1.3/Y7 Listening – (a) interpreting intonation and tone

1.3/Y7 Speaking – (b) using intonation and tone

Grammar

- The present tense of the verb *haben* in the *ich* and *du* forms
- Forming questions with question words

Key language

Days of the week
Was hast du am (Montag)?
Ich habe am (Montag) (Deutsch).
Wie findest du Deutsch?
Ich finde (Deutsch) gut / schlecht / interessant / langweilig / einfach / schwierig / toll / furchtbar.

High-frequency words

was?
ich, du
habe, hast
am
finde, findest
gut, schlecht, interessant, langweilig, einfach, schwierig, toll, furchtbar

Pronunciation

ei/ie

English

Reading and understanding an email

Resources

CD 1, tracks 31–34
Workbooks A and B, p.13
Echo Elektro 1 TPP, Mod 2 2.1–2.7

Starter 1

5.3

Aims

To introduce the days of the week.
To encourage the use of cognates in inferring meaning.

On the board or an OHT, write the days of the week in German, scattered in random order. As the class comes into the room, ask pupils to think about what the words on the board mean. Collect ideas and establish that they are the days of the week. Elicit from the class what the English translation of each day is. *Montag, Freitag, Samstag* and *Sonntag* should be recognisable to pupils; encourage them to guess the remaining three. Invite ideas from the class about the subject of today's lesson (school + days of the week = timetable).

1 Hör zu. Was passt zusammen? (1–7) (AT 1/1) 4.2/Y7

Listening. Pupils listen to the recording and put the days of the week in the correct order.

31

1 Montag
2 Dienstag
3 Mittwoch
4 Donnerstag
5 Freitag
6 Samstag
7 Sonntag

Answers
1 e **2** a **3** d **4** b **5** c **6** f **7** g

2 Hör zu. Welcher Tag ist das? (1–5) (AT 1/2) 1.1/Y7

Listening. Pupils listen to the recording and select the appropriate pictures. In preparation for listening, look at the photos and their labels with the class and establish what each of the subjects is in English: *Wie heißt „Werken" auf Englisch?*, etc. Ask pupils to study the instructions and elicit what they will be listening for (days of the week).

32

1 – Was hast du am Donnerstag?
– Ich habe am Donnerstag Werken.

2 – Und was hast du am Dienstag?
– Ich habe am Dienstag … Informatik.

3 – OK … Was hast du am Montag?
– Ähh … ich habe am Montag Naturwissenschaften.

4 – *Und am Mittwoch? Was hast du am Mittwoch?*
– *Ich habe am Mittwoch Französisch.*

5 – *Und was hast du am Freitag?*
– *Kunst – ich habe am Freitag Kunst.*

Answers
1 Donnerstag
2 Dienstag
3 Montag
4 Mittwoch
5 Freitag

3 Partnerarbeit: Mach Interviews. (AT 2/3) 1.4a/Y7

Speaking. Pupils work together in pairs to interview each other about their timetables. In preparation, elicit how to say 'on Monday', etc., in German: *Wie heißt* „on Monday" *auf Deutsch*? Ask pupils in what other context they have already seen *am* and *was*. Focus pupils' attention on the form of the question and answer in the Key Language panel. With a lower-ability class, gather suggestions for each day and write the subjects on the board or an OHT for pupils to refer to.

Starter 2 4.2/Y7

Aim

To reinforce some high-frequency words.

Present these words on the board, scattered at random:

bin, bist, dein, habe, hast, mein, was, wie

Pupils in higher-ability classes race to compose a correct sentence containing the word. For mixed or lower-ability classes, display the following gapped sentences on an OHT and reveal them one at a time (or write them on the board). Pupils find the word on the board that completes the sentence.

1 *Wann … du Geburtstag?*
2 *… schreibt man das?*
3 *Ich … am ersten Januar Geburtstag.*
4 *Was ist … Lieblingsfach?*
5 *… ist das?*
6 *Wie alt … du?*
7 *… Lieblingsfach ist Sport.*
8 *Ich … elf Jahre alt.*

More able pupils can then compose new sentences using as many of the words on the board as possible.

Suggestion

Introduce the following sentences on an OHT. Read them out with the appropriate gestures and tone of voice, eliciting meaning as you go.

Ich finde Deutsch gut.	(one thumb up)
Ich finde Deutsch schlecht.	(one thumb down)
Ich finde Deutsch interessant.	(wide open eyes, reading textbook avidly)
Ich finde Deutsch langweilig.	(yawning, eyes half closed)
Ich finde Deutsch einfach.	(hands folded behind head, relaxed)
Ich finde Deutsch schwierig.	(mopping sweat from brow)
Ich finde Deutsch toll.	(both thumbs up)
Ich finde Deutsch furchtbar.	(both thumbs down)

Read the sentences through a second time, this time asking the class to copy your gestures. Finally, they provide the gestures themselves. Now ask the class to stand, and read out the sentences in random order. Pupils mime the opinions when they hear the opinion word; pupils who mime the wrong word or hesitate too long must sit down.

4 Hör zu. Wie findet Julia die Fächer? (1–8) (AT 1/2) 1.3a/Y7

Listening. Pupils listen to the recording and identify Julia's opinions about the subjects. Pupils could listen to the recording a first time with their books shut. Does she sound positive or negative about each subject (gist)? They could then listen a second time to note specific adjectives (detail).

1 – *Wie findest du Geschichte?*
– *Ich finde Geschichte gut.*

2 – *Wie findest du … Englisch?*
– *Englisch? Ich finde Englisch schwierig!*

3 – *Und wie findest du Sport?*
– *Ich finde Sport schlecht.*

4 – *Aha. Wie findest du Musik?*
– *Na ja … Ich finde Musik furchtbar!*

5 – *Julia, wie findest du Deutsch?*
– *Ach, ich finde Deutsch einfach.*

6 – *Und Mathe? Wie findest du Mathe?*
– *Ich finde Mathe … langweilig.*

7 – *Wie findest du … Erdkunde?*
– *Ich finde Erdkunde interessant.*

8 – *Und wie findest du Kunst?*
– *Ich finde Kunst toll!*

Answers
1 a 2 f 3 b 4 h 5 e 6 d 7 c 8 g

Aussprache: *ei/ie* 4.1/Y7

This panel explains the difference between ***ei*** and ***ie***. Ask pupils to find other examples of these letter combinations in this unit or chapter, and to read them aloud.

5 Lies die Wörter vor, dann hör zu. 5.1

Listening. Pupils attempt to pronounce the words containing *ei* and *ie* correctly, then listen to the recording and finally repeat the correct pronunciation.

1 *drei, langweilig, einfach*
2 *vier, schwierig, Lieblingsfach*

34

6 Partnerarbeit. (AT 2/3) 1.3b/Y7 1.4b/Y7

Speaking. Pupils work together in pairs to interview each other about their opinions of school subjects. In preparation, go through the **ECHO-Tipp** panel (giving opinions) and the Key Language panel with the class. Encourage pupils to use tone of voice and intonation to convey meaning.

+ In a higher-ability class, the pairs go on to record an interview, using a greater variety of questions (*Wie heißt du?, Wie alt bist du?, Was ist dein Lieblingsfach?,* etc.) and answers. Provide 'stalling' expressions which pupils can use to give themselves time to think, e.g. *Ach … , Na ja … , Tja … , Also … , Weißt du … .*

7 Lies Viktors E-Mail. Mach Notizen über die Fächer auf Englisch. (AT 3/4) 2.2a/Y7

Reading. Pupils read the email and note Viktor's opinion of each subject in English.
With weaker pupils, go through the text first picking out the subjects, then go through it again to look for the corresponding opinions.

Answers
science – difficult; history – bad; maths – easy but boring; English – interesting; art – great

+ Pupils reread the text and list any unknown language. They first try to work out meanings from the context, then use the **Wortschatz** at the back of their books to check meanings. As a further task or for homework, they could write a reply to the email.

8 Schreib Sätze für jeden Tag. (AT 4/3) 4.4/Y7

Writing. Pupils write what subjects they have on each day of the week, and their opinions about them.

+ Higher-ability pupils can mention more than one subject per day.

Plenary 5.8

Play the recording from exercise 4 again, while the class listens with books closed. Ask for opinions about whether the recording is easy or difficult to understand. Ask pupils who say 'easy' to support this with information they have gleaned from the recording. Why did they find it easy or difficult (e.g. slow/fast, clear/unclear, repetition, too much material, known/unknown language)?

Point out that the more you listen to German, the easier it is to understand. Did they find the recording from exercise 4 easier this time? Suggest or elicit strategies for improving listening (relax, and don't try to understand every word; focus on the important language; prepare before you listen, e.g. by looking for clues in the book, thinking about what the listening will be about and what words you are likely to hear).

3 Wie viel Uhr ist es?

Learning targets

- Talking about the school timetable
- Telling the time

Key framework objectives

3.2/Y7 Culture – (a) young people: interests/opinions

Grammar

- The present tense of the verb *sein*: *es ist*
- Forming questions with *wie?* and *wann?*

Key language

Wie viel Uhr ist es?
Es ist … Uhr …
Wann beginnt/endet (Deutsch)?
Um … Uhr …

High-frequency words

wie viel?
wann?
es ist
beginnt
endet

Pronunciation

w/v

Mathematics

Using the 24-hour clock

Citizenship

School routine in German-speaking countries

Resources

Cassette A, side 2
CD 1, tracks 35–38
Workbooks A and B, p.14
Arbeitsblatt 2.2, p.21
Echo Elektro 1 TPP, Mod 2 3.1–3.8

Starter 1 4.2/Y7

Aims

To revise numbers 1–24.

Either present **Arbeitsblatt 2.2** as an OHT for the whole class to work through, or photocopy it for individual pupils or pairs to work through quietly. The exercise revises numbers 1–24 (pupils join the dots to reveal a picture of an object).

You may wish to explain that the 24-hour clock is used a lot more in German-speaking countries than in the UK, e.g. for timetables (school, bus, cinema).

1 Wie viel Uhr ist es? (AT 3/2) 4.2/Y7

Reading. Pupils match the clock faces to the sentences. They can check their own answers by doing exercise 2.

Answers

1 e **2** c **3** a **4** b **5** d **6** f

ECHO-Detektiv 4.5a/Y7

This panel formally introduces *es ist* as part of the verb *sein*. Elicit from the class the other forms of *sein* they have met so far (*ich bin, du bist*). Talk with pupils about which parts of *sein* are easy to remember and which ones are hard to remember, e.g. *ist* should be easy because it looks like 'is'.

2 Hör zu und überprüfe es. (1–6) (AT 1/2) 4.2/Y7

Listening. Pupils listen to the recording to check their answers to exercise 1. Elicit the question pupils heard each time. You could point out that Germans don't ask 'what' time it is but rather 'how much' time it is.

1 – *Wie viel Uhr ist es?*
– *Es ist acht Uhr.*

2 – *Wie viel Uhr ist es?*
– *Es ist elf Uhr.*

3 – *Wie viel Uhr ist es?*
– *Es ist dreiundzwanzig Uhr.*

4 – *Wie viel Uhr ist es?*
– *Es ist vierzehn Uhr dreißig.*

5 – *Wie viel Uhr ist es?*
– *Es ist neun Uhr vierzig.*

6 – *Wie viel Uhr ist es?*
– *Es ist elf Uhr fünfzehn.*

3 Hör zu. Wie viel Uhr ist es? (1–10) (AT 1/2) 1.1/Y7

Listening. Pupils listen and note the clock times, numerically. Encourage them to focus on the actual numbers heard.

36

1 – Wie viel Uhr ist es?
– Es ist sieben Uhr fünf.

2 – Wie viel Uhr ist es bitte?
– Es ist zehn Uhr dreißig.

3 – Wie viel Uhr ist es?
– Ähm… es ist zwei Uhr fünfzehn.

4 – Wie viel Uhr ist es?
– Es ist acht Uhr.

5 – Wie viel Uhr ist es bitte?
– Es ist neun Uhr zwanzig.

6 – Wie viel Uhr ist es?
– Ähm… es ist zwölf Uhr vier.

7 – Wie viel Uhr ist es?
– Es ist fünfzehn Uhr.

8 – Wie viel Uhr ist es bitte?
– Es ist achtzehn Uhr fünfzehn.

9 – Wie viel Uhr ist es?
– Es ist zwanzig Uhr.

10 – Wie viel Uhr ist es?
– Ähm… Es ist zweiundzwanzig Uhr.

Answers

1 07.05	**2** 10.30	**3** 02.15	**4** 08.00	**5** 09.20
6 12.04	**7** 15.00	**8** 18.15	**9** 20.00	**10** 22.00

 Wie viel Uhr ist es? (AT 4/3) 4.4/Y7

Writing. Pupils write down the times in words, as whole sentences. Go through the answers with the whole class, writing the correct answers on the board and focusing on accurate spelling, capitalisation and word division.

Answers

1. Es ist sieben Uhr zwanzig.
2. Es ist acht Uhr fünfzig.
3. Es ist dreizehn Uhr dreiunddreißig.
4. Es ist zwölf Uhr fünfundvierzig.
5. Es ist elf Uhr siebzehn.

Aussprache: w/v 5.1

This panel explains the difference in pronunciation between *w* (covered in Chapter 1, Unit 1, page 6) and *v*.

5 Hör zu und wiederhole dreimal. 5.1

Listening. Pupils listen to the recording and repeat the tongue twister three times, to practise *w* and *v*. Pupils could work in pairs to see who can repeat the tongue twister more times in 30 seconds.

Wie viel Uhr ist es, Volker?
Es ist vier Uhr vierzig, Wilfried.

37

Starter 2 4.2/Y7

Aim

To practise numbers 1–60, prior to further work with digital clock times.

Before starting the game, you may wish to quickly revise key numbers with the class. Then ask for a volunteer 'searcher', who leaves the room briefly while another pupil hides a soft toy or other object somewhere in the classroom. As the volunteer begins to search, the rest of the class count aloud from one upwards in German, getting louder or quieter to assist the searcher, depending on how close he/she is getting to the hidden object. Write the name of the volunteer, and the number the class had reached (if they get as high as 60, go back to 1), on the board when the object is found, and play again with another searcher.

6 Partnerarbeit. (AT 2/2) 1.4b/Y7

Speaking. Pupils work in pairs to practise clock times.

7 Hör zu und lies. Was hat Viktor heute? (AT 3/3) 1.1/Y7

Listening. Pupils listen to the recording and follow the text in their books. They identify Viktor's subjects.

38

– Heute habe ich Kunst … Ach … Julia! Wann beginnt Kunst?
– Um zehn Uhr fünfundvierzig.
– O.K. … Wann endet Kunst?
– Um elf Uhr dreißig.
– Hmm … Und wann beginnt Mathe?
– Um zehn Uhr.
– O nein!
– Was?
– Es ist zehn Uhr fünf!

Answers

Kunst, Mathe

8 Lies noch mal. Was ist nicht im Dialog? (AT 3/3) 2.1/Y7

Reading. Pupils read the dialogue again and identify the clock times which are not mentioned. Ask pupils to identify which word in German means 'at'.

Answers
4 and 5

\+ Pupils work in pairs to write and act out their own dialogues, based on the one in the book. They could include opinions such as *O nein! Deutsch ist furchtbar!,* etc. To support medium-ability pupils, copy the dialogue onto an OHT with certain words blanked out to be filled in by the pupils.

9 Was sagt Julia? Schreib Sätze. (AT 4/3) 4.4/Y7

Writing. Pupils write down Julia's answers to the questions about her timetable, in full sentences. Focus more able pupils on accuracy (spelling, capitals, word division).

Suggestion 3.2a/Y7

Elicit differences between Julia's school day and the pupils' own. Explain that Julia's school day is fairly typical of schools in German-speaking countries: most schools start at 8 and finish at around 1, and pupils go home for lunch. You could elicit opinions (in German), e.g. *Ich finde es gut / schlecht / toll / furchtbar.*

Answers
1 Geschichte beginnt um zwölf Uhr fünfundzwanzig.
2 Geschichte endet um dreizehn Uhr zehn.
3 Religion beginnt um elf Uhr vierzig.
4 Kunst endet um elf Uhr dreißig.
5 Englisch beginnt um acht Uhr fünfundfünfzig.

Plenary: Mini-Test 5.8

Aim

To review language learned to date and identify areas for improvement.

Pupils work in pairs to check the language they have learned so far in this chapter, using the **Mini-Test** checklist. Ask pupils which points their partners found most difficult. Give pupils the task of improving those points by next lesson. Partners could then test them again.

Learning targets

- Talking about what you eat and drink at break
- Checking verb endings

Key framework objectives

4.5/Y7 Language – (a) present tense verbs

Grammar

- Present tense endings of regular verbs (*ich* and *du* forms)
- Present tense endings of irregular verbs: *haben, sein, essen* (*ich* and *du* forms)

Key language

die Kekse
die Chips
der Apfel
die Orange
die Banane
die Schokolade
die Bonbons
das Brötchen
die Cola
der Orangensaft
das Wasser
der Kuchen
Was isst / trinkst du in der Pause?
Ich esse einen Apfel / Kuchen, eine Orange / Banane, ein Brötchen, Schokolade / Kekse / Chips / Bonbons / nichts.
Ich trinke Cola / Orangensaft / Wasser / nichts.
Ja, bitte?
Ein Brötchen, bitte.
Das macht fünfzig Cent.
Bitte. Danke.

High-frequency words

ich, du
in
bitte, danke
das macht
nichts
haben
sein
essen
trinken
wohnen

ICT

Use clipart to create a tuck shop price list.

Mathematics

Prices in euros

Resources

CD 1, tracks 39–41
Workbooks A and B, p.15
Arbeitsblatt 2.3, p.22
Arbeitsblatt 2.4, p.23
Flashcards 35–46
Echo Elektro 1 TPP, Mod 2 4.1–4.8

Starter 1

4.1/Y7

Aim

To focus on sound patterns (vowels) in German.

Display the following gapped nouns on an OHT or the board as pupils come into the class:

Apf_l
K_chen
*Banan_*
Br_tchen
*Schokolad_*
*Keks_*
W_sser

Tell the class that a vowel is missing from each word. Can they guess what it is? (Stress that meaning is not important at this stage.) Working in pairs, pupils write out the words, guessing what the missing vowels will be. Now read the new words slowly several times. Pupils review their guesses, and alter their words as necessary. Finally, collect answers around the class and complete the words on the OHT/board.

Suggestion

Use the flashcards to introduce the new vocabulary. (See the Introduction on page 8 for general suggestions for using flashcards.) You could then stick the flashcards on the board using removable adhesive. Two pupils come to the board and arrange the cards into groups, using principles of their own choosing. The rest of the class guesses what the principle is (e.g. gender, colour, shape, eat/drink, like/dislike). The pupil who guesses correctly chooses a partner to help him/her rearrange the cards, etc.

1 Hör zu. Was passt zusammen? (1–12) (AT 1/2) 1.1/Y7

Listening. Pupils listen to the recording and find the letter to match the items they hear. For further exploitation of this activity, see Mime activities on p.9.

1 *Ich esse Schokolade … mmm!*
2 *Ich esse eine Banane … mmm!*
3 *Ich esse ein Brötchen … mmm!*
4 *Ich trinke Wasser … ahh!*
5 *Ich esse einen Apfel … mmm!*
6 *Ich trinke Cola … ahh!*
7 *Ich trinke Orangensaft … ahh!*
8 *Ich esse Kuchen … mmm!*
9 *Ich esse Bonbons … mmm! Lecker!*

10 Ich esse eine Orange … mmm!
11 Ich esse Kekse … mmm!
12 Ich esse Chips … mmm!

Answers
1 l 2 h 3 e 4 d 5 f 6 a 7 b 8 i
9 k 10 g 11 j 12 c

2 Hör zu. Was essen / trinken sie in der Pause? (AT 1/3) 1.1/Y7

Listening. Pupils listen to the recording and find in the photograph the items mentioned by each speaker. They may find it easier to complete the exercise in two stages: making shorthand notes while listening, then finding the items in the picture afterwards.

Suggestion

Before playing the recording, look at the instructions in the Pupil's Book with the class, and gather ideas about the recording. What do they think it will be about? Who will speak? Write their predictions on the board. Pupils listen to the recording (or part of the recording) a first time with books closed. Emphasise that they are listening to get a general idea of what the recording is about. You could introduce the concept of 'listening for gist'. Afterwards, ask the class whether their predictions proved to be correct. Before playing the recording a second time, elicit from the class that they will be listening for words from exercise 1. You could now introduce the concept of 'listening for detail'.

40

– Peter, was isst du in der Pause?
– Ich esse ein Brötchen und einen Apfel oder eine Orange.

– Und was trinkst du?
– Ich trinke Cola.

– Stefanie, was isst du in der Pause?
– Ich esse nichts.
– Oh! Und was trinkst du?
– Ich trinke Orangensaft.

– Viktor, was isst du in der Pause?
– Ähm … Ich esse Schokolade oder Bonbons.
– Und was trinkst du?
– Ich trinke Cola.

– Und Julia, was isst du in der Pause?
– Ich esse eine Banane und eine Orange.
– Trinkst du auch Cola?
– Nein. Ich trinke Orangensaft.

– Und Nina. Was isst du in der Pause?
– Ich esse Kekse und Chips.
– Und was trinkst du?
– Ich trinke Wasser.

Answers
Peter: e, f, g, a
Stefanie: b
Viktor: l, k, a
Julia: h, g, b
Nina: j, c, d

3 Umfrage. (AT 2/3) 1.4a/Y7 4.5a/Y7

Speaking. Pupils conduct a class survey about what their classmates eat and drink at break, and record the results, e.g. as tally marks. Prepare by looking at the form of the question and answer in detail, using the Key Language panel, and getting pupils to practise the dialogue with a partner.

ECHO-Detektiv 4.5a/Y7

This panel reviews verb forms met so far, including the two new verbs *essen* and *trinken*. You may wish to discuss ideas for learning verb conjugations at this point. **Arbeitsblatt 2.4** provides practice of the singular forms of regular verbs.

4 Pausenbrot: Wähle jeden Tag etwas anderes. (AT 4/3) 2.4a/Y7

Writing. Pupils write about what they eat and drink at break, choosing different items or combinations for each day. Assist less able pupils by showing them how the sentences in the example can be adapted.

\+ More able pupils can be given extra items of food/drink to look up in their dictionaries.

Starter 2 4.2/Y7

Aims
To revise numbers to 69.
To introduce prices in euros.

Use **Arbeitsblatt 2.3** either as an OHT for whole-class use or photocopied as worksheets for individual work or pairwork. With a higher-ability class, you could reverse the OHT to increase the level of difficulty. If using photocopies, the coins could be cut out to enable pairs of pupils to practise further. For example: partner A picks a coin while partner B looks away; partner B says the value of the coin that is missing.

5 Hör zu. Was essen sie? Was kostet das? (1–4) (AT 1/3) 1.1/Y7

Listening. Pupils listen to the recording. They first identify the items each speaker asks for, then note down how much it costs. After completing the exercise, draw pupils' attention to the polite use of *Danke* and *Bitte.*

41

1 – *Ja, bitte?*
– *Ein Brötchen, bitte.*
– *Das macht fünfundsechzig Cent.*
– *Fünfundsechzig Cent. Bitte.*
– *Danke.*
– *Bitte.*

2 – *Ja, bitte?*
– *Bonbons, bitte.*
– *Das macht neununddreißig Cent.*
– *Neununddreißig Cent. Bitte.*
– *Danke.*
– *Bitte.*

3 – *Ja, bitte?*
– *Cola, bitte.*
– *Das macht sechzig Cent.*
– *Sechzig Cent. Bitte.*
– *Danke.*
– *Bitte.*

4 – *Ja, bitte?*
– *Eine Banane, bitte.*
– *Das macht fünfundvierzig Cent.*
– *Fünfundvierzig Cent. Bitte.*
– *Danke.*
– *Bitte.*

Answers
1 Brötchen – 65 Cent
2 Bonbons – 39 Cent
3 Cola – 60 Cent
4 Banane – 45 Cent

Suggestion

To prepare for exercise 6, write the full menu on the board, getting pupils to read out the items and prices for you to write down.

ECHO-Tipp 4.2/Y7

This points out how useful the high-frequency word *bitte* is. It can be used in several different situations.

6 Partnerarbeit: Mach Dialoge. (AT 2/3) 1.4b/Y7

Speaking. Pupils work in pairs to create tuck shop role plays.

ICT Pupils could create their own tuck shop price lists, decorated with clipart. More able pupils could be encouraged to look up their favourite items of food and drink in their dictionaries.

7 Lies die Texte. Welches Bild ist das? (AT 3/3) 2.1/Y7

Reading. Pupils read the texts and find the appropriate picture for each one. Model the process of comparing details of the first text against each picture in turn.

Answers
1 b **2** d **3** a **4** c

Plenary 1.4b/Y7

Aims

To consolidate language introduced in this unit.
To improve fluency in spontaneous speech.

Play 'throw and catch' around the class using a soft toy or ball. One pupil asks *Was isst du?* or *Was trinkst du?* and throws the toy/ball to another pupil, who responds then asks one of the questions and throws the toy/ball again, etc.

Alternatively, pupils could work together in groups to play a 'chain game' with snacks. Each player adds another item to the sentence, until a mistake is made:

Pupil A: *Was isst du in der Pause?*
Pupil B: *Ich esse ein Brötchen.*
Pupil C: *Ich esse ein Brötchen und Schokolade.*
Pupil D: *Ich esse …*

Finish the lesson by eliciting from the class what they have learned from this unit, other than just nouns for food and drink (e.g. verb forms, *bitte* and *danke*, prices).

5 Was trägst du in der Schule?

Learning targets

- Describing what you wear to school
- Revising *einen, eine, ein*

Key framework objectives

4.3/Y7 Language – gender
2.4/Y7 Writing – (b) building text

Grammar

- The accusative of the indefinite article: *einen / eine / ein*
- The indefinite article with plural nouns: *die*
- The verb *sein*: *es ist, sie sind*

Key language

die Jacke
die Hose
das Hemd
der Pullover
die Krawatte
die Schuhe
der Rock
die Socken
das Sweatshirt
das T-Shirt
die Jeans
die Stiefel
die Bluse
die Sportschuhe
das Kleid
(Der Rock) ist …
(Die Schuhe) sind …
blau / braun / gelb / grau / grün / lila / orange / rot / schwarz / weiß.
Was trägst du in der Schule?
Ich trage …
einen Rock / Jeansrock / Pullover
eine Hose / Bluse / Jacke
ein Hemd / T-Shirt / Kleid / Sweatshirt
Jeans / Schuhe / Stiefel / Sportschuhe.
Ich finde das cool / bequem / schick / gut.

High-frequency words

was?
es ist
sie sind
ich trage, du trägst
ich finde das

Citizenship

Differing school culture/rules in other countries

Resources

CD 1, tracks 42–43
Workbooks A and B, p.16
Arbeitsblatt 2.5, p.24
Arbeitsblatt 2.6, p.25
Echo Elektro 1 TPP, Mod 2 5.1–5.6

Starter 1

4.2/Y7

Aim

To revise colours.

Call out the colours which pupils encountered in Chapter 1 (*blau, braun, gelb, grau, grün, orange, rot, schwarz, weiß*) in random order. Pupils race to touch or hold up something of the correct colour. After you have run through each of the colours once, individual pupils can start to take over calling out the colours. The first pupil to touch the correct colour could call out the next one, and so on.

Suggestion

Use people's clothes in the classroom to introduce the new vocabulary. Decide with the class how many of the items are cognates.

1 Hör zu. Was ist die richtige Reihenfolge? (AT 1/1) 4.2/Y7

Listening. Pupils listen to the recording and note the letters of the items of clothing from the picture in the order in which they are mentioned.

der Pullover
die Krawatte
die Schuhe
die Jacke
die Hose
der Rock
das Hemd
das Sweatshirt

das T-Shirt
die Stiefel
die Bluse
das Kleid
die Jeans
die Socken
die Sportschuhe

Answers

j, i, n, a, d, b, f, l, e, o, h, k, g, m, c

2 Sieh dir das Bild in Aufgabe 1 an. Richtig oder falsch? (AT 3/2) 2.1/Y7

+ *Reading.* Pupils study the picture again and decide whether the statements are true or false.

More able pupils can also write correct statements. Draw attention to the fact that they should use *sind* instead of *ist* for items where there is more than one. You may wish to point out at this point that *die Hose* is singular, even though its equivalent in English is plural.

Answers
1 falsch (Die Jacke ist blau.)
2 falsch (Der Rock ist braun.)
3 richtig
4 falsch (Die Jeans sind blau.)
5 richtig
6 falsch (Das Hemd ist weiß.)

ECHO-Detektiv: the + plural nouns

4.3/Y7

This panel explains to pupils that *die* is used with plural nouns. With a more confident group, you might wish to elaborate on this, by also looking at the singular forms of the plural clothing nouns, e.g. comparing *der Schuh* with *die Schuhe*.

3 Partnerarbeit. (AT 2/3) 1.4b/Y7 4.3/Y7

Speaking. Pupils work in pairs to create dialogues. Partner A makes a statement about the colour of an item in the picture, and partner B decides whether the statement is true or false. Then the roles are reversed. Remind pupils to listen carefully to what their partner says, especially the item and the colour. Point out that they can ask for repetition using *Wie bitte?*. Encourage them to speak clearly and attempt good pronunciation. For further exploitation of this activity, see Other games, p. 10.

ECHO-Detektiv: *sie sind* = they are

With a confident class, you may wish to discuss *sie*, meaning 'they', and compare it with the same word to mean 'she'. Weaker pupils just need to understand at this stage that *sind* means 'are'.

Starter 2

1.1/Y7

Aims

To improve understanding of speech.
To consolidate clothing vocabulary and colours.

Play 'true/false sentences': make statements such as *Der Rock ist rot.* (For greater variety than allowed for by the school uniform, you could base the questions on pictures cut from fashion magazines/advertisements.) Pupils stand up if the statement is true and remain sitting if it is false. Alternatively, mini-whiteboards could be marked with T/F. After a few examples, pupils can take over making the statements. This could be a game between two teams, with each team scoring points according to how many members of the opposing team respond incorrectly.

4 Schreib acht Sätze über die Kleidung in Aufgabe 1. (AT 4/3) 4.4/Y7

Writing. Pupils write a sentence about eight of the items in exercise 1. They could state the colour as in the example.

5 Hör zu und lies. Sieh dir die Bilder an. Wo ist der Fehler? (AT 1/3) 2.1/Y7

Listening. Pupils compare the texts with the pictures and identify the deliberate error in each text. After checking answers, you could elicit reactions to the fact that pupils in German-speaking countries do not have school uniform: *Ich finde das cool / toll / gut / schlecht,* etc.

CD 43

1 *Ich trage einen Jeansrock und einen Pullover. Der Pullover ist rot und der Jeansrock ist blau. Ich trage Schuhe, das finde ich schick!*
2 *Ich trage eine Hose und einen Pullover. Die Hose ist grün und der Pullover ist blau. Ich trage Stiefel. Ich finde das cool!*
3 *Ich trage eine Bluse und eine Hose. Die Hose ist grün. Ich trage auch Sportschuhe. Ich finde das bequem.*

Answers
1 Der Pullover ist grün.
2 Ich trage Sportschuhe.
3 Ich trage eine Bluse.

ECHO-Detektiv 5.1

This panel reminds pupils of the accusative forms of the indefinite article. Refer more able pupils to the **Grammatik** on page 126 for more information and practice. You could also refer them back to where they have seen this before in Chapter 1 (page 15). **Arbeitsblatt 2.5** also provides practice of this grammatical point.

6 Gedächtnisspiel: Was trägst du in der Schule? (AT 2/3) 1.4b/Y7

Speaking. Pupils play a 'chain game' about clothing. Each player adds an item of clothing to the sentence until a mistake is made. Focus more able pupils on the accurate use of *einen / eine / ein* and on the forms of the verb: *ich trage, du trägst.*

7 Deine Traumuniform. (AT 4/3–4) 2.4b/Y7 2.5/Y7

Writing. Pupils write about their own ideal school uniform. You could use this exercise to show pupils how to build short texts from notes, e.g.

Sweatshirt – blau; Hose – schwarz; toll

becomes:

Ich trage ein Sweatshirt. Das Sweatshirt ist blau. Ich trage eine Hose. Die Hose ist schwarz. Ich finde das toll!

Plenary 4.2/Y7

Aim

To get used to revising and recycling language.

Set a time limit of about three minutes. Pupils draw up two lists: language that was new in the unit (e.g. clothes, plural nouns) and language that was not new (e.g. colours, *ist*). Then combine pairs into groups of four: the groups put their ideas together, crossing out any duplicates. Again, set a time limit, e.g. two minutes. Finally, one group reads out its lists to the class. Each subsequent group adds any additional items it has noted. List the items on the board.

Discuss the idea that language has to be revised and recycled. Just because you have learnt it once, doesn't mean it's not useful to go over it again!

There is further practice of vocabulary-building skills on **Arbeitsblatt 2.6**.

6 Meine Schule

Learning targets
- Learning about school life in German-speaking countries
- Understanding a longer text

Key framework objectives
4.6/Y7 Language – (b) negatives
5.6 Strategies – reading aloud
5.7 Strategies – planning and preparing

Grammar
- The accusative of *kein*: *keinen / keine / kein*

Key language
Ich heiße … .
Ich bin … Jahre alt.
Ich wohne in …
Ich bin in der Klasse … .
Die Schule beginnt um … .
In der Pause esse / trinke ich … .
Mein Lieblingsfach ist …
Ich finde … schwierig (etc).
Ich trage … in der Schule.
Ich habe keine Schuluniform.

High-frequency words
kein, keine, keinen
ich heiße
ich wohne
ich bin
ich esse
ich trinke
ich finde
ich trage
ich habe
in
um
zur

Pronunciation
Reading aloud

English
Reading and understanding a webpage

Citizenship
School routine in German-speaking countries

ICT
Planning and writing a webpage

Resources
CD 1, track 44
Workbooks A and B, p.17
Echo Elektro 1 TPP, Mod 2 6.1–6.5

Starter 1 5.7

Aims
To consolidate school vocabulary.
To start planning a website in German.

Write in the centre of an OHT: *eine Website für die Schule.* Gather ideas around the class for useful items of language, encouraging use of the target language. Develop a network of ideas on the OHT. Provide categories, e.g. *Schuluniform, Schulfächer, Pausenbrot, Stundenplan, Schultag* to prompt and guide pupils' ideas. The OHT can be used at the end of the unit to assist in planning exercise 6.

1 Hör zu und lies. (AT 3/4) 2.2a/Y7 5.4

Listening. Pupils listen to the recording and read the webpage in their books.

44

Hallo!
Ich heiße Nina Bukowski. Ich bin dreizehn Jahre alt. Ich wohne in Salzburg in Österreich.
Meine Schule heißt das Musische Gymnasium. Ich bin in der Klasse 8a.
Die Schule beginnt um acht Uhr und endet um dreizehn Uhr zehn. In der Pause esse ich ein Brötchen und ich trinke Orangensaft oder Cola.
Mein Lieblingsfach ist Musik. Ich finde Englisch schwierig und Französisch ist furchtbar!
Ich trage ein Sweatshirt und Jeans in der Schule – ich habe keine Schuluniform.

Suggestion
Write the following sentences on the board or an OHT:

1 N. introduces her school.
2 N. introduces herself.
3 N. talks about food and drink.
4 N. talks about her school routine.
5 N. talks about her subjects.
6 N. talks about what she wears.

Uncover them one at a time. Working in pairs, pupils scan the webpage in exercise 1 to find the sentence or sentences which match these descriptions. When pupils think they have found the matching section of the text, they put their hands up and read it out when asked.

ECHO-Tipp: Understanding a text 5.4

This gives advice about preparing to read a text – looking for clues to help with meaning – and about reading for gist.

2 Partnerarbeit. Lies den Text vor.

5.6

Speaking. Pupils practise reading the webpage text aloud in pairs. Able pupils could be encouraged to correct each other's pronunciation. In preparation, play the recording again and ask all pupils to read along under their breath. Ask which words/passages they find particularly difficult to pronounce, and chorus these with the class.

3 Lies den Text noch mal und ordne die Bilder. (Vier Bilder sind nicht im Text.) (AT 3/4) 2.2a/Y7

Reading. Pupils read the text again and put the pictures in the order in which the items occur in the text. In preparation, discuss how best to approach this exercise and help pupils to draw up a sequence of steps to take. For example:

1 Identify chunks of information (e.g. *acht Uhr*).
2 Scan pictures for one that matches.
3 Write down the letter of any matching picture.
4 Double-check at the end that there are only four letters left over.

Answers
d, b, f, i, j, k, h (not in text: a, c, e, g)

ECHO-Detektiv 4.6b/Y7

This panel explains the formation and usage of the negative article *kein*. Pupils could refer to the **Grammatik** on page 127 for detailed explanation and practice. Draw pupils' attention to the fact that this is another word that they will see a lot and can also use often in order to talk about what they don't have.

Starter 2 4.6b/Y7

Aims

To improve pupils' capacity to follow speech.
To introduce *keinen / keine / kein.*

Make a list of eight to ten sentences containing *einen / eine / ein* or *keinen / keine / kein* and known language from Chapters 1 and 2. For example:

Ich habe einen Bleistift.
Ich trage keine Schuluniform.
Es gibt eine Pause um zehn Uhr dreißig.
Ich habe kein Wörterbuch.
Ich esse keine Kekse.
Es gibt keine Pause um elf Uhr.
Ich habe keinen Kuli.
Ich esse einen Kuchen.
Hast du ein Wörterbuch?

Do not show the list to the class at this point. (However, you may find it useful to write the list on an OHT for discussion at the end of the starter.) Pupils work in pairs. They write a large tick on one mini-whiteboard or piece of paper, and a large cross on another. They place these in front of them on the desk. Read out the sentences one at a time, clearly but at close to normal speed. When pupils hear *einen, eine* or *ein* they must hold up the tick; when they hear *keinen, keine* or *kein* they must hold up the cross. Pupils can compete with their partners to grab the correct answer and hold it up. Finally, you could display the sentences on an OHT and elicit English translations from the class.

4 Beantworte die Fragen auf Englisch. (A/T 3/4) 2.2a/Y7

Reading. Pupils answer these questions in English to check their detailed understanding of the text in exercise 1.

Answers
1 Salzburg (in Austria)
2 Grammar school
3 8a
4 Difficult
5 Jeans and a sweatshirt

5 Was ist an deiner Schule anders? Mach eine Liste. (AT 4/3) 3.1/Y7

Writing. Pupils make a list of the differences between Nina's school and their own. Go through the text with the class and elicit what the main points are, so that pupils have a clear basis for comparison. Write a few pointers on the board to support less able pupils. For further exploitation of this activity, see Reading aloud on p. 9.

6 Schreib eine Webseite über deine Schule. (AT 4/4) 2.5/Y7

Writing. Pupils write a webpage about their own school. Discuss how to structure this, and how to present it.

ICT This exercise could be the starting point for a collaborative ICT project, with individual pupils responsible for paragraphs about timetable, subjects, uniform, etc. If practicable, the resulting pages, or a selection of work from them, could be uploaded to the school website as an example of pupils' work. Alternatively pupils could present their work in a PowerPoint presentation. Planning the webpage could be your **plenary** (or see the alternative suggestion below). Refer pupils back to the mindmap created for the starter, and add any refinements or additional ideas prompted by this unit.

You could show a few bookmarked examples of German school homepages, using a computer or digital projector.

Plenary 4.6b/Y7

Aim

To reinforce *keinen / keine / kein.*

Ask for a volunteer to come to the front of the class and explain what he/she has learned about *keinen / keine / kein* in this unit (e.g. meaning, how to use it, examples). He/She can nominate an 'assistant' to help. The volunteers can then test the class by asking questions.

Lernzieltest 5.8

This is a checklist of language covered in Chapter 2. Pupils can work with the checklist in pairs to check what they have learned. Points which directly address grammar and structures are marked with a G. There is a **Lernzieltest** sheet in the Resource and Assessment File (page 29). Encourage pupils to look back at the chapter and to use the grammar section to revise what they are unclear about.

You can also use the **Lernzieltest** as an end-of-chapter plenary.

Resources
CD 1, track 45

Wiederholung

This is a revision page to prepare pupils for the **Kontrolle** at the end of the chapter.

1 Hör zu. Welches Fach ist das? (1–8) (AT 1/2) 1.1/Y7

Listening. Pupils listen to the recording and match the pictures to the subjects mentioned by the speakers.

45

1 *Mein Lieblingsfach ist Französisch.*
2 *Mein Lieblingsfach ist Religion.*
3 *Mein Lieblingsfach ist Werken.*
4 *Mein Lieblingsfach ist Erdkunde.*
5 *Mein Lieblingsfach ist Naturwissenschaften.*
6 *Mein Lieblingsfach ist Deutsch.*
7 *Mein Lieblingsfach ist Sport.*
8 *Mein Lieblingsfach ist Theater.*

Answers
1 c **2** d **3** f **4** a **5** g **6** b **7** e **8** h

2 Partnerarbeit: Mach zwei Interviews. (AT 2/3) 1.4a/Y7

Speaking. Pupils interview each other about their school subjects and school routine, using the two lists of questions provided.

3 Ist das in der E-Mail? (AT 3/4) 2.1/Y7

Reading. Pupils read the email and decide which pictures show things that are mentioned.

Answers
1 ja **2** nein **3** ja **4** ja **5** nein **6** nein
7 ja **8** ja

4 Ergänze die Sätze. Schreib sie aus. (AT 4/3) 2.4a/Y7

Writing. Pupils complete the sentences, using the picture cues.

Answers
1 Mein Lieblingsfach ist Sport.
2 Ich finde Mathe langweilig.
3 Ich esse eine Banane und ich trinke Cola.
4 Die Schule beginnt um neun Uhr und endet um fünfzehn Uhr dreißig.

Learning targets

- Understanding imaginative texts about an ideal school
- Finding out the meanings of unknown words

Key framework objectives

4.4/Y7 Language – sentence formation

Key language

Die Schule beginnt um …
In der Pause esse / trinke ich …
Um … Uhr habe ich Englisch (etc.).

High-frequency words

meine
ich habe
in
um
das ist
sehr
und
keine
wie?

Pronunciation

Reading aloud (singing)

English

Reading and understanding an imaginative text

Resources

CD 1, tracks 46–47
Workbooks A and B, p.18
Arbeitsblatt 2.7, p.26

Starter 1 4.4/Y7

Aims

To encourage pupils to form grammatically correct sentences.
To consolidate school vocabulary.

Present three headings on the board or an OHT: *Schulfächer, Schuluniform, Pausenbrot.*

Elicit and clarify their meanings as necessary. Divide pupils into teams. Give them three minutes to write as many sentences as possible on an OHT about these three topics. The sentences must be grammatically correct (but do not penalise minor errors), be legible and make sense. After the time limit has expired, a representative from each team comes to the OHP and displays the team's sentences. Help the class to spot errors and decide whether sentences are valid. The team with the most correct sentences wins a small prize. The class could also vote for the best/most creative/most difficult/silliest sentence.

1 Hör zu und lies mit. 2.3/Y7

Listening. Pupils listen to the recording and follow the photostory in their books. In preparation, ask them to assess the text for visual clues, gist and level of difficulty.

46

– Wie ist meine Traumschule?
Die Schule beginnt um zehn Uhr. Ich habe Musik – Rockmusik. Sie ist sehr laut!
Um zehn Uhr fünfzig habe ich eine Pause. In der Pause esse ich im Schul-Restaurant Pasta. Lecker!
Um elf Uhr dreißig endet die Pause. Ich habe Englisch. Ich sehe eine TV-Show aus Amerika.
Um zwölf Uhr fünfzehn habe ich Informatik. Ich spiele Computerspiele. Das ist toll!
Um dreizehn Uhr zwanzig endet die Schule …
– Peter! Es ist sieben Uhr vierzig! Die Schule beginnt in zwanzig Minuten. Du kommst zu spät!

2 Schreib Peters Stundenplan für die „Traumschule". (AT 3/4) 2.2a/Y7

Writing. Pupils read the photostory again and note down the times and subjects mentioned.

Answers

10.00 – Rockmusik
10.50 – Pause
11.30 – Englisch
12.15 – Informatik
13.20 – Die Schule endet

3 Rate mal: Wie heißt das auf Englisch? (AT 3/4) 5.4

Reading. Pupils attempt to work out the meanings of unknown words from the photostory, using context and other clues. Look at each of the words with the whole class. Discuss ideas for working out and checking the meanings. **Arbeitsblatt 2.7** could extend this discussion by looking at false friends.

Answers

1 tasty, delicious
2 the computer game
3 you come
4 too late

Starter 2 4.2/Y7

Aims
To improve fluency of speech.
To revise language about school.

Make 'cards' by dividing an A4 sheet into (e.g.) fifteen rows and two columns. There should be half as many cards as there are pupils in the class. On each card, write a cue such as *Lieblingsfach: Englisch*, *Pause: Brötchen* or *Jeans und T-Shirt.* Photocopy the sheet, then cut out the cards to make enough for each pupil to have one.

Pupils draw a card from a bag as they come into the class. (They must conceal it from other pupils.) If there are cards left over, give an extra card to each of the most able pupils.

Pupils circulate in the class, saying sentences such as *Mein Lieblingsfach ist Englisch* to find their 'twin'. Twins sit down together, until finally all pupils are seated.

4 Deine Meinung: Traumschule oder Realität? (AT 3/3) 5.4

Reading. Pupils read the speech bubbles and decide which, in their opinion, belong to 'dream school' and which belong to 'real school'. They identify and look up unknown words.

\+ The most able pupils could go on to write their own sentences for *Traumschule* and *Realität.*

5 Hör zu und sing mit. 2.3/Y7 5.6

Listening. Pupils listen to the song, then sing along. For further ideas on how to use this activity, see Exploiting the songs on page 9.

Ich trage eine Hose.
Wie ist die Hose?
Sie ist bequem und grün.
Ich trage einen Rock.
Wie ist der Rock?
Er ist rot und schön.

Die Schuluniform ist doof, doof, doof!
Die Schuluniform ist toll, toll, toll!

Ich trage eine Jacke.
Wie ist die Jacke?
Sie ist praktisch und blau.
Ich trage einen Pulli.
Wie ist der Pulli?
Er ist hässlich und grau!

Die Schuluniform ist doof, doof, doof!
Die Schuluniform ist toll, toll, toll!

Ich trage ein Hemd.
Wie ist das Hemd?
Es ist cool und weiß.
Ich trage schwarze Socken.
Wie sind die Socken?
Sie sind bequem, aber heiß.

Die Schuluniform ist doof, doof, doof!
Die Schuluniform ist toll, toll, toll!

6 Wie ist deine Traumschule? Schreib einen Stundenplan. (AT 4/3) 2.4a/Y7

Writing. Pupils write a timetable for their own 'dream school'. Discuss the use of dictionaries and other resources to look up unknown words.

\+ Pupils write sentences based on their 'dream school' timetables.

Plenary 1.4b/Y7

Aim
To develop fluency in spontaneous talk.

Pupils work in groups of three. They take it in turns to attempt to speak without pause on the subject of *die Schule.* The first pupil talks for 20 seconds, the second for 40 seconds and the third for a minute.

SELF-ACCESS READING AND WRITING AT TWO LEVELS

A Reinforcement

1 Welches Fach ist das? Schreib das Wort auf. (AT 4/1) 4.2/Y7

Writing. Pupils copy and complete the words for school subjects, using the picture clues for support.

Answers
1 Englisch **2** Erdkunde **3** Geschichte **4** Mathe
5 Religion **6** Deutsch

2 Positiv oder negativ? (AT 3/2) 4.2/Y7

Reading. Pupils read each sentence, and decide whether the opinion expressed is positive or negative.

Answers
1 positiv **2** negativ **3** negativ **4** positiv
5 negativ **6** negativ

3 Wie findest du das? (AT 4/2) 2.4a/Y7

Writing. Pupils write out the sentences from exercise 2, changing the coloured words to reflect their own opinions. They can find ideas in the original versions of the sentences.

4 Finde die richtigen Bilder. (AT 3/2) 2.1/Y7

Reading. Pupils read the sentences, and find the correct two pictures for each one.

Answers
1 f, b **2** e,i **3** g, d **4** a,j **5** h, c

B Extension

1 Lies Valentinas Stundenplan. Richtig oder falsch? Schreib die Sätze richtig auf. (AT 3/2) 2.1/Y7

Reading. Pupils use the school timetable to work out if each sentence is true or false. They write out the false sentences correctly.

Answers
1 Falsch. Deutsch beginnt um acht Uhr zehn.
2 Richtig
3 Falsch. Sport endet um dreizehn Uhr zehn.
4 Falsch. Die erste Pause endet um zehn Uhr.
5 Richtig
6 Falsch. Die zweite Pause beginnt um elf Uhr dreißig.

2 Was sagt Valentina über die Schulfächer? Schreib sechs Sätze. (AT 4/3) 4.4/Y7

Writing. Pupils write six sentences to show what Valentina thinks of the subjects, based on the pictures drawn on her timetable. Accept any suitable adjectives.

Possible answers
Ich finde Deutsch toll.
Ich finde Englisch gut.
Ich finde Mathe schlecht.
Ich finde Erdkunde langweilig.
Ich finde Kunst schwierig.
Ich finde Sport super.

3 Lies die Texte und sieh dir das Bild an. Wer ist das? (AT 3/4) 2.1/Y7

Reading. Pupils read the two texts about school uniform, and decide to whom each item of clothing pictured belongs. As an extra task, they could draw, colour and label pictures of Lea and Marie, using lines from the texts as labels.

Answers
1 Marie **4** Lea
2 Marie **5** Marie
3 Lea **6** Lea

Übungsheft A, Seite 12

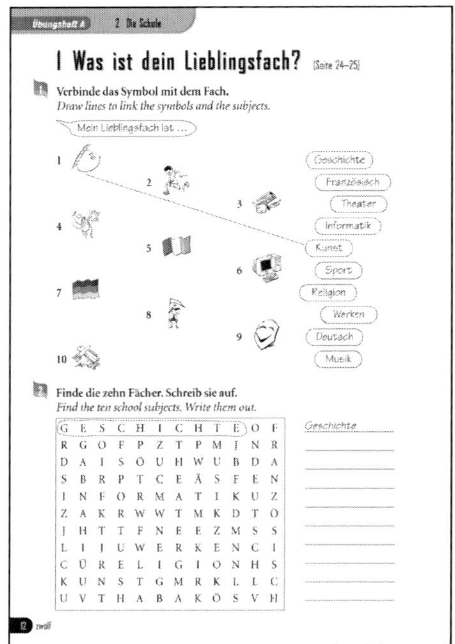

Übungsheft A 2 Die Schule

1 Was ist dein Lieblingsfach? (Seite 24–25)

1 **Verbinde das Symbol mit dem Fach.**
Draw lines to link the symbols and the subjects.

Mein Lieblingsfach ist …

1 2 3 4 5 6 7 8 9 10

Geschichte
Französisch
Theater
Informatik
Kunst
Sport
Religion
Werken
Deutsch
Musik

2 **Finde die zehn Fächer. Schreib sie auf.**
Find the ten school subjects. Write them out.

G	E	S	C	H	I	C	H	T	E	O	F
R	G	O	F	P	Z	T	P	M	J	N	R
D	A	I	S	Ö	U	H	W	U	B	D	A
S	B	R	P	T	C	E	Ä	S	F	E	N
I	N	F	O	R	M	A	T	I	K	U	Z
Z	A	K	R	W	W	T	M	K	D	T	Ö
J	H	T	T	F	N	E	E	Z	M	S	S
L	I	J	U	W	E	R	K	E	N	C	I
C	Ü	R	E	L	I	G	I	O	N	H	S
K	U	N	S	T	G	M	R	K	L	L	C
U	V	T	H	A	B	A	K	Ö	S	V	H

Geschichte

12 zwölf

1 (AT3 Level 1) 1 Kunst **2** Sport **3** Musik **4** Religion **5** Französisch **6** Informatik **7** Deutsch **8** Geschichte **9** Theater **10** Werken

2 (AT3 Level 1, AT4 Level 1) Geschichte, Informatik, Werken, Religion, Kunst, Sport, Theater, Musik, Deutsch, Französisch

Übungsheft B, Seite 12

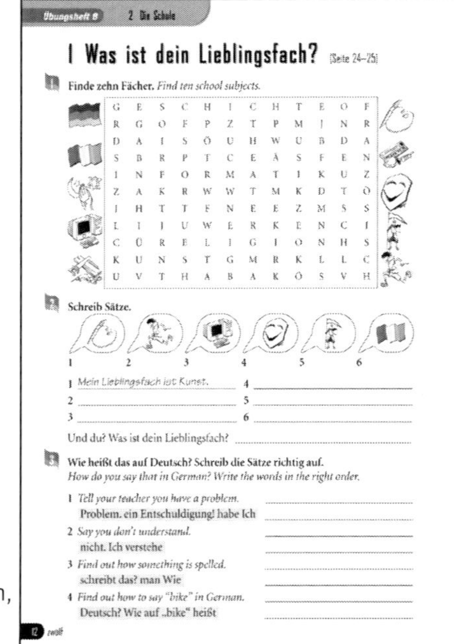

Übungsheft B 2 Die Schule

1 Was ist dein Lieblingsfach? (Seite 24–25)

1 **Finde zehn Fächer.** *Find ten school subjects.*

G	E	S	C	H	I	C	H	T	E	O	F
R	G	O	F	P	Z	T	P	M	J	N	R
D	A	I	S	Ö	U	H	W	U	B	D	A
S	B	R	P	T	C	E	Ä	S	F	E	N
I	N	F	O	R	M	A	T	I	K	U	Z
Z	A	K	R	W	W	T	M	K	D	T	Ö
J	H	T	T	F	N	E	E	Z	M	S	S
L	I	J	U	W	E	R	K	E	N	C	I
C	Ü	R	E	L	I	G	I	O	N	H	S
K	U	N	S	T	G	M	R	K	L	L	C
U	V	T	H	A	B	A	K	Ö	S	V	H

2 **Schreib Sätze.**

1 2 3 4 5 6

1 Mein Lieblingsfach ist Kunst. 4
2 5
3 6

Und du? Was ist dein Lieblingsfach?

3 **Wie heißt das auf Deutsch? Schreib die Sätze richtig auf.**
How do you say that in German? Write the words in the right order.

1 *Tell your teacher you have a problem.*
Problem. ein Entschuldigung! habe Ich
2 *Say you don't understand.*
nicht. Ich verstehe
3 *Find out how something is spelled.*
schreibt das? man Wie
4 *Find out how to say "bike" in German.*
Deutsch? Wie auf „bike" heißt

12 zwölf

1 (AT3 Level 1) Geschichte, Informatik, Werken, Religion, Kunst, Sport, Theater, Musik, Deutsch, Französisch

2 (AT4 Level 2) 1 Mein Lieblingsfach ist Kunst. **2** Mein Lieblingsfach ist Sport. **3** Mein Lieblingsfach ist Informatik. **4** Mein Lieblingsfach ist Theater. **5** Mein Lieblingsfach ist Geschichte. **6** Mein Lieblingsfach ist Französisch.

3 (AT4 Level 2) 1 Entschuldigung! Ich habe ein Problem. **2** Ich verstehe nicht. **3** Wie schreibt man das? **4** Wie heißt „bike" auf Deutsch?

Übungsheft A, Seite 13

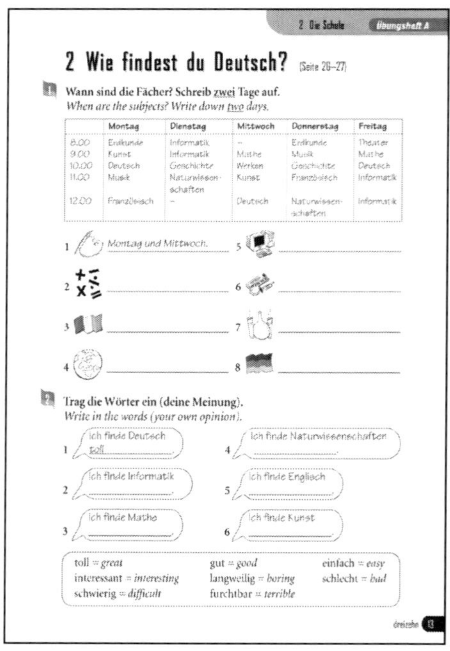

2 Die Schule Übungsheft A

2 Wie findest du Deutsch? (Seite 26–27)

1 **Wann sind die Fächer? Schreib zwei Tage auf.**
When are the subjects? Write down two days.

	Montag	Dienstag	Mittwoch	Donnerstag	Freitag
8.00	Erdkunde	Informatik	–	Erdkunde	Theater
9.00	Kunst	Informatik	Mathe	Musik	Mathe
10.00	Deutsch	Geschichte	Werken	Geschichte	Deutsch
11.00	Musik	Naturwissen-schaften	Kunst	Französisch	Informatik
12.00	Französisch	–	Deutsch	Naturwissen-schaften	Informatik

1 Montag und Mittwoch. 5
2 6
3 7
4 8

2 **Trag die Wörter ein (deine Meinung).**
Write in the words (your own opinion).

1 Ich finde Deutsch toll.
2 Ich finde Informatik .
3 Ich finde Mathe .
4 Ich finde Naturwissenschaften .
5 Ich finde Englisch .
6 Ich finde Kunst .

toll = *great* gut = *good* einfach = *easy*
interessant = *interesting* langweilig = *boring* schlecht = *bad*
schwierig = *difficult* furchtbar = *terrible*

dreizehn 13

1 (AT3 Level 2, AT4 Level 1–2) 1 Montag und Mittwoch. **2** Mittwoch und Freitag **3** Montag und Donnerstag **4** Montag und Donnerstag **5** Dienstag und Freitag **6** Montag und Donnerstag **7** Dienstag und Donnerstag **8** Montag und Freitag

2 (AT3 Level 2, AT4 Level 1) Sentences to be finished with appropriate adjective.

toll / langweilig / interessant / furchtbar / schwierig / einfach / gut / schlecht

Übungsheft B, Seite 13

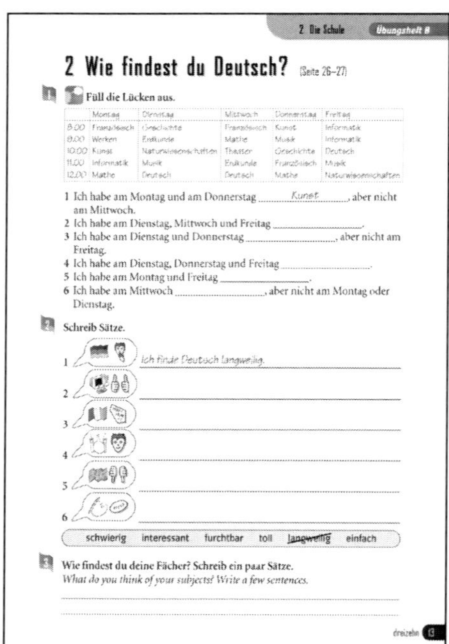

2 Die Schule Übungsheft B

2 Wie findest du Deutsch? (Seite 26–27)

1 **Füll die Lücken aus.**

	Montag	Dienstag	Mittwoch	Donnerstag	Freitag
8.00	Französisch	Geschichte	Französisch	Kunst	Informatik
9.00	Werken	Erdkunde	Mathe	Musik	Informatik
10.00	Kunst	Naturwissenschaften	Theater	Geschichte	Deutsch
11.00	Informatik	Musik	Erdkunde	Französisch	Musik
12.00	Mathe	Deutsch	Deutsch	Mathe	Naturwissenschaften

1 Ich habe am Montag und am Donnerstag Kunst, aber nicht am Mittwoch.
2 Ich habe am Dienstag, Mittwoch und Freitag .
3 Ich habe am Dienstag und Donnerstag , aber nicht am Freitag.
4 Ich habe am Dienstag, Donnerstag und Freitag .
5 Ich habe am Montag und Freitag .
6 Ich habe am Mittwoch , aber nicht am Montag oder Dienstag.

2 **Schreib Sätze.**

1 Ich finde Deutsch langweilig.
2
3
4
5
6

schwierig interessant furchtbar toll ~~langweilig~~ einfach

3 **Wie findest du deine Fächer? Schreib ein paar Sätze.**
What do you think of your subjects? Write a few sentences.

dreizehn 13

1 (AT3 Level 2, AT4 Level 1) 1 Ich habe am Montag und am Donnerstag **Kunst**, aber nicht am Mittwoch. **2** Ich habe am Dienstag, Mittwoch und Freitag **Deutsch**. **3** Ich habe am Dienstag und Donnerstag **Geschichte**, aber nicht am Freitag. **4** Ich habe am Dienstag, Donnerstag und Freitag **Musik**. **5** Ich habe am Montag und Freitag **Informatik**. **6** Ich habe am Mittwoch **Theater**.

2 (AT4 Level 2) 1 Ich finde Deutsch langweilig. **2** Ich finde Informatik toll. **3** Ich finde Französisch schwierig. **4** Ich finde Naturwissenschaften interessant. **5** Ich finde Englisch furchtbar. **6** Ich finde Kunst einfach.

3 (AT4 Level 3)

Übungsheft A, Seite 14

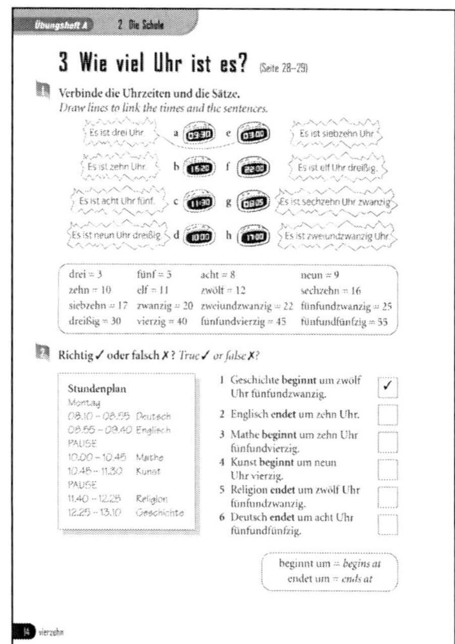

Übungsheft A 2 Die Schule

3 Wie viel Uhr ist es? (Seite 28–29)

1 Verbinde die Uhrzeiten und die Sätze.
Draw lines to link the times and the sentences.

Es ist drei Uhr. a 09:30 e 03:00 Es ist siebzehn Uhr.
Es ist zehn Uhr. b 16:20 f 22:00 Es ist elf Uhr dreißig.
Es ist acht Uhr fünf. c 11:30 g 08:05 Es ist sechzehn Uhr zwanzig.
Es ist neun Uhr dreißig. d 10:00 h 17:00 Es ist zweiundzwanzig Uhr.

drei = 3	fünf = 5	acht = 8	neun = 9
zehn = 10	elf = 11	zwölf = 12	sechzehn = 16
siebzehn = 17	zwanzig = 20	zweiundzwanzig = 22	fünfundzwanzig = 25
dreißig = 30	vierzig = 40	fünfundvierzig = 45	fünfundfünfzig = 55

2 Richtig ✓ oder falsch ✗? *True ✓ or false ✗?*

Stundenplan
Montag
08.10 – 08.55 Deutsch
08.55 – 09.40 Englisch
PAUSE
10.00 – 10.45 Mathe
10.45 – 11.30 Kunst
PAUSE
11.40 – 12.25 Religion
12.25 – 13.10 Geschichte

1 Geschichte **beginnt** um zwölf Uhr fünfundzwanzig. ✓
2 Englisch **endet** um zehn Uhr.
3 Mathe **beginnt** um zehn Uhr fünfundvierzig.
4 Kunst **beginnt** um neun Uhr vierzig.
5 Religion **endet** um zwölf Uhr fünfundzwanzig.
6 Deutsch **endet** um acht Uhr fünfundfünfzig.

beginnt um = *begins at*
endet um = *ends at*

14 vierzehn

1 (AT3 Level 2) a Es ist neun Uhr dreißig. **b** Es ist sechzehn Uhr zwanzig. **c** Es ist elf Uhr dreißig. **d** Es ist zehn Uhr. **e** Es ist drei Uhr. **f** Es ist zweiundzwanzig Uhr. **g** Es ist acht Uhr fünf. **h** Es ist siebzehn Uhr.

2 (AT3 Level 2) 1 ✓ **2** ✗ **3** ✗ **4** ✗ **5** ✓ **6** ✓

Übungsheft B, Seite 14

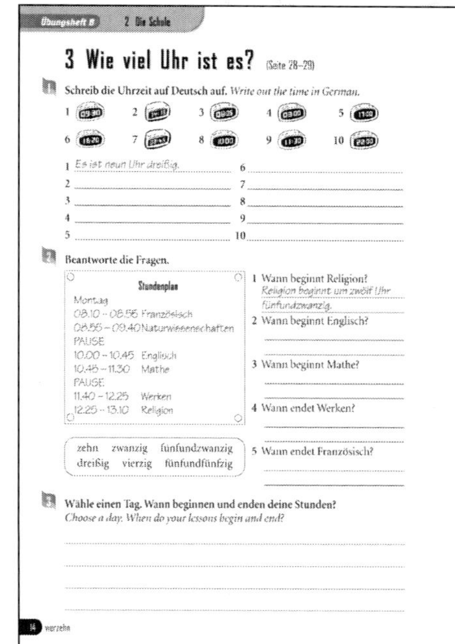

Übungsheft B 2 Die Schule

3 Wie viel Uhr ist es? (Seite 28–29)

1 Schreib die Uhrzeit auf Deutsch auf. *Write out the time in German.*

1 09:30 2 14:15 3 08:05 4 03:00 5 17:00
6 16:20 7 14:45 8 10:00 9 11:30 10 22:00

1 Es ist neun Uhr dreißig. 6 ______
2 ______ 7 ______
3 ______ 8 ______
4 ______ 9 ______
5 ______ 10 ______

2 Beantworte die Fragen.

Stundenplan
Montag
08.10 – 08.55 Französisch
08.55 – 09.40 Naturwissenschaften
PAUSE
10.00 – 10.45 Englisch
10.45 – 11.30 Mathe
PAUSE
11.40 – 12.25 Werken
12.25 – 13.10 Religion

1 Wann beginnt Religion? *Religion beginnt um zwölf Uhr fünfundzwanzig.*
2 Wann beginnt Englisch?
3 Wann beginnt Mathe?
4 Wann endet Werken?
5 Wann endet Französisch?

zehn zwanzig fünfundzwanzig dreißig vierzig fünfundfünfzig

3 Wähle einen Tag. Wann beginnen und enden deine Stunden?
Choose a day. When do your lessons begin and end?

14 vierzehn

1 (AT4 Level 2) 1 Es ist neun Uhr dreißig. **2** Es ist vierzehn Uhr fünfzehn. **3** Es ist acht Uhr fünf. **4** Es ist drei Uhr. **5** Es ist siebzehn Uhr. **6** Es ist sechzehn Uhr zwanzig. **7** Es ist zwei Uhr fünfundvierzig. **8** Es ist zehn Uhr. **9** Es ist elf Uhr dreißig. **10** Es ist zweiundzwanzig Uhr.

2 (AT3 Level 2) 1 Religion beginnt um zwölf Uhr fünfundzwanzig. **2** Englisch beginnt um zehn Uhr. **3** Mathe beginnt um zehn Uhr fünfundvierzig. **4** Werken endet um zwölf Uhr fünfundzwanzig. **5** Französisch endet um acht Uhr fünfundfünfzig.

3 (AT4 Level 3)

Übungsheft A, Seite 15

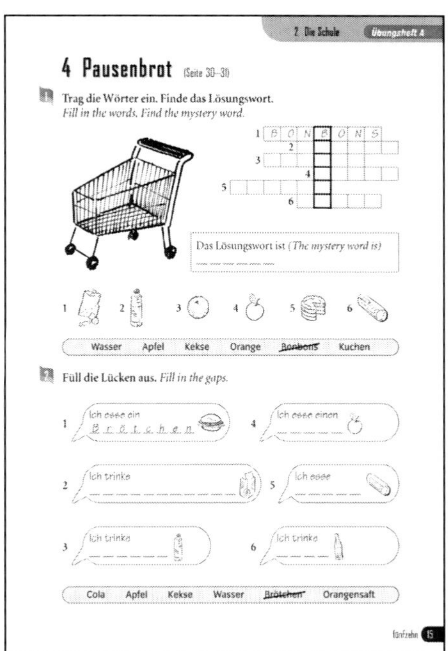

2 Die Schule Übungsheft A

4 Pausenbrot (Seite 30–31)

1 Trag die Wörter ein. Finde das Lösungswort.
Fill in the words. Find the mystery word.

1 B O N B O N S

Das Lösungswort ist (*The mystery word is*) ______

Wasser Apfel Kekse Orange ~~Bonbons~~ Kuchen

2 Füll die Lücken aus. *Fill in the gaps.*

1 Ich esse ein B r ö t c h e n
2 Ich trinke ______
3 Ich trinke ______
4 Ich esse einen ______
5 Ich esse ______
6 Ich trinke ______

Cola Apfel Kekse Wasser ~~Brötchen~~ Orangensaft

fünfzehn 15

1 (AT4 Level 1) 1 Bonbons **2** Wasser **3** Orange **4** Apfel **5** Kuchen **6** Kekse

Das Lösungswort ist Banane.

2 (AT3 Level 2, AT4 Level 1) 1 Ich esse ein **Brötchen**. **2** Ich trinke **Orangensaft**. **3** Ich trinke **Wasser**. **4** Ich esse einen **Apfel**. **5** Ich esse **Kekse**. **6** Ich trinke **Cola**.

Übungsheft B, Seite 15

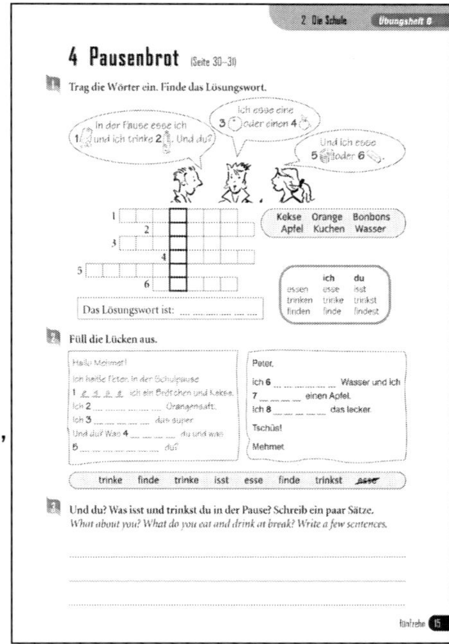

2 Die Schule Übungsheft B

4 Pausenbrot (Seite 30–31)

1 Trag die Wörter ein. Finde das Lösungswort.

In der Pause esse ich 1 ___ und ich trinke 2 ___. Und du?
Ich esse eine 3 ___ oder einen 4 ___.
Und ich esse 5 ___ oder 6 ___.

Kekse Orange Bonbons Apfel Kuchen Wasser

Das Lösungswort ist: ______

	ich	du
essen	esse	isst
trinken	trinke	trinkst
finden	finde	findest

2 Füll die Lücken aus.

Hallo Mehmet!
Ich heiße Peter. In der Schulpause
1 e s s e ich ein Brötchen und Kekse.
Ich 2 ______ Orangensaft.
Ich 3 ______ das super.
Und du? Was 4 ______ du und was
5 ______ du?

Peter,
Ich 6 ______ Wasser und ich
7 ______ einen Apfel.
Ich 8 ______ das lecker.
Tschüs!
Mehmet

trinke finde trinke isst esse finde trinkst ~~esse~~

3 Und du? Was isst und trinkst du in der Pause? Schreib ein paar Sätze.
What about you? What do you eat and drink at break? Write a few sentences.

fünfzehn 15

1 (AT3 Levels 2–3, AT4 Level 1)
1 Bonbons **2** Wasser **3** Orange **4** Apfel **5** Kuchen **6** Kekse

Das Lösungswort ist Banane.

2 (AT3 Level 3, AT4 Level 1) 1 Hallo Mehmet! Ich heiße Peter. In der Schulpause **esse** ich ein Brötchen und Kekse. Ich **trinke** Orangensaft. Ich **finde** das super. Und du? Was **isst** du und was **trinkst** du?

2 Peter, ich **trinke** Wasser und ich **esse** einen Apfel. Ich **finde** das lecker. Tschüs! Mehmet

3 (AT4 Level 3)

Übungsheft A, Seite 16

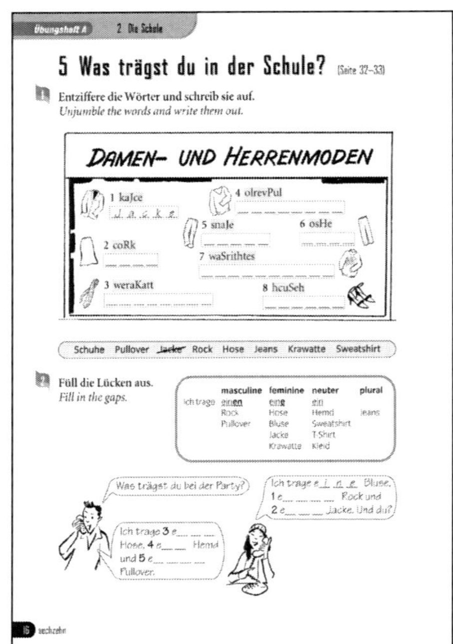
Übungsheft A 2 Die Schule

5 Was trägst du in der Schule? (Seite 32–33)

1 **Entziffere die Wörter und schreib sie auf.**
Unjumble the words and write them out.

DAMEN- UND HERRENMODEN

1 kaJce J a c k e
2 coRk
3 weraKatt
4 olrevPul
5 snaJe
6 osHe
7 waSrithtes
8 hcuSeh

Schuhe Pullover ~~Jacke~~ Rock Hose Jeans Krawatte Sweatshirt

2 **Füll die Lücken aus.**
Fill in the gaps.

	masculine	feminine	neuter	plural
Ich trage	einen	eine	ein	
	Rock	Hose	Hemd	Jeans
	Pullover	Bluse	Sweatshirt	
		Jacke	T-Shirt	
		Krawatte	Kleid	

16 sechzehn

1 (AT4 Level 1) 1 die Jacke **2** der Rock **3** die Krawatte **4** der Pullover **5** die Jeans **6** die Hose **7** das Sweatshirt **8** die Schuhe

2 (AT3 Level 2–3, AT4 Level 1) Ich trage **eine** Bluse, **einen** Rock und **eine** Jacke. Und du?

Ich trage **eine** Hose, **ein** Hemd und **einen** Pullover.

Übungsheft B, Seite 16

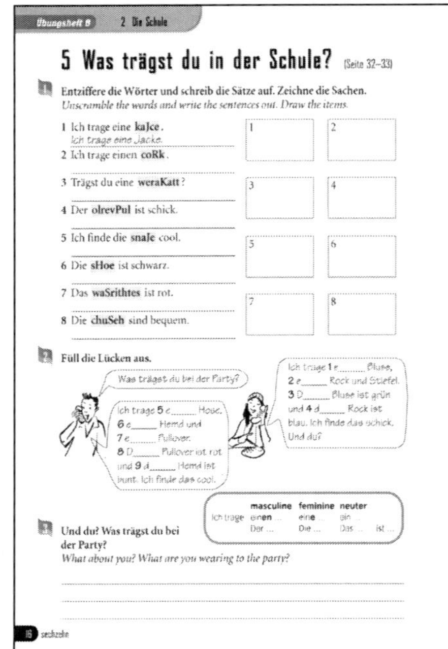
Übungsheft B 2 Die Schule

5 Was trägst du in der Schule? (Seite 32–33)

1 **Entziffere die Wörter und schreib die Sätze auf. Zeichne die Sachen.**
Unscramble the words and write the sentences out. Draw the items.

1 Ich trage eine **kaJce**.
Ich trage eine Jacke.
2 Ich trage einen **coRk**.
3 Trägst du eine **weraKatt**?
4 Der **olrevPul** ist schick.
5 Ich finde die **snaJe** cool.
6 Die **sHoe** ist schwarz.
7 Das **waSrithtes** ist rot.
8 Die **chuSeh** sind bequem.

2 **Füll die Lücken aus.**

	masculine	feminine	neuter	
Ich trage	einen …	eine …	ein …	
	Der …	Die …	Das …	ist …

3 **Und du? Was trägst du bei der Party?**
What about you? What are you wearing to the party?

16 sechzehn

1 (AT3 Level 2, AT4 Level 2) 1 Ich trage eine Jacke. **2** Ich trage einen Rock. **3** Trägst du eine Krawatte? **4** Der Pullover ist schick. **5** Ich finde die Jeans cool. **6** Die Hose ist schwarz. **7** Das Sweatshirt ist rot. **8** Die Schuhe sind bequem.

2 (AT3 Level 3, AT4 Level 1) – Was trägst du bei der Party? – Ich trage **1 eine** Bluse, **2 einen** Rock und Stiefel. **3** D**ie** Bluse ist grün und **4** d**er** Rock ist blau. Ich finde das schick. Und du? – Ich trage **5** e**ine** Hose, **6** e**in** Hemd und **7** e**inen** Pullover. **8** D**er** Pullover ist rot und **9** d**as** Hemd ist bunt. Ich finde das cool.

3 (AT4 Levels 2–3)

Übungsheft A, Seite 17

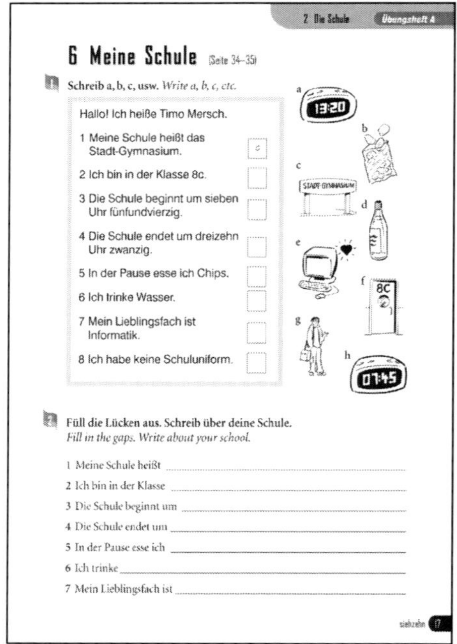
2 Die Schule Übungsheft A

6 Meine Schule (Seite 34–35)

1 **Schreib a, b, c, usw.** *Write a, b, c, etc.*

Hallo! Ich heiße Timo Mersch.
1 Meine Schule heißt das Stadt-Gymnasium. c
2 Ich bin in der Klasse 8c.
3 Die Schule beginnt um sieben Uhr fünfundvierzig.
4 Die Schule endet um dreizehn Uhr zwanzig.
5 In der Pause esse ich Chips.
6 Ich trinke Wasser.
7 Mein Lieblingsfach ist Informatik.
8 Ich habe keine Schuluniform.

2 **Füll die Lücken aus. Schreib über deine Schule.**
Fill in the gaps. Write about your school.

1 Meine Schule heißt
2 Ich bin in der Klasse
3 Die Schule beginnt um
4 Die Schule endet um
5 In der Pause esse ich
6 Ich trinke
7 Mein Lieblingsfach ist

siebzehn 17

1 (AT3 Level 2)

Answers
1 c **2** f **3** h **4** a **5** b **6** d **7** e **8** g

2 (AT3 Level 2, AT4 Level 1–2)

Übungsheft B, Seite 17

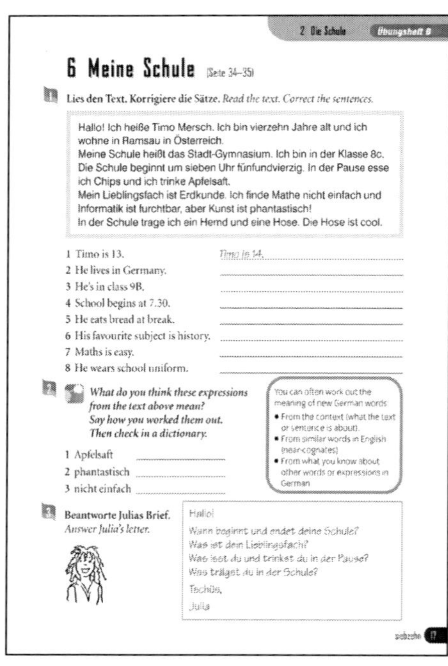
2 Die Schule Übungsheft B

6 Meine Schule (Seite 34–35)

1 **Lies den Text. Korrigiere die Sätze.** *Read the text. Correct the sentences.*

Hallo! Ich heiße Timo Mersch. Ich bin vierzehn Jahre alt und ich wohne in Ramsau in Österreich.
Meine Schule heißt das Stadt-Gymnasium. Ich bin in der Klasse 8c.
Die Schule beginnt um sieben Uhr fünfundvierzig. In der Pause esse ich Chips und ich trinke Apfelsaft.
Mein Lieblingsfach ist Erdkunde. Ich finde Mathe nicht einfach und Informatik ist furchtbar, aber Kunst ist phantastisch!
In der Schule trage ich ein Hemd und eine Hose. Die Hose ist cool.

1 Timo is 13. Timo is 14.
2 He lives in Germany.
3 He's in class 9B.
4 School begins at 7.30.
5 He eats bread at break.
6 His favourite subject is history.
7 Maths is easy.
8 He wears school uniform.

2 ***What do you think these expressions from the text above mean? Say how you worked them out. Then check in a dictionary.***

1 Apfelsaft
2 phantastisch
3 nicht einfach

You can often work out the meaning of new German words:
- From the context (what the text or sentence is about).
- From similar words in English (near-cognates)
- From what you know about other words or expressions in German

3 **Beantworte Julias Brief.**
Answer Julia's letter.

Hallo!
Wann beginnt und endet deine Schule?
Was ist dein Lieblingsfach?
Was isst du und trinkst du in der Pause?
Was trägst du in der Schule?
Tschüs,
Julia

siebzehn 17

1 (AT3 Level 3) 1 Timo is 14. **2** He lives in Austria. **3** He's in class 8c. **4** School begins at 7.45. **5** He eats crisps at break. **6** His favourite subject is geography. **7** Maths is not easy. **8** He doesn't wear school uniform.

2 (AT3 Level 1) 1 apple juice **2** fantastic **3** not easy

3 (AT3 Level 3, AT4 Level 3)

Übungsheft A, Seite 18

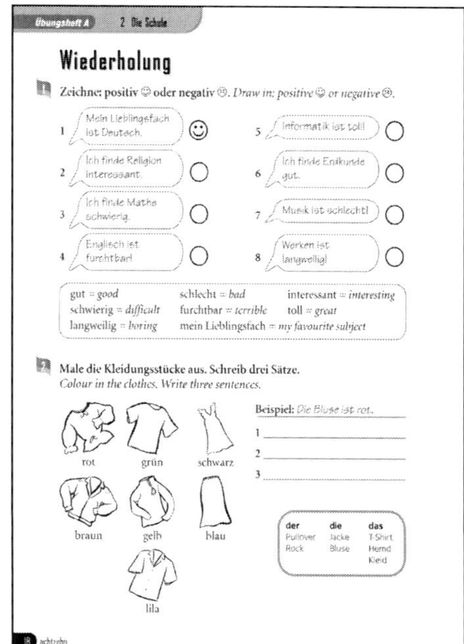

Übungsheft A 2 Die Schule

Wiederholung

1 Zeichne: positiv ☺ oder negativ ☹. *Draw in: positive ☺ or negative ☹.*

1 Mein Lieblingsfach ist Deutsch. ☺
2 Ich finde Religion interessant. ○
3 Ich finde Mathe schwierig. ○
4 Englisch ist furchtbar! ○
5 Informatik ist toll! ○
6 Ich finde Erdkunde gut. ○
7 Musik ist schlecht! ○
8 Werken ist langweilig! ○

gut = *good* schlecht = *bad* interessant = *interesting*
schwierig = *difficult* furchtbar = *terrible* toll = *great*
langweilig = *boring* mein Lieblingsfach = *my favourite subject*

2 Male die Kleidungsstücke aus. Schreib drei Sätze.
Colour in the clothes. Write three sentences.

rot grün schwarz
braun gelb blau
lila

Beispiel: *Die Bluse ist rot.*
1 ___
2 ___
3 ___

der	die	das
Pullover	Jacke	T-Shirt
Rock	Bluse	Hemd
		Kleid

18 achtzehn

1 (AT3 Level 2) 1 ☺ **2** ☺ **3** ☹ **4** ☹ **5** ☺ **6** ☺ **7** ☹ **8** ☹

2 (AT3 Level 1, AT4 Level 2) red blouse, green T-shirt, black dress, brown jacket, yellow pullover, blue skirt, purple shirt

Choose from:
Das T-Shirt ist grün. Das Kleid ist schwarz. Die Jacke ist braun. Der Pullover ist gelb. Der Rock ist blau. Das Hemd ist lila.

Übungsheft B, Seite 18

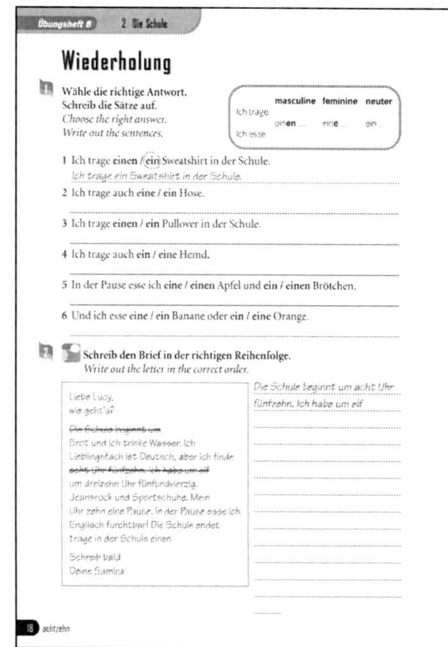

Übungsheft B 2 Die Schule

Wiederholung

1 Wähle die richtige Antwort. Schreib die Sätze auf.
Choose the right answer. Write out the sentences.

	masculine	feminine	neuter
Ich trage / Ich esse	ein**en** ...	ein**e** ...	ein ...

1 Ich trage **einen / ein** Sweatshirt in der Schule.
Ich trage ein Sweatshirt in der Schule.
2 Ich trage auch **eine / ein** Hose.
3 Ich trage **einen / ein** Pullover in der Schule.
4 Ich trage auch **ein / eine** Hemd.
5 In der Pause esse ich **eine / einen** Apfel und **ein / einen** Brötchen.
6 Und ich esse **eine / ein** Banane oder **ein / eine** Orange.

2 Schreib den Brief in der richtigen Reihenfolge.
Write out the letter in the correct order.

Liebe Lucy,
wie geht's?
~~Die Schule beginnt um~~
Brot und ich trinke Wasser. Ich
Lieblingsfach ist Deutsch, aber ich finde
~~acht Uhr fünfzehn. Ich habe um elf~~
um dreizehn Uhr fünfundvierzig.
Jeansrock und Sportschuhe. Mein
Uhr zehn eine Pause. In der Pause esse ich
Englisch furchtbar! Die Schule endet
trage in der Schule einen
Schreib bald
Deine Samira

Die Schule beginnt um acht Uhr fünfzehn. Ich habe um elf

18 achtzehn

1 (AT3 Level 2, AT4 Level 2) 1 Ich trage **ein** Sweatshirt in der Schule. **2** Ich trage auch **eine** Hose. **3** Ich trage **einen** Pullover in der Schule. **4** Ich trage auch **ein** Hemd. **5** In der Pause esse ich **einen** Apfel und **ein** Brötchen. **6** Und ich esse **eine** Banane oder **eine** Orange.

2 (AT3 Level 3, AT4 Levels 3–4) Liebe Lucy, wie geht's? Die Schule beginnt um acht Uhr fünfzehn. Ich habe um elf Uhr zehn eine Pause. In der Pause esse ich Brot und ich trinke Wasser. Ich trage in der Schule einen Jeansrock und Sportschuhe. Mein Lieblingsfach ist Deutsch, aber ich finde Englisch furchtbar! Die Schule endet um dreizehn Uhr fünfundvierzig.

Schreib bald, deine Samira.

(Order could vary, as long as the letter makes sense.)

Arbeitsblatt 2.1

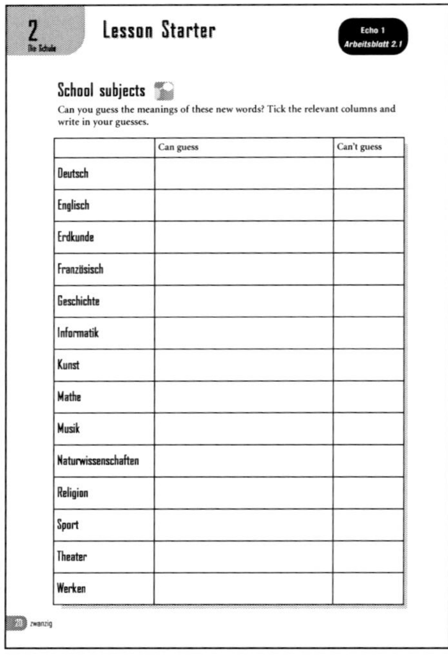

2 Die Schule | Lesson Starter | Echo 1 Arbeitsblatt 2.1

School subjects

Can you guess the meanings of these new words? Tick the relevant columns and write in your guesses.

	Can guess	Can't guess
Deutsch		
Englisch		
Erdkunde		
Französisch		
Geschichte		
Informatik		
Kunst		
Mathe		
Musik		
Naturwissenschaften		
Religion		
Sport		
Theater		
Werken		

20 zwanzig

Arbeitsblatt 2.2

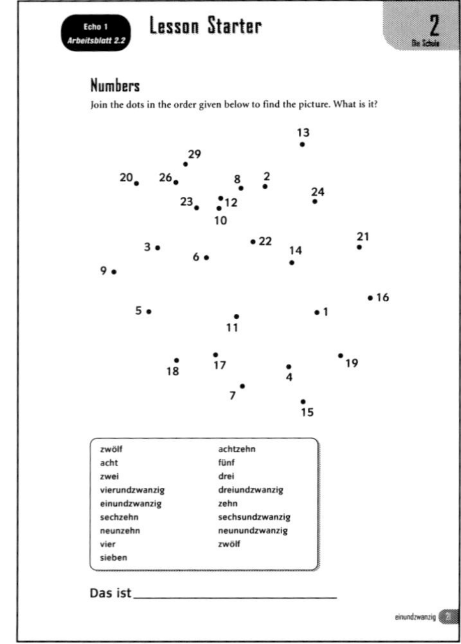

Echo 1 Arbeitsblatt 2.2 | Lesson Starter | 2 Die Schule

Numbers

Join the dots in the order given below to find the picture. What is it?

zwölf	achtzehn
acht	fünf
zwei	drei
vierundzwanzig	dreiundzwanzig
einundzwanzig	zehn
sechzehn	sechsundzwanzig
neunzehn	neunundzwanzig
vier	zwölf
sieben	

Das ist ____________

einundzwanzig 21

Das ist ein Apfel

Arbeitsblatt 2.3

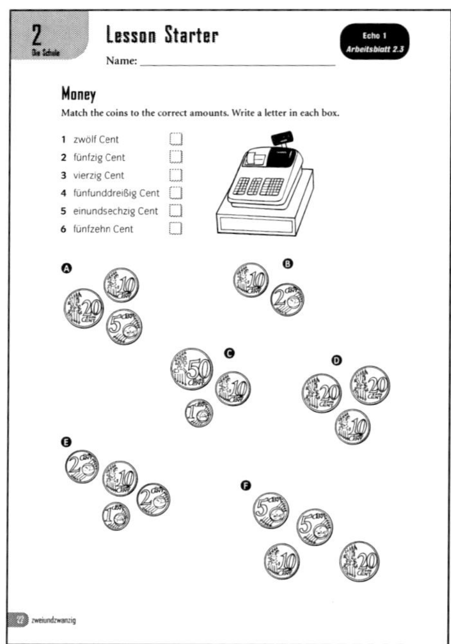

2 Die Schule | Lesson Starter | Echo 1 Arbeitsblatt 2.3

Name: ____________

Money

Match the coins to the correct amounts. Write a letter in each box.

1 zwölf Cent ☐
2 fünfzig Cent ☐
3 vierzig Cent ☐
4 fünfunddreißig Cent ☐
5 einundsechzig Cent ☐
6 fünfzehn Cent ☐

22 zweiundzwanzig

1 B 2 D 3 F 4 A 5 C 6 E

Arbeitsblatt 2.4

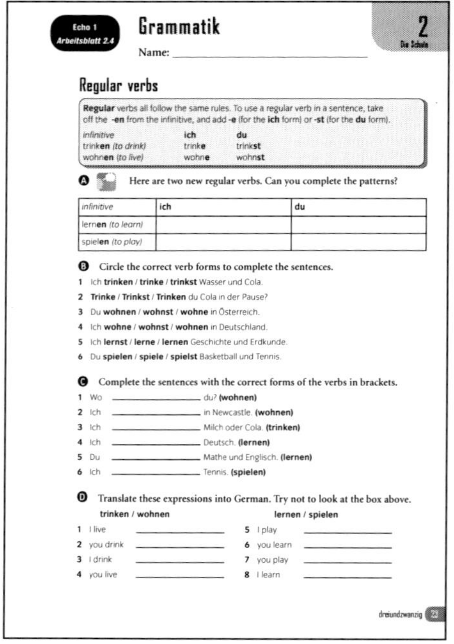

Echo 1 Arbeitsblatt 2.4 | Grammatik | 2 Die Schule

Name: ____________

Regular verbs

Regular verbs all follow the same rules. To use a regular verb in a sentence, take off the **-en** from the infinitive, and add **-e** (for the **ich** form) or **-st** (for the **du** form).

infinitive	ich	du
trink**en** (to drink)	trink**e**	trink**st**
wohn**en** (to live)	wohn**e**	wohn**st**

A Here are two new regular verbs. Can you complete the patterns?

infinitive	ich	du
lern**en** (to learn)		
spiel**en** (to play)		

B Circle the correct verb forms to complete the sentences.

1 Ich **trinken / trinke / trinkst** Wasser und Cola.
2 **Trinke / Trinkst / Trinken** du Cola in der Pause?
3 Du **wohnen / wohnst / wohne** in Österreich.
4 Ich **wohne / wohnst / wohnen** in Deutschland.
5 Ich **lernst / lerne / lernen** Geschichte und Erdkunde.
6 Du **spielen / spiele / spielst** Basketball und Tennis.

C Complete the sentences with the correct forms of the verbs in brackets.

1 Wo ____________ du? **(wohnen)**
2 Ich ____________ in Newcastle. **(wohnen)**
3 Ich ____________ Milch oder Cola. **(trinken)**
4 Ich ____________ Deutsch. **(lernen)**
5 Du ____________ Mathe und Englisch. **(lernen)**
6 Ich ____________ Tennis. **(spielen)**

D Translate these expressions into German. Try not to look at the box above.

trinken / wohnen		lernen / spielen	
1 I live	________	5 I play	________
2 you drink	________	6 you learn	________
3 I drink	________	7 you play	________
4 you live	________	8 I learn	________

dreiundzwanzig 23

A
lerne, lernst, spiele, spielst

B
1 trinke **2** Trinkst **3** wohnst **4** wohne **5** lerne **6** spielst

C
1 wohnst **2** wohne **3** trinke **4** lerne **5** lernst **6** spiele

D
1 ich wohne **2** du trinkst **3** ich trinke **4** du wohnst **5** ich spiele **6** du lernst **7** du spielst **8** ich lerne

Arbeitsblatt 2.5

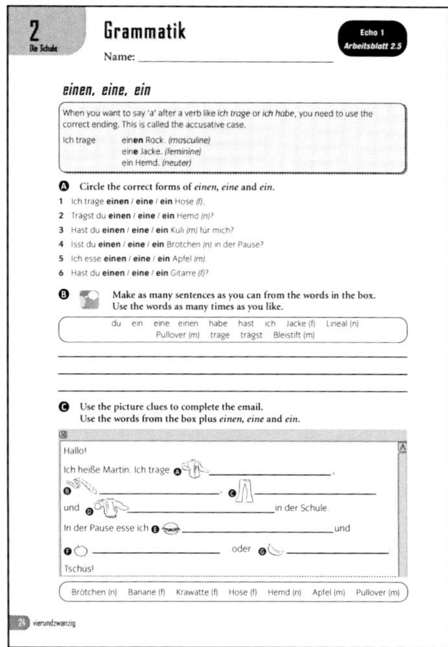

2 Die Schule

Grammatik

Echo 1 Arbeitsblatt 2.5

Name: ____________________

einen, eine, ein

When you want to say 'a' after a verb like *ich trage* or *ich habe*, you need to use the correct ending. This is called the accusative case.

Ich trage ein**en** Rock. *(masculine)*
ein**e** Jacke. *(feminine)*
ein Hemd. *(neuter)*

A Circle the correct forms of *einen*, *eine* and *ein*.

1 Ich trage **einen / eine / ein** Hose *(f)*.
2 Trägst du **einen / eine / ein** Hemd *(n)*?
3 Hast du **einen / eine / ein** Kuli *(m)* für mich?
4 Isst du **einen / eine / ein** Brötchen *(n)* in der Pause?
5 Ich esse **einen / eine / ein** Apfel *(m)*.
6 Hast du **einen / eine / ein** Gitarre *(f)*?

B Make as many sentences as you can from the words in the box. Use the words as many times as you like.

du ein eine einen habe hast ich Jacke (f) Lineal (n) Pullover (m) trage trägst Bleistift (m)

C Use the picture clues to complete the email. Use the words from the box plus *einen*, *eine* and *ein*.

Hallo!
Ich heiße Martin. Ich trage A ____________, B ____________, C ____________
und D ____________ in der Schule.
In der Pause esse ich E ____________ und
F ____________ oder G ____________
Tschüs!

Brötchen (n) Banane (f) Krawatte (f) Hose (f) Hemd (n) Apfel (m) Pullover (m)

24 vierundzwanzig

A

1 eine **2** ein **3** einen **4** ein **5** einen **6** eine

B

Possible answers

Ich trage eine Jacke. Ich trage einen Pullover. Du trägst eine Jacke. Du trägst einen Pullover. Ich habe ein Lineal. Ich habe einen Bleistift. Du hast ein Lineal. Du hast einen Bleistift.

C

A ein Hemd **B** eine Krawatte **C** eine Hose **D** einen Pullover **E** ein Brötchen **F** einen Apfel **G** eine Banane

Arbeitsblatt 2.6

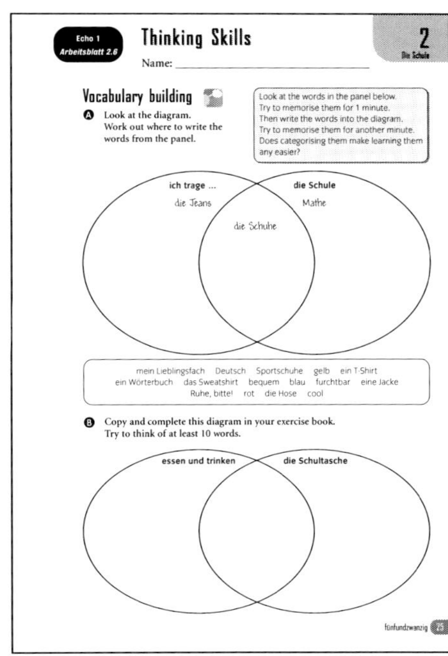

Echo 1 Arbeitsblatt 2.6

Thinking Skills

2 Die Schule

Name: ____________________

Vocabulary building

A Look at the diagram. Work out where to write the words from the panel.

Look at the words in the panel below. Try to memorise them for 1 minute. Then write the words into the diagram. Try to memorise them for another minute. Does categorising them make learning them any easier?

mein Lieblingsfach Deutsch Sportschuhe gelb ein T-Shirt ein Wörterbuch das Sweatshirt bequem blau furchtbar eine Jacke Ruhe, bitte! rot die Hose cool

B Copy and complete this diagram in your exercise book. Try to think of at least 10 words.

fünfundzwanzig 25

A

ich trage die Jeans, Sportschuhe, ein T-Shirt, das Sweatshirt, bequem, cool, gelb, rot

die Schule Mathe, mein Lieblingsfach, Deutsch, ein Wörterbuch, blau, furchtbar, Ruhe, bitte!

could apply to both die Schuhe, eine Jacke, die Hose

Arbeitsblatt 2.7

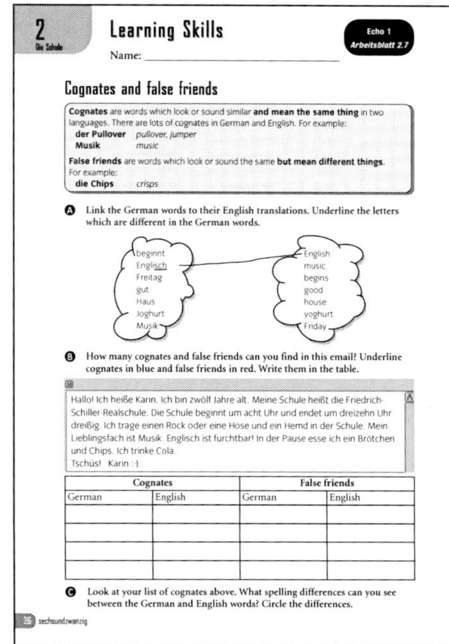

2 Die Schule

Learning Skills

Echo 1 Arbeitsblatt 2.7

Name: ____________________

Cognates and false friends

Cognates are words which look or sound similar **and mean the same thing** in two languages. There are lots of cognates in German and English. For example:
der Pullover *pullover, jumper*
Musik *music*

False friends are words which look or sound the same **but mean different things**. For example:
die Chips *crisps*

A Link the German words to their English translations. Underline the letters which are different in the German words.

B How many cognates and false friends can you find in this email? Underline cognates in blue and false friends in red. Write them in the table.

Hallo! Ich heiße Karin. Ich bin zwölf Jahre alt. Meine Schule heißt die Friedrich-Schiller-Realschule. Die Schule beginnt um acht Uhr und endet um dreizehn Uhr dreißig. Ich trage einen Rock oder eine Hose und ein Hemd in der Schule. Mein Lieblingsfach ist Musik. Englisch ist furchtbar! In der Pause esse ich ein Brötchen und Chips. Ich trinke Cola.
Tschüs! Karin :-)

Cognates		False friends	
German	English	German	English

C Look at your list of cognates above. What spelling differences can you see between the German and English words? Circle the differences.

26 sechsundzwanzig

A

beginnt / *begins*, Englisch / *English*, Freitag / *Friday*, gut / *good*, Haus / *house*, Joghurt / *yoghurt*, Musik / *music*

B

Possible answers. Allow any plausible alternatives / additions.

Cognates		**False friends**	
German	**English**	**German**	**English**
Hallo!	*Hello! / Hi!*	bin	*am*
Schule	*school*	Hose	*trousers*
beginnt	*begins*	Chips	*crisps*
endet	*ends*	Pause	*break*
in	*in*	die	*the*
Musik	*music*	Rock	*skirt*
Englisch	*English*		
trinke	*drink*		
Cola	*cola*		

C

Many possible answers. Help pupils to spot these key differences.

German	**English**	
alt	*old*	t = *d*
trinke	*drink*	
Schule	*school*	u = *oo*
beginnt	*begins*	*different endings on verbs*
endet	*ends*	
Musik	*music*	k = *c*
Englisch	*English*	sch = *sh*

3 Familie und Freunde

Unit Learning targets	Key framework objectives	NC levels and PoS coverage	Grammar and key language	Skills
1 Hast du Geschwister? (pp. 42–43) ● Talking about brothers and sisters ● Using the pronouns *er* and *sie* ('he' and 'she')	**1.4/Y7** Speaking – (a) social and classroom language	**NC levels 2–4** **2.2a** listen for gist **2.2d** pronunciation and intonation **2.2e** ask and answer questions **3b** sounds and writing **3c** apply grammar **4b** communicate in pairs etc. **4g** language for a range of purposes	Plural nouns: *Brüder/Schwestern* Pronouns *er* and *sie* *Er/sie ist …* *Er/sie heißt …* *Ich habe einen / eine* (revisited) *Hast du … ?* *Ich habe …* *einen Bruder / Halbbruder / Stiefbruder* *eine Schwester / Halbschwester / Stiefschwester* *zwei Brüder / Schwestern* *Ich bin Einzelkind.* *Wie heißt er / sie?* *Wie alt ist er / sie?*	Pronunciation: *u/ü* Appreciating the importance of high-frequency words
2 Haustiere (pp. 44–45) ● Talking about pets ● Using plural forms of nouns	**1.1/Y7** Listening – gist and detail **4.3/Y7** Language – plurals	**NC levels 2–4** **2.1b** memorising **2.2a** listen for gist **2.2e** ask and answer questions **2.2g** write clearly and coherently **3c** apply grammar **4b** communicate in pairs etc.	*Ich habe einen / eine / ein …* (revisited) Plural forms of nouns (pets) *Hast du ein Haustier?* *Ich habe einen …* *Goldfisch(-e)* *Hamster(-)* *Hund(-e)* *Wellensittich(-e)* *Ich habe eine …* *Katze(-n)* *Schlange(-n)* *Schildkröte(-n)* *Ich habe ein …* *Kaninchen(-)* *Meerschweinchen(-)* *Pferd(-e)* *Ich habe zwei / drei etc* + plural forms *Ich habe keine Haustiere.* *Er / Sie / Es ist … / heißt …*	Finding out plural forms of nouns
3 Die Familie (pp. 46–47) ● Giving information about family members ● Using the possessive adjectives *mein* and *dein* ('my' and 'your')	**2.4/Y7** Writing – (a) sentences and texts as models	**NC levels 1–3** **2.2a** listen for gist **2.2d** pronunciation and intonation **2.2e** ask and answer questions **2.2i** reuse language they have met **3c** apply grammar **3d** use a range of vocab / structures	Possesive adjectives: *mein(e) / dein(e)* Personal pronouns: *er / sie* (revisited) *Mein Vater / Stiefvater / Bruder / Großvater / Onkel / Cousin* *Das ist mein … / Ist das dein … ?* *Meine Mutter / Schwester / Stiefmutter / Großmutter / Tante / Cousine* *Das ist meine … / Ist das deine … ?* *Er / Sie heißt …* *Er / Sie ist … Jahre alt.* Numbers 1–100	
4 Wie sieht sie aus? (pp. 48–49) ● Describing people's appearance ● Using adjectives with nouns	**1.1/Y7** Listening – gist and detail	**NC levels 2–3** **2.2a** listen for gist **2.2d** pronunciation and intonation **2.2j** adapt previously-learnt language **3b** sounds and writing **3c** apply grammar	Adjectival endings before noun (*lange, braune*, etc) *haben* and *sein: ich / du / er / sie / es* *braune / blonde / rote / schwarze / lange / kurze / glatte / lockige Haare* *grüne / braune / blaue / graue Augen* *groß / mittelgroß / klein / schlank / kräftig / dick*	Pronunciation: *au*

Unit Learning targets	Key framework objectives	NC levels and PoS coverage	Grammar and key language	Skills
5 Er ist lustig (pp. 50–51) ● Talking about people's characteristics ● Making sentences more interesting	2.2/Y7 Reading – (a) unfamiliar language	NC levels 1–4 **2.2a** listen for gist **2.2d** pronunciation and intonation **2.2j** adapt previously-learnt language **3b** sounds and writing **3c** apply grammar **3d** use a range of vocab / structures	Connectives: *und / aber* Qualifiers: *sehr / ziemlich* *nicht* *Wie bist du?* *Wie ist … ?* *Ich bin / Du bist / Er / Sie ist freundlich / lustig / laut / schüchtern / intelligent / sportlich / musikalisch / kreativ / faul / launisch / unpünktlich.* *Herr / Frau*	Using connectives and qualifiers to make sentences longer/more interesting
6 E-Mails (pp. 52–53) ● Understanding a longer email and writing a reply ● Finding out the meanings of new words	3.2/Y7 Culture – (a) young people: interests/ opinions 3.2/Y7 Culture – (b) challenging stereotypes 5.4 Strategies – working out meaning	NC levels 2–4 **2.1d** previous knowledge **2.2b** skim and scan **2.2c** respond appropriately **2.2e** ask and answer questions **2.2j** adapt previously-learnt language **3b** sounds and writing **3d** use a range of vocab / structures **4b** communicate in pairs etc. **4g** language for a range of purposes	*Hallo!* *Ich heiße …* *Ich bin / Er/Sie ist … Jahre alt.* *Ich habe am … Geburtstag.* *Ich wohne in …* *Das ist in …* *Ich habe …* (family and pets) *Ich habe …* (appearance) *Ich bin / Er/Sie ist …* (character) *Wie geht's?* *Hast du Geschwister?* *Hast du ein Haustier?* *Wie siehst du aus?* *Schreib bald!* *dein / deine*	Reading/ Listening to a longer text for gist Deducing the meanings of new words Composing an email in German
Lernzieltest und Wiederholung (pp. 54–55) ● Pupils' checklist and practice test		NC levels 2–4 **3c** apply grammar **3d** use a range of vocab / structures **4b** communicate in pairs etc.		
Mehr (pp. 56–57) ● Information about a famous person	1.5/Y7 Speaking – (a) presenting 1.5/Y7 Speaking – (b) expression/ non-verbal techniques 5.7 Strategies – planning and preparing	NC levels 3–4 **2.2b** skim and scan **2.2c** respond appropriately **2.2e** ask and answer questions **2.2j** adapt previously-learnt language **3c** apply grammar **3d** use a range of vocab / structures **4e** use a range of resources **4f** language of interest / enjoyment **4g** language for a range of purposes	Third person singular verb forms Profile of a famous person: *Name* *Alter* *Geburtstag* *Wohnort* *Freundin* *Geschwister* *Haustiere* *Größe* *Haare* *Augen* *Persönlichkeit*	
Extra (pp. 116–117) Self-access reading and writing at two levels		NC levels 1–4 **2.2e** ask and answer questions **3c** apply grammar **3d** use a range of vocab / structures		

1 Hast du Geschwister?

Learning targets

- Talking about brothers and sisters
- Using the pronouns *er* and *sie* ('he' and 'she')

Key framework objectives

1.4/Y7 Speaking – (a) social and classroom language

Grammar

- Plurals: *Brüder / Schwestern*
- Third person singular of *sein*: *er / sie ist*
- *haben* + *einen / eine* (revisited)

Key language

Hast du Geschwister?
Ich habe …
einen Bruder / Halbbruder / Stiefbruder
eine Schwester / Halbschwester / Stiefschwester
zwei Brüder / Schwestern.
Ich bin Einzelkind.
Wie heißt er / sie?
Er / Sie heißt …
Wie alt ist er / sie?
Er / Sie ist … Jahre alt.

High-frequency words

hast du?
ich habe
einen / eine
ich bin
er/sie ist
wie?
und

Pronunciation

u / ü

Mathematics

Using numbers to give ages
Simple arithmetic

Resources

CD 2, tracks 2–4
Workbooks A and B, p.22
Arbeitsblatt 3.1, p.39
Echo Elektro 1 TPP, Mod 3 1.1–1.7

Starter 1 4.6a/Y7

Aim

To re-cap question forms encountered in Chapters 1 and 2.

Reveal the following list of English questions on the board or an OHT. You may wish to use just the first five with a less confident class. Pupils work in pairs to find and write down the correct German equivalents, using their textbooks for reference. You may then wish to discuss the question words found, and the *hast du?* question form.

What are you called?
How old are you?
Where do you live?
Have you got a ruler?
What is your favourite subject?
How do you find German?
When does geography start?
What do you eat at break?

Suggestion

Before starting exercise 1, get pupils to open their books and look at the illustrations for the task for 5 seconds before shutting their books again, and ask them what they think they will be learning this lesson. Did the words in the speech bubbles give any clues (e.g. prior knowledge of the high frequency words *ich, habe, ein*; similarity to English; links between words)?

1 Hör zu und lies. Wer ist das? (1–7) (AT 1/2) 4.2/Y7 4.3/Y7

Listening. Pupils listen to the recording and match each speaker to the correct picture. If not already discussed through doing the starter activity, discuss what pupils think the words mean before listening. Briefly discuss the reason for *einen / eine* (already encountered in Chapters 1 and 2) and ask what the difference is between *Bruder* and *Brüder*, *Schwester* and *Schwestern* – plural forms are looked at in more detail in Unit 2 of this chapter.

1 – *Hallo! Hast du Geschwister?*
– *Nein! Ich bin Einzelkind.*

2 – *Und hast du Geschwister?*
– *Ja. Ich habe zwei Brüder.*

3 – *Und du, hast du Geschwister?*
– *Ja, sicher. Ich habe zwei Schwestern.*

4 – Hast du Geschwister?
– Ja. Ich habe einen Stiefbruder.

5 – Und hast du Geschwister?
– Ja. Ich habe eine Schwester.

6 – Hast du auch Geschwister?
– Ja. Ich habe eine Halbschwester.

7 – Und du? Hast du Geschwister?
– Ja. Ich habe einen Bruder.

Answers
1 g **2** b **3** e **4** c **5** d **6** f **7** a

Aussprache: u/ü 5.1

Read through this pronunciation tip before moving on to exercise 2.

2 Hör zu und wiederhole dreimal. 5.1

Listening. Pupils listen to and repeat the question and answer illustrating the difference in sound between *u* and *ü*. Pairs could then practise pronouncing the question and answer, competing to see how many times they can repeat them correctly in ten seconds.

*Hast d**u** einen Br**u**der?*
*Ja, ich habe f**ü**nf Br**ü**der!*

3

3 Klassenumfrage. (AT 2/2) 1.4a/Y7

Speaking. Pupils conduct a survey about brothers and sisters and note their findings as shown. Set a time limit, so that all pupils finish at the same time.

\+ Afterwards, pupils could write sentences showing what some of their interviewees actually said (using the *ich* form). Encourage them to focus on accuracy.

Starter 2 4.2/Y7

Aim

To revise numbers 1–20, introduced in Chapter 1, prior to saying and understanding ages of siblings.

Pairs sit back to back, partner A facing the board, B with a pen and paper or mini-whiteboard. On the board, write five simple sums in number form, using + and – (remind the class how to pronounce these signs in the German way), whose answers total no more than 20. Partner A reads out each sum to partner B, who writes down the answers. Tell pairs to swap roles, and put another five sums on the board. The range of numbers could be increased for more able pupils.

4 Hör zu und füll die Tabelle aus. (1–5) (AT 1/3) 1.1/Y7

Listening. This exercise introduces *er/sie heißt* and *er/sie ist*. Pupils make brief notes as shown. The names needed are given in random order in the Pupil's Book for support. Afterwards, elicit the words heard for 'he' and 'she'. Discuss briefly with the class whether these little words are easy or difficult to remember, and why.

4

1 – Peter, hast du Geschwister?
– Ja, ich habe einen Bruder.
– Wie heißt er?
– Er heißt Hanno.
– Wie alt ist er?
– Er ist neunzehn.

2 – Hallo, Stefanie. Hast du Geschwister?
– Ja, ich habe eine Schwester.
– Wie heißt sie?
– Sie heißt Miriam.
– Wie alt ist sie?
– Sie ist elf Jahre alt.

3 – Nina, hast du Geschwister?
– Ja! Ich habe zwei Brüder, Paul und Markus.
– Wie alt ist Paul?
– Er ist acht Jahre alt.
– Und wie alt ist Markus?
– Er ist zehn Jahre alt.

4 – Und Julia, hallo! Hast du Geschwister?
– Ja, ich habe einen Stiefbruder.
– Wie heißt er?
– Er heißt Stefan.
– Und wie alt ist er?
– Er ist vierzehn Jahre alt.

5 – Und Viktor, grüß dich! Hast du Geschwister?
– Nein, ich bin Einzelkind, also ich habe keine Geschwister.

Answers
1 1 Bruder, Hanno, 19
2 1 Schwester, Miriam, 11
3 2 Brüder, Paul 8, Markus 10
4 1 Stiefbruder, Stefan, 14
5 Einzelkind

ECHO-Tipp 5.2

This tip points out the usefulness of *er* and *sie*. Ask pupils if they can suggest ways of remembering these words and how to spell them, e.g. *sie* sounds like she; *sie* spelt 'i' 'e'. You may wish to refer pupils to the vocabulary learning strategy about high-frequency words at the end of the chapter (Pupil's Book page 59).

5 Parternerarbeit. (AT 2/3)

1.4a/Y7 4.6a/Y7

Speaking. In pairs, pupils ask and answer questions to give details of siblings' names and ages. Go over the question that they need to ask before starting the exercise.

+ More able pupils may be able to have a freer conversation, e.g. by giving all details in one long sentence, or by including an opinion. For this, remind them of, or elicit, suitable opinion words already known, e.g. *toll, furchtbar.*

6 Lies den Text. Wer ist das? Wie heißt er / sie? Wie alt ist er / sie? (AT 3/4)

2.1/Y7

Reading. Pupils find the necessary details in a longer text to identify the people in the family picture.

Answers

a Sabine, 16
b Lulu, 12
c Zaki, 13
d Anabel, 4
e Max, 1

7 Schreib Sätze über deine Geschwister mit „er" und „sie". (AT 4/3–4) 2.4a/Y7

Writing. Pupils use the example to write sentences about their own siblings. Those who do not have any, could write in the name of a famous person or TV character. Make sure that they focus on accuracy of pronouns and verb forms.

+ Encourage more able pupils to write a paragraph in the style of the text in exercise 6, including opinions and other details.

Plenary

4.2/Y7

Aim

To recap what pupils know so far about different kinds of German words.

Use **Arbeitsblatt 3.1.** Tell pupils they must work with a partner to write two German words in every box on the sheet. Decide whether you will allow them to refer to the Pupil's Book. Afterwards, use an OHT copy of the **Arbeitsblatt** to collate and discuss their answers for self-marking: two possible marks per box, with bonus marks available for unusual correct answers.

2 Haustiere

Learning targets
- Talking about pets
- Using plural forms of nouns

Key framework objectives
1.1/Y7 Listening – gist and detail
4.3/Y7 Language – plurals

Grammar
- Plural forms of nouns
- *haben* + *einen / eine / ein* (revisited)
- *er / sie / es* = it
- *keine*

Key language
Hast du ein Haustier?
Ich habe einen …
Goldfisch
Hamster
Hund
Wellensittich
Ich habe eine …
Katze
Schlange
Schildkröte
Ich habe ein …
Kaninchen
Meerschweinchen
Pferd
Ich habe zwei / drei etc. + plural forms
Ich habe keine Haustiere.
Er / Sie / Es heißt …
Er / Sie / Es ist … braun / gelb / orange / schwarz

High-frequency words
ich habe
hast du?
du bist
und
er/sie/es
ist
heißt
einen / eine / ein

English
Learning and using plurals of nouns.

ICT
Creating a poster about pets.

Resources
CD 2, tracks 5–7
Workbooks A and B, p.23
Arbeitsblatt 3.2, p.40
Echo Elektro 1 TPP, Mod 3 2.1–2.8

Starter 1 5.1

Aim
To encourage pupils to use their prior knowledge of German pronunciation to try saying 'difficult' new words.

Write these five new words on the board or OHT:

Hund
Katze
Kaninchen
Meerschweinchen
Wellensittich
(Substitute *Schlange / Pferd* for a less able group.)

Pairs (or groups) could attempt to pronounce each word, then consolidate and build confidence through whole-class chorusing (use louder/quieter, etc. to make this fun). Tell them to look for parts of words that they already know how to pronounce, to get them started (e.g. *und, ich*), and remind them that there are no 'silent letters' in German.

At this stage they will not understand the words. Ask if anyone knows what type of words they are (nouns, pets), how they know, and whether they can guess the meanings of any of the words.

Suggestion
Before embarking on exercise 1, you may wish to present the pet words using flashcards you might already have (easily guessed ones could be omitted). Present them in gender groups, allowing plenty of practice time. See the list of ideas for games with flashcards on page 8.

1 Hör zu und wiederhole. (1–10) 1.1/Y7

Listening. Pupils listen to the recording and repeat.

5

1 Ich habe einen Goldfisch.
2 Ich habe einen Hamster.
3 Ich habe einen Hund.
4 Ich habe einen Wellensittich.
5 Ich habe eine Katze.
6 Ich habe eine Schildkröte.
7 Ich habe eine Schlange.
8 Ich habe ein Kaninchen.
9 Ich habe ein Meerschweinchen.
10 Ich habe ein Pferd.

2 Finde die Paare oben. (AT3/2)

4.2/Y7

Reading. Pupils match the words for pets to pictures (this could be done as a research exercise using the vocabulary list, if no prior presentation has been used). You may wish pupils to write down the pairs of German and English words. Ask why the nouns are arranged in three coloured groups, and recap the use of *einen / eine / ein* if necessary. At this point you may want to ask pupils about their own pets (you will need to give them the phrase *Ich habe keine Haustiere*, which comes up in exercises 6 and 7, and to give vocabulary for unusual pets). For further exploitation of this activity, see Vocabulary treasure hunt on p. 10.

Answers
1 i **2** j **3** g **4** a **5** b **6** c **7** h **8** d
9 e **10** f

3 Hör zu. Welche Haustiere hat er / sie? (AT 1/2)

1.1/Y7

Listening. Using the pictures from exercise 1, pupils note down the pets each person has. You might want to advise pupils to note down first the German pet words they hear (or the first few letters of each for speed – using the list in the book), which they can then match to the correct picture later or when listening again. Play the recording at least twice. Alternatively, a weaker class could simply look at the list of German words in exercise 1, and write down the numbers of those heard.

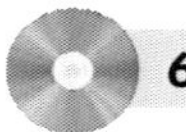

1 – *Hast du ein Haustier, Viktor?*
– *Ja, ich habe einen Hund und eine Katze.*

2 – *Und du, Peter?*
– *Ja, ich habe ein Kaninchen.*

3 – *Stefanie, hast du ein Haustier?*
– *Ja, ich habe einen Goldfisch, einen Hund und ein Meerschweinchen.*

4 – *Und du, Julia?*
– *Ich habe ein Pferd und eine Schildkröte.*

Answers
Viktor – g, b
Peter – d
Stefanie – i, g, e
Julia – f, c

4 Was sagen sie? Schreib Sätze. (AT 4/2)

4.4/Y7

Writing. Pupils write a sentence for each of the characters in exercise 3. Encourage them to copy *einen / eine / ein* and the spellings of the pet words carefully.

Answers
Viktor: Ich habe einen Hund und eine Katze.
Peter: Ich habe ein Kaninchen.
Stefanie: Ich habe einen Goldfisch, einen Hund und ein Meerschweinchen.
Julia: Ich habe ein Pferd und eine Schildkröte.

Starter 2

4.2/Y7

Aim

To recap vocabulary for pets.

Write a pet word on a piece of paper and put it out of sight, e.g. in a drawer. Start to draw that pet on the board or an OHT. You could start with a large circle for the pet's head, or a triangle for the nose, or a small circle for an eye – the images can be quite abstract, with no special drawing skills required! Pupils work in small teams and, after each new line has been added to the picture, a team secretary writes down their bet on which animal it is. Ask all teams to read these out. The first team(s) to get it right wins a point (confirm this by revealing the answer you have hidden). They may guess immediately or it may take a few goes. Pupils could then take over the drawing role from you.

5 Gedächtnisspiel. (AT 2/2)

4.3/Y7 5.2

Speaking. Pupils play this memory game in groups, building up a list of pets. Encourage more able groups to focus on the accurate use of *einen / eine / ein* or on the use of plurals.

6 Hör zu. Wer ist das? (1–5) (AT 1/2–3)

1.1/Y7

Listening. Pupils listen to statements about pets, and match them to the correct pet owner in the picture. More able pupils could also listen for extra details.

1 – *Hast du ein Haustier?*
– *Ja, ich habe zwei Pferde und eine Schildkröte.*

2 – *Und du, hast du ein Haustier?*
– *Ja, ich habe drei Goldfische. Sie sind toll!*

3 – *Hast du ein Haustier?*
– *Nein, ich habe keine Haustiere. Ich finde das langweilig.*

4 – *Und hast du Haustiere?*
– *Ich habe meine zwei Katzen, Franzi und Fritzi, und eine Schlange – sie heißt Susi.*

5 – *Hast du ein Haustier?*
– *Ja, ich habe drei Wellensittiche und zwei Hunde. Ludwig ist vierzehn Jahre alt und Lala ist sieben.*

Answers
1 c **2** d **3** e **4** a **5** b

ECHO-Detektiv: Plurals of nouns

4.3/Y7

This panel introduces three main plural noun endings. Before pupils read it, show them six of the plural forms, scattered in random order on the board or an OHT. Elicit the fact that they are plurals of pet words. Discuss how they managed to guess this correctly (knowing that words in other languages change in the plural). How do German plurals so far seem different from English ones? Do all English words have the same plural ending? Elicit examples. Then look at the grammar box together.

+ With a more able class, ask them where they could find plurals of other pet words. You may wish them to look up some additional plural forms. You could also use **Arbeitsblatt 3.2.**

7 Partnerarbeit: Wer bist du? (AT 2/2)

1.4a/Y7 4.6/Y7

Speaking. This offers oral practice of the plural forms, using the illustration from exercise 6.

+ Pupils could go on to ask and answer questions about their own pets, using plural forms where necessary. This could be a pair / group / survey task. Practise the question *Hast du ein Haustier?* first. To give names and ages, many pupils will at this point simply apply *er* to male pets, and *sie* to female ones, and you might feel it is too early to give a full explanation of gender-related pronouns. With a more able group, you may wish to explain the correct use of *er / sie / es* as pronouns related to the gender of the noun.

8 Lies den Text and füll die Tabelle aus. (Wer ist das aus Aufgabe 6?) (AT 3/3)

2.1/Y7

Reading. Pupils identify which person in the picture used for exercises 6 and 7 is speaking, and fill in the necessary details in the grid.

Answers
Das ist a.

Tier	**Name**	**Alter**	**Farbe**
Schlange	Susi	2	braun, gelb
Katze	Franzi	3	schwarz
Katze	Fritzi	14	orange

ECHO-Detektiv: er / sie / es = *it*

You may wish to draw this to the attention of pupils. More able pupils can then make use of it for exercise 9.

9 Beschreib deine Haustiere oder Traumhaustiere. (AT4/3–4)

2.5/Y7

ICT *Writing.* Pupils write about their own pet, or a dream pet. This could be done in exercise books or for display work, perhaps using ICT. They can use the text from the previous exercise as a model, and include an illustration. Weaker pupils can write short, simple sentences. More able pupils should be able to write a paragraph, and to build in opinions.

Plenary

4.3/Y7

Aim
To look at strategies for researching, recording and learning plural forms of nouns.

Give pupils a few minutes to revise and test each other on the three different types of plural endings seen in this unit. Then conduct a quick-fire quiz to check how many plural forms of nouns for pets the class can remember. You could compete with the class – a point for you every time one of them makes a wrong guess. Discuss why these plurals are important, and how they can be checked – mention regular and irregular plurals in English, too. With a more able class, gather ideas for memorising and recording plural forms.

3 Das ist meine Familie

Learning targets

- Giving information about family members
- Using the possessive adjectives *mein* and *dein* ('my' and 'your')

Key framework objectives

2.4/Y7 Writing – (a) sentences and texts as models

Grammar

- Possessive adjectives: *mein(e) / dein(e)*
- Personal pronouns: *er / sie* (revisited)
- *sein: er / sie ist* (revisited)

Key language

mein Vater / Stiefvater / Bruder / Großvater / Onkel / Cousin
meine Mutter / Stiefmutter / Schwester / Großmutter / Tante / Cousine
Das ist mein / meine …
Ist das dein / deine … ?
Er / Sie heißt …
Er / Sie ist … Jahre alt.
Numbers 1–100

High-frequency words

mein(e)
dein(e)
das ist
ist das?
er / sie ist
er / sie heißt

English

Possessive adjectives

Mathematics

Using numbers 1–100

Resources

CD 2, tracks 8–10
Workbooks A and B, p. 24
Arbeitsblatt 3.3, p.41
Echo Elektro 1 TPP, Mod 3
3.1–3.6

Starter 1 — 5.1

Aim

To reactivate family and pet vocabulary.

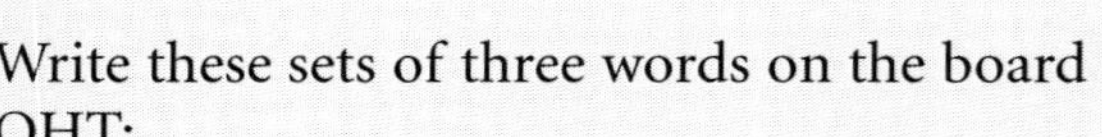

Write these sets of three words on the board or OHT:

1 *Bruder – Kaninchen – Schwester*
2 *Katze – Bruder – Schwester*
3 *Schwestern – Stiefbruder – Brüder*

Working in pairs, pupils try to find the odd one out in each set. Set a time limit; after it has expired, ask for volunteers to provide answers. Encourage a wide variety of answers – this should not be a purely grammatical activity. Possible answers include:

1 *Kaninchen* because it is an animal or because it ends in *-en*
2 *Katze* because it is an animal; *Bruder* because it is masculine
3 *Schwestern* because sisters are female; *Stiefbruder* because only one parent is the same, or because it is singular

1 Finde die Paare. (AT 3/2) 4.2/Y7

Reading. Pupils study the photographs and match Peter's statements to the appropriate photographs. As pupils have not encountered *Mutter*, *Großmutter*, *Vater* or *Großvater* before in this course, give them the hint that they sound similar to their English equivalents. Pupils could work in pairs or small groups. Listen to the exercise 2 recording before discussing the answers.

Answers
1 d **2** a **3** c **4** f **5** b **6** e

2 Hör zu und überprüfe es. (AT 1/2) 1.1/Y7

Listening. Pupils listen to the recording and check their answers to exercise 1.

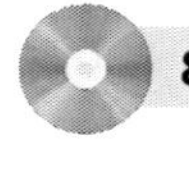

– Foto 1 … wer ist das, Peter?
– Das ist meine Großmutter.
– Und Foto 2?
– Das ist meine Mutter.
– Foto 3 … ist das dein Bruder?
– Ja, das ist mein Bruder, Hanno.
– Und auf Foto 4? Ist das dein Großvater?
– Ja, das ist mein Großvater.
– Und Foto 5. Wer ist das, Peter?
– Das ist mein Kaninchen!
– Und auf Foto 6, wer ist das?
– Das ist mein Vater.

ECHO-Detektiv: mein (*my*) and dein (*your*) 4.3/Y7

Pupils work in pairs to read the box and work out the rule for when to use *mein / dein* and when to use *meine / deine*. (You may need to direct attention to the colour-coding and ask what it means.) Ask for a volunteer to answer, and check that other pupils agree, before confirming the correct answer: *mein* and *dein* are used with masculine and neuter nouns; *meine* and *deine* are used with feminine nouns. There is further practice of this on page 127.

Suggestion 4.1/Y7 5.1/Y7

At this stage, especially with weaker pupils, you might wish to revise the difference in sound between *ei* and *ie*. Write the letter combinations on the board, and read out the following words (or use other examples) – the class should repeat the words after you. A volunteer pupil stands at the front and, after each word, moves to stand under the correct pair of letters, depending on its sound. Ask the class to decide if he/she has chosen correctly.

mein sie deine Stiefbruder sieben heiße

3 Partnerarbeit: Stell Fragen über Peters Fotos. (AT 2/2) 4.6a/Y7

Speaking. Pupils work in pairs to ask each other questions about the photos in exercise 1. Pupil A points to a photo and asks, e.g. *Ist das deine Mutter?* Pupil B answers. After three or four questions, the roles are reversed. You may need to prepare the activity by going through the question forms with the class.

\+ More able pupils could be encouraged to use *Wer ist das?* as an alternative question form. Remind pupils to think carefully about *mein / meine* and *dein / deine.*

Starter 2 5.4/Y7

Aims

To introduce the new vocabulary for family members.
To develop confidence in using cognates and context (other, known words; arrangement on page) to infer meaning.

Write the new relationship words on the board or OHT, along with the ones pupils already know. For a less confident class, divide them into pairs thus:

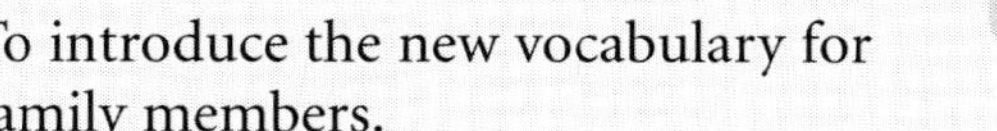

Großmutter – Großvater; Mutter – Vater; Tante – Onkel; Schwester – Bruder; Cousine – Cousin

Starter 2 *continued*

More able learners can sort them into pairs themselves.

Give pupils a moment to confer in pairs or small groups, then ask for volunteers to give the English translations of the words. Ask how they worked out the meanings.

4 Hör zu. Schreib die Bingo-Karte ab und füll sie aus. (AT 1/1) 4.2/Y7

Listening. Pupils copy the bingo card shown, and cross off each number as they hear it. Before playing the recording, go over numbers 70 to 90 in the Key Language box and elicit what some other numbers in between will be. Pupils should call out *Bingo!* when they have crossed off all the numbers (hopefully at the same time!). Practising these higher numbers will be useful for talking about ages of older family members.

Sechsundneunzig
Achtundsiebzig
Zweiundsiebzig
Neunzig
Zweiundachtzig
Siebenundneunzig
Siebzig
Einundneunzig
Fünfundsiebzig
Achtzig
Dreiundneunzig
Hundert

5 Michaels Stammbaum. Hör zu. Wer ist das?(1–10) (AT 1/2) 1.1/Y7

Listening. Pupils listen and identify which family members Michael is talking about. Suggest that they first note the relevant letter, then later, or when listening again, copy the correct word from the key language box. Play the recording at least twice. Before or after listening, you could ask pupils to pretend they are Michael, and to identify who each of the family members is, using the words in the Key Language box, as a whole class or pairwork activity. For example*: a? das ist mein Großvater* or *Wer ist Jochen? Jochen ist mein Vater.*

\+ Additionally, to practise numbers, pupils could work in pairs and ask each other the ages of the family members: *Wie alt ist Hanno?*, etc.

10

1 Meine Großmutter heißt Hedwig. Sie ist dreiundsiebzig.
2 Mein Großvater heißt Wilfried. Er ist einundsiebzig Jahre alt.
3 Mein Vater heißt Jochen. Er ist vierzig.
4 Meine Mutter heißt Heike. Sie ist neununddreißig.
5 Mein Bruder heißt Stefan. Er ist siebzehn Jahre alt.
6 Mein Stiefvater heißt Rolf. Er ist einundvierzig Jahre alt.
7 Meine Tante heißt Birgit. Sie ist sechsunddreißig Jahre alt.
8 Mein Onkel heißt Lutz. Er ist dreiundvierzig Jahre alt.
9 Meine Cousine heißt Marlies. Sie ist nur ein Jahr alt.
10 Mein Cousin heißt Marc. Er ist fünfzehn Jahre alt.

Answers
1 b – meine Großmutter
2 a – mein Großvater
3 e – mein Vater
4 f – meine Mutter
5 k – mein Bruder
6 g – mein Stiefvater
7 d – meine Tante
8 c – mein Onkel
9 i – meine Cousine
10 h – mein Cousin

6 Lies die Texte. Richtig oder falsch? (AT 3/2) 2.1/Y7

Reading. Pupils check their ability to recognise numbers in written form, by comparing Michael's sentences with his family tree. More able pupils could then correct the false answers.

Answers
1 richtig
2 falsch
3 falsch
4 richtig
5 falsch
6 falsch

2 Mein Bruder heißt Stefan. Er ist siebzehn Jahre alt.
3 Meine Mutter heißt Heike. Sie ist neununddreißig Jahre alt.
5 Meine Großmutter heißt Hedwig. Sie ist dreiundsiebzig Jahre alt.
6 Mein Großvater heißt Wilfried. Er ist einundsiebzig Jahre alt.

7 Und du? Zeichne deinen Stammbaum und schreib Sätze. (AT 4/1–3)

2.4a/Y7

Writing. Pupils draw their own family tree, using Michael's as a model and the Key Language box to add *mein Vater*, etc., as well as names and ages. You could give them the option of drawing a fictitious family, e.g. from their favourite soap opera. Most can then write sentences about family members. For some, this could be developed into a short text about a member or members of their own family (relationship, name and age), illustrated with photos.

+ For additional speaking practice, pupils could give a partner information from their own family tree, e.g. *Mein Vater heißt John, er ist 39.* Partners listen and attempt to sketch the family tree. Alternatively, pupils could omit names and ages from their initial family tree, using only *meine Mutter*, etc. They then swap books, and complete each other's family trees by asking and answering questions: *Wie heißt deine Mutter? Wie alt ist sie?*, etc.

Plenary 5.3/Y7

Aim

To build confidence in recognising cognates.

Ask pupils to write down a pair of words, German and English, which sound similar and mean the same thing (e.g. *Mutter* – 'mother', *ist* – 'is'). Collect examples around the class and write them on the board or an OHT.

With a more able group, continue by asking the class to think of examples of word pairs which sound similar, but mean different things (e.g. '*Mutter*' – 'mutter', '*nein*' – 'nine', '*wer*' – 'where'). How can they avoid being misled by these 'false friends'? (e.g. look at the words around the unknown word, think about the situation, work out whether it's a noun or a verb, etc.)

Mini-Test

Alternatively, use the **Mini-Test** as a plenary. Pupils work in pairs to check the language they have learnt so far in the chapter.

4 Wie sieht sie aus?

Learning targets

- Describing people's appearance
- Using adjectives with nouns

Key framework objectives

1.1/Y7 Listening – gist and detail

Grammar

- *haben: ich habe, du hast, er / sie hat*
- *sein: ich bin, du bist, er / sie ist*
- Using adjectives before nouns

Pronunciation

au

Key language

Ich habe …
Du hast …
Er / Sie hat …
braune / blonde / rote / schwarze / lange / kurze / glatte / lockige Haare.
grüne / braune / blaue / graue Augen.
Ich bin …
Du bist …
Er / Sie ist …
groß / mittelgroß / klein / schlank / kräftig / dick

High-frequency words

ich habe
du hast
er/sie hat
ich bin
du bist
er/sie ist
wie
und

English

Adjectives

Resources

CD 2, tracks 11–13
Workbooks A and B, p.25
Arbeitsblatt 3.4, p.42
Echo Elektro 1 TPP, Mod 3 4.1–4.6

Starter 1 (5.4)

Aim

To encourage use of cognates and non-linguistic clues (physical evidence) to work out unknown language items.

Write three or four sentences on the board describing members of the class. The sentences should be factually correct, e.g.

Gavin hat braune Haare.
Paula hat blonde Haare.
Ich habe blaue Augen.

Read the sentences aloud with the whole class. Working in pairs or small groups, pupils try to guess what the sentences mean. Set a time limit and elicit answers. Ask for a class consensus before confirming the correct answers. You could then write additional similar sentences, and give pupils further time to confer. Ask the class to guess what today's lesson will be about, before they open their books.

1 Hör zu. Wie sehen sie aus? (1–8) (AT 1/2) 1.1/Y7

Listening. Pupils listen to the descriptions, and find the 'Identikit' pictures which match the descriptions. When checking answers, you could point out that German speakers say 'hairs' rather than 'hair'.

R Pupils could reinforce the new vocabulary working in pairs: partner A reads out one of the phrases from the 'Identikit'and partner B gives the correct letter; or partner A reads out one of the phrases from the 'Identikit'and partner B (with book closed) identifies someone in the class who has that feature.

1 – *Theo: Wie siehst du aus?*
– *Ich habe grüne Augen.*

2 – *Und du, Vikki? Wie siehst du aus?*
– *Ich habe graue Augen.*

3 – *Bastian, wie siehst du aus?*
– *Ich habe kurze Haare.*

4 – *Und du, Lisa? Wie siehst du aus?*
– *Ich habe lockige Haare.*

5 – *Stefanie, wie siehst du aus?*
– *Ich habe blaue Augen und lange Haare.*

6 – *Und du, Oliver, wie siehst du aus?*
– *Ich habe braune Augen und rote Haare.*

7 – *Wie siehst du aus, Jan?*
– *Ich habe grüne Augen und glatte Haare.*

8 – *Wie siehst du aus, Eva?*
– *Also, ich habe auch grüne Augen und ich habe blonde Haare.*

Answers
1 a **2** d **3** e **4** g **5** b, f **6** c, j **7** a, h **8** a, i

2 Wer ist das – Anja, Manja oder Tanja? (AT3/2) 2.1/Y7

Reading. Pupils read the speech bubbles and match each one to its correct photo.

Answers
1 Tanja **2** Anja **3** Manja

ECHO-Detektiv: Adjective endings

5.1

Pupils read the panel and spot the 'e' ending used with hair and eyes. At this stage, this is the only form they need to know, and you may wish to leave further explanation until later.

Aussprache: au 4.1/Y7

Read through this pronunciation tip before moving on to exercise 3.

3 Hör zu und wiederhole dreimal. (AT 1/) 4.1/Y7

Listening. Pupils listen to the recording and read through the tongue twister. They then repeat it three times.

Blaue Frauen haben immer graue Augen. 12

R Pupils could chorus the colours *blau, braun, grau* for further practice of the *au* sound.

4 Und du? Wie siehst du aus? (AT 4/2–3) 4.4/Y7

Writing. Pupils write a short description of themselves. Encourage them to use more than one adjective when describing hair.

+ Pupils go on to write descriptions of friends, family or their favourite actors or popstars, perhaps in the form of labelled pictures.

Starter 2 4.4/Y7

Aim

To reinforce language for describing hair and eyes.

Select volunteers to be the 'caller' at the front of the class. They make up a sentence about appearance, e.g. *ich habe kurze Haare.* Pupils listen, and stand up if the sentence applies to them. More confident 'callers' will be able to include extra detail in their sentences. Check with the class that the correct pupils have stood up.

5 Hör zu und schau das Bild an. Wer ist das? (1–5) (AT 1/2) 1.1/Y7

Listening. Pupils listen to the descriptions, based on build only, and identify the correct picture. They can use the Key Language box for support. Remind weaker pupils about the meanings of *er* and *sie* – they could listen a first time simply to identify whether each description is of a man or woman, to make the main task easier.

1 – *Wie sieht er aus?*
– *Er ist groß und kräftig!*

2 – *Wie sieht sie aus?*
– *Sie ist mittelgroß und schlank.*

3 – *Wie sieht er aus?*
– *Er ist klein und dick.*

4 – *Wie sieht sie aus?*
– *Sie ist klein und schlank.*

5 – *Wie sieht er aus?*
– *Er ist groß und schlank.*

Answers
1 c **2** d **3** b **4** a **5** e

6 Finde ihn / sie auf dem Bild. (AT 3/3) 2.1/Y7

Reading. Pupils read the more detailed descriptions and identify the band members on the poster. For further exploitation of this activity, see Grammar treasure hunt on page 10.

Answers
1 d **2** c **3** e **4** b **5** a

+ Pupils who finish quickly could write similar sentences describing members of the class, using just *er / sie* (no names). Partners read these and guess who is being described (writing down their guess if the activity needs to be done quietly), or the whole class could later listen and guess.

ECHO-Detektiv: *haben – to have, sein – to be* 4.5a/Y7

Go through these verb paradigms with the class. Pupils could test each other in pairs: partner A closes his/her book, and partner B gives the English verb form; partner A responds with the German verb form. Stress that these are very useful verbs (see the plenary suggestion below). **Arbeitsblatt 3.4** could be used now or as a homework task.

7 Gruppenarbeit. Beschreib jemand auf dem Bild. (AT 2/2–3) 1.4b/Y7 4.4/Y7

Speaking. Pupils work together in small groups or pairs. One pupil formulates a sentence about one of the popstars from the picture (in the *ich* form, as in the example, or in the *er / sie* form). The other members of the group try to guess which band member is being described.

As an additional, or homework task, pupils could name, draw and describe an alien. Remind them of extra colour adjectives they could use, and show how they can adapt the sentence patterns they have already learned:

Er ist [adjective].
Er hat [adjective + e] *Augen / Haare.*

Plenary 4.5a/Y7

Aim

To help pupils appreciate the importance of the high-frequency verbs *haben* or *sein* (or both).

Pupils work together briefly in pairs to write down a sentence using the verb *haben* or *sein.* Collect examples around the class and write them on the board or an OHT, correcting any mistakes.

Can pupils see that these verbs are used in all sorts of different situations? What does this tell them about priorities in their language learning? (e.g. Learn them, and you'll be able to talk about lots of things.) Collect ideas around the class about how to learn verbs, e.g. chanting, testing each other, 'look say cover write check'.

5 Er ist lustig

Learning targets
- Talking about people's characteristics
- Making sentences more interesting

Key framework objectives
2.2/Y7 Reading – (a) unfamiliar language

Grammar
- Connectives: *und, aber*
- Qualifiers: *sehr, ziemlich*
- *nicht*

Key language
Wie bist du?
Wie ist …?
Ich bin …
Du bist …
Er / Sie ist …
freundlich / lustig / laut / schüchtern / intelligent / sportlich / musikalisch / kreativ / faul / launisch / unpünktlich
und
aber
nicht
sehr
ziemlich
Herr / Frau

High-frequency words
wie?
ich bin
du bist
er / sie ist
und
aber
nicht
sehr
ziemlich

English
Connectives and qualifiers

Resources
CD 2, tracks 14–17
Workbooks A and B, p.26
Arbeitsblatt 3.5, p.43
Arbeitsblatt 3.6, p.44
Flashcards 47–57
Echo Elektro 1 TPP, Mod 5 5.1–5.7

Starter 1 5.4

Aim
To introduce the new personality adjectives using prior knowledge of cognates and prefixes.

Write these personality adjectives randomly on the board or an OHT, together with a plus and minus sign, and elicit guesses from the class as to what sort of words they are:

freundlich	laut
faul	intelligent
lustig	sportlich
unpünktlich	kreativ

Then tell them to sort the words into two lists, positive and negative, using their knowledge of cognates and prefixes to make guesses. Does the word sound positive or negative? If they can guess the meaning, do they feel it is a positive or negative characteristic? After a few minutes, elicit or give the meanings, and discuss their decisions and how they arrived at them.

1 Hör zu. Was passt zusammen? (1–11) (AT 1/1) 1.1/Y7

Listening. Pupils listen to the new language, matching numbers to letters. You may wish to play the recording in two parts, discussing the answers after each.

1 – *Wie bist du, Amelie?*
– *Ich bin kreativ.*

2 – *Wie bist du, Tobias?*
– *Ich bin sportlich.*

3 – *Wie bist du, Mareike?*
– *Ich bin lustig.*

4 – *Wie bist du, Felix?*
– *Ich bin freundlich.*

5 – *Wie bist du, Sarah?*
– *Ich bin intelligent.*

6 – *Wie bist du, Christian?*
– *Ich bin musikalisch.*

7 – *Wie bist du, Hannah?*
– *Ich bin unpünktlich.*

8 – *Wie bist du, Wolfgang?*
– *Ich bin schüchtern.*

9 – *Wie bist du, Thomas?*
– *Ich bin launisch.*

10 – *Wie bist du, Leon?*
– *Ich bin faul.*

11 – *Wie bist du, Petra?*
– *Ich bin laut.*

Answers
1 d **2** c **3** j **4** a **5** b **6** h **7** f **8** i
9 g **10** k **11** e

You may wish to reinforce the new vocabulary through mime at this point. After some initial practice and guessing (in pairs or as a whole class), divide the class into two teams to play charades. A volunteer from each team picks characteristics written on cards from a hat and mimes them – team members have to guess within a time limit. See page 9 for further games ideas.

2 Partnerarbeit: Interviews. (AT 2/2) 1.4b/Y7

Speaking. This could be a brief pairwork or group exercise, or it could be extended to multiple interviews with note taking, and reporting back using *er / sie ist …* orally or in writing. Start by practising the question with the class.

3 Hör zu und lies. Wie sind Theos Lehrer? (1–4) (AT 1&3/2) 1.1/Y7 2.1/Y7

Listening/Reading. Pupils listen to Theo and read the sentences, then translate each teacher's characteristics into English. Elicit the meanings of *Herr* and *Frau*, as well as *aber*. Pupils could firstly listen to the recording without looking at the texts. Elicit the personality adjectives heard.

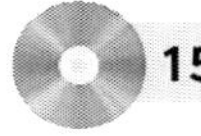
15

1 Herr Heumann ist laut und lustig.
2 Frau Schütte ist freundlich, aber sie ist launisch.
3 Herr Arendt ist kreativ, aber er ist unpünktlich.
4 Frau Schmidt ist intelligent und musikalisch, aber sie ist schüchtern.

Answers
1 loud and funny
2 friendly but moody
3 creative but unpunctual
4 intelligent and musical, but shy

Suggestion
Further work on adjectives can be found on **Arbeitsblatt 3.5.**

ECHO-Tipp 4.4/Y7
Refer pupils to this panel about the use of *und* and *aber* before they do writing exercise 4.

4 Beschreib zwei deiner Lehrer. (AT 4/3–4) 4.4/Y7

Writing. Pupils write sentences about two of their own teachers. Explain the use of *Herr*, and *Frau* (used for all female teachers, regardless of marital status). Some pupils could write more than two sentences.

Suggestion
This could also be done as a speaking task, without including the teacher's name in the sentences. Partners, or the whole class, have to guess who is being described. Physical description could be revised and included here too. You may wish to insist that descriptions are positive! These extra adjectives will be useful:

nett (nice), *hilfsbereit* (helpful), *streng* (strict).

Starter 2 4.2/Y7

Aim
To revise personality words from the last lesson.

Knock-down miming game: divide the class into two or three teams. A volunteer from the first team has one minute to guess what characteristic each of the other team members is miming – by pointing at individuals and saying *Du bist … .* If correct, that pupil sits down. Count up the number of seated team members at the end of the given time. Then the other team tries to beat the score.

5 Hör zu und lies. Wie ist Bart Simpson? (AT 1&3/2) 2.1/Y7 4.2/Y7

Listening/Reading. This task introduces the concept of qualifiers. Pupils listen to the recording about Bart Simpson, and read the text. They decide whether he is not (✗), fairly (✓) or very (✓ ✓) loud, etc.

16

Er ist sehr laut.
Er ist ziemlich intelligent.
Er ist nicht schüchtern.
Er ist ziemlich freundlich.
Er ist sehr lustig.

Answers
laut ✓ ✓ intelligent ✓ schüchtern ✗
freundlich ✓ lustig ✓ ✓

ECHO-Detektiv: Useful qualifiers
Use this panel to consider qualifiers. Ask pupils why they think it is useful to know them. There is further practice of this on **Arbeitsblatt 3.6**.

Wie bist du? Schreib vier Sätze. (AT 4/3) 4.4/Y7

Writing. Pupils write four sentences about themselves, using qualifiers.

Verbinde deine Sätze aus Aufgabe 6 mit „und" und „aber". (AT 4/3) 4.4/Y7

Writing. Pupils then try to join their four sentences using the connectives already encountered.

Suggestion

Ask pupils to read their sentences aloud, using appropriate, even exaggerated, expression when they say *aber*, *sehr*, *ziemlich* or *nicht*.

Hör zu und sing mit. 2.2a/Y7 5.6

Listening/Reading. Pupils listen and read, then sing along to the song. Divide the class in two to sing the two voices of the conversation. For further ideas on using this activity, see Exploiting the songs on p. 9.

17

– Hallo, Georg,
– Hast du Geschwister?
– *Ja, ich habe einen Bruder*
– *Und er heißt Frank*

– Wie sieht er denn aus?
– Hat er blonde Haare?
– *Nein. Er hat grüne Haare!*
– *Er ist groß und sehr schlank!*

– Und hast du ein Haustier?
– Hast du eine Katze?
– *Nein, ich habe eine Schlange*
– *Und sie heißt Klaus.*

– Ach, eine Schlange,
– Wie sieht sie denn aus?
– *Sie ist lang, grün und gelb,*
– *Aber sie ist schüchtern wie eine Maus.*

– Ist sie ziemlich freundlich?
– *Ja, sie ist sehr freundlich*
– Ach wie toll!
– *Ja, Klaus ist toll.*

Plenary 2.1/Y7

Aim

To consolidate the language of this unit.

Prepare three or four brief, positive descriptions of members of the class on an OHT (you could also include physical descriptions), using *er / sie* but not names, and including the connectives and qualifiers learnt. Reveal them one at a time, and ask pupils to write down who they think it is. Reveal the answers, and see how many they guessed correctly. This is a wonderful chance to show quieter pupils that you value their qualities!

Pupils could then write descriptions to read out for the class to guess.

Learning targets

- Understanding a longer email and writing a reply
- Finding out the meanings of new words

Key framework objectives

3.2/Y7 Culture – (a) young people: interests/opinions
3.2/Y7 Culture – (b) challenging stereotypes
5.4 Strategies – working out meaning

Grammar

- Formulating questions
- Using connectives and qualifiers

Key language

Hallo!
Ich heiße …
Ich bin / Er / Sie ist … Jahre alt.
Ich habe am … Geburtstag.
Ich wohne in …
Das ist in …
Ich habe … (family and pets)
Ich habe … (Haare / Augen.)
Ich bin / Er / Sie ist … (character)
Wie geht's?
Hast du Geschwister?
Hast du ein Haustier?
Wie siehst du aus?
Schreib bald!
dein / deine

High-frequency words

sehr
aber
und
auch
ich heiße
ich bin
er / sie / das ist
ich habe
hast du?
wie?
mein / meine
dein / deine

ICT

Word process, or possibly send, an email

English

Structuring an email to a friend

Citizenship

Penfriend links with another country

Resources

CD 2, track 18
Workbooks A and B, p.27
Echo Elektro 1 TPP, Mod 3 6.1–6.3

Starter 1 3.2a+b/Y7

Aim
To introduce the concept, and benefits, of links with pupils in German-speaking countries.

Before pupils open their books, explain that the class will be looking at an email from a German pupil looking for a penfriend. Ask pupils to predict the content of the email – what sort of things would one say? Get pairs of pupils to think of one question and one sentence in German that might be in such an email (using language they already know). Take the opportunity to discuss any links your school has with others abroad, and what pupils might expect to gain from such links.

Suggestion
Before doing exercise 1, ask pupils to assess what the email is about, who it is written to and why, and how difficult they think it is (if you have done Starter 1, they will have been given a head start with some of these). Direct pupils' attention to the **ECHO-Tipp** panel about reading for gist.

1 Hör zu und lies Julias E-Mail. 2.2a/Y7 5.6

Listening/Reading. Pupils listen to the recording and follow the text in their books. They could then read the email aloud in pairs, with emphasis on getting the correct pronunciation and intonation. For further exploitation of this text, see Reading aloud on p. 9.

18

Hallo!
Wie geht's? Ich heiße Julia Döring.
Ich wohne in Leipzig. Das ist in Deutschland.
Ich bin zwölf Jahre alt. Ich habe am ersten September Geburtstag. Ich bin in der Klasse 8C. Ich suche einen Brieffreund oder eine Brieffreundin!
Ich habe eine Schwester, Tanja. Sie ist vierzehn Jahre alt. Sie ist lustig und sehr laut! Hast du Geschwister?

Mein Vater heißt Jens. Er ist achtunddreißig Jahre alt. Er ist sehr groß und kräftig, aber ziemlich schüchtern. Meine Mutter, Bettina, ist sehr kreativ.

Ich habe ein Pferd. Es ist fünf Jahre alt. Es ist braun und ziemlich groß und sehr freundlich. Das Pferd heißt Toby. Ich habe auch eine Schildkröte. Hast du ein Haustier?

Wie siehst du aus? Ich habe rote Haare und blaue Augen. Ich bin ziemlich groß und schlank. Ich bin sehr sportlich, aber sehr unpünktlich!

Schreib bald!

Deine Julia

2 Welcher Absatz ist das? (AT 3/4) 2.1/Y7

Reading. Pupils identify the paragraph in the email that contains each type of information.

Answers
1 b, c **2** d **3** e **4** a

3 Finde die richtige Antwort. (AT 3/4) 2.1/Y7

Reading. Pupils look at the email text in greater detail to find the correct multiple-choice answers. Encourage them to scan for the section where they know they might find the right answer.

Answers
1 b **2** c **3** c **4** a **5** b **6** a

ECHO-Tipp: Finding out what a new word means 5.4

Read the skills box with pupils and encourage them to follow this strategy when doing exercise 4.

4 Was sind diese neuen Wörter auf Englisch? (AT 3/4) 5.4

Reading. Pupils work out what each new word means. Discuss their findings, and how they reached these conclusions.

Answers
Ich suche = I'm looking for / searching for
Brieffreund (in) = penfriend
Schreib bald = write soon

Starter 2 4.6a/Y7

Aim
To practise formation of questions, in preparation for reading and writing tasks.

Divide the class into teams of roughly equal size and ability, seated together. Copy the following words onto slips of paper and put them, folded, into a bag, hat, or similar object. Volunteers pick a word out of the hat, and show it to the class. Each team must write down a question beginning with that word, before you say stop. Listen to each team's answer, and check the spelling of the written version, awarding a point for each correct question – two points if the question has not been used by anybody else. A more able class could see how many questions they can come up with using the word in the time given.

Wie (x 2)
Was (x 2)
Wo
Wann
Hast

5 Welche vier Fragen stellt Julia? (AT 3/2) 4.6a/Y7

Reading. Pupils pick out the questions asked by Julia in her email, prior to answering them in the next task.

Answers
Wie geht's?
Hast du Geschwister?
Hast du ein Haustier?
Wie siehst du aus?

6 Partnerarbeit: Beantworte Julias Fragen. (AT 2/3) 4.6a/Y7

Speaking. Pupils work in pairs, giving their own answers to the questions in Julia's email (as preparation for the writing task to come).

7 Schreib eine Antwort an Julia. (AT 4/4)

2.4b/Y7

Writing. Pupils use the writing frame and Julia's own email as a model to write a reply to her.

R For lower ability pupils, you could write up the beginnings of the sentences in the writing frame on the board or an OHT. Brainstorm ideas that pupils could use in each paragraph and model the writing process, including checking use of capital letters for nouns and other issues that they might need to be reminded about.

+ Encourage more able pupils to include extra information and questions, and to make use of connectives and qualifiers to lengthen their sentences. Refer them back to the earlier pages of this chapter for ideas. They could also think about questions to add to make the letter sound more natural.

ICT Their 'emails' should ideally be word-processed for authenticity. You may even be able to send them to a partner school as real emails.

Plenary

4.4/Y7

Aims

To reinforce the language of this chapter.
To practise the use of connectives and qualifiers.

At this stage of the course, most pupils should be able to successfully build long sentences, using connectives and qualifiers. Select one pupil after another (choose according to how difficult a stage the sentence is at) to add a word to the chain and build sentences around the class. By dividing the class into two teams, and selecting from one team then the other, make it into a competition by awarding a point to the opposing team when someone is unable to take a sentence further.

Lernzieltest 5.8

This is a checklist of language covered in Chapter 3. Pupils can work with the checklist in pairs to check what they have learned. Points which directly address grammar and structures are marked with a G. There is a **Lernzieltest** sheet in the Resource and Assessment File (page 47). Encourage pupils to look back at the chapter and to use the grammar section to revise what they are unclear about.

You can also use this as an end-of-chapter plenary.

Wiederholung

A confidence-building revision test to prepare pupils for the **Kontrolle** at the end of the chapter.

Resources

CD 2, track 19

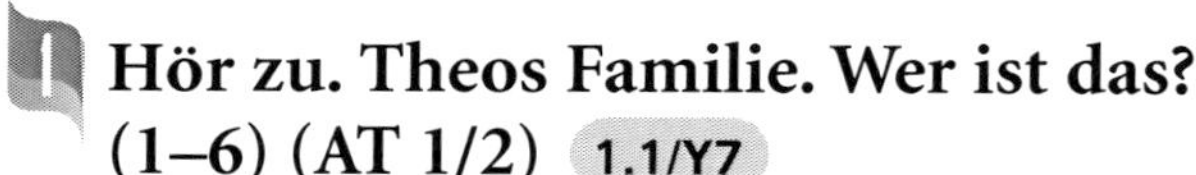

1 Hör zu. Theos Familie. Wer ist das? (1–6) (AT 1/2) 1.1/Y7

Listening. Pupils listen and select the correct picture.

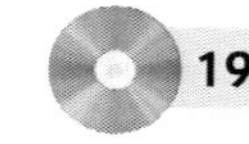

19

1 – *Wer ist das?*
– *Das bin ich. Ich heiße Theo. Ich bin dreizehn Jahre alt.*
2 – *Und wer ist das?*
– *Das ist mein Wellensittich, Willi.*
3 – *Und das?*
– *Das ist mein Vater. Er heißt Volker.*
4 – *Wer ist das, Theo?*
– *Das ist meine Mutter. Sie ist vierzig Jahre alt.*
5 – *Und das?*
– *Das ist meine Katze. Sie ist schüchtern.*
6 – *Und wer ist das?*
– *Das ist meine Schwester, Susi.*

Answers
1 e **2** c **3** b **4** d **5** a **6** f

2 Partnerarbeit: Mach Interviews. (AT 2/3–4) 1.4a/Y7

Speaking. Pupils select five relevant questions from those given, to ask their partners. More able pupils can of course make up other similar questions of their own, and give more extended answers.

3 Richtig oder falsch? (AT 3/2) 2.1/Y7

Reading. Pupils use the pictures to determine if each statement about appearance is true or false. They could correct the two false statements.

Answers
1 falsch **2** richtig **3** richtig **4** richtig
5 falsch **6** richtig

4 Schreib die E-Mail ab und füll die Lücken aus. (AT 3&4/3) 2.1/Y7

Writing. Pupils copy out the email and fill each numbered gap with the correct word from those given in the box.

Answers
1 Hallo **2** habe **3** ist **4** laut **5** nicht
6 bin **7** du **8** Schreib

Learning targets

- Understanding and giving information about a famous person
- Finding out about famous people from German-speaking countries

Key framework objectives

1.5/Y7 Speaking – (a) presenting
1.5/Y7 Speaking – (b) expression/non-verbal techniques
5.7 Strategies – planning and preparing

Grammar

- Further practice of third person present tense verb forms

Key language

Name
Alter
Geburtstag
Wohnort
Freundin
Geschwister
Haustiere
Größe
Haare
Augen
Persönlichkeit

High-frequency words

er / sie
nicht
sehr
wie?
wann?
wo?
wer?
ja, richtig
nein, falsch

Pronunciation

German names

English

Assessing a text for gist, intended audience, and difficulty

Citizenship

Finding out about people who are well known in sport, entertainment and other areas

ICT

Preparing visual material for an oral mini-presentation
Preparing display material

Resources

CD 2, track 20
Workbooks A and B, p.28

Starter 1 4.6a/Y7

Aim
To recap how to ask questions using verb forms in the third person singular.

Display a picture of a person of interest. This could be a German-speaking politician, pop star or sportsperson, possibly unknown to pupils. Volunteers ask questions, e.g. *Wie heißt er?*, *Wie alt ist er?*. Answers can be supplied by you or by members of the class if known. Get a confident pupil to note the answers on the board. Finish by getting the class to tell you facts about the person, in German, using *er* or *sie*.

Suggestion
Before doing exercise 1, look at the *Steckbrief* with the class. Encourage pupils to assess the text for gist, intended audience and difficulty.

1 Hör zu. Richtig oder falsch? (1–6) (AT 1/3, AT 3/3) 3.1/Y7

Listening. Pupils look at the information about the fictional teenage film star Benjamin Braun, and decide whether each statement they hear is true or false. The tasks that follow all focus on use of the third person singular.

CD 20

1 *Benjamin Braun ist neunzehn Jahre alt.*
2 *Er hat am vierzehnten März Geburtstag.*
3 *Er hat eine Freundin. Sie heißt Katharina. Sie ist sechzehn Jahre alt.*
4 *Er hat zwei Schwestern und zwei Brüder.*
5 *Er hat blonde Haare und braune Augen.*
6 *Er ist lustig, laut, launisch und faul.*

Answers
1 richtig 2 falsch 3 falsch 4 falsch
5 falsch 6 falsch

2 Beantworte die Fragen über Benjamin. Schreib einen Absatz. (AT 3/3, AT 4/3) 2.4b/Y7

Writing. Pupils answer these comprehension questions about the **Steckbrief**, in full sentences to give practice in using third person singular forms.

They should form a paragraph with their answers. The questions and answers are useful preparation for the speaking and writing activities which follow.

Answers (accept alternative correct wording)

1. Er ist neunzehn Jahre alt.
2. Er hat am 24. März Geburtstag.
3. Er wohnt in Berlin, in Deutschland.
4. Ja, er hat eine Freundin. Sie heißt Katharina und sie ist 17 Jahre alt.
5. Ja, er hat eine Schwester und zwei Brüder.
6. Ja, er hat eine Katze, Lili.
7. Er ist 1, 80m groß. Er hat braune Haare und braune Augen.
8. Er ist lustig, laut, nicht launisch und sehr faul.

3 Partnerarbeit: berühmte Leute. Wer ist das? (AT 2/3–4) 1.4b/Y7 4.6a/Y7

Speaking. Pupils choose any famous person, and answer their partner's questions about him or her until the identity has been correctly guessed. You may wish to demonstrate with the whole class first – perhaps revealing a picture of the person when they guess correctly. Pupils could select from the questions in the previous task. This could be played competitively, by counting the number of questions needed to guess correctly. Weaker pupils can participate by giving short answers, perhaps paired with a more able pupil to help them.

Starter 2 4.4/Y7

Aim

To recap language for giving information about a famous person, in preparation for creative speaking and writing tasks.

Give pupils one minute to study again the *Steckbrief* of Benjamin Braun in their textbooks, telling them that you will be testing them on how many details they can remember. They then close their books, and work in pairs to write as many sentences as they can about him in German (although you may prefer weaker pupils to write in English), in three minutes. Either collate answers immediately, awarding a point for every factually correct sentence (ignoring minor errors), or collect them in and look through them later in the lesson while pupils are preparing their creative work.

Suggestion

Look at the **ECHO-Tipp** panel about famous people. Discuss the categories of famous person with the class, brainstorming ideas. Aim to use at least some German while doing this (*Ja, er kommt aus Deutschland,* etc). If they don't know current musicians or film stars, you could discuss why that is the case.

4 Minivortrag: eine berühmte Person. (AT 2/4) 1.5a/Y7 5.7

Speaking. This talk will need to be prepared carefully by pupils. Some should be able to learn their talk, rather than simply reading from a script, or perhaps to use brief prompts only. Encourage able pupils to extend their sentences and to use a wide range of previously learnt vocabulary. Presentations could include illustrative material, and could be done to a partner or small group, or to the whole class, as your plenary. Weaker pupils could simply read out a *Steckbrief.*

ICT Numerous images of famous people are available on the Internet for downloading. Pupils could use Powerpoint for their presentation, or make use of ICT for their poster.

5 Poster: Steckbrief einer berühmten Person. (AT 4/3–4) 2.4a/Y7

Writing. This poster could take the form of simple points as in the example about Benjamin Braun, or paragraphs using full sentences. Remind pupils to focus on German they know, rather than trying to translate excess material.

Plenary 1.5a+b/Y7

Aim

To give a short presentation in German.

Volunteers perform their presentation about a famous person to the class or in groups, making use of illustrative material for added interest. Encourage pupils to make their talk more interesting by using expression and non-verbal techniques (e.g. props, pictures, tone, facial expression). Encourage positive feedback and appreciation from the audience.

SELF-ACCESS READING AND WRITING AT TWO LEVELS

A Reinforcement

Was passt zusammen? (AT 3/2) 4.2/Y7

Reading. Pupils match the statements about family members to the pictures.

Answers
1 d **2** e **3** a **4** b **5** c

Verbinde die Worthälften. (AT 4/1) 4.2/Y7

Writing. Pupils match the word halves to copy words for pets.

Answers
Wellensittich, Meerschweinchen, Schildkröte, Kaninchen, Goldfisch, Schlange, Hamster, Katze

3 Richtig oder falsch? (AT 3/3) 2.1/Y7

Reading. Pupils decide whether the sentences are true or false in describing the pictures. Pupils could then write out the false sentences correctly.

Answers
1 richtig **2** falsch **3** richtig **4** falsch
5 falsch **6** falsch

Schreib den Text ab und füll die Lücken aus. Zeichne Boris. (AT 4/2) 4.4/Y7

Writing. Pupils write out the text, filling in each gap with the correct word from those given. They then use the information to draw a picture of Boris.

Answers
Hallo! Ich bin **groß** und kräftig. Ich habe **blonde**, lockige Haare. Ich habe kurze **Haare**. Ich habe **grüne** Augen. Ich bin sehr **musikalisch** und sportlich. Ich bin **freundlich**.

B Extension

Was passt zusammen? Füll die Lücken aus. (AT 4/2) 4.2/Y7

Reading. Pupils match each sentence to a picture, then complete the sentences using the information in the picture.

Answers
1 c Ich habe **zwei** Katzen.
2 d Ich habe eine **Schlange** und ein Kaninchen.
3 a Ich habe **drei** Schildkröten.
4 b Ich habe einen Wellensittich und ein **Pferd**.
5 f Ich habe einen **Hund**.
6 e Ich habe **zwei** Goldfische und eine **Katze**.

2 Lies Annas Brief und beantworte die Fragen. Benutze „er“ oder „sie“. AT 3/4 AT 4/3 2.1/Y7

Reading/Writing. Pupils write answers to comprehension questions in full sentences, using *er* or *sie*.

Answers
1 Sie wohnt in Hamburg, in Deutschland.
2 Sie ist ziemlich klein und schlank.
3 Er heißt Andreas.
4 Er ist sehr launisch.
5 Er hat am vierten April Geburtstag.
6 Er wohnt in Amerika.

3 Schreib den Text ab und füll die Lücken aus. (AT 4/3) 2.4a/Y7

Writing. Pupils copy the text and fill in the missing words, checking the meanings of any they cannot remember.

Answers
Stefan ist **zehn** Jahre alt. Er hat am **zwanzigsten Mai** Geburtstag. Er ist **groß** und **schlank**. Er hat **blaue Augen**. Er hat **kurze**, **schwarze** Haare. Er ist sehr **intelligent** und ziemlich **sportlich**. Er ist auch **musikalisch**. Er hat einen **Hund**, Albi. Albi ist **braun** und **freundlich.**

4 Beschreib einen Freund / eine Freundin. (AT 4/3–4) 2.4a+b/Y7

Writing. Pupils write their own text about a friend, using the one in exercise 3 as a model. Give credit for accuracy, range of vocabulary, and use of connectives and qualifiers to vary structure.

Übungsheft A, Seite 22

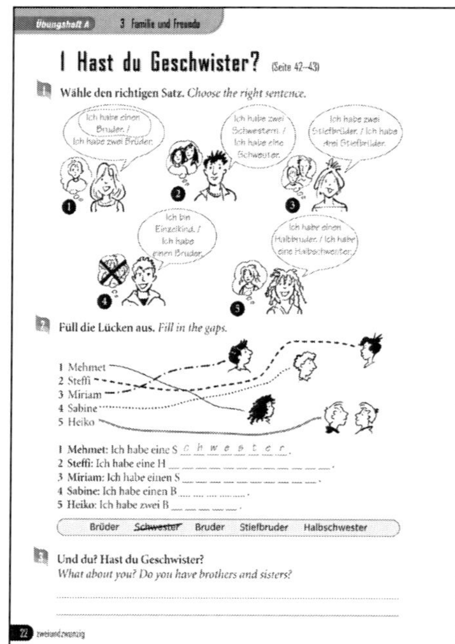
Übungsheft A 3 Familie und Freunde

I Hast du Geschwister? (Seite 42–43)

1 Wähle den richtigen Satz. *Choose the right sentence.*

2 Füll die Lücken aus. *Fill in the gaps.*

1 Mehmet
2 Steffi
3 Miriam
4 Sabine
5 Heiko

1 Mehmet: Ich habe eine S c h w e s t e r.
2 Steffi: Ich habe eine H _ _ _ _ _ _ _ _ _ _ _ _ .
3 Miriam: Ich habe einen S _ _ _ _ _ _ _ _ _ .
4 Sabine: Ich habe einen B _ _ _ _ _ .
5 Heiko: Ich habe zwei B _ _ _ _ _ .

Brüder ~~Schwester~~ Bruder Stiefbruder Halbschwester

3 Und du? Hast du Geschwister?
What about you? Do you have brothers and sisters?

22 zweiundzwanzig

1 (AT3 Level 2) 1 Ich habe einen Bruder. **2** Ich habe zwei Schwestern. **3** Ich habe zwei Stiefbrüder. **4** Ich bin Einzelkind. **5** Ich habe eine Halbschwester.

2 (AT3 Level 2, AT4 Level 1) 1 Mehmet: Ich habe eine Schwester. **2** Steffi: Ich habe eine Halbschwester. **3** Miriam: Ich habe einen Stiefbruder. **4** Sabine: Ich habe einen Bruder. **5** Heiko: Ich habe zwei Brüder.

3 (AT4 Level 2)

Übungsheft B, Seite 22

Übungsheft B 3 Familie und Freunde

I Hast du Geschwister? (Seite 42–43)

1 Wähle ein Wort und füll die Lücken aus. *Choose a word and fill in the gaps.*

Bruder Brüder Schwester Schwestern Einzelkind

masculine feminine
Ich habe einen ... eine ...

2 Schreib die Sätze auf. *Write out the sentences.*

1 Mehmet
2 Steffi
3 Miriam
4 Sabine
5 Heiko

1 Mehmet: Ich habe eine Schwester. Sie heißt Hülya. Sie ist dreizehn Jahre alt.
2 Steffi: Ich
3 Miriam: Ich ______. Er ______
Er ______.
4 Sabine:
5 Heiko: ______. Matthias und Jakob. Matthias ist ______
Jakob ______.

3 Und du? Hast du Geschwister? Wie heißt er / sie? Wie alt ist er / sie?

22 zweiundzwanzig

1 (AT3 Level 2, AT4 Level 2) 1 Ich habe einen **Bruder**. **2** Ich habe zwei **Brüder / Schwestern**. **3** Ich habe drei **Brüder / Schwestern**. **4** Ich bin **Einzelkind**. **5** Ich habe eine **Schwester**.

2 (AT4 Level 2) 1 Mehmet: Ich habe eine Schwester. Sie heißt Hülya. Sie ist dreizehn Jahre alt. **2** Steffi: Ich habe eine Halbschwester. Sie heißt Julia. Sie ist sechzehn Jahre alt. **3** Miriam: Ich habe einen Stiefbruder. Er heißt Kevin. Er ist zwölf Jahre alt. **4** Sabine: Ich habe einen Bruder. Er heißt Maiko. Er ist vierzehn Jahre alt. **5** Heiko: Ich habe zwei Brüder, Matthias und Jakob. Matthias ist siebzehn Jahre alt. Jakob ist elf Jahre alt.

3 (AT4 Level 2–3)

Übungsheft A, Seite 23

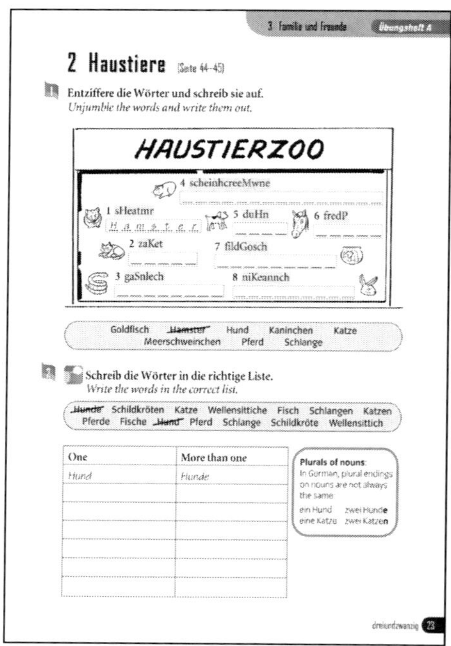
3 Familie und Freunde Übungsheft A

2 Haustiere (Seite 44–45)

1 Entziffere die Wörter und schreib sie auf. *Unjumble the words and write them out.*

HAUSTIERZOO

1 sHeatmr H a m s t e r
2 zaKet
3 gaSnlech
4 scheinhcreeMwne
5 duHn
6 fredP
7 fildGosch
8 niKeannch

Goldfisch ~~Hamster~~ Hund Kaninchen Katze Meerschweinchen Pferd Schlange

2 Schreib die Wörter in die richtige Liste. *Write the words in the correct list.*

~~Hunde~~ Schildkröten Katze Wellensittiche Fisch Schlangen Katzen Pferde Fische ~~Hund~~ Pferd Schlange Schildkröte Wellensittich

One	More than one
Hund	Hunde

Plurals of nouns
In German, plural endings on nouns are not always the same:
ein Hund zwei Hunde
eine Katze zwei Katzen

dreiundzwanzig 23

1 (AT4 Level 1) 1 Hamster **2** Katze **3** Schlange **4** Meerschweinchen **5** Hund **6** Pferd **7** Goldfisch **8** Kaninchen

2 (AT3 Level 1, AT4 Level 1)

One	More than one
Hund	Hunde
Schildkröte	Schildkröten
Wellensittich	Wellensittiche
Schlange	Schlangen
Katze	Katzen
Fisch	Fische
Pferd	Pferde

Übungsheft B, Seite 23

3 Familie und Freunde Übungsheft B

2 Haustiere (Seite 44–45)

1 Entziffere die Wörter und füll die Lücken aus. *Unjumble the words and fill in the gaps.*

fildGosch scheinhcreeMwne sHeatmr niKeannch fredP zaKet duHn ~~gaSnlech~~

2 Und du? Hast du ein Haustier?

dreiundzwanzig 23

1 (AT3 Level 2, AT4 Level 2) 1 Das ist eine Schlange. **2** Das ist ein Kaninchen. **3** Hast du ein Pferd? **4** Hast du eine Katze? **5** Ich habe einen Hund. **6** Ich habe einen Goldfisch. **7** Ich habe einen Hamster. **8** Das ist mein Meerschweinchen.

2 (AT4 Level 2–3)

Übungsheft A, Seite 24

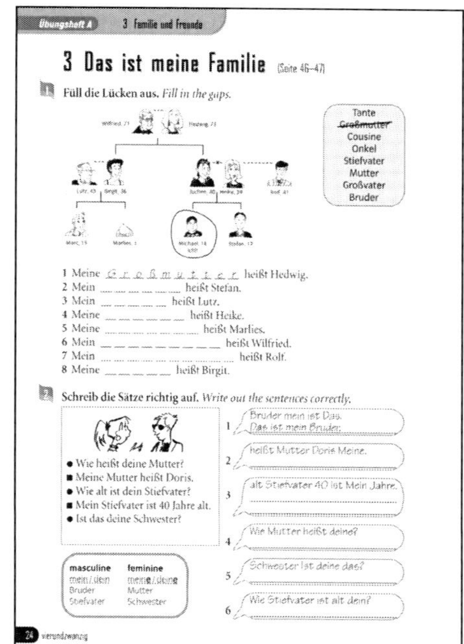
Übungsheft A 3 Familie und Freunde

3 Das ist meine Familie (Seite 46–47)

1 Füll die Lücken aus. *Fill in the gaps.*

Tante, ~~Großmutter~~, Cousine, Onkel, Stiefvater, Mutter, Großvater, Bruder

1 Meine G r o ß m u t t e r heißt Hedwig.
2 Mein ________ heißt Stefan.
3 Mein ________ heißt Lutz.
4 Meine ________ heißt Heike.
5 Meine ________ heißt Marlies.
6 Mein ________ heißt Wilfried.
7 Mein ________ heißt Rolf.
8 Meine ________ heißt Birgit.

2 Schreib die Sätze richtig auf. *Write out the sentences correctly.*

• Wie heißt deine Mutter?
■ Meine Mutter heißt Doris.
• Wie alt ist dein Stiefvater?
■ Mein Stiefvater ist 40 Jahre alt.
• Ist das deine Schwester?

1 Bruder mein ist Das. Das ist mein Bruder.
2 heißt Mutter Doris Meine.
3 alt Stiefvater 40 ist Mein Jahre.
4 Wie Mutter heißt deine?
5 Schwester ist deine das?
6 Wie Stiefvater ist alt dein?

masculine	feminine
mein / dein	meine / deine
Bruder	Mutter
Stiefvater	Schwester

24 vierundzwanzig

1 (AT3 Level 2, AT4 Level 1) 1 Meine **Großmutter** heißt Hedwig. **2** Mein **Bruder** heißt Stefan. **3** Mein **Onkel** heißt Lutz. **4** Meine **Mutter** heißt Heike. **5** Meine **Cousine** heißt Marlies. **6** Mein **Großvater** heißt Wilfried. **7** Mein **Stiefvater** heißt Rolf. **8** Meine **Tante** heißt Birgit.

2 (AT3 Level 2, AT4 Level 2) 1 Das ist mein Bruder. **2** Meine Mutter heißt Doris. **3** Mein Stiefvater ist 40 Jahre alt. **4** Wie heißt deine Mutter? **5** Ist das deine Schwester? **6** Wie alt ist dein Stiefvater?

Übungsheft B, Seite 24

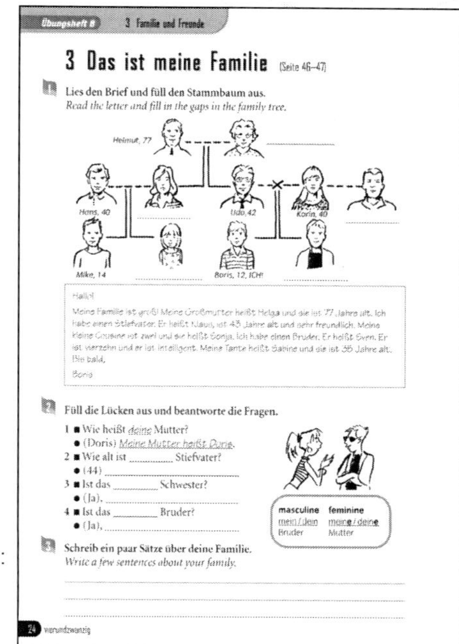
Übungsheft B 3 Familie und Freunde

3 Das ist meine Familie (Seite 46–47)

1 Lies den Brief und füll den Stammbaum aus. *Read the letter and fill in the gaps in the family tree.*

Helmut, 77 / Hans, 40 / Udo, 42 / Karin, 40 / Mike, 14 / Boris, 12, ICH!

Hallo!
Meine Familie ist groß! Meine Großmutter heißt Helga und sie ist 77 Jahre alt. Ich habe einen Stiefvater. Er heißt Klaus, ist 43 Jahre alt und sehr freundlich. Meine kleine Cousine ist zwei und sie heißt Sonja. Ich habe einen Bruder. Er heißt Sven. Er ist vierzehn und er ist intelligent. Meine Tante heißt Sabine und sie ist 35 Jahre alt.
Bis bald,
Boris

2 Füll die Lücken aus und beantworte die Fragen.

1 ■ Wie heißt deine Mutter?
● (Doris) Meine Mutter heißt Doris.
2 ■ Wie alt ist ________ Stiefvater?
● (44) ________
3 ■ Ist das ________ Schwester?
● (Ja). ________
4 ■ Ist das ________ Bruder?
● (Ja). ________

masculine	feminine
mein / dein	meine / deine
Bruder	Mutter

3 Schreib ein paar Sätze über deine Familie. *Write a few sentences about your family.*

24 vierundzwanzig

1 (AT3 Level 3, AT4 Level 1) Top line: Helmut, 77 and **Helga, 77**
Next line, from left: Hans, 40, and **Sabine, 35**; Udo, 42, Karin, 40, and **Klaus, 43**.
Bottom line, from left: Mike, 14, **Sonja, 2,** Boris, 12 (ICH!) and **Sven, 14**.

2 (AT3 Level 2, AT4 Level 2) 1 Wie heißt **deine** Mutter? – **Meine Mutter heißt Doris**. **2** Wie alt ist **dein** Stiefvater? – **Mein Stiefvater ist vierundvierzig Jahre alt**. **3** Ist das **deine** Schwester? – **Ja, das ist meine Schwester**. **4** Ist das **dein** Bruder? – **Ja, das ist mein Bruder**.

3 (AT4 Level 2–3)

Übungsheft A, Seite 25

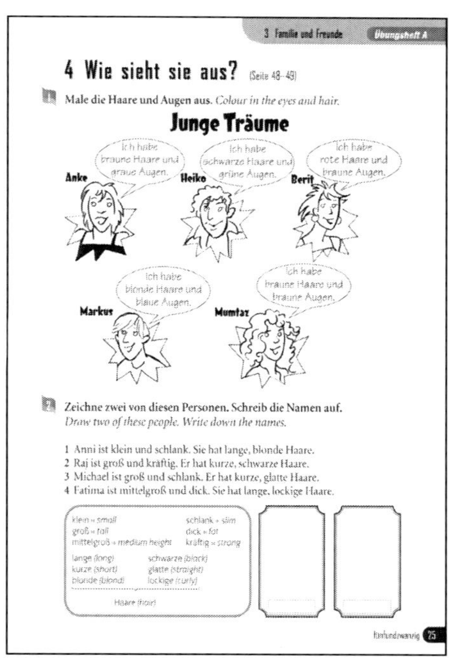
3 Familie und Freunde Übungsheft A

4 Wie sieht sie aus? (Seite 48–49)

1 Male die Haare und Augen aus. *Colour in the eyes and hair.*

Junge Träume

Anke: Ich habe braune Haare und graue Augen.
Heiko: Ich habe schwarze Haare und grüne Augen.
Berit: Ich habe rote Haare und braune Augen.
Markus: Ich habe blonde Haare und blaue Augen.
Mumtaz: Ich habe braune Haare und braune Augen.

2 Zeichne zwei von diesen Personen. Schreib die Namen auf. *Draw two of these people. Write down the names.*

1 Anni ist klein und schlank. Sie hat lange, blonde Haare.
2 Raj ist groß und kräftig. Er hat kurze, schwarze Haare.
3 Michael ist groß und schlank. Er hat kurze, glatte Haare.
4 Fatima ist mittelgroß und dick. Sie hat lange, lockige Haare.

klein = small, groß = tall, mittelgroß = medium height, schlank = slim, dick = fat, kräftig = strong, lange (long), kurze (short), blonde (blond), schwarze (black), glatte (straight), lockige (curly), Haare (hair)

fünfundzwanzig 25

1 (AT3 Level 2) Anke: brown hair, grey eyes. **Heiko**: black hair, green eyes. **Berit**: red hair, brown eyes. **Markus**: blonde hair, blue eyes. **Mumtaz**: brown hair, brown eyes.

2 (AT3 Level 2) *Pupils choose two of these to draw:*
1 Anni: small, slim, long blonde hair. **2** Raj: tall, strong, short black hair. **3** Michael: tall, slim, short straight hair. **4** Fatima: medium height, plump, long curly hair.

Übungsheft B, Seite 25

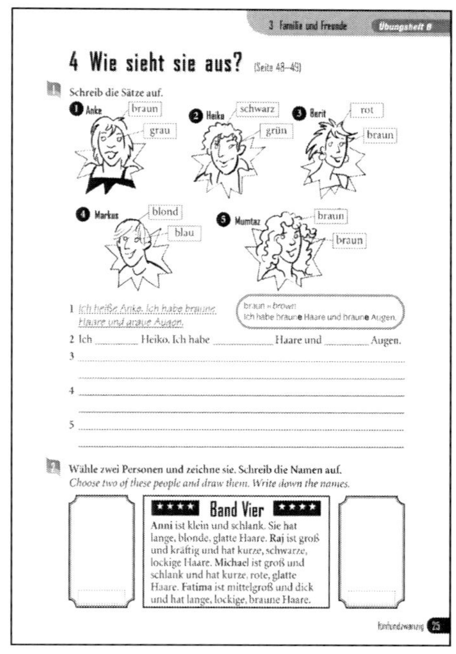
3 Familie und Freunde Übungsheft B

4 Wie sieht sie aus? (Seite 48–49)

1 Schreib die Sätze auf.

1 Anke: braun, grau 2 Heiko: schwarz, grün 3 Berit: rot, braun 4 Markus: blond, blau 5 Mumtaz: braun, braun

1 Ich heiße Anke. Ich habe braune Haare und graue Augen.
2 Ich ________ Heiko. Ich habe ________ Haare und ________ Augen.
3 ________
4 ________
5 ________

braun = brown
Ich habe braun**e** Haare und braun**e** Augen.

2 Wähle zwei Personen und zeichne sie. Schreib die Namen auf. *Choose two of these people and draw them. Write down the names.*

Band Vier
Anni ist klein und schlank. Sie hat lange, blonde, glatte Haare. Raj ist groß und kräftig und hat kurze, schwarze, lockige Haare. Michael ist groß und schlank und hat kurze, rote, glatte Haare. Fatima ist mittelgroß und dick und hat lange, lockige, braune Haare.

fünfundzwanzig 25

1 (AT4 level 3)
1 Ich heiße Anke. Ich habe braune Haare und graue Augen. **2** Ich heiße Heiko. Ich habe schwarze Haare und grüne Augen. **3** Ich heiße Berit. Ich habe rote Haare und braune Augen. **4** Ich heiße Markus. Ich habe blonde Haare und blaue Augen. **5** Ich heiße Mumtaz. Ich habe braune Haare und braune Augen.

2 (AT3 Level 3) *Pupils choose two of these to draw:* **Anni:** small und slim, with long blonde straight hair. **Raj:** big and strong, with short black curly hair. **Michael:** tall und slim, with short red straight hair. **Fatima:** medium-height and fat, with long curly brown hair.

Übungsheft A, Seite 26

1 (AT3 Level 1)
Completed wordsearch below

2 (AT3 Level 2, AT4 Level 1)
1 Mein Bruder ist **ziemlich** freundlich, aber **sehr** laut. Er ist **nicht** musikalisch. **2** Meine Schwester ist sehr **intelligent** und **sportlich**, aber ziemlich **faul**. Sie ist nicht **launisch**.

Übungsheft A 3 Familie und Freunde

5 Er ist lustig (Seite 50–51)

Finde die neun anderen Wörter. *Find the nine other words.*

1 freundlich, 2 intelligent, 3 sportlich, 4 kreativ, 5 musikalisch, 6 lustig, 7 schüchtern, 8 laut, 9 faul, 10 launisch

Füll die Lücken aus. *Fill in the gaps.* ✓ = ziemlich (quite) ✓✓ = sehr (very)

1 Mein Bruder ist ________ ✓ freundlich, aber ______ ✓✓ laut. Er ist ______ ✗ musikalisch.

2 Meine Schwester ist sehr i________ und s________, aber ziemlich f______. Sie ist nicht l________.

faul launisch intelligent sportlich

26 sechsundzwanzig

Übungsheft B, Seite 26

1 (AT3 Level 2, AT4 Level 1)
Completed wordsearch below

2 (AT3 Level 1, AT4 Level 2)
1 Mein Bruder **ist sehr laut**. **2** Meine Schwester **ist nicht musikalisch.** **3** Meine Mutter **ist ziemlich sportlich. 4** Mein Vater **ist sehr intelligent. 5** Kai ist **nicht schüchtern. 6** Manja ist **ziemlich kreativ.**

Übungsheft B 3 Familie und Freunde

5 Er ist lustig (Seite 50–51)

Finde zehn Charakterwörter in dem Puzzle. *Find ten words to describe character in the wordsearch.*

1 Sascha ist **üternschch**. 2 Ich bin **orspichtl**. 3 Karina ist **veatikr**. 4 Mein Vater ist **ellingentit**. 5 Meine Schwester ist **lauf**. 6 Ich bin sehr **taul**. 7 Bist du **unislach**? 8 Olaf ist **slutig**. 9 Bist du **schmuikalis**? 10 Ich bin sehr **reuhfndlic**.

Schreib Sätze mit „ziemlich", „sehr" oder „nicht" + Adjektiv. *Write sentences including ziemlich, sehr or nicht + an adjective.* ✓ = ziemlich ✓✓ = sehr

1 ✓✓ Mein Bruder ist sehr laut. 2 ✗ Meine Schwester 3 ✓ Meine Mutter 4 ✓✓ Mein Vater 5 ✗ Kai 6 ✓ Manja

26 sechsundzwanzig

s	b	m	u	f	a	u	l	e	d	d	o
m	e	p	j	k	r	e	a	t	i	v	c
u	h	k	ö	l	l	a	u	t	c	n	n
s	r	t	b	i	a	f	n	i	z	i	n
i	s	p	o	r	t	l	i	c	h	l	x
k	g	l	p	h	t	h	s	y	w	z	f
a	ö	u	m	g	m	s	c	i	a	l	j
l	p	s	c	h	ü	c	h	t	e	r	n
i	n	t	e	l	l	i	g	e	n	t	h
s	c	i	r	v	o	ü	f	w	e	j	b
c	u	g	w	e	d	z	v	a	k	o	g
h	k	f	r	e	u	n	d	l	i	c	h

s	b	m	u	f	a	u	l	e	d	d	o
m	e	p	j	k	r	e	a	t	i	v	c
u	h	k	ö	l	l	a	u	t	c	n	n
s	r	t	b	i	a	f	n	i	z	i	n
i	s	p	o	r	t	l	i	c	h	l	x
k	g	l	p	h	t	h	s	y	w	z	f
a	ö	u	m	g	m	s	c	i	a	l	j
l	p	s	c	h	ü	c	h	t	e	r	n
i	n	t	e	l	l	i	g	e	n	t	h
s	c	i	r	v	o	ü	f	w	e	j	b
c	u	g	w	e	d	z	v	a	k	o	g
h	k	f	r	e	u	n	d	l	i	c	h

Übungsheft A, Seite 27

1 (AT3 Level 2)
1 Gitti **2** Mirko **3** Gitti **4** Manja **5** Mirko **6** Gitti **7** Manja **8** Mirko **9** Gitti **10** Manja

2 (AT3 Level 1, AT4 Level 1)
Cognates: intelligent (intelligent). **Near-cognates:** freundlich (friendly), sportlich (sporty), laut (loud), kreativ (creative). **Non-cognates:** faul (lazy), launisch (moody), lustig (funny)

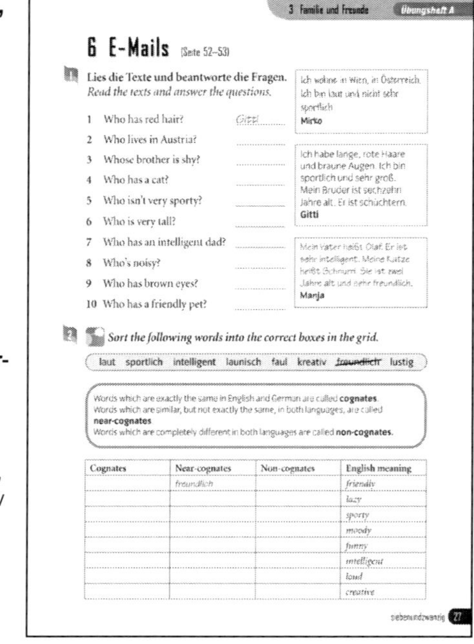

3 Familie und Freunde Übungsheft A

6 E-Mails (Seite 52–53)

Lies die Texte und beantworte die Fragen. *Read the texts and answer the questions.*

1 Who has red hair? Gitti
2 Who lives in Austria?
3 Whose brother is shy?
4 Who has a cat?
5 Who isn't very sporty?
6 Who is very tall?
7 Who has an intelligent dad?
8 Who's noisy?
9 Who has brown eyes?
10 Who has a friendly pet?

Ich wohne in Wien, in Österreich. Ich bin laut und nicht sehr sportlich. Mirko

Ich habe lange, rote Haare und braune Augen. Ich bin sportlich und sehr groß. Mein Bruder ist sechzehn Jahre alt. Er ist schüchtern. Gitti

Mein Vater heißt Olaf. Er ist sehr intelligent. Meine Katze heißt Schnurri. Sie ist zwei Jahre alt und sehr freundlich. Manja

Sort the following words into the correct boxes in the grid.

laut sportlich intelligent launisch faul kreativ ~~freundlich~~ lustig

Words which are exactly the same in English and German are called **cognates**. Words which are similar, but not exactly the same, in both languages, are called **near-cognates**. Words which are completely different in both languages are called **non-cognates**.

Cognates	Near-cognates	Non-cognates	English meaning
	freundlich		friendly
			lazy
			sporty
			moody
			funny
			intelligent
			loud
			creative

siebenundzwanzig 27

Übungsheft B, Seite 27

1 (AT3 Level 2, AT4 Level 2)

2 (AT3 Level 3, AT4 Level 2)
Hallo! Ich heiße **Timo**. Ich wohne in Berlin, das ist in **Deutschland**. Ich bin **vierzehn** Jahre alt. Ich habe am elften **Februar** Geburtstag. Ich habe **einen** Bruder. Er ist fünfzehn **Jahre** alt und er ist ziemlich **laut. Meine** Mutter heißt Elke. Sie hat **blonde** Haare und blaue **Augen.** Mein Vater **heißt** Volker und er ist **sehr** intelligent. Ich habe **eine** Katze. Sie heißt Bonbon. **Hast** du ein Haustier? Wie siehst du aus? Ich habe schwarze **Haare** und **blaue** Augen. Alles Gute, Timo

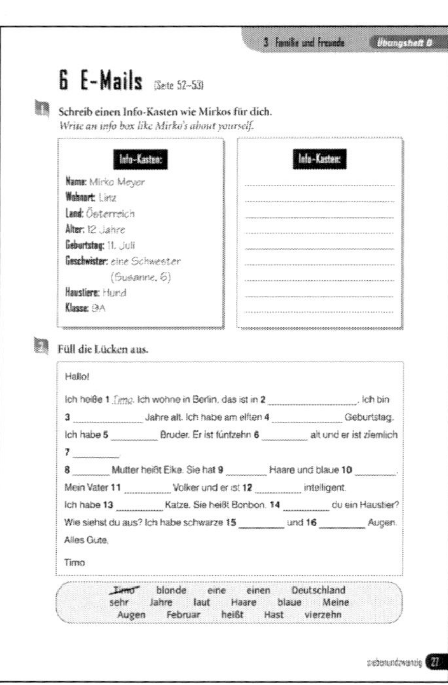

3 Familie und Freunde Übungsheft B

6 E-Mails (Seite 52–53)

Schreib einen Info-Kasten wie Mirkos für dich. *Write an info box like Mirko's about yourself.*

Info-Kasten:
Name: Mirko Meyer
Wohnort: Linz
Land: Österreich
Alter: 12 Jahre
Geburtstag: 11. Juli
Geschwister: eine Schwester (Susanne, 6)
Haustiere: Hund
Klasse: 9A

Info-Kasten:

Füll die Lücken aus.

Hallo!
Ich heiße 1 Timo. Ich wohne in Berlin, das ist in 2 ________. Ich bin 3 ________ Jahre alt. Ich habe am elften 4 ________ Geburtstag. Ich habe 5 ______ Bruder. Er ist fünfzehn 6 ______ alt und er ist ziemlich 7 ______. 8 ______ Mutter heißt Elke. Sie hat 9 ______ Haare und blaue 10 ______. Mein Vater 11 ______ Volker und er ist 12 ______ intelligent. Ich habe 13 ______ Katze. Sie heißt Bonbon. 14 ______ du ein Haustier? Wie siehst du aus? Ich habe schwarze 15 ______ und 16 ______ Augen.
Alles Gute,
Timo

~~Timo~~ blonde eine einen Deutschland sehr Jahre laut Haare blaue Meine Augen Februar heißt Hast vierzehn

siebenundzwanzig 27

Übungsheft A, Seite 28

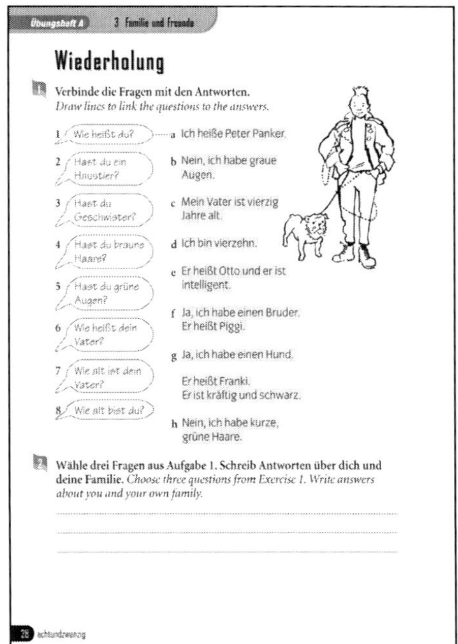

Übungsheft A 3 Familie und Freunde

Wiederholung

1 Verbinde die Fragen mit den Antworten. *Draw lines to link the questions to the answers.*

1 Wie heißt du?
2 Hast du ein Haustier?
3 Hast du Geschwister?
4 Hast du braune Haare?
5 Hast du grüne Augen?
6 Wie heißt dein Vater?
7 Wie alt ist dein Vater?
8 Wie alt bist du?

a Ich heiße Peter Panker.
b Nein, ich habe graue Augen.
c Mein Vater ist vierzig Jahre alt.
d Ich bin vierzehn.
e Er heißt Otto und er ist intelligent.
f Ja, ich habe einen Bruder. Er heißt Piggi.
g Ja, ich habe einen Hund. Er heißt Franki. Er ist kräftig und schwarz.
h Nein, ich habe kurze, grüne Haare.

2 Wähle drei Fragen aus Aufgabe 1. Schreib Antworten über dich und deine Familie. *Choose three questions from Exercise 1. Write answers about you and your own family.*

28 achtundzwanzig

1 **(AT3 Level 2, AT4 Level 2)**

1 a **2** g **3** f **4** h **5** b **6** e **7** c **8** d

2 **(AT 4 Level 2)**

Übungsheft B, Seite 28

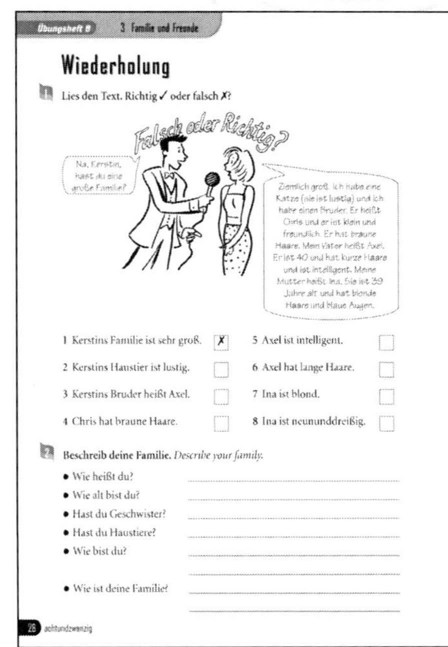

Übungsheft B 3 Familie und Freunde

Wiederholung

1 Lies den Text. Richtig ✓ oder falsch ✗?

1 Kerstins Familie ist sehr groß. ✗
2 Kerstins Haustier ist lustig.
3 Kerstins Bruder heißt Axel.
4 Chris hat braune Haare.
5 Axel ist intelligent.
6 Axel hat lange Haare.
7 Ina ist blond.
8 Ina ist neununddreißig.

2 Beschreib deine Familie. *Describe your family.*

- Wie heißt du?
- Wie alt bist du?
- Hast du Geschwister?
- Hast du Haustiere?
- Wie bist du?
- Wie ist deine Familie?

28 achtundzwanzig

1 **(AT3 Level 3, AT4 Level 1)**

1 ✗ **2** ✓ **3** ✗ **4** ✓ **5** ✓ **6** ✗ **7** ✓ **8** ✓

2 **(AT 4 Level 3)**

Arbeitsblatt 3.1

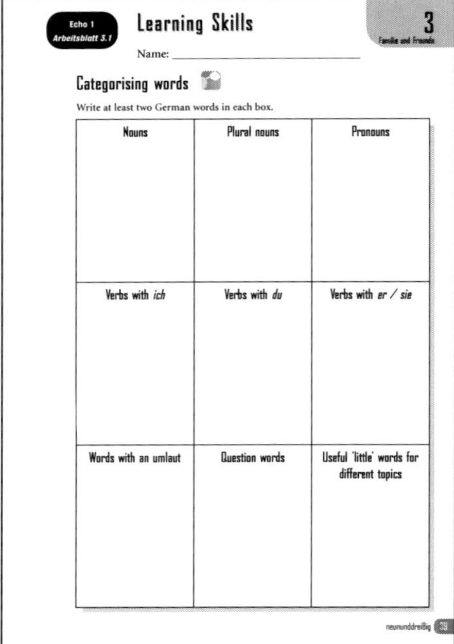
Echo 1 Arbeitsblatt 3.1

Learning Skills

3 Familie und Freunde

Name: ______________________

Categorising words

Write at least two German words in each box.

Nouns	Plural nouns	Pronouns
Verbs with *ich*	Verbs with *du*	Verbs with *er / sie*
Words with an umlaut	Question words	Useful 'little' words for different topics

neununddreißig 39

Arbeitsblatt 3.2

3 Familie und Freunde

Grammatik

Echo 1 Arbeitsblatt 3.2

Name: ______________________

Plural forms of nouns

In German, you usually can't just add an **s** to make a noun plural (cat**s**, dog**s**). You need other endings.

A Label the pictures. Underline anything that is different from the singular forms.

zwei Schlangen / Fußbälle / Hunde / Katzen / Lineale / Bücher

B Write the plural forms of the nouns.

1 Hund (-e) 2 Schere (-n) 3 Kaninchen (-) 4 Gitarre (-n) 5 Idee (-n)

In word lists and dictionaries, the plural ending is shown after the noun in brackets or in bold print. Schlange (-n) – Schlangen. (-) shows that there is no change when you put the word into the plural form.

C Write the plural forms of the nouns.

1 Apfel (¨) 2 Buch (¨er) 3 Fach (¨er) 4 Ball (¨e) 5 Vogel (¨)

Sometimes the plural form of a word has an umlaut added to an **a**, **o** or **u** in the word, or an umlaut as well as another ending. Bruder (¨) – Brüder Haus (¨er) – Häuser

D Sort the words below into three pairs. Write each pair into the 'singular' column of a grid. Then look up the plurals in the *Wortschatz* at the back of Echo 1. Can you think of one more word for each group?

Brötchen Banane Filzstift Mädchen Klebstift Lampe

Singular	Plural	Singular	Plural	Singular	Plural

40 vierzig

A
1 zwei Katzen
2 zwei Bücher
3 zwei Lineale
4 zwei Fußbälle
5 zwei Hunde
6 zwei Schlangen

B
1 Hunde **2** Scheren
3 Kaninchen
4 Gitarren **5** Ideen

C
1 Äpfel **2** Bücher
3 Fächer **4** Fußbälle
5 Vögel

D
Lampe / Lampen, Banane / Bananen; Meerschweinchen / Meerschweinchen, Mädchen / Mädchen; Klebstift / Klebstifte, Filzstift / Filzstifte

Other possible words to add:
Katze, Kaninchen, Bleistift

Arbeitsblatt 3.3

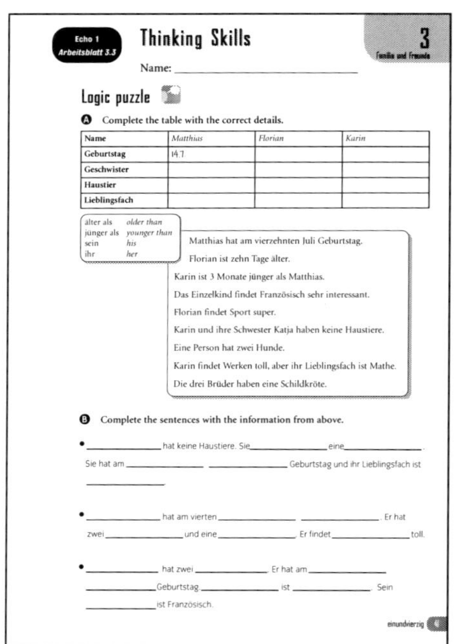
Echo 1 Arbeitsblatt 3.3

Thinking Skills

3 Familie und Freunde

Name: ______________________

Logic puzzle

A Complete the table with the correct details.

Name	Matthias	Florian	Karin
Geburtstag	14.7.		
Geschwister			
Haustier			
Lieblingsfach			

älter als – older than; jünger als – younger than; sein – his; ihr – her

Matthias hat am vierzehnten Juli Geburtstag.
Florian ist zehn Tage älter.
Karin ist 3 Monate jünger als Matthias.
Das Einzelkind findet Französisch sehr interessant.
Florian findet Sport super.
Karin und ihre Schwester Katja haben keine Haustiere.
Eine Person hat zwei Hunde.
Karin findet Werken toll, aber ihr Lieblingsfach ist Mathe.
Die drei Brüder haben eine Schildkröte.

B Complete the sentences with the information from above.

• ________ hat keine Haustiere. Sie ________ eine ________. Sie hat am ________ ________ Geburtstag und ihr Lieblingsfach ist ________

• ________ hat am vierten ________ ________. Er hat zwei ________ und eine ________. Er findet ________ toll.

• ________ hat zwei ________. Er hat am ________ ________ Geburtstag. ________ ist ________. Sein ________ ist Französisch.

einundvierzig 41

A

Name	*Matthias*	*Florian*	*Karin*
Geburtstag	14.7.	4.7.	14.10.
Geschwister	–	2 Brüder	1 Schwester
Haustier	2 Hunde	1 Schildkröte	–
Lieblingsfach	Französisch	Sport	Mathe

B
Karin hat keine Haustiere. Sie **hat** eine **Schwester**. Sie hat am **vierzehnten Oktober** Geburtstag und ihr Lieblingsfach ist **Mathe. Florian** hat am vierten **Juli Geburtstag** . Er hat zwei **Brüder**. Er findet **Sport** toll. **Matthias** hat zwei **Hunde**. Er hat am **vierzehnten Juli** Geburtstag. **Er** ist **Einzelkind**. Sein **Lieblingsfach** ist Französisch.

Arbeitsblatt 3.4

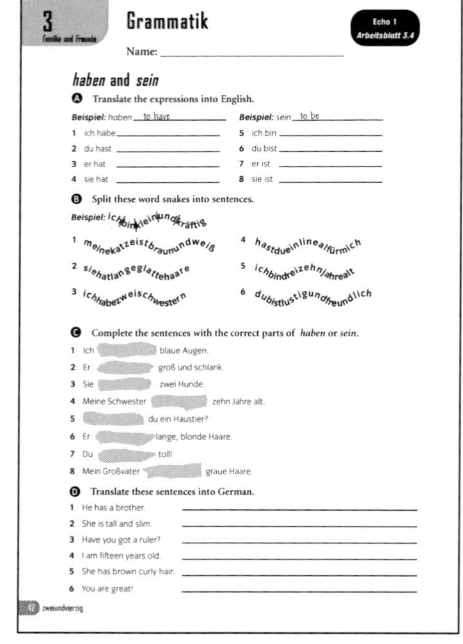
3 Familie und Freunde

Grammatik

Echo 1 Arbeitsblatt 3.4

Name: ______________________

haben and *sein*

A Translate the expressions into English.

Beispiel: haben – to have; sein – to be

1 ich habe 2 du hast 3 er hat 4 sie hat 5 ich bin 6 du bist 7 er ist 8 sie ist

B Split these word snakes into sentences.

Beispiel: ichbinkleinundkräftig

1 meinekatzeistbraunundweiß 2 siehatlangeglattehaare 3 ichhabezweischwestern 4 hastdueinlinealfürmich 5 ichbindreizehnjahrealt 6 dubistlustigundfreundlich

C Complete the sentences with the correct parts of *haben* or *sein*.

1 Ich ____ blaue Augen. 2 Er ____ groß und schlank. 3 Sie ____ zwei Hunde. 4 Meine Schwester ____ zehn Jahre alt. 5 ____ du ein Haustier? 6 Er ____ lange, blonde Haare. 7 Du ____ toll! 8 Mein Großvater ____ graue Haare.

D Translate these sentences into German.

1 He has a brother. 2 She is tall and slim. 3 Have you got a ruler? 4 I am fifteen years old. 5 She has brown curly hair. 6 You are great!

42 zweiundvierzig

A
1 I have **2** you have **3** he has **4** she has **5** I am **6** you are **7** he is **8** she is

B
1 Meine Katze ist braun und weiß. **2** Sie hat lange, glatte Haare. **3** Ich habe zwei Schwestern. **4** Hast du ein Lineal für mich? **5** Ich bin dreizehn Jahre alt. **6** Du bist lustig und freundlich.

C
1 habe **2** ist **3** hat **4** ist **5** Hast **6** hat **7** bist **8** hat

D
1 Er hat einen Bruder. **2** Sie ist groß und schlank. **3** Hast du ein Lineal? **4** Ich bin fünfzehn Jahre alt. **5** Sie hat lockige, braune Haare. **6** Du bist toll!

Arbeitsblatt 3.5

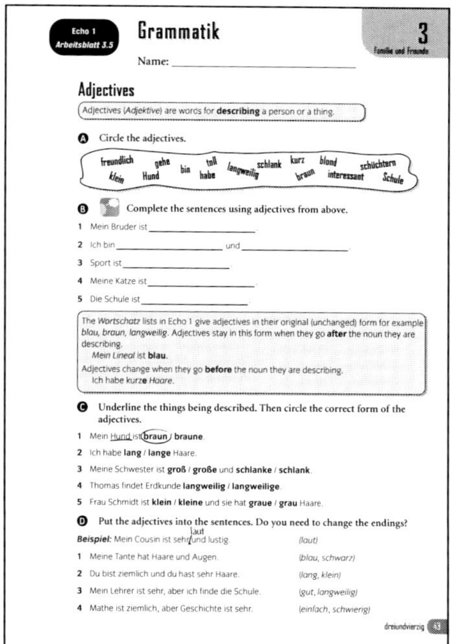
Echo 1 Arbeitsblatt 3.5

Grammatik

3 Familie und Freunde

Name: ____________

Adjectives

Adjectives (*Adjektive*) are words for **describing** a person or a thing.

A Circle the adjectives.

freundlich gehe toll langweilig schlank kurz blond schüchtern klein Hund bin habe braun interessant Schule

B Complete the sentences using adjectives from above.

1 Mein Bruder ist ____________.
2 Ich bin ____________ und ____________.
3 Sport ist ____________.
4 Meine Katze ist ____________.
5 Die Schule ist ____________.

The *Wortschatz* lists in Echo 1 give adjectives in their original (unchanged) form for example *blau, braun, langweilig*. Adjectives stay in this form when they go **after** the noun they are describing.
Mein Lineal ist **blau**.
Adjectives change when they go **before** the noun they are describing.
Ich habe kurz**e** *Haare*.

C Underline the things being described. Then circle the correct form of the adjectives.

1 Mein Hund ist **braun** / **braune**.
2 Ich habe **lang** / **lange** Haare.
3 Meine Schwester ist **groß** / **große** und **schlanke** / **schlank**.
4 Thomas findet Erdkunde **langweilig** / **langweilige**.
5 Frau Schmidt ist **klein** / **kleine** und sie hat **graue** / **grau** Haare.

D Put the adjectives into the sentences. Do you need to change the endings?

Beispiel: Mein Cousin ist sehr laut und lustig. *(laut)*
1 Meine Tante hat Haare und Augen. *(blau, schwarz)*
2 Du bist ziemlich und du hast sehr Haare. *(lang, klein)*
3 Mein Lehrer ist sehr, aber ich finde die Schule. *(gut, langweilig)*
4 Mathe ist ziemlich, aber Geschichte ist sehr. *(einfach, schwierig)*

dreiundvierzig 43

A
braun, interessant, schüchtern, klein, blond, schlank, freundlich, langweilig, kurz, toll

C
1 Hund / braun. **2** Haare / lange. **3** Schwester / groß, schlank. **4** Erdkunde / langweilig. **5** Frau Schmidt / klein, Haare / graue

D
1 Meine Tante hat schwarze Haare und blaue Augen. **2** Du bist ziemlich klein und du hast sehr lange Haare. **3** Mein Lehrer ist sehr gut / langweilig aber ich finde die Schule gut / langweilig. **4** Mathe ist ziemlich einfach / schwierig, aber Geschichte ist sehr einfach / schwierig.

Arbeitsblatt 3.6

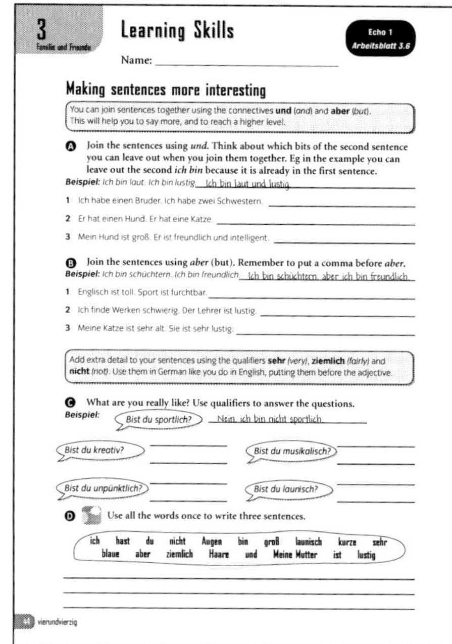
3 Familie und Freunde

Learning Skills

Echo 1 Arbeitsblatt 3.6

Name: ____________

Making sentences more interesting

You can join sentences together using the connectives **und** (*and*) and **aber** (*but*). This will help you to say more, and to reach a higher level.

A Join the sentences using *und*. Think about which bits of the second sentence you can leave out when you join them together. Eg in the example you can leave out the second *ich bin* because it is already in the first sentence.

Beispiel: *Ich bin laut. Ich bin lustig.* Ich bin laut und lustig
1 Ich habe einen Bruder. Ich habe zwei Schwestern. ____________
2 Er hat einen Hund. Er hat eine Katze. ____________
3 Mein Hund ist groß. Er ist freundlich und intelligent. ____________

B Join the sentences using *aber* (but). Remember to put a comma before *aber*.

Beispiel: *Ich bin schüchtern. Ich bin freundlich.* Ich bin schüchtern, aber ich bin freundlich.
1 Englisch ist toll. Sport ist furchtbar. ____________
2 Ich finde Werken schwierig. Der Lehrer ist lustig. ____________
3 Meine Katze ist sehr alt. Sie ist sehr lustig. ____________

Add extra detail to your sentences using the qualifiers **sehr** (*very*), **ziemlich** (*fairly*) and **nicht** (*not*). Use them in German like you do in English, putting them before the adjective.

C What are you really like? Use qualifiers to answer the questions.

Beispiel: *Bist du sportlich?* Nein, ich bin nicht sportlich.

Bist du kreativ? ____________
Bist du musikalisch? ____________
Bist du unpünktlich? ____________
Bist du launisch? ____________

D Use all the words once to write three sentences.

ich hast du nicht Augen bin groß launisch kurze sehr blaue aber ziemlich Haare und Meine Mutter ist lustig

44 vierundvierzig

A
1 Ich habe einen Bruder und zwei Schwestern. **2** Er hat einen Hund und eine Katze. **3** Mein Hund ist groß, freundlich und intelligent.

B
1 Englisch ist toll, aber Sport ist furchtbar. **2** Ich finde Werken schwierig, aber der Lehrer ist lustig. **3** Meine Katze ist sehr alt, aber sie ist sehr lustig.

D
Possible answer

Ich bin nicht groß. Du hast blaue Augen und kurze Haare. Meine Mutter ist ziemlich launisch, aber sehr lustig.

4 Freizeit

Unit Learning targets	Key framework objectives	NC levels and PoS coverage	Grammar and key language	Skills
1 Sport (pp. 60–61) • Talking about sports • Using *gern* to show what you like doing	**2.4/Y7** Writing – (b) building text	**NC l levels** 2–4 **2.1c** knowledge of language **2.2d** pronunciation and intonation **2.2e** ask and answer questions **3b** sounds and writing **3c** apply grammar **3d** use a range of vocab / structures **4b** communicate in pairs etc. **4d** make links with English	Present tense paradigms: *ich / du / er / sie* forms of *spielen / gehen / wohnen* Use of *gern* *Ich spiele …* *Spielst du …?* *Er / Sie spielt …* *gern / nicht gern* *Basketball* *Federball* *Fußball* *Rugby* *Tennis* *Tischtennis* *Volleyball* *Ich gehe …* *Gehst du …?* *Er / Sie geht …* *angeln* *reiten* *schwimmen* *Snowboard fahren* *wandern*	Pronunciation of cognates
2 Hobbys (pp. 62–63) • Talking about what you do in your free time • Using the present tense of regular and irregular verbs	**4.6/Y7** Language – (a) questions **5.5** Strategies – reference materials	**NC levels** 2–3 **2.1c** knowledge of language **2.1e** use reference of language **2.2d** pronunciation and intonation **2.2e** ask and answer questions **3b** sounds and writing **3c** apply grammar **3d** use a range of vocab / structures	*Ich* and *du* forms of other verbs, including some strong verbs Revision of *gern* Forming closed questions *Ich spiele Gitarre.* *Ich spiele am Computer.* *Ich gehe in die Stadt.* *Ich gehe in den Jugendklub.* *Ich gehe ins Kino.* *Ich tanze.* *Ich lese.* *Ich besuche meine Freunde.* *Ich höre Musik.* *Ich sehe fern.* *Ich fahre Rad.* *Ich faulenze.* *Siehst du gern fern?* *Besuchst du gern deine Freunde?* *Liest du gern Bücher?* *Spielst du gern …?* *Gehst du gern …?* *Hörst du gern Musik?*	Looking up the meanings of verbs Pronunciation: *a / ä*
3 Lieblingssachen (pp. 64–65) • Talking about your favourite things • Using *sein* (his) and *ihr* (her)	**5.8** Strategies – evaluating and improving	**NC levels** 1–3 **2.2d** pronunciation and intonation **2.2e** ask and answer questions **2.2j** adapt previously-learnt language **3b** sounds and writing **3c** apply grammar **3d** use a range of vocab / structures **4b** communicate in pairs etc.	Revision of *Lieblings-* *sein / ihr* *Was ist dein(e) / mein(e) / sein(e) / ihr(e)…?* *Lieblingshaustier* *Lieblingsfarbe* *Lieblingssport* *Lieblingssendung* *Lieblingsmannschaft* *Lieblingsmusik* *Lieblingszahl* *Lieblingsauto*	Pronunciation: saying long words

Unit Learning targets	Key framework objectives	NC levels and PoS coverage	Grammar and key language	Skills
4 Brieffreunde (pp. 66–67) • Saying how often you do things • Learning how to write a letter to a penfriend	**2.3/Y7** Reading – text features **2.4/Y7** Writing – (a) sentences and texts as models	**NC levels** 2–4 **2.1d** previous knowledge **2.2e** ask and answer questions **2.2g** write clearly and coherently **3b** sounds and writing **3c** apply grammar **3d** use a range of vocab / structures **4b** communicate in pairs etc. **4f** language of interest / enjoyment	Adverbs of frequency *wir* *Wie oft …?* *jeden Tag* *(ein)mal pro Woche* *am Wochenende* *nie* *Lieber* *Danke für deinen Brief* *Schreib bald* *Dein(e)*	Writing a letter to a penfriend
5 Möchtest du ins Kino gehen? (pp. 68–69) • Arranging to go out and when to meet • Using *möchtest du …?* (would you like …?) with an infinitive	**2.1/Y7** Reading – main points and detail	**NC levels** 2–4 **2.1a** identify patterns **2.2d** pronunciation and intonation **2.2e** ask and answer questions **3b** sounds and writing **3c** apply grammar **3d** use a range of vocab / structures **4b** communicate in pairs etc.	*Möchtest du?* + infinitive Introduction to *in* + accusative *Hast du am Donnerstag / Freitag / Samstag / Sonntag Zeit?* *Möchtest du…* *Fußball / Tennis / Basketball / Cricket spielen?* *in die Stadt / in die Disko / in den Jugendklub / ins Kino gehen?* *Ja, gern.* *Ja, das mag ich.* *Nein, das mag ich nicht.* *Nein, das ist langweilig.* *Wann treffen wir uns?* *Um … Uhr* Revision of digital time Revision of greetings *Bis dann / Bis Samstag*	Expressing wishes and opinions Pronunciation: *o/ö*
6 Abenteuer im Freien (pp. 70–71) • Understanding information about an adventure sports centre • Using *man kann* to say what activities there are	**4.5/Y7** Language – (b) modal verbs	**NC levels** 1–4 **2.1a** identify patterns **2.1c** knowledge of language **2.2c** respond appropriately **2.2e** ask and answer questions **3b** sounds and writing **3c** apply grammar **3d** use a range of vocab / structures **4b** communicate in pairs etc. **4d** make links with English	*Man kann* + infinitive *Man kann* + leisure activity *Kann man …?* *Ich mag* *Mountainbike fahren* *Wildwasser fahren* *Kanu fahren* *klettern* *schwimmen* *segeln* *windsurfen* *Tennis spielen* *Volleyball spielen* *Basketball spielen*	Writing a simple letter of enquiry Receptive introduction of *du / Sie*
Lernzieltest und Wiederholung (pp. 72–73) • Pupil's checklist and practice test		**NC levels** 2–4 **2.1b** memorising		

Unit Learning targets	Key framework objectives	NC levels and PoS coverage	Grammar and key language	Skills
Mehr (pp. 74–75) • Reading a letter about plans for next week • Making plans to go out next week	**2.2/Y7** Reading – (b) text selection **3.1/Y7** Culture – aspects of everyday life **4.5/Y7** Language – (a) future using present tense	**NC levels** 3–4 **2.1c** knowledge of language **2.2e** ask and answer questions **3b** sounds and writing **3c** apply grammar **3d** use a range of vocab / structures **4b** communicate in pairs etc.	Present tense to talk about close future (receptive) Verb as second idea (revision) *Möchtest du* + infinitive? (revision) *Möchtest du am (Montag) (ins Kino gehen)?* *Nein, ich (spiele Fußball).* *Ja, gern.* *Wann treffen wir uns?* *Um (sechs) Uhr.* *Bis dann.*	
Extra (pp. 118–119) • Self-access reading and writing at two levels		**NC levels** 2–4 **2.2e** ask and answer questions **2.2j** adapt previously-learnt language **3c** apply grammar **3d** use a range of vocab / structures		

1 Sport

Learning targets

- Talking about sports
- Using *gern* to say what you like doing

Key framework objectives

2.4/Y7 Writing – (b) building text

Grammar

- Present tense regular verbs: 1st, 2nd, 3rd person
- Using (*nicht*) *gern*

Key language

Ich spiele …
Spielst du …?
Er / Sie spielt …
gern / nicht gern
Basketball
Federball
Fußball
Rugby
Tennis
Tischtennis
Volleyball
Ich gehe …
Gehst du …?
Er / Sie geht …
angeln
reiten
schwimmen
Snowboard fahren
wandern

High-frequency words

gern
nicht gern
ich gehe
gehst du …?
er / sie geht
ich spiele
du spielst
er / sie spielt
das ist …
ich finde das …
sehr
aber

Pronunciation

Sports cognates

Resources

CD 2, tracks 21–23
Workbooks A and B, p.32
Arbeitsblatt 4.1, p.57
Arbeitsblatt 4.3, p.59
Flashcards 58–69
Echo Elektro 1 TPP, Mod 4 1.1–1.7

Starter 1 4.1/Y7

Aim

To build confidence in aural recognition of cognates.

Give each pupil a copy of **Arbeitsblatt 4.1.** Explain that they will hear you read out a list of new German words, and must join the pictures shown on the worksheet in the order that they hear them. First, elicit what type of words they are going to be (evident from the pictures). Read out the following list of sports cognates, allowing time for weaker pupils to find and join the pictures. The sports are listed at the bottom of the worksheet. You may choose to remove these in order to make the exercise listening only. At the end, ask all pupils to hold up their completed worksheet, which should show the outline of a tennis racquet.

Tennis
Basketball
Fußball

Starter 1 *continued*

Schwimmen
Rugby
Tischtennis
Snowboard fahren
Volleyball
Reiten
Tennis

Before looking at exercise 1, ask pupils why they think many of the German sports words are the same as in English, or very similar (common roots of the languages; modern sports with international names). Ask them to guess the meanings of *wandern*, *Federball*, and *angeln*.

1 Hör zu. Was passt zusammen? (1–12) (AT 1/2) 4.2/Y7

Listening. Pupils listen to the statements about sport, and identify the correct picture. Play the recording in two parts, to match the two groups of pictures: 1–7 *ich spiele* and 8–12 *ich gehe.*

1. *Ich spiele Tischtennis.*
2. *Ich spiele Rugby.*
3. *Ich spiele Federball.*
4. *Ich spiele Fußball.*

5 *Ich spiele Volleyball.*
6 *Ich spiele Tennis.*
7 *Ich spiele Basketball.*

Answers
1 f **2** g **3** e **4** b **5** d 6 a **7** c

8 *Ich gehe wandern.*
9 *Ich gehe schwimmen.*
10 *Ich gehe angeln.*
11 *Ich gehe reiten.*
12 *Ich gehe Snowboard fahren.*

Answers
8 k **9** i **10** j **11** h **12** l

To practise this vocabulary, pupils could mime and guess the sports in pairs or small groups.

Aussprache 4.1/Y7 5.3

Before going on to exercise 2, discuss the **Aussprache** panel with pupils. It clarifies the fact that, although a number of words look very similar in English and German, their pronunciation is often different.

2 Hör zu und wiederhole. (AT 2/) 4.1/Y7

Listening. Pupils listen and repeat, to practise the differences in pronunciation between these cognates and their English versions. Encourage pupils to start in a whisper, building up to a crescendo.

Suggestion

Additional activities with this recording are: say each line faster than the previous one; diminish the volume; say each line with expression depending on whether pupils like the sport or not; halves of the class compete.

22

Fußball, Fußball, Fußball
Basketball, Basketball, Basketball
Volleyball, Volleyball, Volleyball
Rugby, Rugby, Rugby!

3 Partnerarbeit: Sportarten. (AT 2/2) 4.2/Y7

Speaking. Pupils work in pairs, practising the sports phrases and identifying the relevant pictures. It would be a good idea to revise letters of the alphabet in German, as pupils will need to say them in this speaking activity (only the letters a–l are needed).

ECHO-Detektiv: Verb endings (regular) 4.5a/Y7

Read the grammar box, then look together at the endings for ***wohnen***. Ask pupils to write or say a sentence using a regular verb form (weaker pupils can stick to ***spielen***). Their sentences could be prepared in advance, and said aloud to you as they pass you at the door to leave at the end of the lesson. For further practice, see page 130.

4 Spielen oder gehen? Schreib Sätze. (AT4/2) 4.5a/Y7

Writing. Pupils construct simple sentences, prompted by the pronouns and illustrations given, using different forms of *spielen* or *gehen*. Encourage them to think carefully about which of these two verbs is needed. Refer them to the grammar box to check verb endings.

Answers
1 Er spielt Tennis.
2 Sie geht reiten.
3 Du spielst Fußball.
4 Ich gehe angeln.
5 Sie geht wandern.

+ Pupils who finish quickly could make up their own sentences using different parts of *wohnen* and *trinken*.

Starter 2 4.5a/Y7 4.2/Y7

Aim

To recap sports vocabulary, and the *du* form of *spielen* and *gehen*.

Quick team game miming sports: divide the class into two teams. The first team has one minute (timed by a volunteer from the opposite team), to mime and guess as many of the 12 sports as possible. As soon as a correct guess has been made, e.g. *Du spielst Tennis*, that person stands up and mimes another. Keep a tally of the number of words guessed. The opposite team then has the same amount of time to do the activity. The team guessing the most is the winner. Adjust the time limit for weaker or more able classes.

+ As an additional activity to focus on this unit's Key framework objectives, higher ability groups could play the game using a specific pronoun that keeps changing. Take away points for using English rather than German pronunciation.

5 Hör zu und lies. Schreib die richtigen Buchstaben auf. (AT 1/3 AT 3/3) 1.1/Y7 2.1/Y7

Listening/Reading. Pupils read the texts about sports likes and dislikes, and select the relevant pictures for each speaker. This can firstly be done as a 'listen and read' – ask pupils to identify the new word *gern* and to speculate as to its meaning. Stronger classes could do the matching task using the audio only. Afterwards, ask pupils to read the texts aloud, using appropriate expression with regard to the likes and dislikes.

23

1. *Ich spiele gern Federball. Ich finde das toll!*
2. *Ich spiele nicht gern Fußball. Das ist so langweilig!*

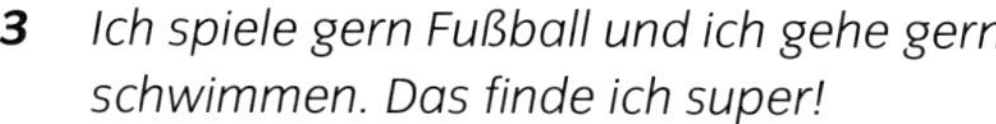

3. *Ich spiele gern Fußball und ich gehe gern schwimmen. Das finde ich super!*
4. *Ich spiele gern Federball, aber ich spiele nicht gern Basketball. Ich finde Federball sehr gut, aber Basketball ist furchtbar!*
5. *Ich gehe nicht gern schwimmen. Das ist doof! Ich spiele gern Federball und Fußball.*

Answers
1 c **2** f **3** a, d **4** c, b **5** e, c, a

ECHO-Detektiv: gern 4.2/Y7

Point out to pupils how useful this word is because they can use it in many situations to give opinions on what they like doing. To help consolidate this fact, pupils could each write or say a sentence with ***gern***, using language they already know, e.g. ***Ich spiele gern Tennis, ich wohne gern in Manchester, ich esse gern Kekse***. For further practice of ***gern***, see page 134. **Arbeitsblatt 4.3** provides general practice of high-frequency words.

Suggestion

As a more challenging alternative, ask pupils to create three sentences with *gern / nicht gern*, one of which is not true. They read them out, and partners or the rest of the class guess which one is false.

6 Partnerarbeit: Stell sechs Fragen und notier die Antworten. (AT 2/3) 1.4a/Y7

Speaking. Pairs interview each other about sports likes and dislikes. They note answers, which are then used in writing exercise 7. This speaking task could be developed into a group or class survey. For further exploitation of this activity, see Other games on page 10.

7 Was macht er / sie gern? Schreib Sätze über deinen Partner / deine Partnerin. (AT 4/3) 4.4/Y7

Writing. Pupils use notes made during the speaking task to write sentences about their partner using *gern / nicht gern*. Remind them to think carefully about their choice of verb and verb ending.

8 Verbinde deine Sätze aus Aufgabe 7 und schreib einen Text. (AT 4/4) 2.4b/Y7

Writing. Pupils link their sentences with *und* and *aber* to write a paragraph about their partner. They could also include opinions. First recap useful language for linking ideas in sentences and making them longer or more interesting.

Plenary 4.5a/Y7

Aim

To consolidate the three regular present tense verb forms learnt, and to look at approaches for remembering them.

Pupils teach and test each other orally in pairs. They must aim to get their partner to 100% accuracy using *spielen, gehen* or *wohnen.* (They should set individual targets of one, two or all three of these verbs.) Start by demonstrating how to 'chant' one verb aloud: *spielen* = to play. *Ich spiele, du spielst, er spielt, sie spielt.* They could point to themselves/their partner/a third person as they do this, to make the pronouns very clear. Finish by asking for volunteers to demonstrate their skills.

2 Hobbys

Learning targets
- Talking about what you do in your free time
- Using the present tense of regular and irregular berbs

Key framework objectives
4.6/Y7 Language – (a) questions
5.5 Strategies – reference materials

Grammar
Regular verbs (*ich, du, er / sie*)
Irregular verbs (*ich, du, er / sie*)
gern
Forming closed questions

Key language
Ich spiele Gitarre.
Ich spiele am Computer.
Ich gehe in die Stadt.
Ich gehe in den Jugendklub.
Ich gehe ins Kino.
Ich tanze.
Ich lese.
Ich besuche meine Freunde.
Ich höre Musik.
Ich sehe fern.
Ich fahre Rad.
Ich faulenze.
Siehst du gern fern?
Besuchst du gern deine Freunde?
Liest du gern Bücher?
Spielst du gern …?
Gehst du gern …?
Hörst du gern Musik?

High-frequency words
ich
du
er / sie
gern
nicht
am
ins
machen
gehen
hören
lesen
sehen
spielen

Pronunciation
a/ä

English
Irregular verbs
Closed questions

Resources
CD 2, tracks 24–26
Workbooks A and B, p. 33
Arbeitsblatt 4.2, p.58
Arbeitsblatt 4.4, p. 60
Echo Elektro 1 TPP, Mod 4 2.1–2.9

Starter 1 5.1

Aim
To familiarise pupils with the infinitives of verbs.

Verb race: show the class these four new infinitives on the board: *hören, lesen, tanzen, besuchen.* Pupils race to find out their meanings. The first five to arrive at the front of the class with the correct meanings (written on paper or mini-whiteboards) are the winners. Afterwards, elicit the fact that these are verbs, and that they are in a different form from those encountered thus far. Explain that all verbs have an infinitive, and ask for other examples, e.g. *spielen, gehen.* Some pupils might be able to give *heißen, wohnen, haben, essen,* etc. Explain that this is the form given in word lists and dictionaries.

Before starting exercise 1, if you have not used Starter 1 you may wish to look at the **ECHO-Tipp** panel with pupils, to prepare them for looking up the meanings of hobby verbs.

1 Rate mal: Was sind diese Hobbys? (AT 3/2) 5.4

Reading. Pupils match phrases about hobbies to pictures. They will probably need to look some of them up. Answers can be checked using listening exercise 2. For further exploitation of this activity, see Mime activities on page 9.

Answers

1	e	Ich gehe ins Kino.
2	d	Ich gehe in den Jugendklub.
3	c	Ich gehe in die Stadt.
4	k	Ich fahre Rad.
5	j	Ich sehe fern
6	i	Ich höre Musik.
7	g	Ich lese.
8	f	Ich tanze.
9	h	Ich besuche meine Freunde.
10	b	Ich spiele am Computer.
11	a	Ich spiele Gitarre.
12	l	Ich faulenze.

2 Hör zu und überprüfe es. (1–12) (AT 1/2) 1.1/Y7

Listening. Pupils listen to the recording, and mark their answers to exercise 1. You could then use the recording for 'listen and repeat' pronunciation practice, pausing it between items. Halves of the class could repeat the question or the answer, alternating between the two.

24

1 – *Was machst du in deiner Freizeit?*
– *Ich gehe ins Kino.*

2 – *Und du, was machst du in deiner Freizeit?*
– *Ich gehe in den Jugendklub.*

3 – *Hallo, was machst du in deiner Freizeit?*
– *Ich gehe in die Stadt.*

4 – *Was machst du in deiner Freizeit?*
– *Ich fahre Rad.*

5 – *Und du, was machst du in deiner Freizeit?*
– *Ähm, … ich sehe fern.*

6 – *Hallo, was machst du in deiner Freizeit?*
– *Ich höre Musik.*

7 – *Was machst du in deiner Freizeit?*
– *Ich lese.*

8 – *Und du, was machst du in deiner Freizeit?*
– *Ich tanze.*

9 – *Was machst du in deiner Freizeit?*
– *Ich besuche meine Freunde.*

10 – *Und du, was machst du in deiner Freizeit?*
– *Ich spiele am Computer.*

11 – *Was machst du in deiner Freizeit?*
– *Ich spiele Gitarre.*

12 – *Hallo, was machst du in deiner Freizeit?*
– *Ich faulenze.*

ECHO-Tipp: Looking up the meaning of a verb 5.5

Practise examples with pupils – working out what the infinitive would be, in order to find it in the vocabulary list or a dictionary. You could also direct them to the vocabulary strategy on page 77.

3 Partnerarbeit. (AT 2/2) 1.4b/Y7

Speaking. In pairs, pupils practise the new vocabulary and question form using the pictures from exercise 1. They could then ask and answer the question for real, in pairs, groups, or as a class survey activity.

4 Hör zu. Was machen sie? (1–8) (AT 1/2) 1.1/Y7

Listening. Pupils note the hobbies mentioned, using the numbered pictures in exercise 1. Encourage weaker pupils to just focus on the hobby words themselves, and tell them that some speakers will say more than one hobby.

25

1 – *Was machst du in deiner Freizeit?*
– *Ich gehe ins Kino.*

2 – *Und du? Was machst du in deiner Freizeit?*
– *Ähm … ich faulenze!*

3 – *Hallo. Was machst du in deiner Freizeit?*
– *Ich besuche meine Freunde.*

4 – *Besuchst du auch deine Freunde in deiner Freizeit?*
– *Nein. Ich spiele am Computer.*

5 – *Und was machst du?*
– *Ich höre Musik und ich lese gern.*

6 – *Hallo, was machst du in deiner Freizeit?*
– *Ich gehe gern in die Stadt und ich fahre Rad.*

7 – *Was machst du in deiner Freizeit?*
– *Ich spiele gern Gitarre und ich sehe fern.*

8 – *Und du? Was machst du in deiner Freizeit?*
– *Ich gehe in den Jugendklub und ich tanze gern.*

Answers
1 1 **2** 12 **3** 9 **4** 10 **5** 6, 7 **6** 3, 4
7 11, 5 **8** 2, 8

Starter 2 5.2

Aim

To recap and consolidate spellings of the hobby vocabulary (*ich* forms only).

Copy these six hobby phrases with vowels missing onto the board or an OHT. Set a time limit for pupils to write out the phrases correctly. Pairs then correct each other's work and award a mark out of six – they must focus on accuracy, including umlauts and capital letters for nouns. Reveal the answers so that they can double check.

ch spl Gtrr	*(Ich spiele Gitarre)*
ch gh grn ns Kn	*(Ich gehe gern ins Kino)*
ch ls grn	*(Ich lese gern)*
ch hr grn Msk	*(Ich höre gern Musik)*
ch tnz grn	*(Ich tanze gern)*
ch spl m Cmptr	*(Ich spiele am Computer)*

5 Lies den Text und füll die Tabelle aus. (AT 3/3) 2.2a/Y7

Reading. Pupils read the text, which includes third person singular forms of the hobby verbs, and decide which pictures apply to Anja and which to Karl.

Answers
Anja – b, e, f   Karl – c, d, a

ECHO-Detektiv: Irregular verbs

4.5a/Y7

This panel shows pupils how three useful hobby-related verbs change their stem vowels in the second and third person singular forms. Ask pupils to pick out examples of these from Anja's text. There is further practice of regular and irregular verbs on **Arbeitsblatt 4.2**.

\+ More able learners could also write or say 'leisure' sentences about a partner to practise the three irregular verbs.

Aussprache: a/ä 4.1/Y7

Go over these two sounds with the class before they tackle exercise 6.

6 Hör zu. Ist das „a" oder „ä"? (1–5) (AT 1/) 4.1/Y7

Listening. Pupils identify which of the two sounds they hear in each case. You may wish to write the words on the board without umlauts, and ask a group of pupils to come to the front and fill in an umlaut where they think they have heard one.

26

1. *fahre*
2. *fährst*
3. *Vater*
4. *fährt*
5. *Äpfel*

7 Schreib sechs Fragen. (AT4/2) 4.6a/Y7

Writing. Pupils find the correct picture to complete each question, then choose the relevant word in order to write the question out in full.

Answers
1. Siehst du gern **fern**?
2. Liest du gern **Bücher**?
3. Spielst du gern **Gitarre**?
4. Fährst du gern **Rad**?
5. Hörst du gern **Musik**?
6. Gehst du gern ins **Kino**?

\+ Pupils could use these or similar questions to interview a partner or conduct a class survey. Remind them about the use of *gern* and *nicht gern*.

ECHO-Detektiv: Asking questions

4.6a/Y7

This reminds pupils that the subject and verb change places when you are asking a question. **Arbeitsblatt 4.4** provides further practice of this.

8 Beantworte die sechs Fragen. 4.4/Y7

Writing. Pupils write their own answers to the six questions in the previous task. Encourage longer answers, and the use of connectives. Those who have done the extension task could write answers about their interviewee, using *er / sie*.

Plenary 4.6a/Y7

Aim

To consolidate questions and answers about free time, and to improve fluency.

Play 'throw and catch' around the class using a soft toy or ball. Throw it to a pupil and ask him/her a question about free time activities. The pupil answers and throws the ball back to you. Use a range of questions depending on pupils' ability, e.g. *Was machst du in deiner Freizeit? Spielst du gern Hockey? Liest du gern?*. After a few turns, pupils follow their answers with a question to another pupil, with the aim of getting everyone involved. To support weaker pupils, elicit some example questions before starting, and write them on the board.

3 Lieblingssachen

Learning targets

- Talking about your favourite things
- Using *sein* (his) and *ihr* (her)

Key framework objectives

5.8 Strategies – evaluating and improving

Grammar

Possessive adjectives: *sein(e) / ihr(e)*

Key language

Was ist …?
dein(e)
mein(e)
sein(e)
ihr(e)
Lieblingsauto
Lieblingsfarbe
Lieblingshaustier
Lieblingsmannschaft
Lieblingsmusik
Lieblingssendung
Lieblingssport
Lieblingszahl

High-frequency words

was?
ist
mein
dein
sein
ihr

Pronunciation

Saying long words in German

English

Possessive adjectives

ICT

Word-process text about hobbies with illustrations from the Internet

Resources

CD 2, tracks 27–29
Workbooks A and B, p. 34
Echo Elektro 1 TPP, Mod 4 3.1–3.4

Starter 1 **3.1/Y7**

Aim

To find out what pupils know about some popular aspects of everyday life in German-speaking countries.

Tell the class that today's lesson will be about people's favourite things. Give small groups three minutes to brainstorm ideas of what German-speaking young people might say is their favourite in each of the categories below (i.e. what German-related names do they know in each category?). Start by eliciting the meanings of the categories, perhaps by giving examples. With a weaker class, you may prefer to give the categories in English.

Auto	*Sendung*
Mannschaft	*Musik*

Discuss their answers, and which ones are likely to be similar to their own (e.g. T.V. programme, car). If there was a category for which they could think of no ideas at all (possibly music), why do they think that is?

1 Hör zu und lies. **2.1/Y7**

Listening/Reading. Pupils read and listen to the cartoon about favourite things. Afterwards, ask for a volunteer to explain what it was about.

CD 27

– *Mein Lieblingssport ist Fuzball.*
Mein Lieblingshaustier is eine Katze.
Mein Lieblingsauto ist ein Porsche.
Meine Lieblingsmusik ist Beethoven.
Meine Lieblingsfarbe ist Schwarz.
Meine Lieblingsmannschaft ist Bayern München.
Meine Lieblingszahl ist dreizehn.
– *Und was ist deine Lieblingssendung?*
– *Meine Lieblingssendung ist „Tom und Jerry".*

2 Was sagt Maxi Maus? (AT 3/2) **4.2/Y7**

Reading. Pupils find the details of favourite things from the cartoon. This could be followed by oral questions to pupils about their own favourite things.

Answers

1 Porsche	**4** Schwarz
2 Bayern München	**5** Katze
3 dreizehn	**6** Tom und Jerry

Aussprache: Saying long German words

Use this panel, and listening exercise 3, to help pupils feel more confident about 'having a go' at saying longer words, which can appear daunting.

3 Hör zu und zähl die Silben. (1–4) (AT1/) 4.1/Y7

Listening. Encouraging pupils to focus on the number of syllables in these longer words will remind them to pronounce every part of such words. After listening, get pupils to chant the words, clearly pronouncing every syllable. The first syllable is usually stressed.

1 *Lieblingsmannschaft*
2 *Lieblingsfarbe*
3 *Lieblingssendung*
4 *Lieblingszahl*

\+ You could write other long German words on the board (not necessarily familiar ones), building up the number of syllables. Set pupils the challenge of pronouncing each one as correctly as possible. You could start with *Schwarz-wäld-er-kirsch-tor-te*, writing it on the board a syllable at a time until the pupils are saying the whole word.

4 Partnerarbeit: Interviews über Lieblingssachen. (AT 2/2) 1.4a/Y7

Speaking. Pupils interview each other about favourite things. This could be developed into a group or whole class survey (limit the number of questions to be asked). If not already discussed, ask for a volunteer to explain when *mein* and *meine* are used.

\+ Pupils note the answers given and write up an interview from their notes as a follow-up task.

5 Sieh dir die Bilder an. Schreib ein Interview mit Fritz Faulenzer oder Selma Sportlich. (AT 4/3) 2.4b/Y7

Writing. Pupils use the information in the illustrations to write relevant questions and the correct answers in interview form. You could also make use of these illustrations for work on *sein* and *ihr* later. Pupils could use dictionaries to help them look up new vocabulary.

ICT As a homework task, pupils could write about and illustrate their own favourite things, perhaps using a DTP package and importing relevant pictures from the Internet.

Starter 2 4.6a/Y7

Aim

To revise questions and answers about favourite things, from the previous lesson.

Tell pupils they are going to find out how well they know others in the class. Write any five questions about favourite things on the board (the class could choose them). Working with a different partner from last lesson, pupils write down what they think his/her answers will be to each. Then pairs interview each other to see how many of these guesses are correct, and award each other marks out of five.

ECHO-Detektiv: sein = *his*, ihr = *her*

Look at this panel with the class, either before or after listening to exercise 6. You may want to focus on the meanings of the two words, rather than on the different endings.

6 Hör zu. Sein oder ihr? (1–5) (AT 1/1) 1.1/Y7

Listening. Pupils listen for the words *sein* and *ihr* in the statements. Before listening, you could write the first one on the board, and elicit the meaning of *ihr* from pupils. At this stage, the difference between *ihr* and *ihre* is not vital – although you may wish to ask a more able group to pick this out, too.

1 *Das ist Nina. Ihre Lieblingsmannschaft ist Borussia Dortmund.*
2 *Und hier ist Julia. Ihre Lieblingsfarbe ist Gelb.*
3 *Das ist Viktor. Sein Lieblingshaustier ist ein Hund.*
4 *Und das ist Peter. Sein Lieblingssport ist Schwimmen.*
5 *Das ist Stefanie. Ihr Lieblingsauto ist ein Volkswagen.*

Answers
1 ihr **2** ihr **3** sein **4** sein **5** ihr

7 Lies die Sätze. Niklas oder Marie? Mach zwei Gruppen. (AT 3/3) 2.1/Y7

Reading. Pupils sort the sentences according to whether they are about Niklas or Marie, by looking for the relevant pronoun or possessive adjective. They could then write out the sentences, in logical order, to form a paragraph about each character.

Answers
Niklas: 3, 5, 6, 8 Marie: 1, 2, 4, 7

R Pupils refer back to the pictures of Fritz Faulenzer or Selma Sportlich (exercise 5), and write sentences about them using *er* and *sie*, *sein* and *ihr*.

\+ Pupils create a poster about a famous person's favourite things (using *sein* / *ihr*).

Suggestion

To help less confident learners consolidate their understanding of the possessive adjectives learnt so far, give groups of pupils a limited time to prepare and practise a short and simple 'rap', using only the line *mein*, *dein*, *sein*, *ihr* (with gestures etc. to make their meanings clear). Groups then perform to the class.

Plenary Mini-Test 5.8

Aim

To review language learned to date and identify areas for improvement.

Pupils work in pairs to check the language they have learned so far in this chapter, using the **Mini-Test** checklist. Ask pupils which points their partners found most difficult. Give pupils the task of improving those points by next lesson. Partners could then test them again.

4 Brieffreunde

Learning targets

- Saying how often you do things
- Learning how to write a letter to a penfriend

Key framework objectives

2.3/Y7 Reading – text features
2.4/Y7 Writing – (a) sentences and texts as models

Grammar

Adverbs of frequency
wir with regular verbs

Key language

Wie oft … spielst du Fußball? / gehst du schwimmen? / spielst du am Computer? / siehst du fern? / liest du ein Buch? / fährst du Rad?
jeden Tag
(ein)mal pro Woche
am Wochenende
nie
Liebe(r)
Danke für deinen Brief
Schreib bald
Dein(e)

High-frequency words

ich
du
ist
wir
auch
wie?
oft
jeden
nie
einmal
zweimal
dreimal
pro
am
für
dein
spielen

ICT

Word-process or DTP a letter

English

Letter-writing conventions

Resources

CD 2, tracks 30–32
Workbooks A and B, p. 35
Arbeitsblatt 4.5, p. 61
Echo Elektro 1 TPP, Mod 4 4.1–4.7

Starter 1 1.1/Y7

Aim
To revise leisure activities in preparation for the tasks in this unit.

Play *Simon sagt:* say sports/leisure activity phrases to the class, who have to instantly mime them, as long as the instruction is prefaced with *Simon sagt*. Anybody who gets it wrong or doesn't know what to mime, sits down, until only three are left – the winners. Phrases could include *du / er / sie*.

1 Hör zu und lies. 1.1/Y7

Listening/Reading. Pupils listen to the recording and look at the pictures and text.

CD 30

1 – *Nina, wie oft spielst du Fußball?*
– *Ich spiele nie Fußball.*

2 – *Julia, wie oft spielst du Fußball?*
– *Ich spiele dreimal pro Woche Fußball.*

3 – *Wie oft spielst du Fußball, Peter?*
– *Ich spiele jeden Tag Fußball.*

4 – *Und Stefanie, wie oft spielst du Fußball?*
– *Ich spiele am Wochenende Fußball.*

5 – *Und wie oft spielst du Fußball, Viktor?*
– *Ich spiele einmal pro Woche Fußball.*

2 Wer ist das? (AT 3/2) 2.1/Y7

Reading. Pupils look again at how often each character plays football, and identify which line of the grid represents each one.

Answers
a Peter **b** Stefanie **c** Julia **d** Nina **e** Viktor

3 Hör zu und mach Notizen. (1–6) (AT 1/3) 1.1/Y7

Listening. Pupils listen to the recording and make brief notes to show the hobbies and frequencies mentioned. Make sure weaker learners focus specifically on the hobbies mentioned, and then on the frequency – play the recording twice.

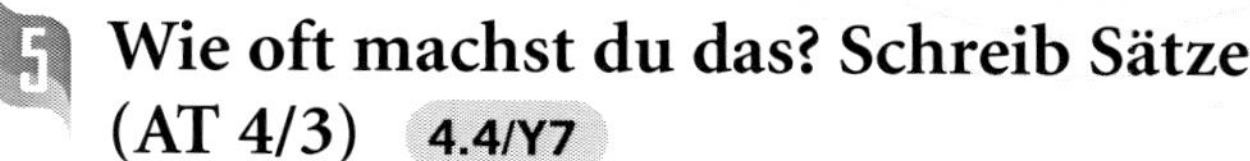

31

1 – *Was machst du in deiner Freizeit?*
– *Ich gehe schwimmen.*
– *Schwimmen? Toll! Wie oft gehst du schwimmen?*
– *Ich gehe zweimal pro Woche schwimmen.*

2 – *Was machst du in deiner Freizeit?*
– *Ich fahre Rad.*
– *Und wie oft fährst du Rad?*
– *Ich fahre am Wochenende Rad.*

3 – *Was machst du in deiner Freizeit?*
– *Ich sehe gern fern.*
– *Fernsehen. Gut. Wie oft siehst du fern?*
– *Ähm ... ich sehe jeden Tag fern. Meine Mutter findet das furchtbar!*

4 – *Was machst du in deiner Freizeit?*
– *Ich gehe reiten.*
– *Reiten? Das ist klasse! Wie oft gehst du reiten?*
– *Ich gehe dreimal pro Woche reiten. Meine Schwester hat ein Pferd.*

5 – *Hallo. Gehst du auch in deiner Freizeit reiten?*
– *Ähm, nein. Ich hore Musik.*
– *Ist das Popmusik?*
– *Ja.*
– *Und wie oft hörst du Musik?*
– *Jeden Tag. Das ist mein Lieblingshobby.*

6 – *Und du? Was machst du in deiner Freizeit?*
– *Ich spiele gern Tennis und Federball.*
– *Sehr gut. Du bist also sehr sportlich. Wie oft machst du das?*
– *Ich spiele am Wochenende Tennis, und einmal pro Woche spiele ich Federball.*

Answers

1 schwimmen, zeimal pro Woche
2 Rad fahren, am Wochenende
3 fernsehen, jeden Tag
4 reiten, dreimal pro Woche
5 Musik hören, jeden Tag
6 Tennis, am Wochenende; Federball, einmal pro Woche

4 Partnerarbeit. (AT 2/3) 1.4a/Y7

Speaking. Pairs ask and answer questions about frequency of leisure activities. Start by pointing out the examples of questions that could be asked in the Key Language box (which is revision from Units 1 and 2). Less confident learners could keep to sports and hobbies that use *spielen* and *gehen.*

Suggestion

This task could be developed into a class survey, with pupils selecting a single question, or a list of questions, to ask, and recording results in their books.

5 Wie oft machst du das? Schreib Sätze. (AT 4/3) 4.4/Y7

Writing. Pupils write sentences to say how often they do each of the given activities, selecting the correct phrase for each from the Key Language box and inserting a frequency expression. At this point you could draw pupils' attention to the adverb of frequency coming immediately after the verb.

+ Those who finish quickly could write additional sentences of their own, perhaps including extra information (places, opinions). They could also check each other's work.

Starter 2 5.4 5.7

Aim

To use prior knowledge of context as preparation for reading a letter in German.

Write the following (mostly familiar) items from Viktor's letter (p. 67) on the board or an OHT. Tell the class that these words come from something they will be looking at this lesson, and ask what it is. Give pupils 20 seconds to put the words in the most logical order (before having seen the letter). Discuss why they know how to do this.

Viktor
D-35921 Rotesheim, den 23. März
dein Viktor
Wie geht's?
Lieber James
Schreib bald!

6 Hör zu und lies den Brief von Viktor. 2.2a/Y7 2.3/Y7

Listening/Reading. Before you play the recording, pupils take a first look at the letter and tell you what they can about its purpose, audience and content. Clarify that this is a postal letter rather than an email. Is it the first contact he has had with James? They then listen to the recording and read through the letter.

32

Rotesheim, den 23. März
Lieber James,
danke für deinen Brief. Wie geht's?
Ich spiele gern Fußball. Meine Lieblingsmannschaft ist Dynamo Dresden. Sie spielen gut!
Meine Cousine spielt jeden Tag Basketball, aber das finde ich langweilig! Wir spielen am Wochenende Tischtennis.
Ich faulenze gern! Ich sehe auch jeden Tag fern. Meine Lieblingssendung heißt „Sportschau“.

Hast du eine Lieblingssendung? Ich besuche zweimal pro Woche meine Freunde.
Was machst du gern in deiner Freizeit?
Schreib bald!
Dein Viktor

7 Finde diese Wörter in Viktors Brief. (AT 3/4) 5.4

Reading. Pupils find the German for useful letter phrases in the text, using prior knowledge and context. When discussing the answers, you may wish to show by example the changes to *lieber / liebe* and *dein / deine* according to gender.

Answers
Dear = *Lieber*
Thank you for your letter = *Danke für deinen Brief*
Write soon = *Schreib bald*
Yours = *Dein*

ECHO-Detektiv: Saing 'we' in German 5.1

This formalises for pupils the verb ending after *wir*.

8 Was passt zusammen? (AT 3/4) 4.4/Y7

Reading. Pupils match the sentence halves about the content of Viktor's letter.

Answers
1 e **2** c **3** b **4** a **5** d

9 Schreib einen Brief an Viktor. Beantworte seine Fragen. (AT 4/4) 2.4a/Y7 5.7

Writing. Pupils write their own letter to an imaginary penfriend, using Viktor's as a model. Firstly discuss what types of information to include, and whether it is a first or later letter. For those in need of more support, a writing frame is available on **Arbeitsblatt 4.5.** This may be a suitable point to take up contact with real penfriends in a German-speaking country and send pupils' letters.

ICT Letters could be word-processed or desktop published, perhaps with illustrations, for display.

Plenary 2.3/Y7

Aim

To review German letter-writing conventions, and useful letter phrases.

Discuss letter-writing in German. Ask pupils to come up with two key elements to remember, e.g. *liebe(r), dein(e),* and two differences in the way German addresses are written, e.g. house number after street name; postcode in front of place name. Ask them to write down their key facts.

5 Möchtest du ins Kino gehen?

Learning targets

- Arranging to go out and when to meet
- Using *möchtest du ...* ? (would you like ...?) with an infinitive

Key framework objectives

2.1/Y7 Reading – main points and detail

Grammar

Möchtest du? + infinitive
Introduction to *in* + accusative

Key language

Hast du am ... Zeit?
Donnerstag / Freitag / Samstag / Sonntag
Möchtest du ...
Fußball / Tennis / Basketball / Cricket spielen?
in die Stadt / in die Disko / in den Jugendklub / ins Kino gehen?
Ja, gern.
Ja, das mag ich.
Nein, das mag ich nicht.
Nein, das ist langweilig.
Wann treffen wir uns?
Um ... Uhr
Bis dann / Bis Samstag

High-frequency words

hast du?
möchtest du?
spielen
gehen
in
ins
ja
nein
gern
ich mag
nicht
wann?
um
bis
dann
wir

Pronunciation

o/ö

Mathematics

Digital time

Resources

CD2, tracks 33–35
Workbooks A and B, p. 36
Echo Elektro 1 TPP, Mod 4 5.1–5.6

Starter 1 4.2/Y7

Aim

To practise vocabulary for accepting or declining invitations.

Start by inviting the class to do different things using *Möchtest du ...*? Pupils stand to show that they would like to take up the invitation or remain sitting if they don't want to do that activity, depending on whether they want to take up the invitation or not. After a while, you could introduce the following responses:

Ja, gern.
Ja, das mag ich.
Nein, danke, das ist langweilig.
Nein, das mag ich nicht.

Encourage pupils to repeat one of them after an invitation. The rest of the class should listen to see if the response corresponds with whether or not that pupil is standing or sitting.

1 Hör zu und lies 2.1/Y7

Listening/Reading. Before playing the recording, tell the class that you will want to know afterwards what it is about. Pupils listen and follow the dialogue in their books.

33

– *Hallo Peter. Hast du am Samstag Zeit? Möchtest du Fußball spielen?*
– *Nein, das mag ich nicht.*
– *Hm ... Möchtest du in die Disko gehen?*
– *Nein, danke, das ist langweilig!*
– *Möchtest du ins Kino gehen?*
– *Ja, gern!*
– *Wann treffen wir uns?*
– *Hm ... Um sieben Uhr?*
– *Ja, gut. Tschüs, bis Samstag!*

2 Finde Stefanies Frage für jede Antwort. (AT 3/3) 4.6a/Y7

Reading. Pupils scan through the dialogue in order to find the question that goes with each of four answers. Elicit the meanings of the questions and answers.

Answers
1 Möchtest du ins Kino gehen?
2 Möchtest du in die Disko gehen?
3 Möchtest du Fußball spielen?
4 Wann treffen wir uns?

ECHO-Detektiv: Möchtest du ... ? = *Would you like ... ?* 4.6a/Y7

Pupils could practise this question form by pretending to ask you out – encourage more confident learners to demonstrate possible questions. You could start by revealing questions with the infinitives missing, and asking pupils to supply them.

Aussprache: o / ö 4.1/Y7

Check this panel briefly with pupils before doing exercise 3.

3 Hör zu. Is das „o“ oder „ö“? (1–5) (AT 1/) 4.1/Y7

Listening. Pupils note down which sound each of the words has. You could then display the words on the board/OHT, and chorus them with the class. You may wish initially to show pupils all the words, without any umlauts, and get them to add an umlaut where they have heard one.

34

1 *möchtest*
2 *hör zu*
3 *rot*
4 *zwölf*
5 *orange*

Answers
1 ö 2 ö 3 o 4 ö 5 o

Suggestion

Use this, or a similar, tongue twister for further practice of the two sounds:

Oma möchte zwölf rote Hosen.

4 Partnerarbeit: Mach vier Dialoge. (AT 2/3) 1.4a/Y7

Speaking. Pupils work in pairs. They practise just the first part of arranging to go out – when to meet will be introduced later. Encourage them to turn down their partner's first few suggestions, and to use the full range of language in the Key Language box. They could work with a number of different partners.

Starter 2 4.1/Y7

Aim

To practise key sounds from the language of this unit.

Write some or all of these tongue twisters on the board or an OHT. Start by practising them with the whole class, to clarify any punctuation issues. Pairs can then work together to refine their accuracy and speed. Afterwards, ask for volunteers to demonstrate their skills to the class.

Am vierten November wird Vati vierundvierzig.
Monika möchte mit Michael Musik machen.
Hast du um zwanzig vor zwölf Zeit?
Susi spricht Spanisch und spielt in der Sporthalle.
Möchtest du Öl aus Österreich?

5 Hör zu und füll die Tabelle aus. (1–3) (AT 1/4) 1.1/Y7

Listening. Pupils listen to the recording and note brief answers in German to show the day, activity and time of each arrangement heard. Remind them to focus on picking out the details needed, and not to worry about extra words. Answers can firstly be jotted down in abbreviated form. Less confident learners could listen for just one specific item each time the audio is repeated.

35

1 – *Hallo, Viktor. Hast du am Samstag Zeit?*
– *Möchtest du Fußball spielen?*
– *Ja, gern.*
– *Wann treffen wir uns?*
– *Um zehn Uhr?*
– *Ja, gut. Tschüs, bis Samstag.*
– *Tschüs.*

2 – *Hallo, Julia. Hast du am Freitag Zeit? Möchtest du in die Disko gehen?*
– *Ja, das mag ich!*
– *Wann treffen wir uns?*

- *Um sechs Uhr dreißig?*
- *Ja, prima. Bis dann.*
- *Tschüs, bis dann.*

3
- *Hallo Nina, wie geht's?*
- *Gut, danke. Und dir?*
- *Auch gut, danke. Hast du am Sonntag Zeit? Möchtest du in die Stadt gehen?*
- *Nein, das ist langweilig.*
- *Möchtest du Tennis spielen?*
- *Ja, gern!*
- *Wann treffen wir uns? Um elf Uhr?*
- *Ja, gut. Bis Sonntag um elf Uhr.*
- *Tschüs, bis dann.*

Answers

1	Sa. Fußball	10.00
2	Fr. Disko	6.30
3	So. Tennis	11.00

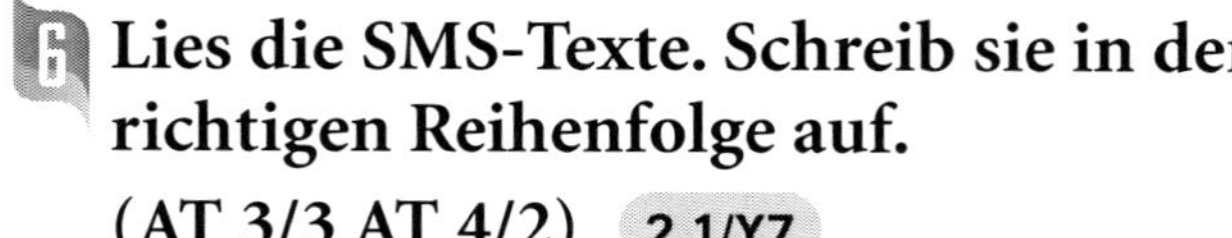

6 Lies die SMS-Texte. Schreib sie in der richtigen Reihenfolge auf. (AT 3/3 AT 4/2) 2.1/Y7

Reading. Pupils work out the correct order of the text messages, and write them out.

Answers

e Hi! Möchtest du am Samstag in die Stadt gehen?
c Nein, das ist langweilig.
a Hm, okay. Möchtest du schwimmen gehen?
g Ja, gern!
b Wann treffen wir uns?
f Um elf Uhr?
d Tschüs, bis dann!

7 Schreib Dialog 1 oder 2 und lern ihn auswendig. Du kannst ihn in der Klasse vortragen. (AT 4/4) 2.4b/Y7

Writing. Pupils use the prompts given to write a dialogue for making arrangements to go out. Remind them to use the Key Language boxes and examples in the unit for support. Pairs could then rehearse and perform one of their dialogues to the class – encourage appropriate expression, and the use of extra words and opinons.

Plenary 5.1

Aim

To focus on the difference between *ich möchte* and *ich mag.*

Write the two sentences below on the board or an OHT. Ask for volunteers to translate them, and elicit the difference between the two forms of the same irregular verb, *mögen.* Have they heard of the conditional? Then give them pairs of sentences (e.g. I like tennis, I'd like to play tennis) to translate into (or from) German.

Ich mag Pommes.
Ich möchte Pommes essen.

6 Abenteuer im Freien

Learning targets

- Understanding information about an adventure sports centre
- Using *man kann* to say what activities there are

Key framework objectives

4.5/Y7 Language – (b) modal verbs

Grammar

man kann + infinitive

Key language

Man kann …
Kann man … ?
Ich mag …
Basketball spielen
Kanu fahren
klettern
Mountainbike fahren
schwimmen
segeln
Tennis spielen
Tischtennis spielen
Volleyball spielen
Wildwasser fahren
windsurfen

High-frequency words

ich
mag
man
kann
fahren
spielen

English

Letters of enquiry

Resources

CD 2, track 36
Workbooks A and B, p. 37
Echo Elektro 1 TPP, Mod 4 6.1–6.3

Starter 1

2.1/Y7 2.3/Y7

Aim

To encourage pupils to pay close attention when reading a text.

Memory test: give pupils 30 seconds to look at the *Abenteuerzentrum* webpage on page 70. Tell them you will be testing their memory of what they have seen. When they have closed their books, ask them about the text. What kind of text was it? How do they know? What is it advertising? Who might it be aimed at? What German words can they remember for activities available at the centre? Collate their answers on the board, then pupils open their books to check.

1 Finde die richtigen Wörter für die Fotos. (AT 3/1) 2.1/Y7

Reading. Pupils find the correct word for each photo on the webpage. They should look up any they cannot guess. A more confident class could do exercises 1 and 2, then listening exercise 3, before any discussion of the meanings of the words.

Answers

1 schwimmen
2 segeln
3 Wildwasser fahren
4 Kanu fahren
5 klettern
6 windsurfen
7 Mountainbike fahren

2 Sport im Abenteuerzentrum Spitzberg. Mach drei Listen. (AT 3/2) 4.2/Y7

Writing. Pupils now use all the sports vocabulary from the text, building three categories of sports. Use listening exercise 3 to check their answers. Ask pupils how putting words into these kinds of category makes them easier to learn. For further exploitation of this activity, see Mime activities on page 9.

Answers

Alltagssport	*Bergsport*	*Wassersport*
Tennis	Mountainbike fahren	Wildwasser fahren
Basketball	klettern	Kanu fahren
Tischtennis		schwimmen
Volleyball		segeln
		windsurfen

3 Hör zu und überprüfe es. (AT 1/4) 1.1/Y7

Listening. Pupils listen to see if they have put the sports from the webpage under the correct headings (in any order). Remind them to listen out for the key words needed, and pause the recording between each of the three sections. Pupils award themselves a mark out of 10. If you have not already done so, elicit the meanings of the headings and new sports words.

Was kann man im Abenteuerzentrum Spitzberg machen? In der Sporthalle treiben wir Alltagssport: Man kann Tennis spielen, Tischtennis spielen und auch Volleyball oder Basketball spielen.

36

Dann haben wir auch Bergsport mit Abenteuer in den Bergen! Man kann Mountainbike fahren und klettern.

Es gibt auch Wassersport. Man kann Wildwasser fahren. Man kann auch Kanu fahren, schwimmen, segeln und windsurfen.

ECHO-Detektiv: Man kann ... (*one can / people can ...*) 4.5b/Y7

After looking at this grammar panel with pupils, you could give them further sentences using this structure to translate from German to English.

4 Partnerarbeit: Stell Fragen über das Abenteuerzentrum Spitzberg. (AT 2/3–4) 1.4b/Y7 4.5b/Y7

Speaking. Pairs use the pictures as prompts for questions and answers about the sports available.

Starter 2

4.5b/Y7

Aim

To reinforce *man kann* plus infinitive.

Divide the class into three teams across the room, and allocate one of the three locations below to each group. Read out the ten statements, and perhaps other similar ones, with a pause between each. When pupils hear an activity that is done in their team's location, they must quickly stand up, then sit down again. If any team member is slow to stand up, that team loses a life (give each team three lives). The winning group is that with the most lives left at the end.

Kantine
Sporthalle
Berge

Hier kann man Tennis spielen.
Hier kann man Volleyball lernen.
Hier kann man Orangensaft trinken.
Hier kann man Mountainbike fahren.
Hier kann man Volleyball spielen.
Hier kann man klettern.
Hier kann man Kekse essen.
Hier kann man Basketball spielen.
Hier kann man wandern.
Hier kann man Chips essen.

5 Lies den Brief. Was ist das auf Deutsch? (AT 3/3) 5.4

Reading. Pupils look through Stefanie's letter and pick out the German phrases to match the English translations given. Before they do so, elicit first impressions of the type and content of this text.

Answers
1. Sehr geehrte Damen und Herren!
2. Können Sie mir bitte helfen?
3. Ich mag Mountainbike fahren.
4. Kann man auch Kanu fahren?
5. Ich klettere sehr gern.
6. Danke schön.

Suggestion 5.3

Write the words *du* and *Sie* on the board. Elicit what the class think the difference in their meanings might be. (*Sie* is briefly used in the letter of enquiry, although it has not yet been formally taught.) Have they heard of this in any other language? Pupils could suggest specific situations where they think *Sie* would be used. With an able group, discuss possible advantages and disadvantages of having more than one word for 'you'.

6 Schreib einen Brief ans Abenteuerzentrum Spitzberg. (AT 4/3–4) 2.4b/Y7

Writing. Pupils write a similar letter of enquiry. Less confident learners can follow the writing frame given in the Pupil's Book; others should be encouraged to add extra sentences of their own, including further opinions.

Plenary

4.2/Y7

Aim

To review the language for adventure activities.

Charades: ask a volunteer to mime one of the activities mentioned on the webpage in this unit. The rest of the class guess the activity (*Kann man Kanu fahren*? or just *Kanu fahren*, depending on ability). The pupil who guesses correctly does the next mime, or nominates someone else. This could be played as a timed team game. You may wish to allow pupils to refer to their books. Finally, you could ask pupils which of the words they have been miming are cognates.

Lernzieltest und Wiederholung

Lernzieltest 5.8

This is a checklist of language covered in Chapter 4. Pupils can work with the checklist in pairs to check what they have learned. Points which directly address grammar and structures are marked with a G. There is a **Lernzieltest** sheet in the Resource and Assessment File (page 65). Encourage pupils to look back at the chapter and to use the grammar section to revise what they are unclear about.

You can also use the **Lernzieltest** as an end-of-chapter plenary.

Wiederholung

This is a revision page to prepare pupils for the **Kontrolle** at the end of the chapter.

Resources

CD 2, track 37

1 Hör zu. Wer ist das? (1–5) (AT1/2) 1.1/Y7

Listening. Pupils listen and match each statement heard to the correct picture.

37

1 – *Was ist dein Lieblingssport?*
– *Mein Lieblingssport ist Schwimmen.*

2 – *Und du, was ist dein Lieblingssport?*
– *Mein Lieblingssport ist Federball.*

3 – *Und du, was ist dein Lieblingssport?*
– *Mein Lieblingssport ist Fußball.*

4 – *Und du, was ist dein Lieblingssport?*
– *Mein Lieblingssport ist Tennis.*

5 – *Und du, was ist dein Lieblingssport?*
– *Mein Lieblingssport is Angeln.*

Answers
1 Thomas **2** Birgit **3** Elke **4** Sabine **5** Jakob

2 Partnerarbeit: Was machst du gern? (AT2/2) 1.4b/Y7

Speaking. Pupils practise dialogues to revise leisure vocabulary with *gern* and identify the correct pictures.

3 Macht Lisa das gern (✓) oder nicht gern (✗)? (AT3/4) 2.1/Y7

Reading. Pupils read the letter to find out whether Lisa likes or dislikes each activity.

Answers
1 ✓ 2 ✗ 3 ✓ 4 ✓ 5 ✓ 6 ✗

4 Schreib die Sätze auf. (AT4/2) 2.4a/Y7

Writing. Pupils identify individual statements in the 'word snake', and copy them out correctly. Encourage pupils to check for capital letters.

Answers
Ich spiele gern Volleyball.
Er geht gern schwimmen.
Sie hört gern Musik.
Ich sehe gern fern.
Ich gehe gern reiten.

5 Beantworte Lisas drei Fragen. (AT4/2–3) 2.4a/Y7

Writing. Pupils identify the three questions in the letter of exercise 3, and write their own answers to them.

Learning targets

- Reading a letter about plans for next week
- Making plans to go out next week

Key framework objectives

2.2/Y7 Reading – (b) text selection
3.1/Y7 Culture – aspects of everyday life
4.5/Y7 Language – (a) future using present tense

Grammar

Present tense to talk about close future (receptive)
Verb as second idea (revision)
Möchtest du (+ infinitive)? (revision)

High-frequency words

am
bis
dann
gehen
gern
haben
möchtest du?
sein
spielen
wann?
was?
wie?

English

Letters of enquiry

Resources

CD 2, tracks 38–39
Workbooks A and B, p. 38
Arbeitsblatt 4.6, p. 62

Starter 1 **2.2a/Y7**

Aim

To practise a two-staged approach to reading a longer text – firstly scanning for gist, purpose and difficulty; then focusing on the meanings of individual words.

Vocabulary search: ask pupils to have a preliminary look at Julia's letter for 30 seconds. Ask them what type of text it is, who it is to and from, and for the gist of what each paragraph is about. Then read out the following list of English words, some of which they may already know in German. After each one, pupils search through the letter to find its German equivalent, write it on a piece of paper or a mini-whiteboard, and hold it up – accept only correctly spelt versions, with capital letters for nouns. Award points to the first five (or more) correct answers each time (pupils could win points for a team or as individuals).

plans	*Pläne*
until	*bis*
the 30th of March	*den 30. März*
visit	*Besuch*
new	*neu(en)*
next	*nächste*

1 Hör zu und lies. **2.2a+b/Y7 3.1/Y7 5.6**

Listening/Reading. Play the recording of Julia's letter, while pupils read along. They could then read the letter aloud in pairs – you may wish first to chorus the words with umlauts for practice.

38

Leipzig, den dreißigsten März
Liebe Nina,
wie geht's? Danke für deinen Brief. Ich habe große Pläne für deinen Besuch nächste Woche!
Am Montag gehen wir ins Kino. Möchtest du den neuen Film von Benjamin Braun sehen? Er ist bestimmt super! Am Dienstag spielen wir vielleicht Tennis. Ich spiele sehr gern Tennis, es ist mein Lieblingssport. Am Mittwoch besuchen wir Stefanie. Sie hat drei Haustiere – einen Goldfisch, einen Hund und ein Meerschweinchen. Am Donnerstag gehen wir in die Stadt.
Gehst du gern in die Disko? Am Freitag haben wir eine Disko im Jugendklub. Man kann tanzen, Tischtennis spielen und auch essen und trinken. Am Samstag gehen wir ins Konzert. Wir treffen Viktor und Peter um sieben Uhr.
Möchtest du am Sonntag faulenzen? Ich mag fernsehen. Meine Lieblingssendung, „Die Simpsons", ist am Sonntag um achtzehn Uhr! Auf Deutsch!
Bis Montag!
Deine
Julia

ECHO-Tipp: using the present tense to talk about future plans

4.5a/Y7

Before looking at exercise 2, you could discuss the fact that the present tense is being used to talk about the close future. (This will be more formally presented in Chapter 6.)

2 Was sind die Pläne? (AT3/3) 2.1/Y7

Reading. Pupils reread Julia's plans, and match the correct activity to each day.

Answers

Montag	c	Freitag	g
Dienstag	d	Samstag	e
Mittwoch	a	Sonntag	f
Donnerstag	b		

3 Beantworte die Fragen. (AT 3/4) 2.1/Y7

Reading. Pupils answer the comprehension questions about the letter in German. More able pupils could answer in full sentences.

Answers

1 den neuen Film von Benjamin Braun
2 Tennis
3 drei Haustiere – einen Goldfisch, einen Hund und ein Meerschweinchen
4 Man kann tanzen, Tischtennis spielen und auch essen und trinken.
5 um sieben Uhr
6 faulenzen

Starter 2 1.4a/Y7

Aim

To recap language for arranging to go out, in preparation for exercises 4 and 5.

Use a copy of **Arbeitsblatt 4.6**, a diary page, on an OHT. Cover it up. Divide the class into two teams. Explain that teams must find out on which night you are free next week, taking it in turns to ask *Möchtest du am (Montag) …?*. No team member may contribute more than once. Award one point for every correctly phrased question (reply *Nein, ich …* if you are not free), two points for the team which discovers the free night (reply *Ja, gern* and reveal your 'diary'), and finally, a bonus point if they can then continue the conversation to make an arrangement to meet you (fill in the time and activity on your OHT). If time allows, play again, using the second 'diary page' on the OHT.

4 Was sind deine Pläne nächste Woche? Du hast einen Tag frei. (AT 4/3) 4.4/Y7

Writing. In preparation for exercise 5, pupils write their own imaginary diary for next week, filling each day except one with a leisure phrase from earlier in this chapter. Make sure they do not all copy the example and leave Wednesday free. They can refer back to Units 1 and 2 for ideas. Quick finishers could add extra activities, still keeping one day free, until everyone is ready. You could use an OHT copy of **Arbeitsblatt 4.6** (see Starter 2) to demonstrate.

5 Gruppenarbeit: Wer hat am (Mittwoch) auch frei? Stell Fragen in der Klasse. (AT 2/4) 1.4b/Y7

Speaking. Pupils use the example dialogues as models and aim to fill the 'free' day in their diary. Use your OHT copy of **Arbeitsblatt 4.6** to demonstrate the procedure with volunteers. It will be most realistic if pupils move around the class until they find a person who is free on the same day as them, and then arrange what to do and when to meet, writing the details into their diary page. More confident pupils should be able to use greetings, opinions and other extra language of their own.

6 Hör zu und sing mit. 2.2a+b/Y7 2.3/Y7

This song may lend itself to singing with actions, or to the other suggestions for using songs, on page 9.

Meine Lieblingszahl ist vierzehn.
Deine Lieblingszahl ist zwei.
Seine Lieblingszahl ist zwanzig.
Ihre Lieblingszahl ist drei.

Farbe, Sport, Tier und Zahl,
Lieblingssachen überall.

Mein Lieblingssport ist Schwimmen.
Dein Lieblingssport ist Wandern.
Sein Lieblingssport ist Tennis.
Ihr Lieblingssport ist Angeln.

Farbe, Sport, Tier und Zahl.
Lieblingssachen überall.

Meine Lieblingsfarbe ist Orange.
Deine Lieblingsfarbe ist Blau.
Seine Lieblingsfarbe ist Lila.
Ihre Lieblingsfarbe ist Grau.

Farbe, Sport, Tier und Zahl.
Lieblingssachen überall.

Mein Lieblingshaustier ist eine Maus.
Dein Lieblingshaustier, eine Giraffe.
Sein Lieblingshaustier ist eine Schlange.
Ihr Lieblingshaustier ist ein Affe.

Farbe, Sport, Tier und Zahl
Lieblingssachen überall.

Plenary 5.8

Aim
To encourage pupils to evaluate and improve the quality of written work.

Spot the mistake: write several sentences containing language from this chapter on the board or an OHT. Depending on the level of the group, the sentences should each contain one or more mistakes. Pupils work alone or in pairs for five minutes to identify the mistakes in each sentence, and correct them. Discuss answers (get volunteers to come up to the front and circle the mistakes) and award points for mistakes spotted and corrections.

SELF-ACCESS READING AND WRITING AT TWO LEVELS

A Reinforcement

1 Was macht Matthias gern oder nicht gern? Schreib sechs Sätze. (AT4/2) 4.4/Y7

Writing. Pupils use the information in the picture of Matthias to build sentences about his leisure likes and dislikes.

Answers
(Six of these in any order)
Er spielt gern Tennis.
Er geht gern angeln.
Er spielt gern Fußball.
Er geht gern reiten.
Er geht gern schwimmen.
Er spielt nicht gern Hockey.
Er spielt nicht gern Rugby.
Er geht nicht gern wandern.

2 Wie ist es richtig? Schreib die Sätze richtig aus. (AT3/2 AT4/2) 4.4/Y7

Writing. Pupils rearrange the mixed-up endings of sentences about favourite things, and copy each one out so that it makes sense.

Answers
1 Meine Lieblingsfarbe ist **Grün**.
2 Mein Lieblingsauto ist ein **Mercedes**.
3 Meine Lieblingszahl ist **dreizehn**.
4 Meine Lieblingsmannschaft ist **Bayern München**.
5 Mein Lieblingshaustier ist eine **Katze**.
6 Meine Lieblingsmusik ist **Mozart**.

3 Was passt zusammen? (AT3/2) 4.6a/Y7

Reading. Pupils match each question to the correct answer.

Answers
1 b **2** d **3** e **4** c **5** a **6** f

4 Beantworte die Fragen. (AT4/2–3) 4.4/Y7

Writing. Pupils write their own answers to the six questions from the previous task.

B Extension

1 Wer mag was? Schreib die Tabelle ab und füll sie mit Häkchen (✓) aus. (AT3/4) 2.1/Y7 2.2a/Y7

Reading. Pupils read Anton's note and Karin's reply then copy and complete the grid to show who likes what.

Answers

	Anton	Karin
Die Simpsons	✓	
Fußball	✓	
Klassische Musik		✓
Windsurfen		✓
Der Jugendklub	✓	
Heavy Metal	✓	

2 Lies noch mal die Briefe aus Aufgabe 1. Schreib die Sätze ab und füll die Lücken aus. (AT3/4) 2.1/Y7

Reading. Pupils reread the letters in order to complete the sentences about Anton and Karin correctly. More able pupils should refer to the support box only to check their answers.

Answers
1 **Anton** spielt **Fußball** in der Schulmannschaft.
2 Karin **geht** gern am Wochenende windsurfen **und** Kanu fahren.
3 Anton ist sehr **schüchtern** in der **Schule.**
4 Karin ist zu **alt** für den Jugendklub.
5 Anton **hört** gern **Heavy Metal** Musik.
6 **Karin** findet **Fußball** furchtbar.
7 Anton findet Karin **toll** und **lustig**.

3 Schreib einen Brief und eine Antwort. (AT4/3–4) 2.4b/Y7 2.5/Y7

Writing. Pupils invent their own scenario to write a note inviting somebody out, and either an enthusiastic acceptance, perhaps a more reluctant acceptance, or a rejection note in reply. Suggest using made-up names, or their own name plus the name of a famous person. Remind them to keep to language they know, and to use the notes they have read as models.

Übungsheft A, Seite 32

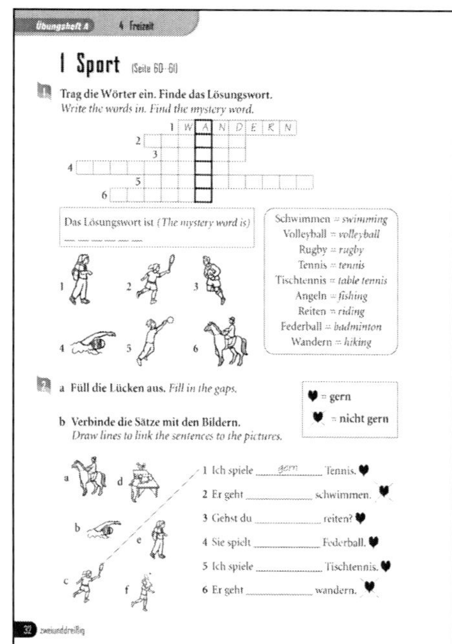
Übungsheft A 4 Freizeit

1 Sport (Seite 60–61)

1 Trag die Wörter ein. Finde das Lösungswort. *Write the words in. Find the mystery word.*

1 WANDERN

Das Lösungswort ist (*The mystery word is*) _ _ _ _ _ _

Schwimmen = *swimming*
Volleyball = *volleyball*
Rugby = *rugby*
Tennis = *tennis*
Tischtennis = *table tennis*
Angeln = *fishing*
Reiten = *riding*
Federball = *badminton*
Wandern = *hiking*

2 a Füll die Lücken aus. *Fill in the gaps.*

b Verbinde die Sätze mit den Bildern. *Draw lines to link the sentences to the pictures.*

♥ = gern
♥̸ = nicht gern

1 Ich spiele __gern__ Tennis. ♥
2 Er geht ______ schwimmen. ♥̸
3 Gehst du ______ reiten? ♥
4 Sie spielt ______ Federball. ♥
5 Ich spiele ______ Tischtennis. ♥
6 Er geht ______ wandern. ♥̸

32 zweiunddreißig

1 (AT3 Level 1, AT4 Level 1) 1 Wandern **2** Tennis **3** Rugby **4** Schwimmen **5** Volleyball **6** Reiten

Das Lösungswort ist angeln.

2 (AT3 Level 2, AT4 Level 1) 1 Ich spiele **gern** Tennis – **c. 2** Er geht **nicht gern** schwimmen – **b. 3** Gehst du **gern** reiten? – **a. 4** Sie spielt **gern** Federball – **f. 5** Ich spiele **gern** Tischtennis – **d. 6** Er geht **nicht gern** wandern – **e.**

Übungsheft B, Seite 32

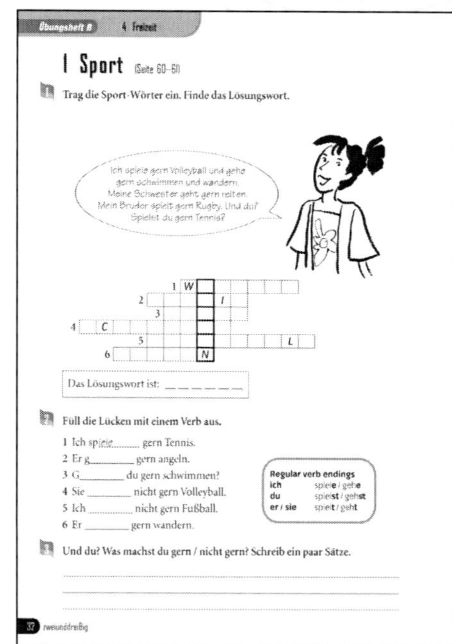
Übungsheft B 4 Freizeit

1 Sport (Seite 60–61)

1 Trag die Sport-Wörter ein. Finde das Lösungswort.

Das Lösungswort ist: _ _ _ _ _ _

2 Füll die Lücken mit einem Verb aus.

1 Ich spiele gern Tennis.
2 Er g______ gern angeln.
3 G______ du gern schwimmen?
4 Sie ______ nicht gern Volleyball.
5 Ich ______ nicht gern Fußball.
6 Er ______ gern wandern.

Regular verb endings
ich spiele / gehe
du spielst / gehst
er / sie spielt / geht

3 Und du? Was machst du gern / nicht gern? Schreib ein paar Sätze.

32 zweiunddreißig

1 (AT3 Level 3, AT4 Level 1) 1 Wandern **2** Tennis **3** Rugby **4** Schwimmen **5** Volleyball **6** Reiten

Das Lösungswort ist angeln.

2 (AT3 Level 2, AT4 Level 1) 1 Ich **spiele** gern Tennis. **2** Er **geht** gern angeln. **3 Gehst** du gern schwimmen? **4** Sie **spielt** nicht gern Volleyball. **5** Ich **spiele** nicht gern Fußball. **6** Er **geht** gern wandern.

3 (AT4 Level 3)

Übungsheft A, Seite 33

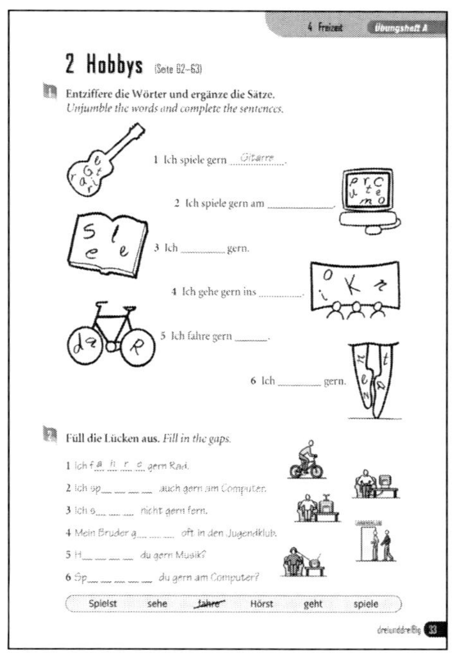
4 Freizeit Übungsheft A

2 Hobbys (Seite 62–63)

1 Entziffere die Wörter und ergänze die Sätze. *Unjumble the words and complete the sentences.*

1 Ich spiele gern __Gitarre__.
2 Ich spiele gern am ______.
3 Ich ______ gern.
4 Ich gehe gern ins ______.
5 Ich fahre gern ______.
6 Ich ______ gern.

2 Füll die Lücken aus. *Fill in the gaps.*

1 Ich f a h r e gern Rad.
2 Ich sp_ _ _ _ auch gern am Computer.
3 Ich s_ _ _ nicht gern fern.
4 Mein Bruder g_ _ _ oft in den Jugendklub.
5 H_ _ _ _ du gern Musik?
6 Sp_ _ _ _ _ du gern am Computer?

Spielst sehe fahre Hörst geht spiele

dreiunddreißig 33

1 (AT3 Level 2, AT4 Level 2) 1 Ich spiele gern **Gitarre**. **2** Ich spiele gern am **Computer**. **3** Ich **lese** gern. **4** Ich gehe gern ins **Kino**. **5** Ich fahre gern **Rad**. **6** Ich **tanze** gern.

2 (AT3 Level 2, AT4 Level 1) 1 Ich **fahre** gern Rad. **2** Ich **spiele** auch gern am Computer. **3** Ich **sehe** nicht gern fern. **4** Mein Bruder **geht** oft in den Jugendklub. **5 Hörst** du gern Musik? **6 Spielst** du gern am Computer?

Übungsheft B, Seite 33

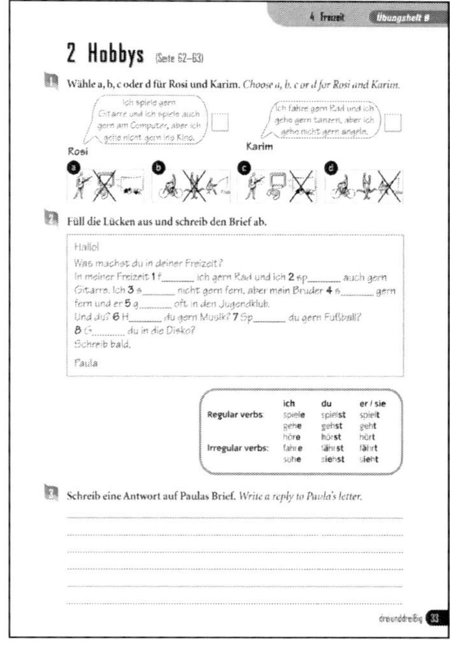
4 Freizeit Übungsheft B

2 Hobbys (Seite 62–63)

1 Wähle a, b, c oder d für Rosi und Karim. *Choose a, b, c or d for Rosi and Karim.*

2 Füll die Lücken aus und schreib den Brief ab.

Hallo!
Was machst du in deiner Freizeit?
In meiner Freizeit **1** f______ ich gern Rad und ich **2** sp______ auch gern Gitarre. Ich **3** s______ nicht gern fern, aber mein Bruder **4** s______ gern fern und er **5** g______ oft in den Jugendklub.
Und du? **6** H______ du gern Musik? **7** Sp______ du gern Fußball?
8 G______ du in die Disko?
Schreib bald.
Paula

	ich	du	er / sie
Regular verbs:	spiele	spielst	spielt
	gehe	gehst	geht
	höre	hörst	hört
Irregular verbs:	fahre	fährst	fährt
	sehe	siehst	sieht

3 Schreib eine Antwort auf Paulas Brief. *Write a reply to Paula's letter.*

dreiunddreißig 33

1 (AT3 Level 2, AT4 Level 1) Rosi c; **Karim** d

2 (AT3 Level 3, AT4 Level 1) Hallo! Was machst du in deiner Freizeit? In meiner Freizeit **fahre** ich gern Rad und ich **spiele** auch gern Gitarre. Ich **sehe** nicht gern fern, aber mein Bruder **sieht** gern fern und er **geht** oft in den Jugendklub. Und du? **Hörst** du gern Musik? **Spielst** du gern Fußball? **Gehst** du in die Disko? Schreib bald, Paula.

3 (AT4 Level 3–4)

Übungsheft A, Seite 34

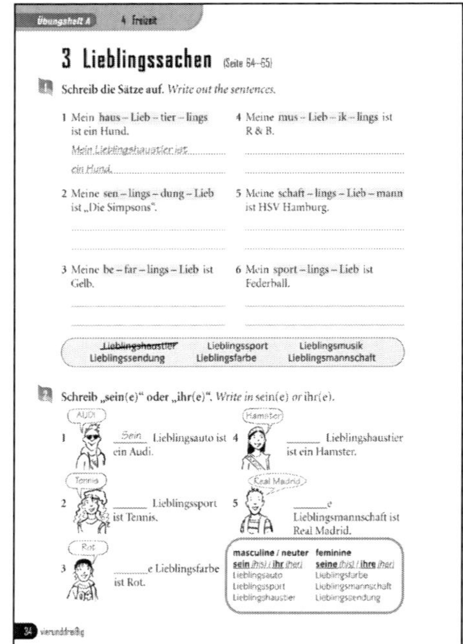
Übungsheft A 4 Freizeit

3 Lieblingssachen (Seite 64–65)

1 Schreib die Sätze auf. *Write out the sentences.*

1 Mein haus – Lieb – tier – lings ist ein Hund.
Mein Lieblingshaustier ist ein Hund.

2 Meine sen – lings – dung – Lieb ist „Die Simpsons".

3 Meine be – far – lings – Lieb ist Gelb.

4 Meine mus – Lieb – ik – lings ist R & B.

5 Meine schaft – lings – Lieb – mann ist HSV Hamburg.

6 Mein sport – lings – Lieb ist Federball.

~~Lieblingshaustier~~ Lieblingssport Lieblingsmusik Lieblingssendung Lieblingsfarbe Lieblingsmannschaft

2 Schreib „sein(e)" oder „ihr(e)". *Write in* sein(e) *or* ihr(e).

1 *Sein* Lieblingsauto ist ein Audi.

2 ______ Lieblingssport ist Tennis.

3 ______e Lieblingsfarbe ist Rot.

4 ______ Lieblingshaustier ist ein Hamster.

5 ______e Lieblingsmannschaft ist Real Madrid.

masculine / neuter	feminine
sein *(his)* / **ihr** *(her)*	**seine** *(his)* / **ihre** *(her)*
Lieblingsauto	Lieblingsfarbe
Lieblingssport	Lieblingsmannschaft
Lieblingshaustier	Lieblingssendung

34 vierunddreißig

1 (AT3 Level 2, AT4 Level 2) 1 Mein **Lieblingshaustier** ist ein Hund. **2** Meine **Lieblingssendung** ist „Die Simpsons". **3** Meine **Lieblingsfarbe** ist Gelb. **4** Meine **Lieblingsmusik** ist R & B. **5** Meine **Liebslingsmannschaft** ist HSV Hamburg. **6** Mein **Lieblingssport** ist Federball.

2 (AT3 Level 2, AT4 Level 1) 1 Sein Lieblingsauto ist ein Audi. **2 Ihr** Lieblingssport ist Tennis. **3 Ihre** Lieblingsfarbe ist Rot. **4 Ihr** Lieblingshaustier ist ein Hamster. **5 Seine** Lieblingsmannschaft ist Real Madrid.

Übungsheft A, Seite 35

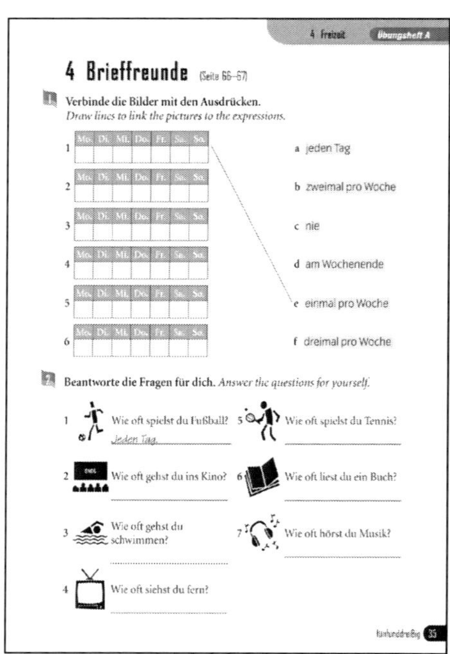
4 Freizeit Übungsheft A

4 Brieffreunde (Seite 66–67)

1 Verbinde die Bilder mit den Ausdrücken. *Draw lines to link the pictures to the expressions.*

	Mo.	Di.	Mi.	Do.	Fr.	Sa.	So.
1							
2							
3							
4							
5							
6							

a jeden Tag
b zweimal pro Woche
c nie
d am Wochenende
e einmal pro Woche
f dreimal pro Woche

2 Beantworte die Fragen für dich. *Answer the questions for yourself.*

1 Wie oft spielst du Fußball? *Jeden Tag.*
2 Wie oft gehst du ins Kino?
3 Wie oft gehst du schwimmen?
4 Wie oft siehst du fern?
5 Wie oft spielst du Tennis?
6 Wie oft liest du ein Buch?
7 Wie oft hörst du Musik?

fünfunddreißig 35

1 (AT3 Level 2) 1 e **2** c **3** d **4** a **5** f **6** b

2 (AT3 Level 2, AT4 Level 1)

Übungsheft B, Seite 34

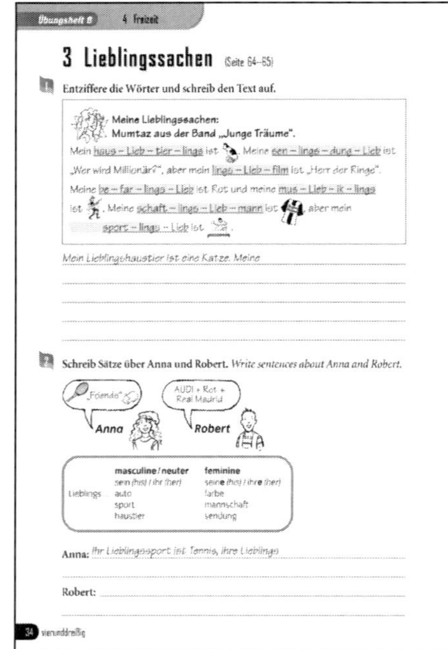
Übungsheft B 4 Freizeit

3 Lieblingssachen (Seite 64–65)

1 Entziffere die Wörter und schreib den Text auf.

Meine Lieblingssachen:
Mumtaz aus der Band „Junge Träume".
Mein haus – Lieb – tier – lings ist [picture]. Meine sen – lings – dung – Lieb ist „Wer wird Millionär?", aber mein lings – Lieb – film ist „Herr der Ringe". Meine be – far – lings – Lieb ist Rot und meine mus – Lieb – ik – lings ist [picture]. Meine schaft – lings – Lieb – mann ist [picture], aber mein sport – lings – Lieb ist [picture].

Mein Lieblingshaustier ist eine Katze. Meine

2 Schreib Sätze über Anna und Robert. *Write sentences about Anna and Robert.*

	masculine / neuter	feminine
	sein *(his)* / ihr *(her)*	seine *(his)* / ihre *(her)*
Lieblings...	auto	farbe
	sport	mannschaft
	haustier	sendung

Anna: *Ihr Lieblingssport ist Tennis, ihre Lieblings*

Robert:

34 vierunddreißig

1 (AT3 Level 3, AT4 Level 3) Main **Lieblingshaustier** ist eine Katze. Meine **Lieblingssendung** is „Wer wird Millionär?", aber mein **Lieblingsfilm** ist „Herr der Ringe". Meine **Lieblingsfarbe** ist Rot und meine **Lieblingsmusic** ist Rockmusik. Meine **Lieblingsmannschaft** ist Bayern München, aber mein **Lieblingssport** ist Tischtennis.

2 (AT3 Level 2, AT4 Level 2) Anna: Ihr Lieblingssport ist Tennis, ihre Lieblingssendung ist „Friends" und ihr Lieblingshaustier ist ein Hamster. **Robert:** Sein Lieblingsauto ist ein Audi, seine Lieblingsfarbe ist Rot und seine Lieblingsmannschaft ist Real Madrid.

Übungsheft B, Seite 35

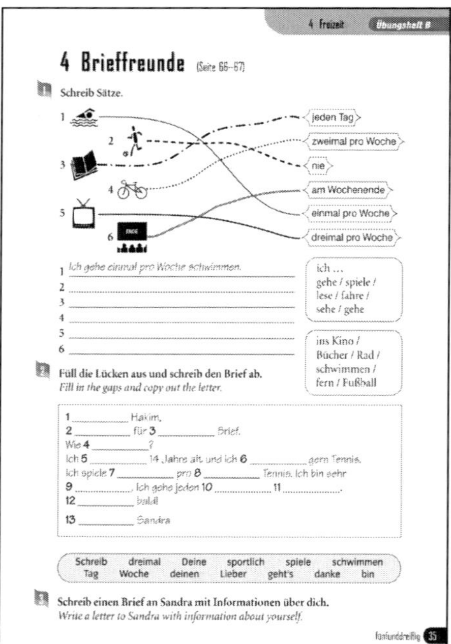
4 Freizeit Übungsheft B

4 Brieffreunde (Seite 66–67)

1 Schreib Sätze.

1 *Ich gehe einmal pro Woche schwimmen.*
2
3
4
5
6

ich …
gehe / spiele / lese / fahre / sehe / gehe

ins Kino / Bücher / Rad / schwimmen / fern / Fußball

2 Füll die Lücken aus und schreib den Brief ab. *Fill in the gaps and copy out the letter.*

1 ______ Hakim,
2 ______ für 3 ______ Brief.
Wie 4 ______?
Ich 5 ______ 14 Jahre alt und ich 6 ______ gern Tennis.
Ich spiele 7 ______ pro 8 ______ Tennis. Ich bin sehr
9 ______. Ich gehe jeden 10 ______ 11 ______.
12 ______ bald!
13 ______ Sandra

Schreib dreimal Deine sportlich spiele schwimmen Tag Woche deinen Lieber geht's danke bin

3 Schreib einen Brief an Sandra mit Informationen über dich. *Write a letter to Sandra with information about yourself.*

fünfunddreißig 35

1 (AT3 Level 1, AT4 Level 2) 1 Ich gehe einmal pro Woche schwimmen. **2** Ich spiele nie Fußball. **3** Ich lese jeden Tag ein Buch. **4** Ich fahre zweimal pro Woche Rad. **5** Ich sehe dreimal pro Woche fern. **6** Ich gehe am Wochenende ins Kino.

2 (AT3 Level 3, AT4 Level 3) Lieber Hakim, **danke** für **deinen** Brief. Wie **geht's**? Ich **bin** 14 Jahre alt und ich **spiele** gern Tennis. Ich spiele **dreimal** pro **Woche** Tennis. Ich bin sehr **sportlich**. Ich gehe jeden **Tag schwimmen**. **Schreib** bald! **Deine** Sandra.

3 (AT4 Level 4)

Übungsheft A, Seite 36

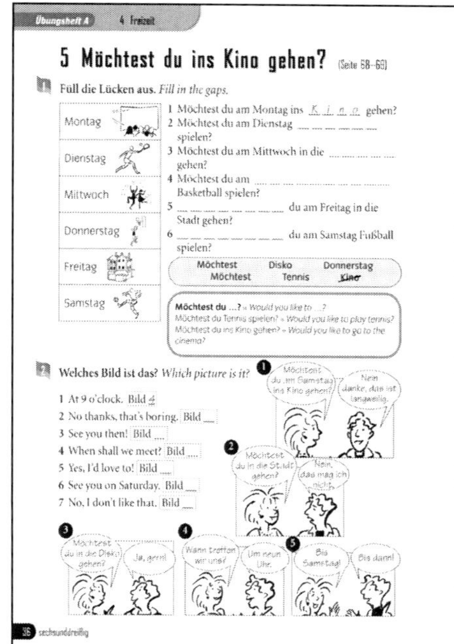

Übungsheft A   4 Freizeit

5 Möchtest du ins Kino gehen? (Seite 68–69)

1 Füll die Lücken aus. *Fill in the gaps.*

Montag / Dienstag / Mittwoch / Donnerstag / Freitag / Samstag

1 Möchtest du am Montag ins K i n o gehen?
2 Möchtest du am Dienstag ______ spielen?
3 Möchtest du am Mittwoch in die ______ gehen?
4 Möchtest du am ______ Basketball spielen?
5 ______ du am Freitag in die Stadt gehen?
6 ______ du am Samstag Fußball spielen?

Möchtest   Disko   Donnerstag   Möchtest   Tennis   ~~Kino~~

Möchtest du …? = *Would you like to …?*
Möchtest du Tennis spielen? = *Would you like to play tennis?*
Möchtest du ins Kino gehen? = *Would you like to go to the cinema?*

2 Welches Bild ist das? *Which picture is it?*

1 At 9 o'clock. Bild 4
2 No thanks, that's boring. Bild __
3 See you then! Bild __
4 When shall we meet? Bild __
5 Yes, I'd love to! Bild __
6 See you on Saturday. Bild __
7 No, I don't like that. Bild __

36 sechsunddreißig

1 (AT3 Level 2, AT4 Level 1) Möchtest du am Montag ins **Kino** gehen? Möchtest du am Dienstag **Tennis** spielen? Möchtest du am Mittwoch in die **Disko** gehen? Möchtest du am **Donnerstag** Basketball spielen? **Möchtest** du am Freitag in die Stadt gehen? **Möchtest** du am Samstag Fußball spielen?

2 (AT3 Level 2) 1 Bild 4 **2** Bild 1 **3** Bild 5 **4** Bild 4 **5** Bild 3 **6** Bild 5 **7** Bild 2

Übungsheft B, Seite 36

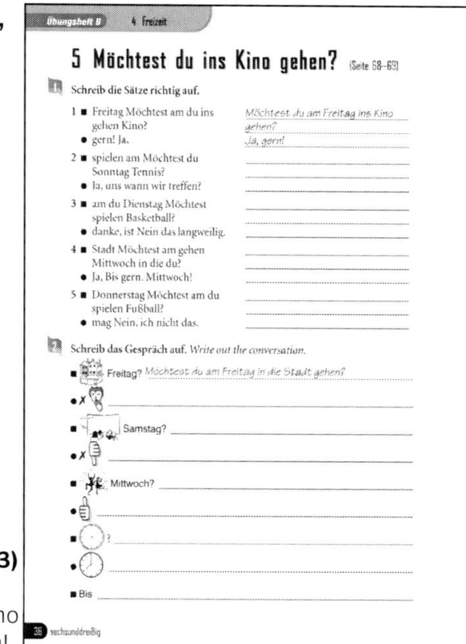

Übungsheft B   4 Freizeit

5 Möchtest du ins Kino gehen? (Seite 68–69)

1 Schreib die Sätze richtig auf.

1 ■ Freitag Möchtest am du ins gehen Kino? — *Möchtest du am Freitag ins Kino gehen?*
● gern! Ja. — *Ja, gern!*
2 ■ spielen am Möchtest du Sonntag Tennis?
● Ja, uns wann wir treffen?
3 ■ am du Dienstag Möchtest spielen Basketball?
● danke, ist Nein das langweilig.
4 ■ Stadt Möchtest am gehen Mittwoch in die du?
● Ja, Bis gern. Mittwoch!
5 ■ Donnerstag Möchtest am du spielen Fußball?
● mag Nein, ich nicht das.

2 Schreib das Gespräch auf. *Write out the conversation.*

■ Freitag? *Möchtest du am Freitag in die Stadt gehen?*
● ✗
■ Samstag?
● ✗
■ Mittwoch?
●
■ ?
●
■ Bis

36 sechsunddreißig

1 (AT4 Level 2–3)
1 – Möchtest du am Freitag ins Kino gehen? – Ja, gern! **2** – Möchtest du am Sonntag Tennis spielen? – Ja, wann treffen wir uns? **3** – Möchtest du am Dienstag Basketball spielen? – Nein danke, das ist langweilig. **4** – Möchtest du am Mittwoch in die Stadt gehen? – Ja, gern. Bis Mittwoch! **5** – Möchtest du am Donnerstag Fußball spielen? – Nein, das mag ich nicht.

2 (AT4 Level 4) ■ Möchtest du am Freitag in die Stadt gehen? ● Nein danke, das ist langweilig. ■ Möchtest du am Samstag ins Kino gehen? ● Neine danke, das mag ich nicht. ■ Möchtest du am Mittwoch in die Disko gehen? ● Ja, gern! ■ Wann treffen wir uns? ● Um acht Uhr. ■ Bis dann! / Bis acht Uhr! / Bis Mittwoch!

Übungsheft A, Seite 37

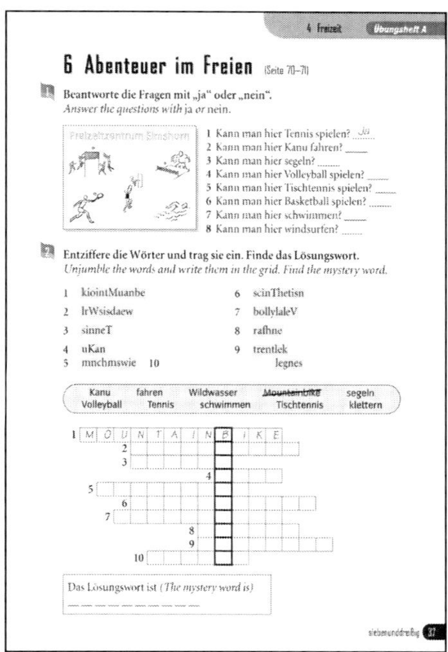

4 Freizeit   Übungsheft A

6 Abenteuer im Freien (Seite 70–71)

1 Beantworte die Fragen mit „ja" oder „nein".
Answer the questions with ja *or* nein.

Freizeitzentrum Elmshorn

1 Kann man hier Tennis spielen? *Ja*
2 Kann man hier Kanu fahren? ____
3 Kann man hier segeln? ____
4 Kann man hier Volleyball spielen? ____
5 Kann man hier Tischtennis spielen? ____
6 Kann man hier Basketball spielen? ____
7 Kann man hier schwimmen? ____
8 Kann man hier windsurfen? ____

2 Entziffere die Wörter und trag sie ein. Finde das Lösungswort.
Unjumble the words and write them in the grid. Find the mystery word.

1 kiointMuanbe   6 scinThetisn
2 lrWsisdaew   7 bollylaleV
3 sinneT   8 rafhne
4 uKan   9 trentlek
5 mnchmswie   10 legnes

Kanu   fahren   Wildwasser   ~~Mountainbike~~   segeln
Volleyball   Tennis   schwimmen   Tischtennis   klettern

1 M O U N T A I N B I K E

Das Lösungswort ist (*The mystery word is*) ______

siebenunddreißig 37

1 (AT3 Level 2, AT4 Level 1) 1 Ja **2** Nein **3** Nein **4** Ja **5** Ja **6** Ja **7** Ja **8** Nein

2 (AT3 Level 2, AT4 Level 1) 1 Mountainbike **2** Wildwasser **3** Tennis **4** Kanu **5** schwimmen **6** Tischtennis **7** Volleyball **8** fahren **9** klettern **10** segeln

Das Lösungswort ist Basketball.

Übungsheft B, Seite 37

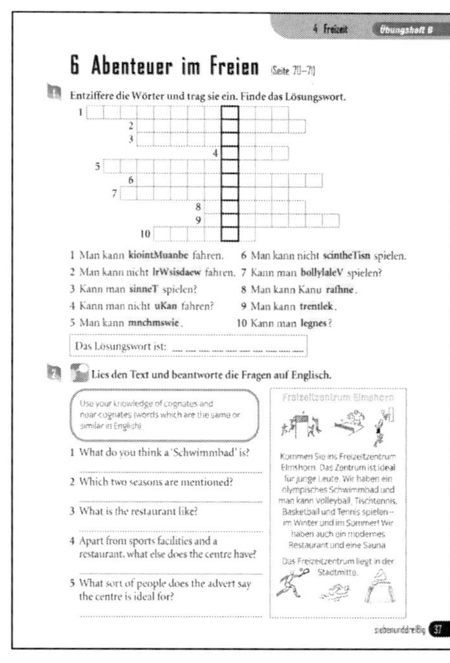

4 Freizeit   Übungsheft B

6 Abenteuer im Freien (Seite 70–71)

1 Entziffere die Wörter und trag sie ein. Finde das Lösungswort.

1 Man kann **kiointMuanbe** fahren.   6 Man kann nicht **scintheTisn** spielen.
2 Man kann nicht **lrWsisdaew** fahren.   7 Kann man **bollylaleV** spielen?
3 Kann man **sinneT** spielen?   8 Man kann Kanu **rafhne**.
4 Kann man nicht **uKan** fahren?   9 Man kann **trentlek**.
5 Man kann **mnchmswie**.   10 Kann man **legnes**?

Das Lösungswort ist: ______

2 Lies den Text und beantworte die Fragen auf Englisch.

Use your knowledge of cognates and near cognates (words which are the same or similar in English).

1 What do you think a 'Schwimmbad' is?
2 Which two seasons are mentioned?
3 What is the restaurant like?
4 Apart from sports facilities and a restaurant, what else does the centre have?
5 What sort of people does the advert say the centre is ideal for?

Freizeitzentrum Elmshorn

Kommen Sie ins Freizeitzentrum Elmshorn. Das Zentrum ist ideal für junge Leute. Wir haben ein olympisches Schwimmbad und man kann Volleyball, Tischtennis, Basketball und Tennis spielen – im Winter und im Sommer! Wir haben auch ein modernes Restaurant und eine Sauna.

Das Freizeitzentrum liegt in der Stadtmitte.

siebenunddreißig 37

1 (AT3 Level 1, AT4 Level 2) 1 Mountainbike **2** Wildwasser **3** Tennis **4** Kanu **5** schwimmen **6** Tischtennis **7** Volleyball **8** fahren **9** klettern **10** segeln

Das Lösungswort ist Basketball.

2 (AT3 Level 4)

1 swimming pool **2** winter and summer **3** modern **4** a sauna **5** young people

Übungsheft A, Seite 38

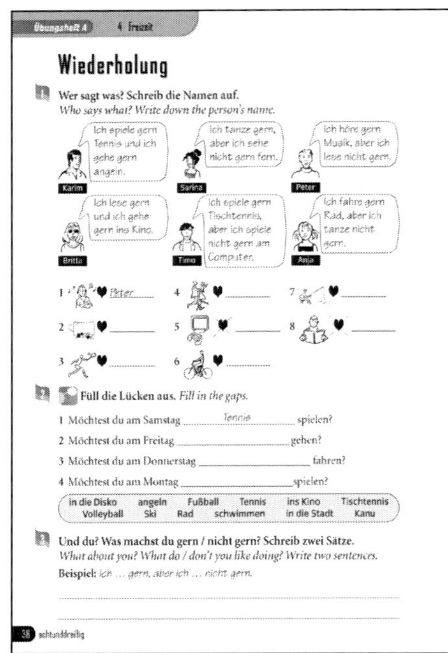

Übungsheft A 4 Freizeit

Wiederholung

1 Wer sagt was? Schreib die Namen auf.
Who says what? Write down the person's name.

1 Peter
2
3
4
5
6
7
8

2 Füll die Lücken aus. *Fill in the gaps.*

1 Möchtest du am Samstag Tennis spielen?
2 Möchtest du am Freitag ________ gehen?
3 Möchtest du am Donnerstag ________ fahren?
4 Möchtest du am Montag ________ spielen?

in die Disko angeln Fußball Tennis ins Kino Tischtennis Volleyball Ski Rad schwimmen in die Stadt Kanu

3 Und du? Was machst du gern / nicht gern? Schreib zwei Sätze.
What about you? What do / don't you like doing? Write two sentences.
Beispiel: ich ... gern, aber ich ... nicht gern.

38 achtunddreißig

1 (AT3 Level 2, AT4 Level 1)

1 Peter **2** Britta **3** Karim **4** Sarina **5** Timo **6** Anja **7** Karim **8** Peter

2 (AT3 Level 2, AT4 Level 1)

2 *Any of*: in die Disko, angeln, ins Kino, schwimmen, in die Stadt **3** *Any of*: Ski, Rad **4** *Any of*: Fußball, Tennis, Tischtennis, Volleyball

3 (AT4 Level 2)

Übungsheft B, Seite 38

Übungsheft B 4 Freizeit

Wiederholung

1 Was kann man hier machen?

Man kann hier Tennis spielen, Kanu

Tennis spielen
Mountainbike fahren
Tischtennis spielen
Kanu fahren
segeln gehen
schwimmen gehen

2 Lies die Texte und finde die Ausdrücke unten.
Read the texts and find the expressions below.

1 At least four expressions saying what these people **like** doing.
2 At least three expressions saying what these people **don't like** doing.
3 Two **invitations** to do something.
4 Four expressions saying **how often** they do something.
5 Two expressions saying what their **favourite** things are.

38 achtunddreißig

1 (AT4 Level 2)

Man kann hier Tennis spielen, Kanu fahren, schwimmen, segeln, Mountainbike fahren und Tischtennis spielen.

2 (AT3 Level 4, AT4 Level 2) 1 ich gehe gern angeln / ich spiele gern Tennis / ich tanze gern / ich höre gern Musik / ich gehe gern ins Kino / ich lese gern / ich spiele gern Tischtennis. **2** ich lese nicht gern / ich sehe nicht gern fern / ich spiele nicht gern am Computer / (ich tanze nie). **3** Möchtest du angeln gehen? / Möchtest du ins Kino gehen? **4** ich spiele einmal pro Woche / am Wochenende tanze ich gern / ich fahre jeden Tag Rad / ich tanze nie. **5** Tennis ist mein Lieblingssport / Mein Liblingsbuch ist „Harry Potter".

Arbeitsblatt 4.1

Echo 1 Arbeitsblatt 4.1

Lesson Starter

4 Freizeit

Sports

Join the dots in the order you hear to find the picture. What sport is it?

Das ist ____________

siebenundfünfzig 57

Das ist Tennis

Arbeitsblatt 4.2

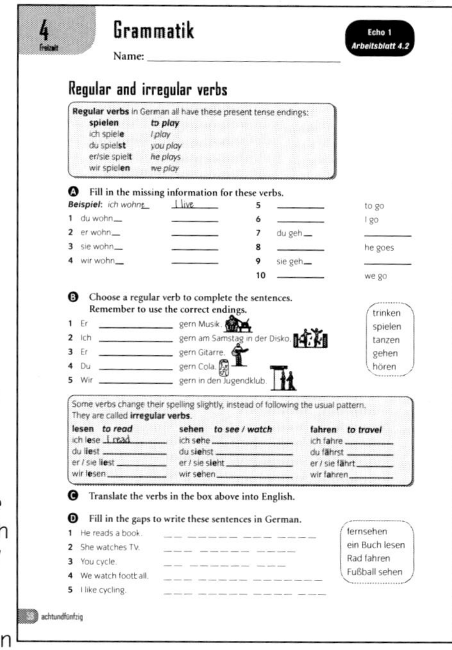

4 Freizeit

Grammatik

Echo 1 Arbeitsblatt 4.2

Name: ____________

Regular and irregular verbs

Regular verbs in German all have these present tense endings:

spielen	***to play***
ich spiel**e**	*I play*
du spiel**st**	*you play*
er/sie spiel**t**	*he plays*
wir spiel**en**	*we play*

A Fill in the missing information for these verbs.

Beispiel: ich wohn_ I live

1 du wohn__ ______
2 er wohn__ ______
3 sie wohn__ ______
4 wir wohn__ ______
5 ______ to go
6 ______ I go
7 du geh__ ______
8 ______ he goes
9 sie geh__ ______
10 ______ we go

B Choose a regular verb to complete the sentences. Remember to use the correct endings.

1 Er ______ gern Musik.
2 Ich ______ gern am Samstag in der Disko.
3 Er ______ gern Gitarre.
4 Du ______ gern Cola.
5 Wir ______ gern in den Jugendklub.

trinken / spielen / tanzen / gehen / hören

Some verbs change their spelling slightly, instead of following the usual pattern. They are called **irregular verbs**.

lesen ***to read***	**sehen** ***to see / watch***	**fahren** ***to travel***
ich l**e**se I read	ich s**e**he ______	ich f**a**hre ______
du l**ie**st ______	du s**ie**hst ______	du f**ä**hrst ______
er / sie l**ie**st ______	er / sie s**ie**ht ______	er / sie f**ä**hrt ______
wir l**e**sen ______	wir s**e**hen ______	wir f**a**hren ______

C Translate the verbs in the box above into English.

D Fill in the gaps to write these sentences in German.

1 He reads a book.
2 She watches TV.
3 You cycle.
4 We watch football.
5 I like cycling.

fernsehen / ein Buch lesen / Rad fahren / Fußball sehen

58 achtundfünfzig

A
1 du wohnst / *you live* **2** er wohnt / *he lives* **3** sie wohnt / *she lives* **4** wir wohnen / *we live* **5** gehen **6** ich gehe **7** du gehst / *you go* **8** er geht **9** sie geht / *she goes* **10** wir gehen

B
1 hört **2** tanze **3** spielt **4** trinkst **5** gehen

C
I read, you read, he / she reads, we read; I see you see, he / she sees, we see; I travel, you travel, he / she travels, we travel

D
1 Er liest ein Buch. **2** Sie sieht fern. **3** Du fährst Rad. **4** Wir sehen Fußball. **5** Ich fahre gern Rad.

Arbeitsblatt 4.3

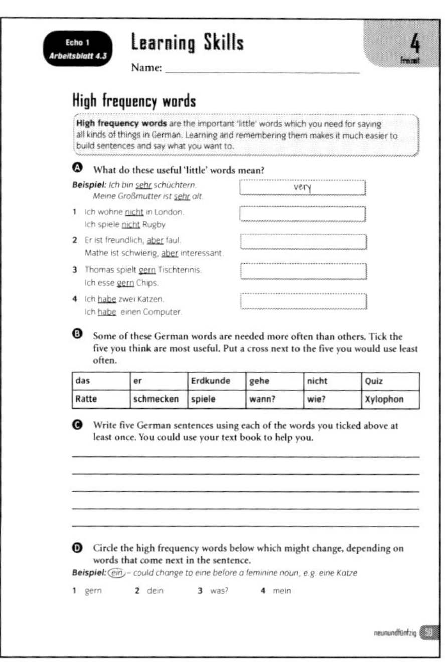

Echo 1 Arbeitsblatt 4.3

Learning Skills

4 Freizeit

Name: ____________

High frequency words

High frequency words are the important 'little' words which you need for saying all kinds of things in German. Learning and remembering them makes it much easier to build sentences and say what you want to.

A What do these useful 'little' words mean?

Beispiel: *Ich bin sehr schüchtern. Meine Großmutter ist sehr alt.* very

1 Ich wohne nicht in London. Ich spiele nicht Rugby
2 Er ist freundlich, aber faul. Mathe ist schwierig, aber interessant.
3 Thomas spielt gern Tischtennis. Ich esse gern Chips.
4 Ich habe zwei Katzen. Ich habe einen Computer.

B Some of these German words are needed more often than others. Tick the five you think are most useful. Put a cross next to the five you would use least often.

das	er	Erdkunde	gehe	nicht	Quiz
Ratte	schmecken	spiele	wann?	wie?	Xylophon

C Write five German sentences using each of the words you ticked above at least once. You could use your text book to help you.

D Circle the high frequency words below which might change, depending on words that come next in the sentence.

Beispiel: ein – *could change to eine before a feminine noun, e.g. eine Katze*

1 gern 2 dein 3 was? 4 mein

neunundfünfzig 59

A
1 not **2** but **3** like(s) **4** have

C
2 was? *could change to* wann? / wie? *etc.* **3** sie *could change to* er / ich *etc.* **4** mein *could change to* meine / deine *etc.*

Arbeitsblatt 4.4

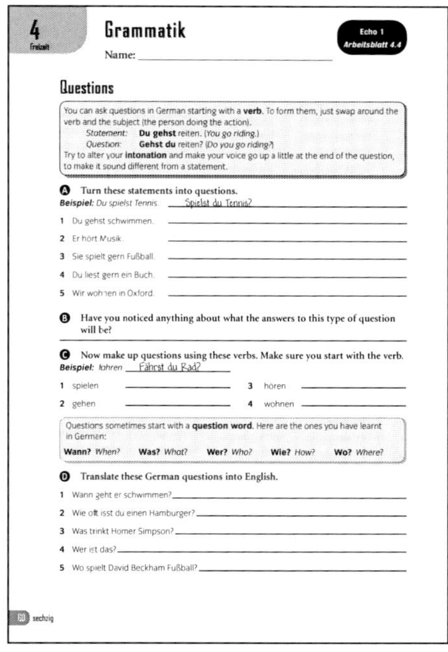

4 Freizeit

Grammatik

Echo 1 Arbeitsblatt 4.4

Name: ____________

Questions

You can ask questions in German starting with a **verb**. To form them, just swap around the verb and the subject (the person doing the action).
Statement: **Du gehst** reiten. (*You go riding.*)
Question: **Gehst du** reiten? (*Do you go riding?*)
Try to alter your **intonation** and make your voice go up a little at the end of the question, to make it sound different from a statement.

A Turn these statements into questions.

Beispiel: *Du spielst Tennis.* Spielst du Tennis?

1 Du gehst schwimmen.
2 Er hört Musik.
3 Sie spielt gern Fußball.
4 Du liest gern ein Buch.
5 Wir wohnen in Oxford.

B Have you noticed anything about what the answers to this type of question will be?

C Now make up questions using these verbs. Make sure you start with the verb.

Beispiel: fahren Fährst du Rad?

1 spielen
2 gehen
3 hören
4 wohnen

Questions sometimes start with a **question word**. Here are the ones you have learnt in German:
Wann? *When?* **Was?** *What?* **Wer?** *Who?* **Wie?** *How?* **Wo?** *Where?*

D Translate these German questions into English.

1 Wann geht er schwimmen?
2 Wie oft isst du einen Hamburger?
3 Was trinkt Homer Simpson?
4 Wer ist das?
5 Wo spielt David Beckham Fußball?

60 sechzig

A
1 Gehst du schwimmen? **2** Hört er Musik? **3** Spielt sie gern Fußball? **4** Liest du gern ein Buch? **5** Gehen wir in die Stadt?

B
Yes or *no*.

C
1 When does he go swimming? **2** How often do you eat a hamburger? **3** What does Homer Simpson drink? **4** Who is that? **5** Where does David Beckham play football?

Arbeitsblatt 4.5

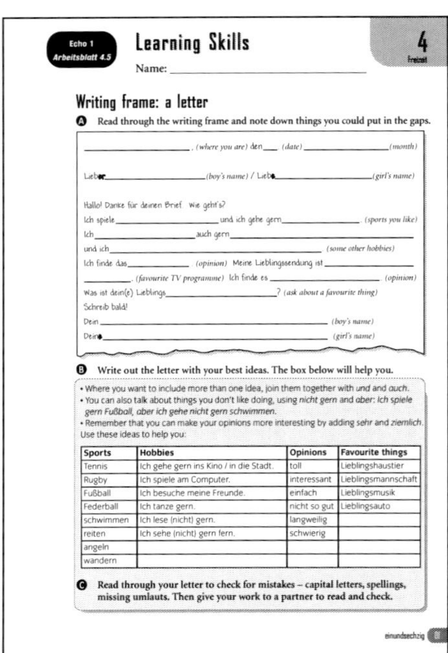

Echo 1
Arbeitsblatt 4.5

Learning Skills

4
Freizeit

Name: ____________________

Writing frame: a letter

A **Read through the writing frame and note down things you could put in the gaps.**

____________, *(where you are)* den___ *(date)* ____________ *(month)*

Lieber____________ *(boy's name)* / Liebe____________ *(girl's name)*

Hallo! Danke für deinen Brief. Wie geht's?
Ich spiele____________ und ich gehe gern____________. *(sports you like)*
Ich____________ auch gern____________
und ich____________ *(some other hobbies)*
Ich finde das____________ *(opinion)* Meine Lieblingssendung ist____________
____________. *(favourite TV programme)* Ich finde es ____________. *(opinion)*
Was ist dein(e) Lieblings____________? *(ask about a favourite thing)*
Schreib bald!
Dein ____________ *(boy's name)*
Deine____________ *(girl's name)*

B **Write out the letter with your best ideas. The box below will help you.**

- Where you want to include more than one idea, join them together with *und* and *auch*.
- You can also talk about things you don't like doing, using *nicht gern* and *aber*: *Ich spiele gern Fußball, aber ich gehe nicht gern schwimmen.*
- Remember that you can make your opinions more interesting by adding *sehr* and *ziemlich*.

Use these ideas to help you:

Sports	Hobbies	Opinions	Favourite things
Tennis	Ich gehe gern ins Kino / in die Stadt.	toll	Lieblingshaustier
Rugby	Ich spiele am Computer.	interessant	Lieblingsmannschaft
Fußball	Ich besuche meine Freunde.	einfach	Lieblingsmusik
Federball	Ich tanze gern.	nicht so gut	Lieblingsauto
schwimmen	Ich lese (nicht) gern.	langweilig	
reiten	Ich sehe (nicht) gern fern.	schwierig	
angeln			
wandern			

C **Read through your letter to check for mistakes – capital letters, spellings, missing umlauts. Then give your work to a partner to read and check.**

einundsechzig 61

Arbeitsblatt 4.6

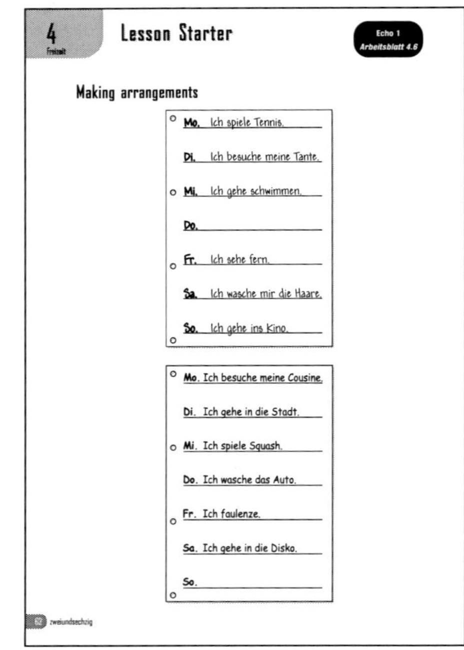

4
Freizeit

Lesson Starter

Echo 1
Arbeitsblatt 4.6

Making arrangements

Mo. Ich spiele Tennis.
Di. Ich besuche meine Tante.
Mi. Ich gehe schwimmen.
Do.
Fr. Ich sehe fern.
Sa. Ich wasche mir die Haare.
So. Ich gehe ins Kino.

Mo. Ich besuche meine Cousine.
Di. Ich gehe in die Stadt.
Mi. Ich spiele Squash.
Do. Ich wasche das Auto.
Fr. Ich faulenze.
Sa. Ich gehe in die Disko.
So.

62 zweiundsechzig

5 Mein Zuhause

Unit Learning targets	Key framework objectives	NC levels and PoS coverage	Grammar and key language	Skills
1 Wo wohnst du? (pp. 78–79) • Saying where you live • Learning to read long words	1.3/Y7 Listening – (a) interpreting intonation and tone 1.3/Y7 Speaking – (b) using intonation and tone 1.4 /Y7 Speaking – (b) using prompts	NC levels 2–4 **2.2a** listen for gist **2.2d** pronunciation and intonation **2.2e** ask and answer questions **2.2f** intiate / sustain conversations **3b** sounds and writing **3c** apply grammar **3d** use a range of vocab / structures **3e** different countries' cultures **4b** communicate in pairs etc. **4g** language for a range of purposes	*mein, dein* *Wo wohnst du?* *Ich wohne in einem Dorf / in einer Stadt / in einer Großstadt / an de Küste / in den Bergen / auf dem Land.* *Meine Adresse ist … .* *Wie ist deine Telefonnummer?* *Meine Telefonnummer ist …* *Wie bitte?* *Langsamer, bitte.*	Pronunciation: question intonation Asking for clarification and repetition Letter writing: addresses
2 Mein Haus (pp. 80–81) • Describing your home • Using *es gibt* to say what there is	1.5/Y7 Speaking – (a) presenting 1.5/Y7 Speaking – (b) expression / non-verbal techniques 4.6/Y7 Language – (b) negatives	NC levels 1–4 **2.2a** listen for gist **3b** sounds and writing **3c** apply grammar **3d** use a range of vocab / structures **3f** compare experiences **4b** communicate in pairs etc.	*Es gibt* + accusative Indefinite article: accusative Negative article: accusative *der Garten / Balkon / Keller / Dachboden* *die Küche / Toilette / Garage* *das Wohnzimmer / Schlafzimmer / Badezimmer / Esszimmer* *Es gibt einen / keinen Garten / Balkon / Keller / Dachboden.* *Es gibt eine / keine Küche / Toilette / Garage.* *Es gibt ein / kein Wohnzimmer / Schlafzimmer / Badezimmer / Esszimmer.* *Ich wohne in einer Wohnung.* *Ich wohne in einem Einfamilienhaus / Doppelhaus / Reihenhaus / Bungalow.* *Mein Haus ist groß / mittelgroß / klein.*	Improving pronunciation by recording and reviewing own speech Giving a presentation Types of accommodation in German-speaking countries
3 Oma schläft im Garten (pp. 82–83) • Describing what you do at home • Using irregular verbs	4.5/Y7 Language – (a) present tense verbs	NC levels 2–3 **2.2a** listen for gist **2.2b** skim and scan **2.2e** ask and answer questions **3b** sounds and writing **3c** apply grammar **3d** use a range of vocab / structures	Irregular verbs in 1st, 2nd, 3rd person singular: *essen, sehen, lesen, schlafen* *Ich höre im Keller Musik.* *Ich spiele im Schlafzimmer am Computer.* *Ich koche in der Küche.* *Ich arbeite im Garten.* *Ich esse im Esszimmer.* *Ich lese im Badezimmer.* *Ich sehe im Wohnzimmer fern.* *Ich schlafe im Schlafzimmer.*	Looking up verbs
4 In meinem Zimmer (pp. 84–85) • Describing your room • Understanding that the verb has to be the second idea	5.1 Strategies – patterns	NC levels 2–3 **2.2a** listen for gist **2.2b** skim and scan **2.2c** respond appropriately **3b** sounds and writing **3c** apply grammar **3d** use a range of vocab / structures **4b** communicate in pairs etc.	Word order: verb as second idea *der Schreibtisch / Kleiderschrank / Stuhl / Computer / Fernseher / Spiegel* *die Lampe / Kommode / Stereoanlage* *das Bett / Regal / Sofa* *In meinem Zimmer habe ich …* *einen Schreibtisch / Kleiderschrank / Stuhl / Computer / Fernseher / Spiegel.* *eine Lampe / Kommode.* *ein Bett / Regal / Sofa.* *Wie ist dein Zimmer?* *Mein Zimmer ist klein / groß / hell / dunkel / ordentlich / unordentlich.* *sehr / ziemlich / nicht sehr*	Revising and improving written work

Unit Learning targets	Key framework objectives	NC levels and PoS coverage	Grammar and key language	Skills
5 Wo ist es? (pp. 86–87) • Saying what is in your room • Using prepositions to describe where things are	2.1/Y7 Reading – main points and detail	**NC levels** 2–4 **2.2a** listen for gist **2.2b** skim and scan **2.2c** respond appropriately **2.2e** ask and answer questions **2.2g** write clearly and coherently **3b** sounds and writing **3d** use a range of vocab / structures **4b** communicate in pairs etc.	Prepositions with the dative Definite article: dative *Wo ist die Katze?* *Die Katze ist ...* *auf dem Regal / unter dem Bett / in dem Kleiderschrank / neben dem Stuhl / zwischen dem Bett und dem Schreibtisch / hinter dem Computer.* *Wo ist der Bleistift?* *Der Bleistift is auf / unter / in / neben / hinter dem Buch.*	Describing a picture
6 Grüße aus Salzburg (pp. 88–89) • Describing where you live • Listening for different types of information	1.2/Y7 Listening – unfamiliar language 4.5/Y7 Language – (a) set phrases about the past	**NC level** 4 **2.2a** listen for gist **2.2b** skim and scan **2.2e** ask and answer questions **3b** sounds and writing **3e** different countries' cultures **3f** compare experiences **4b** communicate in pairs etc.	Recognising references to the past (*war, letzte Woche*, etc.) General consolidation of language from Units 1–5	Listening for specific information Reading a longer text Visualisation and memory skills
Lernzieltest und Wiederholung (pp. 90–91) • Pupils' checklist and practice test		**NC levels** 2–4 **2b** skim and scan **3c** apply grammar **3d** use a range of vocab / structures **4b** communicate in pairs etc.		
Mehr (pp. 92–93) • Extension material	2.2/Y7 Reading – (a) unfamiliar language 2.2/Y7 Reading – (b) text selection 2.5/Y7 Writing – different text types 5.5 Strategies – reference materials	**NC levels** 4–5 **2.1d** previous knowledge **2.1e** use reference materials **2.2a** listen for gist **2.2b** skim and scan **2.2c** respond appropriately **2.2e** ask and answer questions **2.2j** adapt previously-learnt language **3d** use a range of vocab / structures	Consolidation of language from Units 1–6	Reading a longer text for gist and detail Creative writing Recording and reviewing speech
Extra (pp. 120–121) • Self-access reading and writing at two levels		**NC levels** 2–4 **2.2b** skim and scan **2.2c** respond appropriately **2.2e** ask and answer questions **3c** apply grammar **3d** use a range of vocab / structures		

1 Wo wohnst du?

Learning targets

- Saying where you live
- Learning to read long words

Key framework objectives

1.3/Y7 Listening – (a) interpreting intonation and tone
1.3/Y7 Speaking – (b) using intonation and tone
1.4/Y7 Speaking – (b) using prompts

Grammar

mein, dein (revision)

Key language

Wo wohnst du?
Ich wohne …
in einem Dorf / in einer Stadt / in einer Großstadt / an der Küste / in den Bergen / auf dem Land.
Wie ist deine Adresse?
Meine Adresse ist …
Wie ist deine Telefonnummer?
Meine Telefonnummer ist …
Wie bitte?
Langsamer, bitte.

High-frequency words

Cardinal numbers 0–100
an
auf
bitte
deine
du
in
meine
wie?
wie bitte?
wo?
wohnen

Pronunciation

Question intonation

Mathematics

Mental arithmetic
Telephone numbers, addresses

Citizenship

The physical geography of German-speaking countries
The formats of postal addresses and phone numbers in German-speaking countries.

Resources

CD 3, tracks 2–4
Workbooks A and B, p. 79
Arbeitsblatt 5.2, p.79
Echo Elektro 1 TPP, Mod 5 1.1–1.5

Starter 1

4.1/Y7

Aim

To build confidence in recognising and using compound nouns.

Present section A of **Arbeitsblatt 5.1** as an OHT or make individual photocopies for pupils. Pupils form as many compound nouns as they can from the fragments provided. Explain that each compound must be meaningful, i.e. pupils should be able to give an English translation if asked. Set a time limit, then gather compounds around the class and write them on the board.

To stretch more able pupils, you could then present some new compounds and elicit their meaning, e.g. *Lieblingsbruder, Computersendung, Lieblingssportsendung.*

Suggestion

Use OHT 23 from the Colour OHT File or alternatively flashcards that you might already have to introduce *in einem Dorf, in einer Stadt, in einer Großstadt, an der Küste, in den Bergen* and *auf dem Land.*

1 Was passt zusamman? (AT 3/2) 5.4

Reading. Pupils match the speech bubbles to the photos. They can check their own answers by doing exercise 2.

Answers

1 b **2** c **3** d **4** f **5** a **6** e

2 Hör zu und überprüfe es. (AT1/2)

1.1/Y7

Listening. Pupils listen to the recording to check their answers to exercise 1.

CD track 2

1 – *Wo wohnst du, Carsten?*
– *Ich wohne in einer Großstadt.*

2 – *Und du, Beyhan? Wo wohnst du?*
– *Ich wohne in einer Stadt.*

3 – *Olaf, wo wohnst du?*
– *Ich wohne an der Küste.*

4 – *Maren, wohnst du an der Küste?*
– *Nein. Ich wohne auf dem Land.*

5 – *Und du, Heiko? Wo wohnst du?*
– *Ich? Also, ich wohne in einem Dorf.*

6 – *Und Carola? Wo wohnst du?*
– *Ich wohne in Thalkirch in der Schweiz, in den Bergen.*

3 Partnerarbeit. (AT 2/2) 1.4b/Y7

Speaking. Pupils work together in pairs to create dialogues based on the teenagers and locations shown in exercise 1.

> **ECHO-Tipp: Long words**
> This panel builds pupils' confidence in tackling long words. Part A of **Arbeitsblatt 5.1** provides further practice.

4 Schreib Sätze. (AT 4/3) 4.4/Y7

Writing. Pupils write sentences about the teenagers from exercise 1. They could finish with a sentence about where they themselves live. Draw pupils' attention to the sentence structure and the use of *und* to join together two statements.

Starter 2 4.2/Y7

Aim
To revise numbers 0 to 99.

Write six phone numbers on an OHT, each consisting of three two-digit numbers, e.g.

Max	*24 10 39*
Inge	*92 23 48*
Susi	*23 63 55*
Heiko	*42 23 24*
Hanna	*94 23 11*
Lexi	*82 87 77*

Pupils work together in pairs. Partner A sits facing the front of the class; partner B faces the back. When you call out a name, Partner A dictates the telephone number in German to partner B. Partner B writes it on paper or a mini-whiteboard and passes it to partner A to check (or holds it up for you to check). After three numbers, the partners swap seats.

5 Hör zu und lies. 1.3a/Y7

Listening. Pupils listen to the recording and follow the dialogue in their books. Elicit from pupils the differences in address and phone number format in German (road name before number; telephone numbers read as two-digit numbers). Draw pupils' attention to the expressions *Wie bitte?* and *Langsamer, bitte* and how they are used.

CD 3

- *Wie ist deine Adresse, Julia?*
- *Meine Adresse ist Gartenstraße 50.*
- *Wie bitte?*
- *Gartenstraße 50.*
- *O.K. ... Und wie ist deine Telefonnummer?*
- *Meine Telefonnummer ist 80 70 95.*
- *Langsamer, bitte.*
- *80 70 95.*
- *Danke.*

Aussprache 1.3a+b/Y7

This panel draws pupils' attention to question intonation. Practise this with the whole class by chorusing *Wie bitte?* and *Langsamer, bitte,* exaggerating the difference in intonation.

6 Hör zu. Ergänze das Adressbuch. (AT 1/3) 1.1/Y7 1.3a/Y7

Listening. Pupils listen to the recording and note the missing numbers for the address book.

CD 4

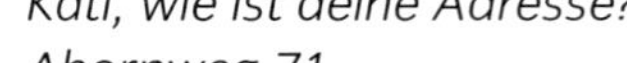

1 – *Kati, wie ist deine Adresse?*
– *Ahornweg 71.*
– *Ahornweg 71 ... Und deine Telefonnummer?*
– *Meine Telefonnummer ist 42 29 93.*
– *Wie bitte?*
– *42 29 93.*

2 – *Wie ist deine Adresse, Alex?*
– *Meine Adresse ist Lindenring 23.*
– *23?*
– *Ja. Und meine Telefonnummer ist 45 03 42.*
– *Langsamer, bitte.*
– *45 03 42. O.K.?*
– *Ja, danke.*

3 – *Und du, Ulli? Wie ist deine Adresse?*
– *Hafenstraße 90.*
– *Hafenstraße ... 90.*
– *Ja.*
– *Und deine Telefonnummer?*
– *Meine Telefonnummer ist 41 92 78.*
– *Wie bitte?*
– *41 92 78.*
– *O.K., danke.*
– *Bitte.*

4 – *Hi, Jana!*
– *Hi!*
– *Du, wie ist deine Adresse?*
– *Meine Adresse? Adlerweg 89!*
– *Ach, ja, natürlich! ... Adlerweg 89.*
– *Ja. Und meine Telefonnummber ist ...*
– *35 23 65!*
– *Richtig! 35 23 65*

> ***Answers***
> **a** 71 **b** 29 **c** 23 **d** 45 **e** 90 **f** 78 **g** 89 **h** 65

R To reinforce question intonation, play the recording again and ask the class to put their hands up whenever they hear a question. Pause the recording at the end of each dialogue and ask for volunteers to repeat any questions asked.

7 Partnerarbeit. (AT 2/3) 1.3b/Y7 1.4a/Y7

Speaking. Pupils work in pairs, asking each other their address and phone number. You may wish pupils to write down the information they hear and then show their notes to their partners to confirm its correctness. Remind pupils that they can use *Wie bitte?* and *Langsamer, bitte* if they have difficulty understanding what their partner says. Encourage them to start using these expressions spontaneously in their pairwork and in their responses to you. Encourage pupils to use the correct intonation when using these expressions. If time permits, pupils could exchange this information with several classmates.

8 Schreib einen Text über dich. (AT 4/3–4) 2.4b/Y7

Writing. Pupils write a short text about themselves, saying what their name is, where they live and giving their address and phone number. Encourage them to use *und* at least once to join statements together.

More able pupils can include any other relevant language they have learned, e.g. favourite things, age, etc. They can build more complex sentences using *und* and *aber.*

Plenary 4.2/Y7

Aim

To emphasise the importance of numbers as high-frequency words.

In English, brainstorm contexts in which the class has met numbers in German (e.g. ages, birthdays, prices, times, pets, family, addresses, phone numbers). Note the contexts on the board or an OHT. Pupils could then produce a sentence for as many of these contexts as possible within a time limit. Each sentence should contain at least one number.

2 Mein Haus

Learning targets

- Describing your home
- Using *es gibt* to say what there is

Key framework objectives

1.5/Y7 Speaking – (a) presenting
1.5/Y7 Speaking – (b) expression / non-verbal techniques
4.6/Y7 Language – (b) negatives

Grammar

- *Es gibt* + accusative
- *einen / eine / ein* (accusative)
- *keinen / keine / kein* (accusative)

Key language

der Garten / Balkon / Keller / Dachboden
die Küche / Toilette / Garage
das Wohnzimmer / Schlafzimmer / Badezimmer / Esszimmer
Es gibt einen / keinen Garten / Balkon / Keller / Dachboden.
Es gibt eine / keine Küche / Toilette / Eingangshalle.
Es gibt ein / kein Wohnzimmer / Schlafzimmer / Badezimmer / Esszimmer.
Ich wohne in einer Wohnung.
Ich wohne in einem Einfamilienhaus / Doppelhaus / Reihenhaus / Bungalow.
Mein Haus ist groß / mittelgroß / klein.

High-frequency words

es gibt	*in*
ein	*kein*
wo?	*wohne, wohnst*
wie	*aber*
nicht	*mein, dein*
das ist	

Pronunciation

Improving pronunciation by recording and reviewing own speech

ICT

Using a program to produce a plan of an ideal home

Citizenship

Homes in German-speaking countries

Resources

CD 3, tracks 5–7
Workbooks A and B, p. 43
Arbeitsblatt 5.1, p. 79
Arbeitsblatt 5.2, p. 80
Flashcards 70–80
Echo Elektro 1 TPP, Mod 5 2.1–2.8

Starter 1 5.4

Aim

To introduce the new vocabulary needed for this lesson. 

To build confidence in inferring the meanings of unknown words.

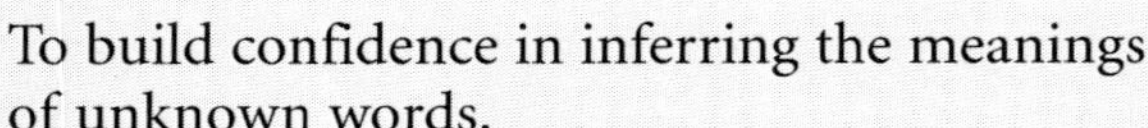

Prepare an OHT with the names of these rooms listed:

die Garage	*das Badezimmer*
der Garten	*das Esszimmer*
die Toilette	*das Schlafzimmer*
der Balkon	*das Wohnzimmer*
der Keller	*der Dachboden*
die Küche	

Distribute photocopies of **Arbeitsblatt 5.1**, section B, one copy per pair of pupils. Reveal the rooms on the OHT one word at a time, reading the word aloud. Pupils speculate which room it is, and hold up the letter of the room on paper or a mini-whiteboard.

1 Hör zu. Welches Zimmer ist das? (1–11) (AT 2/1) 4.2/Y7

Listening. Pupils listen to the recording and find the matching rooms in their books.

Draw attention particulary to the *z* in *Zimmer.*

CD 5

1 das Esszimmer
2 das Wohnzimmer
3 das Badezimmer
4 der Dachboden
5 der Garten
6 der Keller
7 die Garage
8 die Küche
9 der Balkon
10 das Schlafzimmer
11 die Toilette

Answers
1 h **2** f **3** g **4** a **5** k **6** j **7** i **8** e
9 c **10** b **11** d

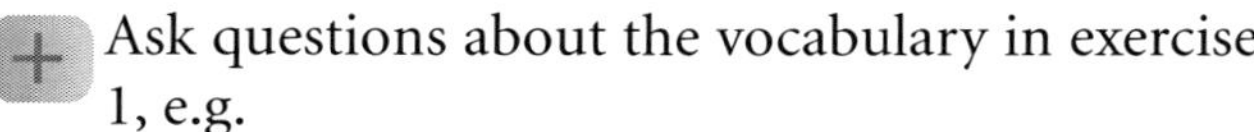

\+ Ask questions about the vocabulary in exercise 1, e.g.

- How many cognates are there?
- Find three masculine / two feminine / four neuter nouns.

– Find a noun with four syllables.

In a higher-ability class, this could be done as a team or individual 'fastest finger first' game.

2 Lies die E-Mails. Ist das Viktors oder Stefanies Wohnung? (AT 3/3) 2.1/Y7

Reading. Pupils read the two emails and decide whose flat is shown in the plan. Draw pupils' attention to the **ECHO-Detektiv** panel on page 81, where *es gibt* and the negative article *kein* are explained. For further exploitation of this activity, see Reading follow-up on page 9.

Answer
Stefanie

2 Hör zu. Welche Zimmer gibt es? (AT 1/4) 1.1/Y7

Listening. Pupils listen to the interviews and note the rooms in each speaker's home, matching them to the house diagram in exercise 1. Draw pupils' attention to the use of *kein* in the first dialogue.

6

- *Welche Zimmer gibt es in deinem Haus, Peter?*
  Also ... es gibt ein Esszimmer ...
  Es gibt ein Wohnzimmer. Es gibt eine Küche, ein Badezimmer und drei Schlafzimmer.
- *Gibt es einen Keller?*
- *Nein, es gibt keinen Keller.*

- *Hallo, Julia. Welche Zimmer gibt es in deinem Haus?*
- *Hallo. Es gibt eine Küche, es gibt ein Esszimmer ... es gibt view Schlafzimmer ... es gibt einen Keller – und es gibt drei Badezimmer.*
- *Drei Badezimmer!*
- *Ja. Mein Haus ist groß.*

Answers
Peter: h, f, e, g, b
Julia: e, h, b, j, g

ECHO-Detektiv 4.6b/Y7

This panel explains how to say that there is / isn't something in German, using *es gibt*. If you wish, refer pupils to the **Grammatik** on page 133 for more information and practice. See also **Arbeitsblatt 5.2.**

Starter 2 4.6b/Y7

Aim
To reinforce *es gibt (k)einen / (k)eine / (k)ein.*

Make an OHT of **Arbeitsblatt 5.1**, section B. Cross out some of the rooms. Pupils work in teams. Read out a number of *Es gibt ...* sentences describing the house diagram, including some which are false, e.g.:

Es gibt einen Keller.
Es gibt kein Wohnzimmer.

Pupils put up their hands as soon as they hear a false sentence. If working in pairs, they could write a T or F on a mini-white board or piece of paper after each sentence. The first pupil to spot a false sentence scores a point for his/her team. If any team member can correct the sentence, the team also scores a bonus point.

+ For a higher-ability class, the game can be made more complex by writing numbers in some rooms to signify *zwei Schlafzimmer*, etc. To extend the game, pupils could make up their own true/false sentences.

4 Wie ist dein Haus / deine Wohnung? Halte einen Vortrag. (AT 2/3–4) 1.5a+b/Y7

Speaking. Pupils prepare and give a presentation about their own home. Give them the option of describing their 'dream home' instead. Pupils' presentations could be recorded (audio or video) and played back to enable them to review and improve their pronunciation. Encourage pupils also to make their talks more interesting through expression and non-verbal techniques, e.g. facial expression, using their hands, using props.

ICT Pupils use a graphics application to produce a plan of their ideal home, colour-coding the rooms and using a key to label the rooms.

5 Hör zu. Was passt zusammen? (1–5) (AT 1/2) 1.1/Y7

Listening. Pupils listen to the recording and match the house pictures to the speakers.

7

1 – *Wo wohnst du, Birgit?*
– *Ich wohne in einem Doppelhaus.*

2 – *Wo wohnst du, Alex?*
– *Ich wohne in enem Reihenhaus.*

3 – *Wo wohnst du, Bastian?*
– *Ich wohne in einem Bungalow.*

4 – *Wo wohnst du, Maja?*
– *Ich wohne in einer Wohnung.*

5 – *Wo wohnst du, Tim?*
– *Ich wohne in einem Einfamilienhaus.*

Answers
1 c **2** a **3** e **4** d **5** b

ECHO-Tipp 3.1/Y7

Discuss the **ECHO-Tipp** panel on types of home with the class. If you have any photos of German/Austrian/Swiss homes, these could be shown to the class. Discuss with the class what kinds of home are most common in their area.

Pupils could conduce a survey amongst their classmates about which type of accommodation they live in:

– *(John), wo wohnst du?*
– *Ich wohne in (einer Wohnung).*

ICT The results could be recorded on a form (a row for each type of accommodation and a tally mark for each interviewee) and then presented in visual form. This could be done using a spreadsheet, then producing a bar or pie chart.

6 Wo wohnst du? Schreib einen Text. (AT 4/3–4) 2.4b/Y7

Writing. Pupils write a short text about their own home. Draw their attention to the form of *in **einem** Bungalow / in **einer** Wohnung*, etc. (The dative case after prepositions and the dative form of the definite article are discussed in Unit 5.)

More able pupils write more complex sentences (including connectives and qualifiers) and look up additional vocabulary in their dictionaries as required.

Plenary 4.6b/Y7

Aim

To reinforce the structure *es gibt (k)einen / (k)eine / (k)ein.*

Pupils work in small groups to prepare a mini-presentation on *es gibt*, including meaning, how to use it and at least one example sentence. Each group writes key points on an OHT or a whiteboard. After five minutes, ask for representatives of one or more groups (depending on time available) to volunteer to give their presentations. Members of other groups can suggest corrections, improvements and additions, or ask questions.

3 Oma schläft im Garten

Learning targets

- Describing what you do at home
- Using irregular verbs

Key framework objectives

4.5/Y7 Language – (a) present tense verbs

Grammar

Irregular verbs in 1st, 2nd, 3rd person singular: *essen, sehen, lesen, schlafen*

Key language

Ich höre im Keller Musik.
Ich spiele im Schlafzimmer am Computer.
Ich koche in der Küche.
Ich arbeite im Garten.
Ich esse im Esszimmer.
Ich lese im Badezimmer.
Ich sehe im Wohnzimmer fern.
Ich schlafe im Schlafzimmer.

High-frequency words

am
das (= that)
ein bisschen
essen
hören
im
lesen
machen
sehen
was?
wo?

English

Irregular verbs

Resources

CD 3, tracks 8–9
Workbooks A and B, p. 44
Arbeitsblatt 5.3, p. 81
Echo Elektro 1 TPP, Mod 5 3.1–3.5

Starter 1 4.5a/Y7

Aim
To revise verbs for leisure activities from Chapter 4.
To introduce new verbs for leisure activities.

Present these sentences on an OHT. The sentences marked * are new:

Ich höre Musik.
Ich koche. *
Ich arbeite im Garten. *
Ich esse.
Ich lese.
Ich schlafe. *

Elicit the meanings from the class, using mime to show the meanings of the new verbs. Go over pronunciation of the new phrases with the class. Pupils then take turns to come to the front of the class to mime the activities, prompting a response. Other class members should monitor pronunciation. This activity could then continue in pairs.

1 Was passt zusammen? (AT3/2) 4.4/Y7

Reading. Pupils match the speech bubbles to the cartoon characters. They can check their own answers by doing exercise 2.

Answers
1 b **2** h **3** c **4** d **5** e **6** f **7** g **8** a

2 Hör zu und überprüfe es. (1–8) (AT 1/2) 4.5a/Y7 5.4

Listening. Pupils listen to the recording to check their answers to exercise 1. You could then elicit the meanings of the verbs. *Ich lese, ich sehe fern, ich höre Musik, ich esse* and *ich spiele am Computer* are known from earlier chapters; *ich koche, ich arbeite* and *ich schlafe* are unknown. Can pupils infer the meanings of the new verbs from context and the illustrations?

1 – *Was machst du, Wolfi?*
– *Ich spiele im Schlafzimmer am Computer.*
2 – *Was machst du, Mutti?*
– *Ich schlafe im Schlafzimmer.*
3 – *Oma! Was machst du, Oma?*
– *Ich koche in der Küche.*
4 – *Und was machst du, Opa?*
– *Ich arbeite im Garten.*
5 – *Was machst du, Vati?*
– *Ich esse im Esszimmer.*
6 – *Ulrika! … Ulrika! … Was machst du, Ulrika?*
– *Ich lese … im Badezimmer.*

7 – *Und was machst du, Onkel Fritz?*
– *Ich sehe im Wohnzimmer fern.*
8 – *Tante Frieda! Was machst du?*
– *Ich höre im Keller Musik.*

Discuss *im* and *in der* with the class. Can pupils work out that they both mean 'in the', and suggest rules for when to use *im* and when to use *in der*?

3 Partnerarbeit. (AT 2/2–3) 1.4b/Y7

Speaking. Pupils work in pairs to create dialogues based on the cartoon pictures in exercise 1.

4 Wo machst du das? (AT 4/2) 4.4/Y7

Writing. Pupils write sentences about where they do various activities. All of the verbs should be familiar from the previous exercises or earlier chapters. You may wish them to choose about five of the verbs, rather than writing sentences for all of them.

R In preparation, run through the meanings of the verbs and elicit the *ich* form of each one. Less able pupils may need to be given the beginning of each sentence to complete, or even the beginnings and ends of sentences to join together in their own combinations.

Starter 1 4.4/Y7

Aim

To revise the structures and language from the previous lesson.
To reinforce basic sentence word order.

Photocopy **Arbeitsblatt 5.3** and distribute a copy to each pair of pupils. Pupils complete the puzzle by linking the words to form sentences. Set a time limit, e.g. five minutes. After the time limit has expired, check answers with the whole class. The grid could be copied onto an OHT to do this. Alternatively, pupils race to complete the puzzle and put their hands up when finished.

5 Hör zu und lies. Wo macht Tobias das? Verbinde die Bilder mit den Verben. (AT 3/3) 2.1/Y7

Listening/Reading. Pupils listen and read the text about brother Tobias and what he does in different rooms. They match the picture of each room with the infinitive to show what he does where. With weaker classes you could go through the meaning of the infinitives beforehand and make it clear that they won't be looking for exactly the same word in the text, but the version of the verb in the third person. The **ECHO-Detektiv** panel will help them to recognise these.

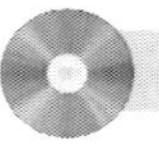

Mein Bruder Tobias ist sehr komisch! Er sieht im Badezimmer fern. Das findet er toll! Er kocht im Wohnzimmer. (Sein Lieblingsessen ist Spaghetti.) Er spielt in der Küche am Computer. Das mag er! Er liest auf dem Dachboden und er schläft im Garten. Das findet er praktisch! Tobias is ein bisschen seltsam!

Answers
1 c **2** b **3** a **4** e **5** d

ECHO-Detektiv 4.5a/Y7

This panel review the irregular verbs ***essen***, ***sehen***, ***lesen*** and ***schlafen*** in the first, second and third person singular. You could ask pupils which regular verbs they also know.

6 Was macht er? Schreib Sätze. (AT 4/2) 4.5a/Y7

Writing. Pupils write sentences, using the pictures as cues. In preparation, elicit from the class the verbs they will need and their *er / sie / es* forms, referring to the **ECHO-Detektiv** panel as necessary. Less able pupils could instead be given the sentence beginnings and ends to match together.

Answers
1. Er isst in der Küche.
2. Er sieht im Schlafzimmer fern.
3. Er spielt im Wohnzimmer am Computer.
4. Er hört im Garten Musik.
5. Er schläft im Badezimmer.

Plenary: Mini-Test 5.8

Aim

To review language learned to date and identify areas for improvement.

Pupils work in pairs to check the language they have learned so far in the chapter, using the **Mini-Test** checklist. Ask pupils which points their partners found most difficult. Give pupils the task of improving those points by next lesson. Partners could then test them again.

4 In meinem Zimmer

Learning targets

- Describing your room
- Understanding that the verb has to be the second idea

Key framework objectives

5.1 Strategies – patterns

Grammar

- Word order: verb as second idea

Key language

der Schreibtisch / Kleiderschrank / Stuhl / Computer / Fernseher / Spiegel
die Lampe / Kommode / Stereoanlage
das Bett / Regal / Sofa
In meinem Zimmer habe ich …
einen Schreibtisch / Kleiderschrank / Stuhl / Computer / Fernseher / Spiegel.
eine Lampe / Stereoanlage / Kommode.
ein Bett / Regal / Sofa.
Wie ist dein Zimmer?
Mein Zimmer ist klein / groß / hell / dunkel / ordentlich / unordentlich.
sehr / ziemlich / nicht sehr

High-frequency words

dein
groß
haben
in
klein
mein
nicht sehr
sehr
wie?
ziemlich

Resources

CD 3, tracks 10–12
Workbooks A and B, p. 45
Arbeitsblatt 5.4, p. 82
Echo Elektro 1 TPP, Mod 5
4.1–4.7

Starter 1 5.4

Aim

To introduce new vocabulary needed for this lesson.

To explore ways of deducing meaning.

Present the following quiz on an OHT. Reveal the questions one by one. Alternatively, you could write the German nouns one by one on the board and read out the three options for the English meaning. Pupils confer in pairs to decide the correct option. Check the answers with the whole class at the end. Ask pupils how they got the correct answer (e.g. deduction, cognate, lucky guess).

Quiz

1 der Stuhl
a TV b chair c sausage
2 der Fernseher
a chair b TV c wardrobe
3 der Spiegel
a mirror b computer c TV
4 die Stereoanlage
a piano b DVD player c hi-fi
5 die Lampe
a wardrobe b fish c lamp

Starter 1 *continued*

6 das Bett
a stool b bed c table
7 der Schreibtisch
a desk b wardrobe c computer
8 der Kleiderschrank
a wardrobe b guinea pig c dining table

Suggestion

Use OHT 25 from the Colour OHT File, or alternatively flashcards you might already have to present the furniture vocabulary.

1 Hör zu und lies. 4.2/Y7

Listening/Reading. Pupils listen to the recording and follow the text in their books.

CD 10

a	*der Fernseher*	*g*	*die Lampe*
b	*der Kleiderschrank*	*h*	*der Spiegel*
c	*die Kommode*	*i*	*das Regal*
d	*das Bett*	*j*	*das Sofa*
e	*die Stereoanlage*	*k*	*der Computer*
f	*der Stuhl*	*l*	*der Schreibtisch*

2 Hör zu. Welche Sachen werden genannt? (1–6) (AT 1/3) 1.1/Y7

Listening. Pupils listen to the recording and note down the letters (from exercise 1) of the items of furniture mentioned.

11

1 – *Was hast du in deinem Zimmer, Carsten?*
– *In meinem Zimmer habe ich ein Bett … ein Sofa und … einen Schreibtisch.*

2 – *Und du, Beyhan? Was hast du in deinem Zimmer?*
– *O.K. … also … in meinem Zimmer habe ich ein Bett und ein Regal – und einen Computer.*

3 – *Und Olaf, was hast du in deinem Zimmer?*
– *Tja, in meinem Zimmer habe ich einen Kleiderschrank, eine Stereoanlage und ein Bett.*

4 – *Maren, was hast du in deinem Zimmer?*
– *Uff! … In meinem Zimmer? … In meinem Zimmer habe ich einen Spiegel, eine Kommode … und einen Stuhl.*

5 – *Was hast du in deinem Zimmer, Heiko?*
– *In meinem Zimmer habe ich einen Fernseher, ein Bett und einen Kleiderschrank.*

6 – *Und Carola. Was hast du in deinem Zimmer, Carola?*
– *In meinem Zimmer habe ich einen Schreibtisch, einen Stuhl und … und ein Regal.*

Answers

1	d, j, l	**4**	h, c, f
2	d, i, k	**5**	a, d, b
3	b, e, d	**6**	l, f, i

3 Gedächtnisspiel. (AT 2/4) 5.1 5.2

Speaking. Pupils work in groups to play a 'chain game' with items of furniture. The first pupil says *In meinem Zimmer habe ich …* and names an item of furniture; subsequent pupils repeat the sentence, each adding another item of furniture to the end, and so on until a pupil forgets the order, hesitates or makes a mistake. He/She restarts the game with a new sentence. Whilst less able pupils may use this exercise purely to improve their fluency and reinforce furniture vocabulary, encourage more able pupils to focus on the accurate use of *einen / eine / ein* as well. For further exploitation of this activity, see Other games on page 10.

ECHO-Detektiv 5.1

This panel looks at inverted word order and the 'verb second' rule. Pupils can be referred to the **Grammatik** on page 132 and **Arbeitsblatt 5.4** for further information and practice.

4 Schreib einen langen Satz über dein Zimmer. (AT 4/3) 4.4/Y7

Writing. Pupils use connectives to write long sentences about their rooms. Remind the class about the use of the connectives *und* and *aber*. Less able pupils may simply string sentences together using *und*.

+ Encourage more able pupils to make their sentences as long and complex as possible, using *aber ich habe keinen / keine / kein* and giving opinions. Pupils could then work in pairs to extend, improve and correct each other's sentences.

Starter 2 5.4

Aim

To introduce the new vocabulary needed for this lesson.

To foster thinking skills (pattern recognition, deduction).

Write these six adjectives on the board, or display them on six small pieces of acetate on the OHP. Make sure they are scattered at random:

klein
hell
unordentlich
dunkel
groß
ordentlich

Explain that these are six adjectives (elicit a definition of an adjective), and that there are three pairs of opposites. Can the class find the pairs, without looking up any meanings? Give pupils 30 seconds to confer with a partner and write down the pairs. Check answers with the class. Ask pupils how they arrived at their answers and whether they could use the same processes in other activities they do in language classes. For example:

- Remembering from another situation: *klein* and *groß* are known from describing people (Chapter 3)
- Recognising a pattern: *ordentlich* and *unordentlich* are identical except for *un-*, which usually makes an opposite.
- Deduction: *hell* and *dunkel* must be the other pair, because they are the only ones left.

Finally, ask pupils to look up *ordentlich* and *hell*. Can they now work out the meanings of *unordentlich* and *dunkel*?

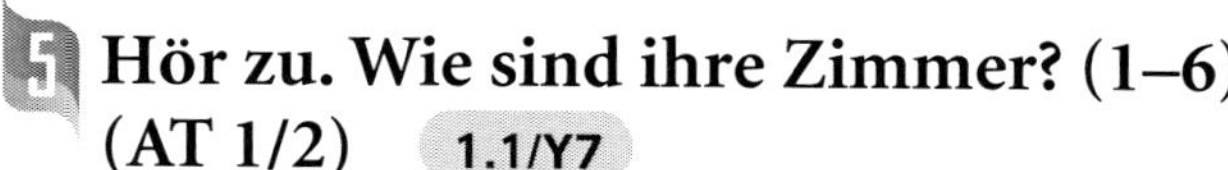

5 Hör zu. Wie sind ihre Zimmer? (1–6) (AT 1/2) 1.1/Y7

Listening. Pupils listen to the recording and note the characteristics of each speaker's room. Encourage pupils to jot down brief notes, going back to write out the adjectives in full after they have done the listening.

1 – Wie ist dein Zimmer, Micha?
– Mein Zimmer? Also, mein Zimmer ist klein.

2 – Und du, Britta? Wie ist dein Zimmer?
– Mein Zimmer ist … unordentlich.

3 – Wie ist dein Zimmer, Fabian?
– Mein Zimmer ist hell.

4 – Und Silke. Wie ist dein Zimmer, Silke?
– Ach … mein Zimmer ist dunkel.

5 – Wie ist dein Zimmer, Matthias?
– Mein Zimmer ist groß.

6 – Wie ist dein Zimmer, Heike?
– Ähmm … mein Zimmer ist ordentlich.

Answers
1 klein
2 unordentlich
3 hell
4 dunkel
5 groß
6 ordentlich

+ Pupils conduct a survey amongst their classmates, asking *Wie ist dein Zimmer?* and writing sentences about their findings. Encourage more confident pupils to also use other adjectives they know.

6 Wessen Zimmer ist das? (AT 3/4) 2.1/Y7

Reading. Pupils read the descriptions and decide whose bedroom is illustrated.

Answer
Viktor

+ Give the class five minutes to read the texts again thoroughly. They use the **Wortschatz** to look up any words they do not recognise. After five minutes, ask individual pupils to translate sentences into English. If they get stuck, you could allow them to nominate another pupil to help them – give the class the sentence *(Jim), kannst du mir helfen?* to enable them to do this in German.

7 Korrigiere die Sätze. (AT 3/4) 2.1/Y7

Reading. Pupils correct the false sentences about the boys' rooms.

Answers
(*Accept any alternatives that make sense.*)
1 Peters Zimmer ist sehr unordentlich.
2 Peter hat einen Schreibtisch, einen Computer, einen Fernseher und ein Bett.
3 Viktors Zimmer ist klein und sehr unordentlich.
4 Viktor findet sein Zimmer toll.
5 Heikos Zimmer ist nicht sehr groß / ziemlich klein und ziemlich dunkel.
6 Heiko hat einen Computer (aber keinen Fernseher).

8 Wie ist dein Zimmer? Schreib einen Text. (AT4/3–4) 2.4b/Y7

Writing. Pupils write a short text describing their own room. Encourage more able pupils to write complex sentences, give opinions and use inverted word order with *In meinem Zimmer habe ich / gibt es …* Pupils could swap their work with a partner to check for specific mistakes: word order, capitalisation of nouns and endings of articles, for example.

Plenary 5.8

Aim

To encourage pupils to evaluate and improve their written work.

Look at the **ECHO-Tipp** panel with the class and discuss the ideas for making sentences more interesting. Then write a simple sentence on the board or an OHT, e.g. *Mein Zimmer ist klein.* Pupils work in pairs to make the sentence more interesting and complex, writing the revised sentence on whiteboards. Examples might include:

Mein Zimmer ist klein, aber ordentlich.
Mein Zimmer ist sehr klein und ich finde es doof.
Mein Zimmer ist klein und schwarz – das ist furchtbar!

Set a time limit of about two minutes. After the time limit has expired, collect suggestions around the class, writing them below the original sentence (and correcting minor errors without comment). The class could then have a vote on which they think was the most interesting sentence.

5 Wo ist es?

Learning targets

- Saying what is in your room
- Using prepositions to describe where things are

Key framework objectives

2.1/Y7 Reading – main points and detail

Grammar

- Prepositions with the dative
- Definite article: dative

Key language

Wo ist die Katze?
Die Katze ist …
auf dem Regal / unter dem Bett / in dem Kleiderschrank / neben dem Stuhl / zwischen dem Bett und dem Schreibtisch / hinter dem Computer.
Wo ist der Bleistift?
Der Bleistift ist auf / unter / in / neben / hinter dem Buch.

High-frequency words

auf
hinter
in
ist
neben
unter
wo?
zwischen

English

Prepositions

Resources

CD 3, track 13
Workbooks A and B, p. 46
Arbeitsblatt 5.5, p. 83
Echo Elektro 1 TPP, Mod 5 5.1–5.5

Starter 1 4.2/Y7

Aim

To revise furniture vocabulary

Option 1: Pupils mime an item of furniture and their classmates ask closed questions such as *Bist du ein Kleiderschrank?*, etc.

Option 2: Play hangman using items of furniture and items in a schoolbag.

Suggestion

Present the six prepositions *auf, hinter, in, neben, unter* and *zwischen* on an OHT or on the board. Demonstrate their meaning using simple diagrams on the board, or objects in the classroom, while chorusing the preposition with the class. Continue to demonstrate the prepositions without saying them – pupils have to call out the correct preposition.

1 Hör zu und lies. Wo ist die Katze? (AT 3/2) 1.1/Y7

Listening. Pupils listen to the recording, following the conversation and focusing on the key phrases under each picture in the Pupil's Book. Emphasise that they should concentrate on hearing and understanding the key phrases as the conversation progresses.

13

– *Wo is die Katze?*
– *Die Katze ist auf dem Regal. Nein … die Katze ist unter dem Bett. Ach, die Katze is in dem Kleiderschrank!*
– *Und jetzt? Wo ist die Katze jetzt?*
– *Die Katze ist neben dem Stuhl. Nein … die Katze ist zwischen dem Bett und dem Schreibtisch. Ach, nein! Die Katze ist hinter dem Computer!*

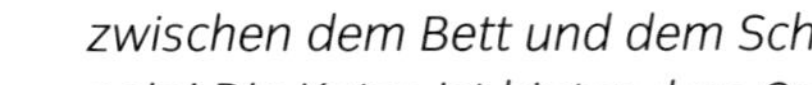

2 Wie heißt das auf Englisch? (AT 3/3) 4.2/Y7

Reading. Pupils translate the prepositions into English, using the illustrations from exercise 1 to infer the meanings.

Answers

1	on (top of)	**4**	next to
2	under	**5**	behind
3	in	**6**	between

3 Partnerarbeit. (AT 2/3) 1.4b/Y7

Speaking. Pupils work in pairs to practise prepositions, using the Key Language panel for support. Partner A positions a pencil relative to a schoolbook and partner B says where it is. Then the roles are reversed. Pupils could practise further with other pairs of objects.

Suggestion

For further practice, partner A says a sentence describing the position of the object, and partner B moves the object accordingly.

4 Sieh dir Zogs Zimmer an und lies die Sätze auf Seite 87. Was ist richtig? (AT 3/2) 4.4/Y7

Reading. Pupils compare the sentences with the picture and choose the correct preposition to complete each sentence.

Answers

1 neben	**4** unter
2 auf	**5** hinter
3 auf	**6** zwischen

Starter 2 4.2/Y7

Aim

To reinforce the meanings of prepositions.

Draw two simple identical sketches of items of furniture (e.g. two wardrobes) on the board side by side. Divide the class into two teams. Each team elects a representative who goes to the board. The teams take turns to call out a German preposition e.g. *auf dem Kleiderschrank* – the representative who draws a cross in the correct place first wins a point for his/her team. Alternatively, the representatives could demonstrate the prepositions using two objects, e.g. a pencil and a schoolbag. Encourage stronger pupils to say a whole phrase rather than just one preposition.

ECHO-Detektiv: Prepositions 4.3/Y7

This panel shows the change in the definite article after a preposition which takes the dative case. You could check comprehension of the term 'preposition' by asking for examples in English, or by calling out words in English including some prepositions – pupils must put up their hands whenever you say a preposition. If you wish, refer pupils to the **Grammatik** on page 126 for more information and practice.

5 Sieh dir das Bild noch mal an. Beantworte die Fragen. (AT 4/3) 4.3/Y7 4.4/Y7

Writing. Pupils answer the questions about the picture from exercise 4 in full sentences. In preparation, go through the **ECHO-Detektiv** panel with the class. With less able pupils, you may wish to concentrate further on the meaning of the prepositions; with more able pupils, focus also on accuracy in the form of the definite article.

Answers

1 Die Gitarre ist unter dem Bett.
2 Der Taschenrechner ist auf dem Bett.
3 Die Jacke ist in dem Kleiderschrank.
4 Die Diskette ist neben dem Computer.

6 Lies den Text und zeichne das Zimmer. (AT 3/4) 2.1/Y7

Reading. Pupils read the description, then draw the bedroom. You could draw the outline of the room and one or two items in it on the board to help pupils get started. For further exploitation of this exercise see Writing follow-up on pages 9–10.

7 Zeichne dein Zimmer. Beschreib es. (AT 4/3–4) 2.4a/Y7

Writing. Pupils draw a picture of their bedroom, then write a description based on the one in exercise 6.

Plenary 4.2/Y7

Aim

To consolidate furniture vocabulary.

Photocopy **Arbeitsblatt 5.5** and cut it in half at the dotted line. Pupils work in pairs. Partner A receives the top half of the worksheet and partner B the bottom half. Each pupil must ask their partner questions in German to locate and draw in the missing items on their sheet. Finally pairs can check their partner's picture against their own.

Alternative: pairs revise changes to articles when they are used with the prepositions in this unit. An able pupil can then be elected to report the rule back to the whole class.

6 Grüße aus Salzburg

Learning targets

- Describing where you live
- Listening for different types of information

Key framework objectives

1.2/Y7 Listening – unfamiliar language
4.5/Y7 Language – (a) set phrases about the past

Grammar

- *sein: ich war* (receptive only)
- Time expressions which signal past reference (receptive only)

Key language

General consolidation of language from Units 1–5

High-frequency words

dort
es gibt
gern
groß
haben
in
klein
mit
nicht sehr
sehr
spielen
was?
wie?
wo?
wohnen
ziemlich

Citizenship

Towns in German-speaking countries

Resources

CD 3, tracks 14–16
Wrokbooks A and B, p. 47
Arbeitsblatt 5.6, p.84
Arbeitsblatt 5.7, p.85
Echo Elektro 1 TPP, Mod 5 6.1–6.5

Starter 1

4.2/Y7

Aim
To recycle language from the chapter.

To foster lateral thinking, logic and word association.

Present the following words/expressions on the board or an OHT:

was?
rot
meine Adresse
eine Lampe
klein
wo?
mein Schlafzimmer
das Reihenhaus
fernsehen
ich lese

Pupils work in pairs to put the items in three groups, using principles of their own choosing. Set a time limit of three minutes. After the time limit has expired, ask for volunteers to demonstrate and explain their groupings.

1 Hör zu. Wo wohnt Martin? (AT 1/4)

1.2/Y7

Listening. Pupils listen to the recording and then decide which of the photos best matches the dialogue (listening for gist). In preparation, elicit any vocabulary pupils can offer to describe the three photos (e.g. type of dwelling, likely situation – town, city, village, country).

14

- *Martin, wo wohnst du?*
- *Ich wohne in Salzburg. Das ist eine Stadt in Österreich, in den Bergen.*
- *Aha. Salzburg. Das muss bestimmt schön sein.*
- *Ja, Salzburg ist sehr schön.*
- *Und wie ist dein Haus?*
- *Mein Haus? Also … ich wohne mit meiner Familie in einem Einfamilienhaus. Es ist ziemlich groß.*
- *Und welche Zimmer gibt es?*
- *Also, es gibt vier Schlafzimmer … Es gibt auch zwei Badezimmer, eine Küche und ein Wohnzimmer … Ach ja, und es gibt einen Keller.*
- *Schön … Und wie ist dein Zimmer?*
- *Mein Zimmer ist klein. Es ist lila und grün.*
- *Lila und grün? Ahh, das ist sehr … originell.*

Answer
c

2 Hör noch mal zu. Notiere fünf Zimmer und zwei Farben. (AT1/4)

1.1/Y7

Listening. Pupils listen to the recording again and note down five rooms and two colours mentioned (listening for detail).

Answers

Rooms: Schlafzimmer, Badezimmer, Küche, Wohnzimmer, Keller
Colour: lila, grün

ECHO-Tipp 1.1/Y7

This panel offers advice about how to approach listening for detail.

3 Hör zu. Füll die Lücken aus. (AT 1/4)

1.1/Y7 1.2/Y7

Listening. Pupils listen to the recording and supply the missing words from the text in their books. More able pupils could read the text first and attempt to predict the missing words, before listening to the recording to check their answers. Encourage pupils to think carefully about the likely part of speech (noun, verb, etc.) represented by each of the gaps.

Salzburg, den 14. Mai
Hallo!
Ich wohne in Salzburg. Das ist eine Stadt in Österreich. Salzburg ist nicht sehr groß, aber sehr interessant. Hier ist viel los! Ich war letzte Woche in der Disko. Ich war auch gestern mit meinen Freunden im Kino. Das war ganz toll!
Ich wohne mit meiner Familie in einer Wohnung hier in Salzburg. Die Wohnung ist ziemlich groß. Es gibt drei Schlafzimmer.
Mein Zimmer ist klein und hell. Es ist blau und gelb. (Blau ist meine Lieblingsfarbe.) Es ist ziemlich ordentlich. Mein Hund, Rollo, schläft immer in meinem Zimmer.
Es gibt ein Bett, einen Schreibtisch, einen Kleiderschrank und ein Sofa in meinem Zimmer. Ich habe auch einen Computer und ein Radio. Ich habe eine Gitarre – ich spiele sehr gern Gitarre. Meine Mutter findet das furchtbar!
Schreib bald!
Deine Nina

Answers

1. Stadt
2. interessant
3. Disko
4. zeimlich
5. Schlafzimmer
6. hell
7. gelb
8. gibt
9. Kleiderschrank
10. Computer
11. gern

ECHO-Detektiv 4.5a/Y7

This panel draws pupils' attention to the way in which Nina refers to the past using ***war*** and phrases like ***letzte Woche***. This idea is introduced receptively only on this spread, but could be developed further using the **Grammatik** on page 132 and **Arbeitsblatt 5.6.**

Starter 2 4.5a/Y7

Aim

To foster thinking skills (visualisation and memory). 
To provide further exposure to the past tense.

Arrange a series of objects on the desk, for pupils to look at as they come into the room. They should all be objects which pupils know the German for, e.g. a reading lamp, a book, a toy animal or a picture of an animal, items of food or drink, items from a schoolbag, etc. When all pupils are seated, cover the desk with a cloth so that the items cannot be seen. Make true/false statements about the objects in the imperfect tense, using *war*, e.g.:

Eine Lampe war auf dem Schreibtisch.
Ein Bleistift war auf dem Buch.

Pupils respond e.g. by thumbs up for 'true' and thumbs down for 'false', or by holding up a tick or cross on their whiteboards. More able pupils could be encouraged to make up their own sentences on the same pattern.

4 and 5 Gedächtnisspiel. (AT2/4)

1.4b/Y7 5.2

Speaking. Pupils work together in pairs. Partner A looks at picture A and attempts to memorise the details, then closes his/her book, while partner B asks him/her the questions and confirms whether his/her answers are correct. Then the roles are reversed in exercise 5 with picture B.

Answers

A		B	
1	ja	**1**	nein
2	gelb	**2**	lila
3	nein	**3**	ja
4	rot	**4**	braun
5	unter dem Schreibtisch	**5**	auf dem Regal

6 Hör zu und sing mit. (AT 2/)

1.2/Y7

Listening. Pupils listen to the song and sing along. For further ideas on using this activity, see Exploiting the songs on page 9.

16

Hier ist der Garten.
Ach, wie bunt!
Was machst du dort?
Ich spiele mit dem Hund!

Das ist unser Haus,
wir wohnen hier!
Das ist unser Haus,
hier wohnen wir!

Hier ist das Wohnzimmer.
Das mag ich gern!
Was machst du dort?
Ich sehe immer fern!

Das ist unser Haus, etc.

Hier ist die Küche.
Ach, wie schick!
Was machst du dort?
Ich höre Musik!

Das ist unser Haus, etc.

Hier ist das Schlafzimmer.
Ach, wie nett!
Was machst du dort?
Ich schlafe in dem Bett!

Das is unser Haus, etc.

\+ Ask pupils to identify unknown words in the song (*ach, bunt, unser, immer, schick, nett*), then race to look them up in the **Wortschatz** at the back of their books.

Plenary

2.2b/Y7 2.3/Y7

Aim

To analyse a text (vocabulary and grammar).

Pupils analyse the song text to find e.g. 4 activities, 4 rooms, 4 adjectives, 4 examples of the dative case, 1 example of inversion, 5 cognates. (Adapt this list to the ability level of the pupils.) This could take the form of a race between two or more teams.

Lernzieltest 5.8

This is a checklist of language covered in Chapter 5. Pupils can work with the checklist in pairs to check what they have learned. Points which directly address grammar and structures are marked with a G. There is a **Lernzieltest** sheet in the Resource and Assessment File (page 88). Encourage pupils to look back at the chapter and to use the grammar section to revise what they are unclear about.

You can also use the **Lernzieltest** as an end-of-chapter plenary.

Widerholung

This is a revision page to prepare pupils for the **Kontrolle** at the end of the chapter.

Resources

CD 3, tracks 17–18

1 Hör zu. Finde die Bilder. (1–8) (AT 1/2) 1.1/Y7

Listening. Pupils listen to the recording and find the picture to match each sentence.

17

1. *Es gibt ein Schlafzimmer.*
2. *Es gibt eine Küche.*
3. *Wir haben einen Dachboden.*
4. *Wir haben einen Garten.*
5. *Wir haben zwei Badezimmer.*
6. *In meinem Haus gibt es ein Esszimmer.*
7. *Wir haben eine Garage.*
8. *Es gibt ein Wohnzimmer.*

Answers
1 d **2** b **3** h **4** f **5** e **6** c **7** g **8** a

2 Hör zu. Schreib die Zahlen auf. (1–8) 1.1/Y7

Listening. Pupils listen to the recording and write down the numbers they hear.

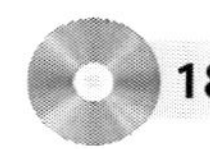
18

1 – *Wie ist deine Adresse?*
– *Meine Adresse ist Bachmannstraße 82.*

2 – *Und wie ist deine Adresse?*
– *Meine Adresse ist Joachimstraße 19.*

3 – *Und du, wie ist deine Adresse?*
– *Meine Adresse ist Märzweg 23.*

4 – *Wie ist deine Adresse?*
– *Meine Adresse ist Ingolfsweg 36.*

5 – *Wie ist deine Adresse?*
– *Meine Adresse ist Marchenallee 47.*

6 – *Und wie ist deine Adresse?*
– *Meine Adresse ist Seestraße 53.*

7 – *Wie ist deine Adresse?*
– *Meine Adresse ist Adlerstraße 43.*

8 – *Und wie ist deine Adresse?*
– *Meine Adresse ist Josephstraße 56.*

Answers
1 82 **2** 19 **3** 23 **4** 36 **5** 47 **6** 53 **7** 43 **8** 56

3 Partnerarbeit: Mach Interviews. (AT 2/3) 1.4b/Y7

Speaking. Pupils work in pairs. They interview each other using the questions provided and respond using the information on the cue cards in their books.

4 Lies den Brief. Beantworte die Fragen auf Englisch. (AT 3/3) 2.1/Y7

Reading. Pupils read the letter and answer the questions in English.

Answers
1. a flat
2. three bedrooms, a bathroom, a toilet, a kitchen, a dining room, a living room, balcony
3. small and untidy
4. desk, wardrobe, chair, bed

5 Wie ist dein Zimmer? Was gibt es in deinem Zimmer? (AT 4/3–4) 2.4a/Y7

Writing. Pupils write a short text about their bedrooms.

Learning targets

- Understanding a cartoon
- Celebrity homes: composing interviews

Key framework objectives

2.2/Y7 Reading – (a) unfamiliar language
2.2/Y7 Reading – (b) text selection
2.5/Y7 Writing – different text types
5.5 Strategies – reference materials

Key language

Consolidation of language from Units 1–6

High-frequency words

auch
das (= that)
dein
dort
es gibt
groß
haben
hallo!
mein
mit
schön
sehr
toll
war
wer?
wo?
wohnen

English

Reading a magazine interview

Resources

CD 3, track 19
Workbooks A and B, p. 48.

Starter 1 2.2a/Y7

Aim
To practise scanning and summarising texts.
To improve recall of written language.

Ask the class to read the story in exercise 1. Set a time limit of about two minutes. At the end of the time limit, pupils close their books. Ask pupils what they remember from the text, including individual words/phrases, details of illustrations and gist (characters, subject matter, plot). Write this on the board or an OHT for review after exercise 1.

1 Hör zu und lies. 2.2b/Y7 4.5a/Y7

Listening. Pupils listen to the recording and follow the cartoon strip in their books.

1 – *Hi, Bork!*
– *Kika! Hallo! Komm 'rein.*
2 – *Wow, dein Haus ist groß!*
– *Ja, es gibt vier Schlafzimmer und drei Badezimmer.*
– *Drei Badezimmer?!*
3 – *Das ist das Gästezimmer. Du schläfst dort. Du hast auch ein eigenes Badezimmer.*
– *He, toll!*
4 – *Das ist mein Schlafzimmer.*
– *Sehr schön.*
– *Das ist mein Computer auf dem Schreibtisch, das ist mein Fernseher und das ... He! Warte mal ... Wo ist meine Stereoanlage? Sie war neben dem Schreibtisch!*
5 – *Ungli!! Das ist meine Stereoanlage!*

2 Richtig, falsch oder nicht im Text? (AT 3/5) 2.1/Y7 5.5

Reading. Pupils read the statements about the cartoon strip and decide whether they are true, false or not mentioned in the text. In preparation, you may wish to check that pupils are clear about the difference between *falsch* (i.e. contradicted by the text) and *nicht im Text* (i.e. not mentioned in the text). Pupils should look up any words they do not understand in the **Wortschatz** at the back of their books.

Answers

1 nicht im Text
2 falsch
3 nicht im Text
4 falsch
5 richtig
6 richtig

3 Welches Haus gehört Benjamin Braun? (AT 3/4) 2.2a+b/Y7 5.5

Reading. Pupils read the magazine interview and decide which house belongs to the fictitious teen actor, Benjamin Braun. They look up any unfamiliar words in the **Wortschatz** at the back of their books. In preparation for this exercise, you could ask the class to assess the text for gist, purpose, intended audience and degree of difficulty (e.g. unknown words).

Answer
b

+ Pupils work in pairs to translate the interview into English for a teen magazine in England.

Wie ist dein Traumhaus? Schreib ein Interview. (AT 4/4) 2.5/Y7

Writing. Pupils write a magazine interview with themselves, as if they were a celebrity with a luxurious house.

Suggestion

You could prepare for this exercise by brainstorming desirable features for the dream house with the class, in English. Write their suggestions on the board or an OHT. Two volunteers then look up the necessary German vocabulary in dictionaries; a 'secretary' writes up the German next to the English.

5 Partnerarbeit: Nimm dein Interview auf. (AT 2/4) 1.4b/Y7

Speaking. Pupils act out and record their interviews in pairs, on audio or video cassette.

Plenary 5.8

Aim

To encourage pupils to evaluate and improve the quality and fluency of their speech.

Play a selection of the recorded interviews to the class. The 'actors' in each interview can ask the class comprehension questions about it in English. The class can offer critiques of pronunciation and content.

SELF-ACCESS READING AND WRITING AT TWO LEVELS

A Reinforcement

Was passt zusammen? (AT 3/3) 2.1/Y7

Reading. Pupils read the 'small ads' for accommodation, and match them to the correct illustrations.

Answers
1 d **2** c **3** a **4** b

Schreib Untertitel für die Bilder. (AT 4/2) 4.4/Y7

Writing. Pupils use the pictures and Key Language box to construct sentences about activities and rooms.

Answers
1. Ich spiele im Wohnzimmer am Computer.
2. Ich lese in der Toilette.
3. Ich höre im Badezimmer Musik.
4. Ich sehe in der Küche fern.
5. Ich schlafe im Garten.
6. Ich arbeite in der Garage.

Schreib die Sätze aus. (AT 4/2) 4.4/Y7

Writing. Pupils copy out the sentences, inserting gaps to separate the words. More confident learners should be expected to use correct capital letters.

Answers
1. Ich wohne in einem Einfamilienhaus auf dem Land.
2. Wir haben sieben Schlafzimmer und sechs Badezimmer.
3. Mein Zimmer ist sehr klein und unordentlich.
4. Meine Adresse ist Teichstraße fünfundneunzig.
5. Mein Computer ist zwischen dem Bett und dem Schreibtisch.

B Extension

Welches Zimmer ist das? Was macht man in dem Zimmer? (AT3/2) 4.2/Y7

Reading. Pupils unjumble the words for rooms and write them out correctly. They then match the most logical activity to each room.

Answers
1. Die Küche – b
2. Das Schlafzimmer – e
3. Das Wohnzimmer – d
4. Das Esszimmer – a
5. Der Garten – c

2 Wo ist das im Zimmer? Was passt zusammen? (AT 3/4) 2.1/Y7

Reading. Pupils read the description of the bedroom, and work out which item each number in the picture represents.

Answers
1. der Stuhl
2. der Fernseher
3. das Regal
4. eine Diskette
5. die Stereoanlage
6. meine Bücher

3 Wie ist die richtige Reihenfolge? Schreib den Text ab und füll die Lücken aus. (AT 3/4 AT 4/2) 4.4/Y7

Reading/ Writing. Pupils firstly scan through the text and work out how to re-order the lines so that it makes sense. They then copy the text out in the correct order, replacing each picture with the correct word (checking spellings as necessary by looking words up).

Answers
5, 1, 3, 2, 4, 6

Hallo! Ich bin Zorka. Mein **Hund** heißt Zluk. Ich wohne in Bloork, das ist ein Dorf auf dem Planeten Blik. Wir haben einen großen **Garten**. Ich wohne in einem Einfamilienhaus. Wir haben ein **Wohnzimmer**, eine Küche, ein **Badezimmer** und zwei Schlafzimmer. Wir haben keinen **Keller**. Mein Schlafzimmer ist sehr unordentlich, aber es ist groß und hell. Es gibt ein **Bett** und einen Stuhl. Auf dem **Schreibtisch** habe ich einen **Fernseher**. Ich sehe gern fern. Mein Zimmer ist toll!

Übungsheft A, Seite 42

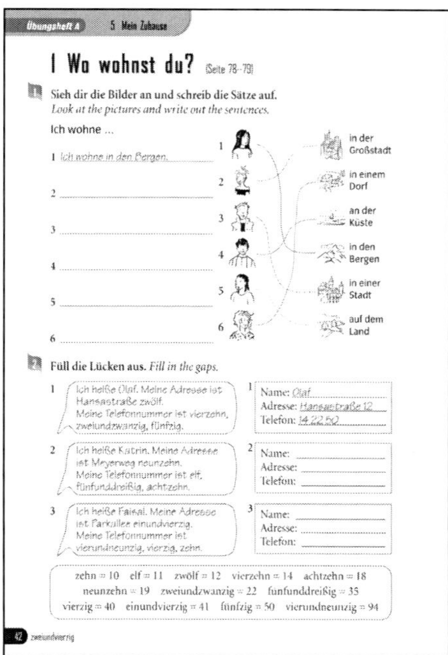
Übungsheft A 5 Mein Zuhause

I Wo wohnst du? (Seite 78–79)

1 Sieh dir die Bilder an und schreib die Sätze auf. *Look at the pictures and write out the sentences.*

Ich wohne …

1 Ich wohne in den Bergen.
2
3
4
5
6

in der Großstadt / in einem Dorf / an der Küste / in den Bergen / in einer Stadt / auf dem Land

2 Füll die Lücken aus. *Fill in the gaps.*

1 Ich heiße Olaf. Meine Adresse ist Hansastraße zwölf. Meine Telefonnummer ist vierzehn, zweiundzwanzig, fünfzig.
Name: Olaf
Adresse: Hansastraße 12
Telefon: 14 22 50

2 Ich heiße Katrin. Meine Adresse ist Meyerweg neunzehn. Meine Telefonnummer ist elf, fünfunddreißig, achtzehn.
Name:
Adresse:
Telefon:

3 Ich heiße Faisal. Meine Adresse ist Parkallee einundvierzig. Meine Telefonnummer ist vierundneunzig, vierzig, zehn.
Name:
Adresse:
Telefon:

zehn = 10 elf = 11 zwölf = 12 vierzehn = 14 achtzehn = 18
neunzehn = 19 zweiundzwanzig = 22 fünfunddreißig = 35
vierzig = 40 einundvierzig = 41 fünfzig = 50 vierundneunzig = 94

42 zweiundvierzig

1 (AT3 Level 2, AT4 Level 2) **1** Ich wohne in den Bergen. **2** Ich wohne in der Großstadt. **3** Ich wohne in einer Stadt. **4** Ich wohne an der Küste. **5** Ich wohne auf dem Land. **6** Ich wohne in einem Dorf.

2 (AT3 Level 3, AT4 Level 1) **1** Name: Olaf. Adresse: Hansastraße 12. Telefon 14 22 50 **2** Name: Katrin. Adresse: Meyerweg 19. Telefon 11 35 18 **3** Name: Faisal. Adresse: Parkallee 41. Telefon 94 40 10

Übungsheft B, Seite 42

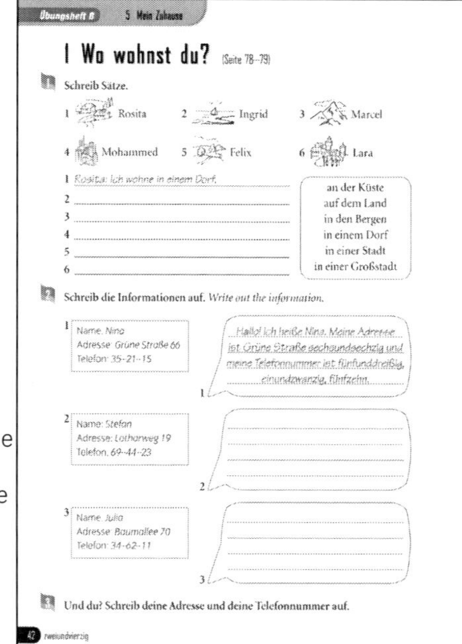
Übungsheft B 5 Mein Zuhause

I Wo wohnst du? (Seite 78–79)

1 Schreib Sätze.

1 Rosita 2 Ingrid 3 Marcel
4 Mohammed 5 Felix 6 Lara

1 Rosita: Ich wohne in einem Dorf.
2
3
4
5
6

an der Küste / auf dem Land / in den Bergen / in einem Dorf / in einer Stadt / in einer Großstadt

2 Schreib die Informationen auf. *Write out the information.*

1 Name: Nina
Adresse: Grüne Straße 66
Telefon: 35-21-15
Hallo! Ich heiße Nina. Meine Adresse ist Grüne Straße sechsundsechzig und meine Telefonnummer ist fünfunddreißig, einundzwanzig, fünfzehn.

2 Name: Stefan
Adresse: Lotharweg 19
Telefon: 69-44-23

3 Name: Julia
Adresse: Baumallee 70
Telefon: 34-62-11

3 Und du? Schreib deine Adresse und deine Telefonnummer auf.

42 zweiundvierzig

1 (AT4 Level 2)
1 Rosita: Ich wohne in einem Dorf. **2** Ingrid: Ich wohne an der Küste. **3** Marcel: Ich wohne in den Bergen. **4** Mohammed: Ich wohne in einer Großstadt. **5** Felix: Ich wohne auf dem Land. **6** Lara: Ich wohne in einer Stadt.

2 (AT3, Level 2, AT4 Level 3) **1** Hallo! Ich heiße Nina. Meine Adresse ist Grüne Straße sechsundsechzig und meine Telefonnummer ist fünfunddreißig, einundzwanzig, fünfzehn. **2** Hallo! Ich heiße Stefan. Meine Adresse ist Lotharweg neunzehn und meine Telefonnummer ist neunundsechzig, vierundvierzig, dreiundzwanzig. **3** Hallo! Ich heiße Julia. Meine Adresse ist Baumallee siebzig und meine Telefonnummer ist vierunddreißig, zweiundsechzig, elf.

3 (AT4 Level 2–3)

Übungsheft A, Seite 43

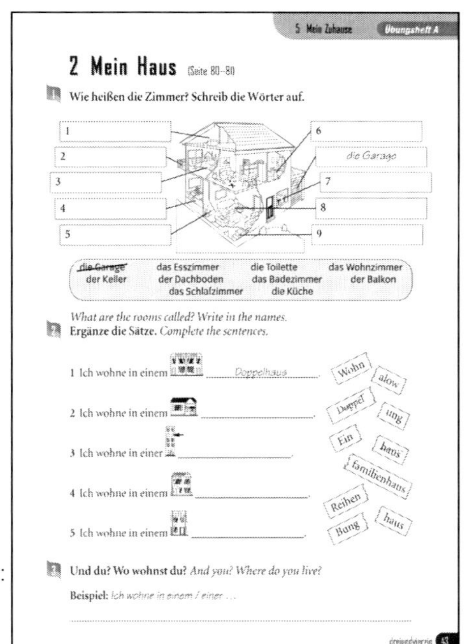
5 Mein Zuhause Übungsheft A

2 Mein Haus (Seite 80–81)

1 Wie heißen die Zimmer? Schreib die Wörter auf.

1 / 2 / 3 / 4 / 5 / 6 die Garage / 7 / 8 / 9

~~die Garage~~ das Esszimmer die Toilette das Wohnzimmer der Keller der Dachboden das Badezimmer der Balkon das Schlafzimmer die Küche

What are the rooms called? Write in the names.

2 Ergänze die Sätze. *Complete the sentences.*

1 Ich wohne in einem Doppelhaus.
2 Ich wohne in einem
3 Ich wohne in einer
4 Ich wohne in einem
5 Ich wohne in einem

Wohn / alow / Doppel / ung / Ein / haus / familienhaus / Reihen / Bung / haus

3 Und du? Wo wohnst du? *And you? Where do you live?*

Beispiel: Ich wohne in einem / einer …

dreiundvierzig 43

1 (AT3 Level 1, AT4 Level 1)
1 attic: *der Dachboden*; **2** balcony: *der Balkon*; **3** bedroom: *das Schlafzimmer*; **4** kitchen: *die Küche*; **5** toilet: *die Toilette*; **6** bathroom: *das Badezimmer*; **7** dining room: *das Esszimmer*; **8** living room: *das Wohnzimmer*; **9** cellar: *der Keller*

2 (AT3 Level 2, AT4 Level 2) **1** Ich wohne in einem **Doppelhaus**. **2** Ich wohne in einem **Bungalow**. **3** Ich wohne in einer **Wohnung**. **4** Ich wohne in einem **Einfamilienhaus**. **5** Ich wohne in einem **Reihenhaus**.

3 (AT4 Level 3)

Übungsheft B, Seite 43

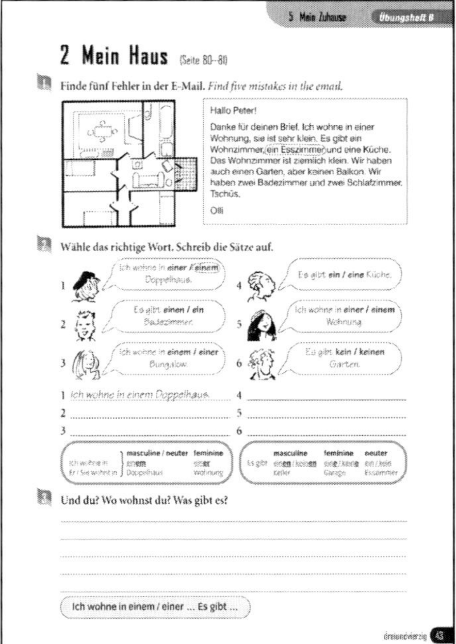
5 Mein Zuhause Übungsheft B

2 Mein Haus (Seite 80–81)

1 Finde fünf Fehler in der E-Mail. *Find five mistakes in the email.*

Hallo Peter!
Danke für deinen Brief. Ich wohne in einer Wohnung, sie ist sehr klein. Es gibt ein Wohnzimmer, ein Esszimmer und eine Küche. Das Wohnzimmer ist ziemlich klein. Wir haben auch einen Garten, aber keinen Balkon. Wir haben zwei Badezimmer und zwei Schlafzimmer.
Tschüs,
Olli

2 Wähle das richtige Wort. Schreib die Sätze auf.

1 Ich wohne in einer / einem Doppelhaus.
2 Es gibt einen / ein Badezimmer.
3 Ich wohne in einem / einer Bungalow.
4 Es gibt ein / eine Küche.
5 Ich wohne in einer / einem Wohnung.
6 Es gibt kein / keinen Garten.

1 Ich wohne in einem Doppelhaus.

3 Und du? Wo wohnst du? Was gibt es?

Ich wohne in einem / einer … Es gibt …

dreiundvierzig 43

1 (AT3 Level 3)
Hallo Peter! Danke für deinen Brief. Ich wohne in einer Wohnung, sie ist sehr klein. Es gibt ein Wohnzimmer, (ein Esszimmer) und eine Küche. Das Wohnzimmer ist ziemlich klein. Wir haben auch (einen Garten) aber (keinen Balkon) Wir haben (zwei Badezimmer) und (zwei Schlafzimmer) Tschüs, Olli.

2 (AT3 Level 2, AT4 Level 2) **1** Ich wohne in **einem** Doppelhaus. **2** Es gibt **ein** Badezimmer. **3** Ich wohne in **einem** Bungalow. **4** Es gibt **eine** Küche. **5** Ich wohne in **einer** Wohnung. **6** Es gibt **keinen** Garten.

3 (AT4 Level 3–4)

Übungsheft A, Seite 44

1 **(AT3 Level 3, AT4 Level 1)** **1** Ich **schlafe** im Schlafzimmer. **2** Ich **lese** im Badezimmer. **3** Ich **esse** im Esszimmer. **4** Ich **koche** in der Küche. **5** Ich **arbeite** im Garten. **6** Ich **höre** im Keller Musik. **7** Ich **sehe** im Wohnzimmer fern **8** Ich **spiele** im Schlafzimmer am Computer.

2 **(AT4 Level 1–2)** **1** Ich schlafe **2** Ich esse **3** Ich sehe **4** Ich arbeite **5** Ich höre **6** Ich koche **7** Ich lese

3 **(AT3 Level 1, AT4 Level 1)** **1** Wohn- **2** Ess- **3** Bade- **4** -zimmer

Übungsheft B, Seite 44

1 **(AT4 Level 2)** **1** Ich schlafe im Schlafzimmer. **2** Ich lese im Badezimmer. **3** Ich esse im Esszimmer. **4** Ich koche in der Küche. **5** Ich arbeite im Garten. **6** Ich höre im Keller Musik. **7** Ich sehe im Wohnzimmer fern **8** Ich spiele im Schlafzimmer am Computer.

2 **(AT3 Level 2, AT4 Level 1)** **1** Was **isst** du? Ich **esse** Kuchen. **2** Was **isst** Papa? Er **isst** einen Apfel. **3** Was **liest** du? Ich **lese** ein Buch. **4** Was **sieht** Oma? Sie **sieht** fern. **5** Wo **schläfst** du? Ich **schlafe** im Schlafzimmer. **6** Wo **schläft** Olli? Er **schläft** im Keller.

3a **(AT3 Level 1, AT4 Level 1)** **1** eat room **2** bath room **3** living room
3b **4** playroom **5** classroom **6** staff room (in school) **7** TV room

Übungsheft A, Seite 45

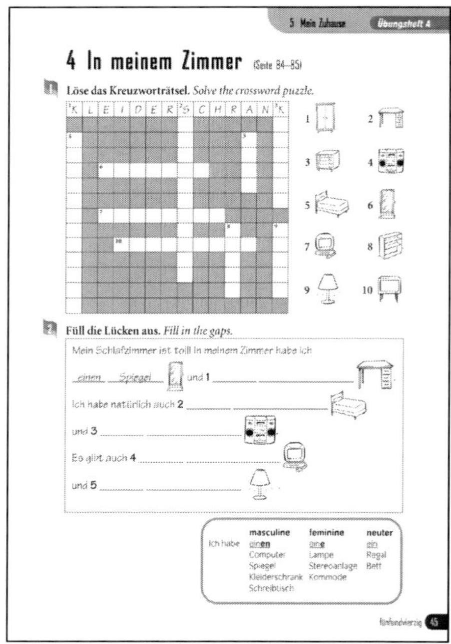
Übungsheft A 5 Mein Zuhause

4 In meinem Zimmer (Seite 84–85)

1 Löse das Kreuzworträtsel. *Solve the crossword puzzle.*

2 Füll die Lücken aus. *Fill in the gaps.*

Mein Schlafzimmer ist toll! In meinem Zimmer habe ich einen Spiegel und 1 ______

Ich habe natürlich auch 2 ______

und 3 ______

Es gibt auch 4 ______

und 5 ______

	masculine	feminine	neuter
Ich habe	einen	eine	ein
	Computer	Lampe	Regal
	Spiegel	Stereoanlage	Bett
	Kleiderschrank	Kommode	
	Schreibtisch		

fünfundvierzig 45

1 **(AT4 Level 1)**

K	L	E	I	D	E	R	S	C	H	R	A	N	K
							C						O
S							H				B		M
T							R				E		M
E		S	P	I	E	G	E	L			T		O
R							I				T		D
E							B						E
O		C	O	M	P	U	T	E	R				
A							I			R			L
N			F	E	R	N	S	E	H	E	R		A
L							C			G			M
A							H			A			P
G										L			E
E													

2 **(AT3 Level 3, AT4 Level 1)** Mein Schlafzimmer ist toll! In meinem Zimmer habe ich **einen Spiegel** und **einen Schreibtisch**. Ich habe natürlich auch **ein Bett** und **eine Stereoanlage**. Es gibt auch **einen Computer** und **eine Lampe**.

Übungsheft B, Seite 45

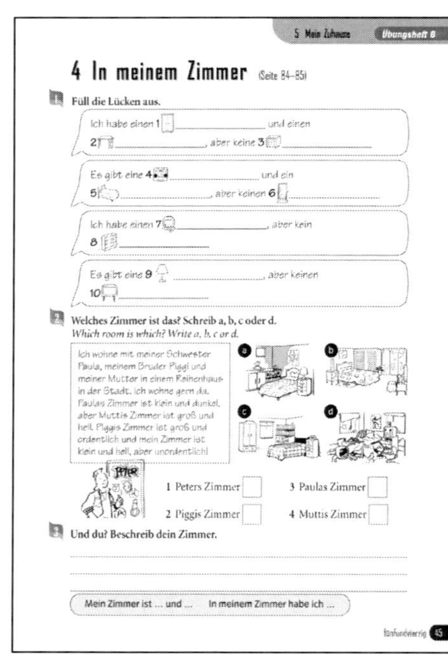
5 Mein Zuhause Übungsheft B

4 In meinem Zimmer (Seite 84–85)

1 Füll die Lücken aus.

Ich habe einen 1 ______ und einen 2 ______, aber keine 3 ______

Es gibt eine 4 ______ und ein 5 ______, aber keinen 6 ______

Ich habe einen 7 ______, aber kein 8 ______

Es gibt eine 9 ______, aber keinen 10 ______

2 Welches Zimmer ist das? Schreib a, b, c oder d.
Which room is which? Write a, b, c or d.

Ich wohne mit meiner Schwester Paula, meinem Bruder Piggi und meiner Mutter in einem Reihenhaus in der Stadt. Ich wohne gern da. Paulas Zimmer ist klein und dunkel, aber Muttis Zimmer ist groß und hell. Piggis Zimmer ist groß und ordentlich und mein Zimmer ist klein und hell, aber unordentlich.

1 Peters Zimmer ☐ 2 Piggis Zimmer ☐ 3 Paulas Zimmer ☐ 4 Muttis Zimmer ☐

3 Und du? Beschreib dein Zimmer.

Mein Zimmer ist ... und ... In meinem Zimmer habe ich ...

fünfundvierzig 45

1 **(AT3 Level 3, AT4 Level 1)** Ich habe einen **1 Kleiderschrank** und einen **2 Schreibtisch**, aber keine **3 Kommode**. Est gibt eine **4 Stereoanlage** und ein **5 Bett**, aber keinen **6 Spiegel**. Ich habe einen **7 Computer**, aber kein **8 Regal**. Es gibt eine **9 Lampe**, aber keinen **10 Fernseher**.

2 **(AT3 Level 3)** **1** d **2** c **3** a **4** b

3 **(AT4 Level 3–4)**

Übungsheft A, Seite 46

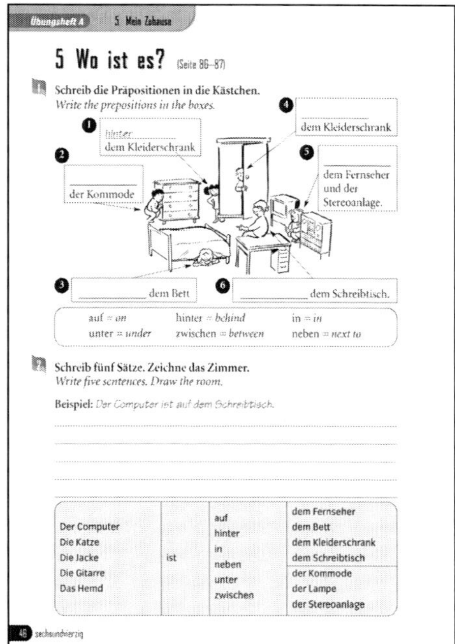
Übungsheft A 5 Mein Zuhause

5 Wo ist es? (Seite 86–87)

1 Schreib die Präpositionen in die Kästchen.
Write the prepositions in the boxes.

1 hinter dem Kleiderschrank
2 der Kommode
3 dem Bett
4 dem Kleiderschrank
5 dem Fernseher und der Stereoanlage.
6 dem Schreibtisch.

auf = *on* hinter = *behind* in = *in*
unter = *under* zwischen = *between* neben = *next to*

2 Schreib fünf Sätze. Zeichne das Zimmer.
Write five sentences. Draw the room.

Beispiel: *Der Computer ist auf dem Schreibtisch.*

Der Computer Die Katze Die Jacke Die Gitarre Das Hemd	ist	auf hinter in neben unter zwischen	dem Fernseher dem Bett dem Kleiderschrank dem Schreibtisch der Kommode der Lampe der Stereoanlage

46 sechsundvierzig

1 (AT3 Level 2, AT4 Level 1) 1 hinter dem Kleiderschrank **2 neben** der Kommode **3 unter** dem Bett **4 in** dem Kleiderschrank **5 zwischen** dem Fernseher und der Stereoanlage **6 auf** dem Schreibtisch

2 (AT4 Level 2) Pupils choose their own sentences.

Übungsheft B, Seite 46

Übungsheft B 5 Mein Zuhause

5 Wo ist es? (Seite 86–87)

1 Lies den Text. Was ist wo? Schreib a, b, c, d oder e in die Kästchen.
Read the text. What is where? Write a, b, c, d or e in the boxes.

Hier ist mein Schlafzimmer. Ich mag mein Zimmer gern. Auf dem Schreibtisch ist ein Buch und die Gitarre ist unter dem Bett. Mein Hemd ist hinter dem Computer. Die Jacke ist in dem Kleiderschrank und meine Katze ist zwischen dem Bett und der Kommode. Wo ist …?

Der, die und das change as follows after the prepositions auf, hinter, in, neben, unter und zwischen:
masculine / neuter: der → dem; feminine: die → der
Schreibtisch, Bett; Kommode
Beispiele: hinter **dem** Bett; auf **der** Kommode

2 Schreib die Sätze in die Kästchen.
Write the sentences in the boxes.

1 Tina ist in dem Auto.
2 Die Katze
3 Carl
4 Der Mechaniker
5 Das Rad … Auto und … Motorrad.

46 sechsundvierzig

1 (AT3 Level 3)
1 b **2** a **3** e **4** c **5** d

2 (AT4 Level 2) 1 Tina **ist in dem Auto**. **2** Die Katze **ist auf dem Auto**. **3** Carl **ist hinter dem Auto**. **4** Der Mechaniker **ist unter dem Auto**. **5** Das Rad ist **zwischen dem Auto** und **dem** Motorrad.

Übungsheft A, Seite 47

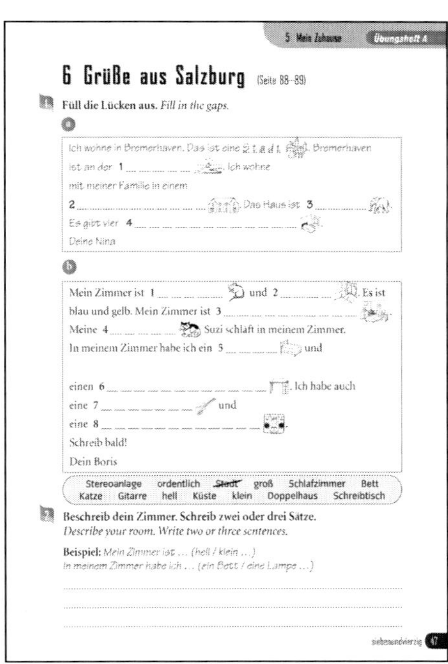
5 Mein Zuhause Übungsheft A

6 Grüße aus Salzburg (Seite 88–89)

1 Füll die Lücken aus. *Fill in the gaps.*

a
Ich wohne in Bremerhaven. Das ist eine S t a d t. Bremerhaven ist an der 1 ______. Ich wohne mit meiner Familie in einem 2 ______. Das Haus ist 3 ______. Es gibt vier 4 ______.
Deine Nina

b
Mein Zimmer ist 1 ______ und 2 ______. Es ist blau und gelb. Mein Zimmer ist 3 ______. Meine 4 ______ Suzi schläft in meinem Zimmer. In meinem Zimmer habe ich ein 5 ______ und einen 6 ______. Ich habe auch eine 7 ______ und eine 8 ______.
Schreib bald!
Dein Boris

Stereoanlage ordentlich ~~Stadt~~ groß Schlafzimmer Bett Katze Gitarre hell Küste klein Doppelhaus Schreibtisch

2 Beschreib dein Zimmer. Schreib zwei oder drei Sätze.
Describe your room. Write two or three sentences.

Beispiel: *Mein Zimmer ist … (hell / klein …)*
In meinem Zimmer habe ich … (ein Bett / eine Lampe …)

siebenundvierzig 47

1 (AT3 Level 3, AT4 Level 3) a Ich wohne in Bremerhaven. Das ist eine **Stadt**. Bremerhaven ist an der **Küste**. Ich wohne mit meiner Familie in einem **Doppelhaus**. Das Haus ist **groß**. Es gibt vier **Schlafzimmer**. Deine Nina. **b** Mein Zimmer ist **klein** und **hell**. Es ist blau und gelb. Mein Zimmer ist **ordentlich**. Meine **Katze** Suzi schläft in meinem Zimmer. In meinem Zimmer habe ich ein **Bett** und einen **Schreibtisch**. Ich habe auch eine **Gitarre** und eine **Stereoanlage**. Schreib bald! Dein Boris.

2 (AT4 Level 3)

Übungsheft B, Seite 47

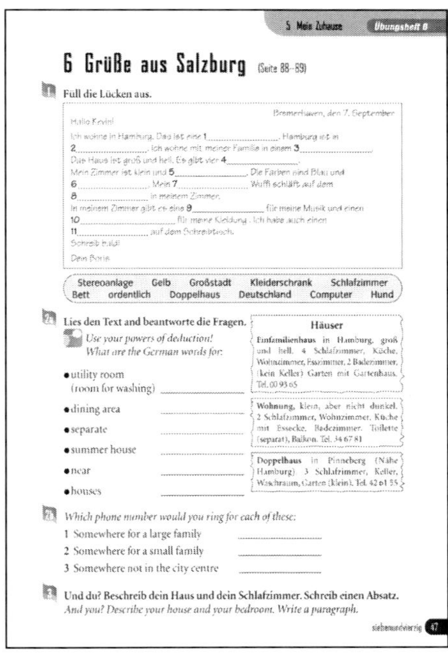
5 Mein Zuhause Übungsheft B

6 Grüße aus Salzburg (Seite 88–89)

1 Füll die Lücken aus.

Stereoanlage Gelb Großstadt Kleiderschrank Schlafzimmer Bett ordentlich Doppelhaus Deutschland Computer Hund

2 Lies den Text und beantworte die Fragen.
Use your powers of deduction! What are the German words for:
utility room (room for washing)
dining area
separate
summer house
near
houses

Häuser

3 *Which phone number would you ring for each of these:*
1 Somewhere for a large family
2 Somewhere for a small family
3 Somewhere not in the city centre

4 Und du? Beschreib dein Haus und dein Schlafzimmer. Schreib einen Absatz.
And you? Describe your house and your bedroom. Write a paragraph.

siebenundvierzig 47

1 (AT3 Level 3, AT4 Level 1) Bremerhaven, den 7. September. Hallo Kevin! Ich wohne in Hamburg. Das ist eine **1 Großstadt**. Hamburg ist in **2 Deutschland**. Ich wohne mit meiner Familie in einem **3 Doppelhaus**. Das Haus ist groß und hell. Es gibt vier **4 Schlafzimmer**. Mein Zimmer ist klein und **5 ordentlich**. Die Farben sind Blau und **6 Gelb**. Mein **7 Hund** Wuffi schläft auf dem **8 Bett** in meinem Zimmer. In meinem Zimmer gibt es eine **9 Stereoanlage** für meine Musik und einen **10 Kleiderschrank** für meine Kleidung. Ich habe auch einen **11 Computer** auf dem Schreibtisch. Schreib bald! Dein Boris

2 (AT3 Level 4) a Waschraum, Essecke, separat, Gartenhaus, Nähe, Häuser **b 1** 00 93 65 **2** 34 67 81 **3** 42 61 55

3 (AT4 Level 4)

Übungsheft A, Seite 48

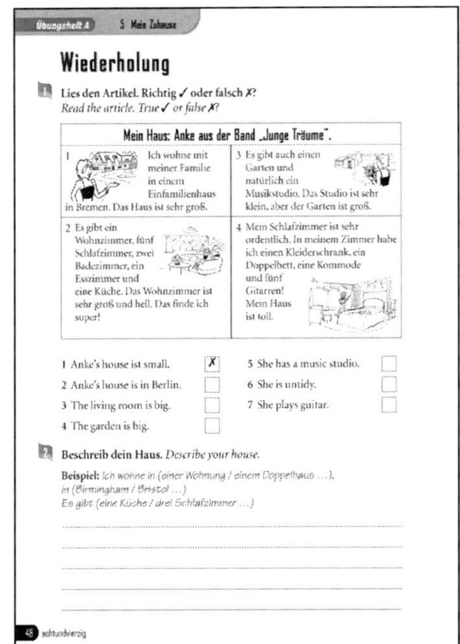

Übungsheft A 5 Mein Zuhause

Wiederholung

1 Lies den Artikel. Richtig ✓ oder falsch ✗?
Read the article. True ✓ or false ✗?

Mein Haus: Anke aus der Band „Junge Träume".

1 Ich wohne mit meiner Familie in einem Einfamilienhaus in Bremen. Das Haus ist sehr groß.

2 Es gibt ein Wohnzimmer, fünf Schlafzimmer, zwei Badezimmer, ein Esszimmer und eine Küche. Das Wohnzimmer ist sehr groß und hell. Das finde ich super!

3 Es gibt auch einen Garten und natürlich ein Musikstudio. Das Studio ist sehr klein, aber der Garten ist groß.

4 Mein Schlafzimmer ist sehr ordentlich. In meinem Zimmer habe ich einen Kleiderschrank, ein Doppelbett, eine Kommode und fünf Gitarren! Mein Haus ist toll.

1 Anke's house ist small. ✗
2 Anke's house is in Berlin. ☐
3 The living room is big. ☐
4 The garden is big. ☐
5 She has a music studio. ☐
6 She is untidy. ☐
7 She plays guitar. ☐

2 Beschreib dein Haus. *Describe your house.*

Beispiel: *Ich wohne in (einer Wohnung / einem Doppelhaus …).*
in (Birmingham / Bristol …)
Es gibt (eine Küche / drei Schlafzimmer …)

48 achtundvierzig

1 (AT3 Level 3) 1 ✗ 2 ✗ 3 ✓ 4 ✓ 5 ✓ 6 ✗ 7 ✓

2 (AT4 Level 3)

Übungsheft B, Seite 48

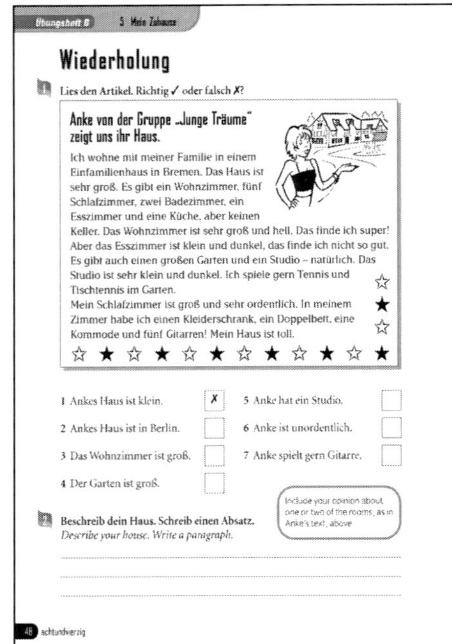

Übungsheft B 5 Mein Zuhause

Wiederholung

1 Lies den Artikel. Richtig ✓ oder falsch ✗?

Anke von der Gruppe „Junge Träume" zeigt uns ihr Haus.

Ich wohne mit meiner Familie in einem Einfamilienhaus in Bremen. Das Haus ist sehr groß. Es gibt ein Wohnzimmer, fünf Schlafzimmer, zwei Badezimmer, ein Esszimmer und eine Küche, aber keinen Keller. Das Wohnzimmer ist sehr groß und hell. Das finde ich super! Aber das Esszimmer ist klein und dunkel, das finde ich nicht so gut. Es gibt auch einen großen Garten und ein Studio – natürlich. Das Studio ist sehr klein und dunkel. Ich spiele gern Tennis und Tischtennis im Garten.
Mein Schlafzimmer ist groß und sehr ordentlich. In meinem Zimmer habe ich einen Kleiderschrank, ein Doppelbett, eine Kommode und fünf Gitarren! Mein Haus ist toll.

1 Ankes Haus ist klein. ✗
2 Ankes Haus ist in Berlin. ☐
3 Das Wohnzimmer ist groß. ☐
4 Der Garten ist groß. ☐
5 Anke hat ein Studio. ☐
6 Anke ist unordentlich. ☐
7 Anke spielt gern Gitarre. ☐

2 Beschreib dein Haus. Schreib einen Absatz.
Describe your house. Write a paragraph.

Include your opinion about one or two of the rooms, as in Anke's text, above

48 achtundvierzig

1 (AT3 Level 4) 1 ✗ 2 ✗ 3 ✓ 4 ✓ 5 ✓ 6 ✗ 7 ✓

2 (AT4 Level 4)

Arbeitsblatt 5.1

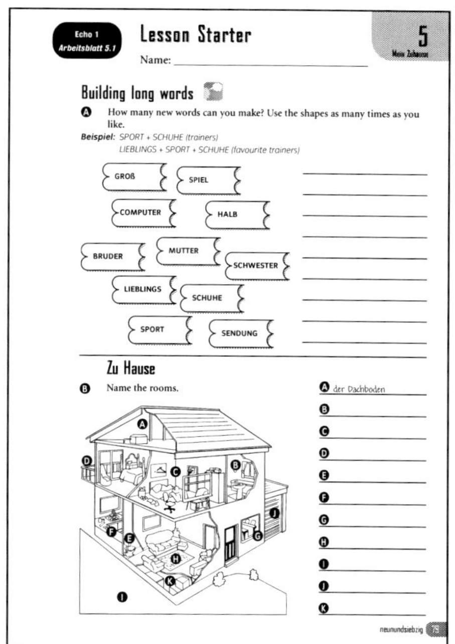
Echo 1
Arbeitsblatt 5.1

Lesson Starter

Name: ____________

5
Mein Zuhause

Building long words

A How many new words can you make? Use the shapes as many times as you like.

Beispiel: *SPORT + SCHUHE (trainers)*
LIEBLINGS + SPORT + SCHUHE (favourite trainers)

GROß SPIEL COMPUTER HALB BRUDER MUTTER SCHWESTER LIEBLINGS SCHUHE SPORT SENDUNG

Zu Hause

B Name the rooms.

A der Dachboden
B
C
D
E
F
G
H
I
J
K

neunundsiebzig 79

A

Halbschwester, Halbbruder, Grossmutter, Computerspiel, Lieblingssendung

B

A *der Dachboden* **B** das Badezimmer **C** das Schlafzimmer **D** der Balkon **E** die Toilette **F** die Küche **G** das Esszimmer **H** das Wohnzimmer **I** der Garten **J** die Garage **K** der Keller

Arbeitsblatt 5.2

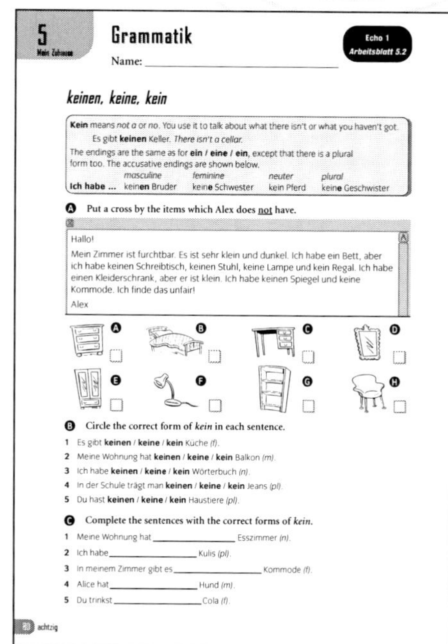
5
Mein Zuhause

Grammatik

Name: ____________

Echo 1
Arbeitsblatt 5.2

keinen, keine, kein

Kein means *not a* or *no*. You use it to talk about what there isn't or what you haven't got.

Es gibt **keinen** Keller. *There isn't a cellar.*

The endings are the same as for **ein / eine / ein**, except that there is a plural form too. The accusative endings are shown below.

	masculine	*feminine*	*neuter*	*plural*
Ich habe ...	kein**en** Bruder	kein**e** Schwester	kein Pferd	kein**e** Geschwister

A Put a cross by the items which Alex does not have.

Hallo!

Mein Zimmer ist furchtbar. Es ist sehr klein und dunkel. Ich habe ein Bett, aber ich habe keinen Schreibtisch, keinen Stuhl, keine Lampe und kein Regal. Ich habe einen Kleiderschrank, aber er ist klein. Ich habe keinen Spiegel und keine Kommode. Ich finde das unfair!

Alex

A B C D E F G H

B Circle the correct form of *kein* in each sentence.

1 Es gibt **keinen / keine / kein** Küche *(f)*.
2 Meine Wohnung hat **keinen / keine / kein** Balkon *(m)*.
3 Ich habe **keinen / keine / kein** Wörterbuch *(n)*.
4 In der Schule trägt man **keinen / keine / kein** Jeans *(pl)*.
5 Du hast **keinen / keine / kein** Haustiere *(pl)*.

C Complete the sentences with the correct forms of *kein*.

1 Meine Wohnung hat ____________ Esszimmer *(n)*.
2 Ich habe ____________ Kulis *(pl)*.
3 In meinem Zimmer gibt es ____________ Kommode *(f)*.
4 Alice hat ____________ Hund *(m)*.
5 Du trinkst ____________ Cola *(f)*.

80 achtzig

A

A, C, D, F, G, H

B

1 keine **2** keinen **3** kein **4** keine **5** keine

C

1 kein **2** keine **3** keine **4** keinen **5** keine

Arbeitsblatt 5.3

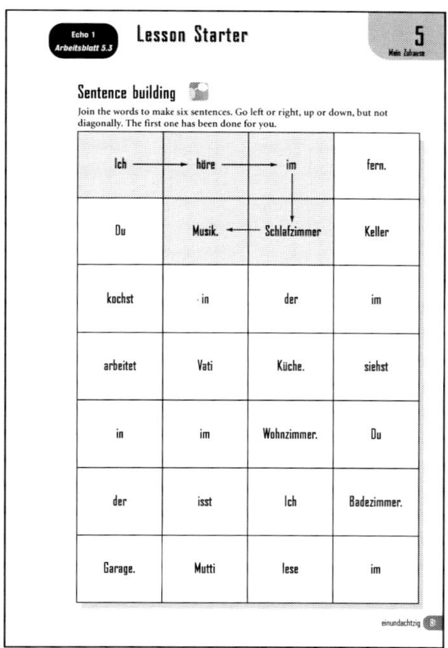
Echo 1
Arbeitsblatt 5.3

Lesson Starter

5
Mein Zuhause

Sentence building

Join the words to make six sentences. Go left or right, up or down, but not diagonally. The first one has been done for you.

Ich	hüre	im	fern.
Du	Musik.	Schlafzimmer	Keller
kochst	in	der	im
arbeitet	Vati	Küche.	siehst
in	im	Wohnzimmer.	Du
der	isst	Ich	Badezimmer.
Garage.	Mutti	lese	im

einundachtzig 81

Ich höre im Schlafzimmer Musik. Du kochst in der Küche. Vati arbeitet in der Garage. Mutti isst im Wohnzimmer. Ich lese im Badezimmer. Du siehst im Keller fern.

Arbeitsblatt 5.4

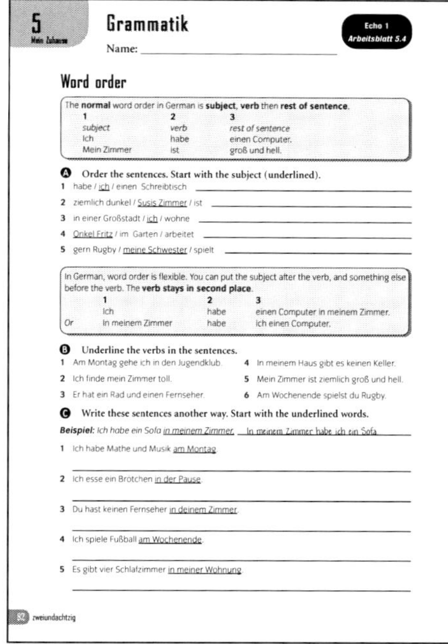
5
Mein Zuhause

Grammatik

Name: ____________

Echo 1
Arbeitsblatt 5.4

Word order

The **normal** word order in German is **subject**, **verb** then **rest of sentence**.

1	2	3
subject	*verb*	*rest of sentence*
Ich	habe	einen Computer.
Mein Zimmer	ist	groß und hell.

A Order the sentences. Start with the subject (underlined).

1 habe / ich / einen Schreibtisch ____________
2 ziemlich dunkel / Susis Zimmer / ist ____________
3 in einer Großstadt / ich / wohne ____________
4 Onkel Fritz / im Garten / arbeitet ____________
5 gern Rugby / meine Schwester / spielt ____________

In German, word order is flexible. You can put the subject after the verb, and something else before the verb. The **verb stays in second place**.

	1	2	3
	Ich	habe	einen Computer in meinem Zimmer.
Or	In meinem Zimmer	habe	ich einen Computer.

B Underline the verbs in the sentences.

1 Am Montag gehe ich in den Jugendklub.
2 Ich finde mein Zimmer toll.
3 Er hat ein Rad und einen Fernseher.
4 In meinem Haus gibt es keinen Keller.
5 Mein Zimmer ist ziemlich groß und hell.
6 Am Wochenende spielst du Rugby.

C Write these sentences another way. Start with the underlined words.

Beispiel: *Ich habe ein Sofa in meinem Zimmer.* In meinem Zimmer habe ich ein Sofa.

1 Ich habe Mathe und Musik am Montag.
2 Ich esse ein Brötchen in der Pause.
3 Du hast keinen Fernseher in deinem Zimmer.
4 Ich spiele Fußball am Wochenende.
5 Es gibt vier Schlafzimmer in meiner Wohnung.

82 zweiundachtzig

A

1 Ich habe einen Schreibtisch. **2** Susis Zimmer ist ziemlich dunkel. **3** Ich wohne in einer Großstadt. **4** Onkel Fritz arbeitet im Garten. **5** Meine Schwester spielt gern Rugby.

B

1 gehe **2** finde **3** hat **4** gibt **5** ist **6** spielst

C

1 Am Montag habe ich Mathe und Musik. **2** In der Pause esse ich ein Brötchen. **3** In deinem Zimmer hast du keinen Fernseher. **4** Am Wochenende spiele ich Fußball. **5** In meiner Wohnung gibt es vier Schlafzimmer.

Arbeitsblatt 5.5

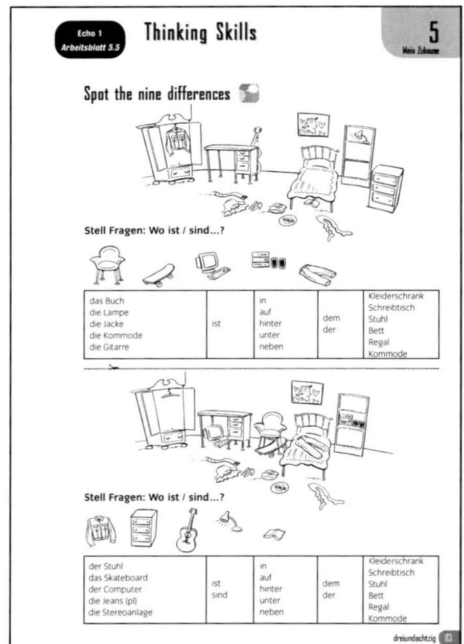

Die Jacke ist in dem Kleiderschrank.
Die Kommode ist neben dem Regal.
Die Gitarre ist hinter dem Schreibtisch.
Die Lampe ist auf dem Regal.
Das Buch ist unter dem Bett.

Der Stuhl ist neben dem Bett / dem Schreibtisch.
Das Skateboard ist unter dem Stuhl.
Der Computer ist unter dem Schreibtisch.
Die Jeans sind auf dem Bett.
Die Stereoanlage ist auf dem Regal.

Arbeitsblatt 5.7

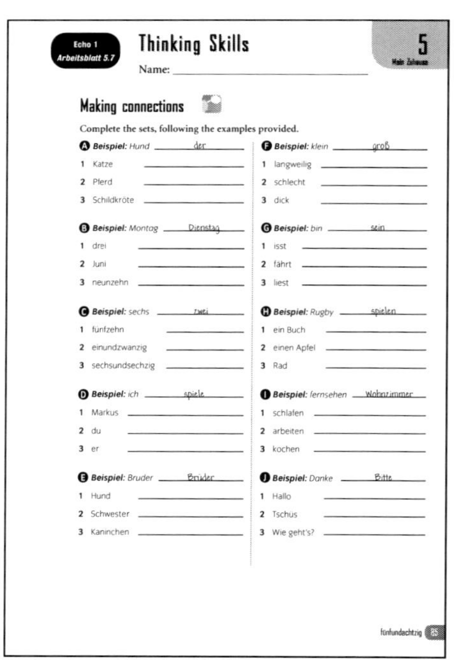

A 1 die **2** das, **3** die **B 1** vier, **2** Juli, **3** zwanzig **C 1** fünf, **2** sieben, **3** zweiundzwanzig **D 1** spielt, **2** spielst, **3** spielt **E 1** Hunde, **2** Schwestern, **3** Kaninchen **F 1** interessant, **2** gut, **3** schlank **G 1** essen, **2** fahren, **3** lesen **H 1** lesen, **2** essen, **3** fahren **I 1** Schlafzimmer **2** Garage / Garten, **3** Küche **J 1** Hallo, **2** Tschüs, **3** Gut, danke (*or similar*)

Arbeitsblatt 5.6

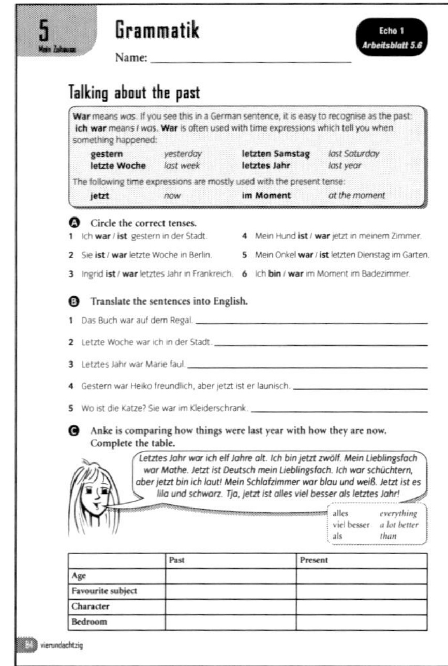

A

1 war **2** war **3** war **4** ist **5** war **6** bin

B

1 The book was on the shelf / bookcase. **2** I was in town last week. **3** Marie was lazy last year. **4** Heiko was friendly yesterday, but now he's moody. **5** Where's the cat? It was in the wardrobe.

C

	Past	**Present**
Age	11	12
Favourite subject	maths	German
Character	shy	noisy
Bedroom	blue and white	purple and black

6 Stadt und Land

Unit Learning targets	Key framework objectives	NC levels and PoS coverage	Grammar and key language	Skills
1 Wo liegt das? (pp. 96–97) • Describing where a town is situated • Learning about some towns and cities in Germany, Austria and Switzerland	4.5/Y7 Language – (b) modal verbs	NC levels 2–4 **2.2d** pronunciation and intonation **2.2e** ask and answer questions **3b** sounds and writing **3c** apply grammar **3d** use a range of vocab / structures **3e** different countries' cultures **4b** communicate in pairs etc.	Revision of *man kann* + infinitive Revision of verb as second idea (*hier kann man…*) *Leipzig, Berlin, Kiel (Wassersport), München (Fußball, Bier), Wien, Salzburg (Mozart), Bern, Klosters (Wintersport)* *Wo liegt (Leipzig)?* *Das liegt in Deutschland / Österreich / der Schweiz* *im Norden / Süden / Osten / Westen von* *die Stadt / die Großstadt / das Dorf* *Das ist die Hauptstadt von …* *bekannt für* (receptive only) *Man kann / Hier kann man …* *ins Kino / ins Sportzentrum gehen* *toll / super / langweilig / interessant*	Learning some basic geographical facts about the main German-speaking countries Pronunciation: names of cities Formulating basic questions Picking out details, including opinions, from longer texts
2 In der Stadt (pp. 98–99) • Saying what there is in a town, and talking about types of transport • Recognising plural forms	4.3/Y7 Language – plurals 5.2 Strategies – memorising	NC levels 1–4 **2.1c** knowledge of language **2.1e** use reference materials **2.2a** listen for gist **2.2e** ask and answer questions **2.2g** write clearly and coherently **3b** sounds and writing **3c** apply grammar **3d** use a range of vocab / structures **4b** communicate in pairs etc. **4d** make links with English	Revision of *es gibt* + accusative Further revision of *man kann* + infinitive *der Bahnhof(¨e)* *der Markt(¨e)* *der Park(-s)* *der Supermarkt(¨e)* *die Kirche(-n)* *die Post* *das Rathaus(¨er)* *das Schloss(¨er)* *das Schwimmbad(¨er)* *das Verkehrsamt(¨er)* *Es gibt …* *einen / eine / ein /* plural *keinen / keine / kein* *mit dem Auto / Bus / Zug / Taxi / Flugzeug* *mit der Straßenbahn / U-Bahn* *zu Fuß* *Man kann … fahren / gehen / fliegen*	Checking/ looking up plurals of nouns Using a dictionary/ other resources appropriately
3 Das Leipzigspiel (pp. 100–101) • Using German to play a board game	1.4/Y7 Speaking – (b) using prompts 5.8 Strategies – evaluating and improving	NC levels 2–4 **2.2e** ask and answer questions **2.2j** adapt previously-learnt language **3c** apply grammar **3d** use a range of vocab / structures **4b** communicate in pairs etc.	Further revision of *es gibt* and *man kann* Consolidation of town-related and transport language from Unit 2 *Ich bin / Du bist dran* *Du beginnst* *Ich habe eine (Drei).* *Das ist (Rot).* *schwarz / rot / gold* *Was gibt es in Leipzig?* *Es gibt …* *Wie kann man in Leipzig fahren?* *Man kann …* *richtig / falsch* *zwei Felder zurück* *einmal aussetzen*	Spontaneous talk

Unit Learning targets	Key framework objectives	NC levels and PoS coverage	Grammar and key language	Skills
4 Wo ist der Markt? (pp. 102–103) • Asking for and giving directions • Understanding the difference between *du* and *Sie*	5.6 Strategies – reading aloud	NC levels 1–3 **2.2e** ask and answer questions **2.2i** reuse language they have met **2.2j** adapt previously-learnt language **3b** sounds and writing **3c** apply grammar **3d** use a range of vocab / structures **4b** communicate in pairs etc.	Use of *du* and *Sie* Introduction to the imperative *Wo ist … ?* *der Markt / Park* *die Kirche / Post / Rathaus* *das Schwimmbad / Verkehrsamt* *Geh / Gehen Sie* *Nimm / Nehmen Sie* *links* *rechts* *geradeaus* *die erste / zweite / dritte Straße* *bitte* *danke*	Social conventions Polite 'little words'
5 An der Imbissbude (pp. 104–105) • Buying food and drink at a snack stand using euros • Using *ich möchte* to say what you would like	3.2/Y7 Culture – (b) challenging stereotypes 5.3 Strategies – English/other languages	NC levels 1–4 **2.1c** knowledge of language **2.2g** write clearly and coherently **3b** sounds and writing **3c** apply grammar **3f** compare experiences **3d** use a range of vocab / structures **4b** communicate in pairs etc. **4f** language of interest / enjoyment	*ich möchte* + direct object *sie sind* (receptive) Identifying nouns, verbs, adjectives Nouns written with capital letter (revision) *Ich möchte …* *einmal / zweimal* *Bratwurst / Hamburger / Pizza / Pommes frites / Schaschlik / Ketchup / Mayonnaise / Senf / Kaffee / Tee* *mit Milch / Zitrone* *Cola* *Limonade* *Das macht …* *Euro/Cent*	Speaking skills Cultural information about currency, snacks and snack stands Identifying words already known from other languages Revision of numbers for prices Polite 'little words'
6 In den Sommerferien (pp. 106–107) • Talking about your plans for the summer holidays • Talking about the future (using the present tense)	1.2/Y7 Listening – unfamiliar language 2.5/Y7 Writing – different text types 4.5/Y7 Language – (a) future using present tense	NC levels 2–5 **2.1a** identify patterns **2.1c** knowledge of language **2.2e** ask and answer questions **2.2g** write clearly and coherently **2.2h** redraft to improve writing **2.2i** reuse language they have met **2.2j** adapt previously-learnt language **3b** sounds and writing **3c** apply grammar **3d** use a range of vocab / structures **4c** use more complex language **4b** communicate in pairs etc. **4d** make links with English	Using the present tense to talk about the future *Was machst du in den Sommerferien?* *Für wie lange?* *Wie fährst du dahin?* *Ich fahre / Wir fahren nach …* *Schottland / Wales / Devon / Spanien / Österreich* *für … Tage / Wochen* *Ich bleibe zu Hause.* *mit dem Auto / Bus / Flugzeug / Zug* *in den Sommerferien* *am Montag / Dienstag / Mittwoch*	
Lernzieltest und Wiederholung (pp. 108–109) • Pupils' checklist and practice test		NC levels 2–5 **2.1b** memorising		
Extra (pp. 122–123) • Self-access reading and writing at two levels		NC levels 1–5 **2.2b** skim and scan **2.2e** ask and answer questions **3c** apply grammar **3d** use a range of vocab / structure		

1 Wo liegt das?

Learning targets

- Describing where a town is situated
- Learning about some towns and cities in Germany, Austria and Switzerland

Key framework objectives

4.5/Y7 Language – (b) modal verbs

Grammar

- Revision of *man kann* + infinitive
- Revision of verb as second idea (*hier kann man …*)

Key language

Berlin, Bern, Kiel, Klosters, Leipzig, München, Salzburg, Wien
bekannt für
Bier, Fußball, Wassersport, Wintersport
Wo liegt (Leipzig)?
Das liegt in Deutschland / Österreich / der Schweiz
im Norden / Süden / Osten / Westen von
die Stadt / die Großstadt / das Dorf
Das ist die Hauptstadt von …
Man kann / Hier kann man …
ins Kino / Sportzentrum gehen
toll / super / langweilig / interessant

High-frequency words

für
gehen
hier
im
in
ins
ist
ich finde es
von
man kann
wo?

Pronunciation

Names of cities

Citizenship

Learning about towns and cities in other countries

Resources

CD 3, tracks 20–22
Workbooks A and B, p.52
Arbeitsblatt 6.1, p.101
Echo Elektro 1 TPP, Mod 6 1.1–1.5

Starter 1 3.1/Y7

Aim
To recap what pupils already know about German-speaking countries, and to introduce them to more geographical facts in preparation for this unit.

Give the class one minute to look at the map on page 96 of the Pupil's Book – tell them they will be tested on how many country and city names they can remember. They then close their books. Give a copy of **Arbeitsblatt 6.1** to each pupil, and ask them to fill in as many names as they can in the correct places on the map. Now, or later, they can also colour in the three flags correctly. Answers could be quickly checked by referring back to the Pupil's Book. Alternatively, a volunteer pupil completes an OHT copy of the **Arbeitsblatt** as you speak. Give information about the cities to introduce new vocabulary as the class mark their answers:

Berlin ist die Hauptstadt von Deutschland.
Kiel liegt im Norden von Deutschland.

1 Welche Stadt ist das? (1–8) (AT 1/2) 1.1/Y7

Listening. Pupils listen to the recording and look at the map in their book. They identify the towns being described, and write down the names. Weaker pupils may prefer to write on **Arbeitsblatt 6.1** instead, and number the towns. They can listen to the recording for exercise 2 to check their answers.

1 *Das liegt im Osten von der Schweiz.*
2 *Das liegt im Norden von Deutschland.*
3 *Das liegt im Süden von Deutschland.*
4 *Das liegt im Osten von Deutschland.*
5 *Das liegt im Westen von Österreich.*
6 *Das ist die Hauptstadt von der Schweiz.*
7 *Das ist die Hauptstadt von Deutschland.*
8 *Das liegt im Osten von Österreich und ist die Hauptstadt von Österreich.*

2 Hör zu und überprüfe es. (AT 1/2)

1.1/Y7

Listening. Pupils check their answers to exercise 1. Then refer pupils to the Key Language box and ask questions about where the towns are, to reinforce the new language.

21

1. *Also, das liegt im Osten von der Schweiz. Ach ja, das ist Klosters.*
2. *Und das liegt im Norden von Deutschland, im Norden von Deutschland – das ist Kiel.*
3. *Das liegt im Süden von Deutschland. Das ist München.*
4. *Und das ist in Deutschland, im Osten. Das ist Leipzig.*
5. *Das ist im Westen von Österreich. Also, im Westen das ist Salzburg.*
6. *Das ist die Hauptstadt von der Schweiz. Das ist Bern.*
7. *Das ist die Hauptstadt von Deutschland. Das ist Berlin.*
8. *Und das ist die Hauptstadt von Österreich, und liegt im Osten. Ähm, das ist Wien.*

Answers
1 Klosters **2** Kiel **3** München **4** Leipzig
5 Salzburg **6** Bern **7** Berlin **8** Wien

Aussprache 4.1/Y7

Look at this panel with the class before going on to listening exercise 3 which practises the pronunciation of the names of these cities in German.

3 Hör zu und wiederhole. (AT 1/ )

4.1/Y7

Listening. Pupils listen to the German pronunciation of European city names that are commonly pronounced differently in English. They could then chorus them for practice.

Berlin
Salzburg
Bern
London
Paris

ECHO-Tipp

This points out the rather different names we use for *München* and *Wien* in English.

4 Partnerarbeit: Erdkundequiz. (AT 2/3)

1.4b/Y7

Speaking. In pairs, pupils quiz each other on the location of the towns and cities on the map, collecting points for immediately correct answers.

+ More confident learners could extend this activity to other cities and countries.

5 Wo wohnen sie? Schreib Sätze. (AT 4/3) 4.4/Y7

Writing. Pupils write sentences describing where people live, using the third person singular.

Answers
1. Ingrid wohnt im Norden von Deutschland.
2. Paul wohnt im Osten von der Schweiz.
3. Anita wohnt im Süden von Deutschland.
4. Markus wohnt im Westen von Österreich.

Starter 2

1.1/Y7

Aim

To encourage pupils to pay close attention when listening.

True or false. Pupils look at the map on page 96 for one minute to refresh their memories about where places are. They then take turns to come to the front and read aloud the following statements about towns in the German-speaking countries. After each one, the rest of the class must stand up if they think it is false. Ask a volunteer to correct it (to make this easier for weaker pupils, you could at this stage reveal the false sentence on an OHT). Less confident learners could be allowed to refer to the map in the Pupil's Book. More able pupils could themselves prepare some true/false statements to be used.

München ist die Hauptstadt von Deutschland. (Berlin)
Bern liegt in Österreich. (in der Schweiz)
Kiel liegt im Norden von Deutschland. (richtig)
Wien ist die Hauptstadt von der Schweiz. (Österreich)
Salzburg ist bekannt für Mozart. (richtig)
Leipzig liegt im Westen von Deutschland. (im Osten)

6 Lies die Texte. Schreib die Tabelle ab und füll sie auf Englisch aus. (AT3/4)

2.1/Y7 4.5b/Y7

Reading. Pupils read the texts in order to find the information needed to complete a copy of the grid in English. For further exploitation of this exercise, see Vocabulary treasure hunt on page 10.

Answers

	1	**2**	**3**
Country	Germany	Switzerland	Germany
N/S/E/W	North	East	South
City/Village	city	village	city
Famous for	water sports	winter sports	football beer
Activities	sailing windsurfing	snow-boarding skiing	cinema sports centre
Opinion	great	super	never boring
Place name	Kiel	Klosters	Munich

7 Schreib den Text ab und füll die Lücken aus. (AT4/2) **2.4b/Y7 4.4/Y7**

Writing. Pupils copy out the text about Berlin, replacing each picture with the correct word from the panel. Encourage more able pupils to cover up the panel, revealing the words only to check answers afterwards.

+ Pupils could write a similar short text about their own town or village. To extend this further, write a list of three places known to them on the board, and ask them to write about each one. You may wish to quickly recap opinion words, or elicit some examples of leisure activities and write them on the board for support.

Answers

Berlin

Berlin ist eine **Großstadt** in **Deutschland**. Sie liegt im **Osten**. Berlin ist die **Hauptstadt** von **Deutschland.** Man kann ins **Kino** und in die **Disko** gehen. Berlin ist **super**.

Plenary

4.1/Y7

Aim

To practise sound–spelling links encountered in this unit, and extend pupils' knowledge of places in Germany.

Read out to pupils some, or all, of the following list of towns and cities in Germany, slowly and clearly. They listen carefully to each one and write it down, aiming to spell it correctly. Tell them to focus on each syllable, and to think whether they already know how to spell that syllable from other words or place names. Reveal each one after reading it out and discuss the pronunciation – what word did it sound like? Offer a reward to any pupil who can show you on a map where the places are, by next lesson.

Bernau	*(Bern, 'au' blau)*
Düsseldorf	*('ü' München, Dorf)*
Freiburg	*('ei' Leipzig, 'burg' Salzburg)*
Schwerin	*(Berlin)*
Trier	*(Kiel)*
Weimar	*('ei' Leipzig)*

2 In der Stadt

Learning targets

- Saying what there is in a town, and talking about types of transport
- Recognising plural forms

Key framework objectives

4.3/Y7 Language – plurals
5.2 Strategies – memorising

Grammar

- *es gibt* + accusative (revision)
- *man kann* + infinitive (revision)

Key language

der Bahnhof(¨-e)
der Markt(¨-e)
der Park(-s)
der Supermarkt(¨-e)
die Kirche(-n)
die Post(-en)
das Rathaus(¨-er)
das Schloss(¨-er)
das Schwimmbad(¨-er)
das Verkehrsamt(¨-er)
Es gibt einen / eine / ein / zwei / drei …
Es gibt keinen / keine / kein …
Man kann … fahren
mit dem Auto / Bus / Zug / Taxi
mit der Straßenbahn / U-Bahn
Man kann mit dem Flugzeug fliegen.
Man kann zu Fuß gehen.

High-frequency words

was?
wie?
auch
es gibt
ein
kein
man
kann
mit
gehen
fahren

ICT

Word-processing a poster

Resources

CD 3, tracks 23–24
Workbooks A and B, p.53
Arbeitsblatt 6.2, p.102
Flashcards 81–88
Echo Elektro 1 TPP, Mod 6 2.1–2.6

Starter 1 4.1/Y7

Aim

To encourage pupils to predict the pronunciation of 'difficult' new words.

Write these six new words on the board:

Kirche
Rathaus
Schloss
Schwimmbad
Supermarkt
Verkehrsamt

In pairs or groups, pupils attempt to pronounce each word. They then consolidate and build their confidence through whole-class chorusing (you can use louder/quieter, etc. to make this fun). Before starting, look at potential problem areas, such as *sch, w, v, s*.

At this stage pupils may not understand the words. Ask if anyone knows what type of words they are (e.g. nouns, places in a town), and whether they can guess the meanings of any of the words. If you are using OHT pieces on a projector, volunteers could come to the front of the class and try to match words to pictures.

1 Wie heißt das auf Deutsch? (AT3/1 AT4/1) 5.4

Writing. Pupils match each word to the correct picture, and copy the word correctly. They will need to look up the meanings of some of the words. After checking answers, you could chorus the words with the class, perhaps firstly asking them to predict the correct pronunciation of each one. For further exploitation of this exercise, see Mime activities on page 9.

Answers

a der Supermarkt
b die Kirche
c der Park
d das Schloss
e der Bahnhof
f das Schwimmbad
g die Post
h der Markt
i das Verkehrsamt
j das Rathaus

Suggestion

Photocopy **Arbeitsblatt 6.2** (two for each pair of pupils), and cut up the copies to make playing cards. Pupils shuffle their set of cards and spread them face down on the table. They then play Pelmanism to collect matching pairs of cards, turning two cards face up each time, and saying the word to go with the picture on each card aloud. The cards could be used again later in the unit, with pupils forming *es gibt* sentences as they turn them over.

Was gibt es in der Stadt? (1–3) (AT1/3)

1.1/Y7

Listening. Pupils listen to the interviews about people's towns, and identify the pictures for the features each town has by writing down the letters each time. Before starting, elicit from the class the meaning of *es gibt*, and remind them about the difference between *ein* and *kein.*

1 – *Andreas, was gibt es in deiner Stadt?*
– *Ähm ... Es gibt ein Schwimmbad. ... Es gibt auch einen Supermarkt und einen Park.*

2 – *Und Herr Detmold, was gibt es in Ihrer Stadt?*
– *Also, es gibt ein Verkehrsamt. Ja, und es gibt auch ein Schloss, eine alte Kirche und ein Rathaus. Das ist sehr interessant.*

3 – *Frau Schmidt, was gibt es in Ihrer Stadt?*
– *Es gibt eine Post. Es gibt auch zwei Supermärkte, aber wir haben keinen Markt.*

Answers
1 f, a, c **2** i, d, b, j **3** g, a (x2)

Gedächtnisspiel: Was gibt es in der Stadt? (AT2/3–4) 5.2

Speaking. Small groups play a memory game, building up a chain of places in a town – this information could be made up, or be based on a place they all know. Draw attention to the Key Language box for support. Weaker pupils can focus on simply using the correct items of vocabulary, while more able learners should aim for accuracy in their use of the indefinite article, and could also include *kein* and plural forms of nouns.

Starter 2

5.2

Aim

To consolidate the vocabulary for places in a town.

Use an OHT copy of **Arbeitsblatt 6.2.** Cut up the individual cards (with or without the words), and scatter them on the projector. Start by running through the vocabulary, using *es gibt.* Then turn the projector off, remove one card, and turn it on again. Pairs of pupils write a sentence on mini-whiteboards or paper to say what is missing, using *es gibt + keinen / keine / kein,* and hold up their answers. With a less able group, you may prefer not to focus on the correct endings for *kein.*

4 Wie viele gibt es? (AT3/4)

4.3/Y7

Reading. Pupils read the tourist information leaflet and record how many of each of the features a–j pictured in exercise 1 there are in Parkstadt. Before starting, draw their attention to the **ECHO-Tipp** panel about the plural forms of nouns.

Answers
a 4 **b** 3 **c** 1 **d** 0 **e** 0 **f** 2 **g** 1 **h** 1
i 1 **j** 1

ECHO-Tipp: Recognising plurals

4.3/Y7

This panel reminds pupils about the range of plural noun forms in German. Discuss with pupils where and how to find the plural forms of nouns. They could then note the plural forms of places in a town – by picking out those used in the text for exercise 4, and looking up others themselves.

5 Hör zu. Finde den richtigen Untertitel für jedes Foto. (1–8) (AT1/2)

4.2/Y7 4.5b/Y7

Listening. Pupils listen to the statements about transport, and identify the correct transport noun for each photo from those given on the right. You may then wish to chorus the new vocabulary to practise pronunciation. Ask more able pupils why some are *mit dem* and others are *mit der.* Also focus on the difference in verb for modes of transport and for going by foot.

1 – *Wie kann man in die Stadt fahren?*
– *Man kann mit dem Auto fahren.*

2 – *Wie kann man in die Stadt fahren?*
– *Man kann mit dem Bus fahren.*

3 – *Wie kann man in die Stadt fahren?*
– *Man kann mit dem Zug fahren.*

4 – *Wie kann man in die Stadt fahren?*
– *Man kann mit dem Taxi fahren.*

5 – *Wie kann man in die Stadt fahren?*
– *Man kann mit dem Flugzeug fliegen.*

6 – *Wie kann man in die Stadt fahren?*
– *Man kann mit der Straßenbahn fahren.*

7 – *Wie kann man in die Stadt fahren?*
– *Man kann mit der U-Bahn fahren.*

8 – *Wie kann man in die Stadt fahren?*
– *Man kann zu Fuß gehen.*

Answers
1 Auto
2 Bus
3 Zug
4 Taxi
5 Flugzeug
6 Straßenbahn
7 U-Bahn (short for Untergrund-Bahn)
8 zu Fuß

6 Partnerarbeit. (AT2/3) 4.3/Y7 4.5b/Y7

Speaking. Using the Key Language box for support, pupils ask and answer questions about transport, using the pictures from exercise 5. Before starting, ask pupils what question they heard each time during the listening exercise. Remind weaker pupils about *man kann*, and that the verb (*fahren*, *gehen* or *fliegen*) goes to the end of the sentence.

7 Schreib Sätze über deine Stadt. (AT4/2) 2.4a/Y7

Writing. Pupils write sentences stating what there is in their town and how they can travel there. They should also add information about what you can do there, and what they think of it. They must focus on accuracy by checking genders and plurals, the correct use of *es gibt* and *man kann*, and other verb forms.

ICT Pupils could use their sentences to produce a word-processed poster about their town, perhaps also including illustrations.

Plenary 5.1

Aims

To recap vocabulary from the unit.
To focus thinking on why one word in a group of three is the odd one out.

Write the following groups of three words from this unit on the board or an OHT. In pairs, pupils work out which word is the odd one out, and why. There may be more than one possible answer – accept any valid reasons when you discuss them. Then give pairs two minutes to come up with their own set of three, referring to their book if necessary, for the class to try.

Rathaus
Verkehrsamt
Parks
(*Park* – not a place you go to for advice; not a *das* word; cognate; plural)

Straßenbahn
Bus
U-Bahn
(*Bus* – does not travel on rails; *der* word; cognate)

3 Das Leipzigspiel

Learning targets

- Using German to play a board game

Key framework objectives

1.4/Y7 Speaking – (b) using prompts
5.8 Strategies – evaluating and improving

Grammar

- *es gibt* and *man kann* (revision)

Key language

Consolidation of town-related and transport language from Unit 2

Ich bin / Du bist dran.
Du beginnst.
Ich habe eine (Drei).
Das ist (Rot).
schwarz / rot / gold
Was gibt es in Leipzig?
Es gibt …
Wie kann man in Leipzig fahren?
Man kann …
richtig / falsch
zwei Felder zurück
einmal aussetzen

High-frequency words

Cardinal numbers 1–6
haben
sein
fahren
es gibt
einen / eine / ein
man kann
richtig, falsch
was?
wie?

Mathematics

Using a die, counting spaces in a board game

Resources

CD 3, track 25
Workbooks A and B, p.54
Dice or spinners, counters
Echo Elektro 1 TPP, Mod 6 3.1–3.4

Starter 4.4/Y7

Aim
To introduce the language needed for playing a board game in German.

Before tackling exercise 1, ask pupils to look at the double-page spread and to tell you what they think they will be doing in this lesson (i.e. playing a board game about towns and transport). Explain that they will start by learning some phrases they need to play the game. Write the following jumbled phrases on the board or an OHT. Ask pupils to arrange each phrase correctly, using prior knowledge of word order and high frequency words, and to guess their meanings.

beginnst du	(*Du beginnst* – You start)
eine habe ich Vier	(*Ich habe eine Vier* – I've got a four)
das Rot ist	(*Das ist Rot* – That's red)
aussetzen einmal falsch	(*Falsch! Einmal aussetzen* – Wrong! Miss one turn)
bin dran ich	(*Ich bin dran* – My turn)

Hör zu und lies. 1.1/Y7

Listening/Reading. Pupils listen to and read the conversation. With a weaker class, you may wish to then translate the conversation, whilst looking at the game board, to make sure they are absolutely clear about how the game progresses. At this stage, or after completing exercise 2, ask a volunteer 'spokesperson' to tell the class key facts about the coloured squares in the game.

Schwarz = Go back 2 spaces and wait until your next turn.

Rot = Reply with *es gibt* + the place pictured.

Gold = Reply with *man kann … fahren* + the transport pictured.

Miss a turn if answers are incorrect.

CD 25

- *Du beginnst.*
- *Ich habe eine Vier. Eins, zwei, drei, vier.*
- *Das ist Rot. Was gibt es in Leipzig?*
- *Es gibt eine Kirche.*
- *Richtig! Ich bin dran. Ich habe eine Sechs. Eins, zwei, drei, vier, fünf, sechs.*
- *Das ist Gold. Wie kann man in Leipzig fahren?*
- *Man kann mit dem Zug fahren.*
- *Falsch! Man kann mit der Straßenbahn fahren. Einmal aussetzen! Ich bin dran.*

2 Wie heißt das auf Englisch? Was passt zusammen? (AT3/2) 5.4

Reading. Pupils check their understanding of key phrases for playing a board game by matching them to the correct English translation. They could then chorus the phrases to practise pronunciation.

Answers
1 c **2** a **3** e **4** b **5** d

3 Gruppenarbeit: das Leipzigspiel. (AT2/3–4) 1.4b/Y7

Speaking. Pupils play the game in pairs or groups of 3. Each group needs a die or spinner, and each pupil a counter. Remind weaker pupils that they will find all the words they need in the previous unit of their book. More able pupils should aim for accuracy in their use of *es gibt* and *mit der / dem,* and could extend their conversations considerably by including opinions and other conversational language.

Plenary: Mini-Test 5.8

Aim

To review language learned to date and identify areas for improvement.

Pupils work in pairs to check the language they have learned so far in this chapter, using the **Mini-Test** checklist. Ask pupils which points their partners found most difficult. Give pupils the task of improving those points by next lesson. Partners could then test them again.

4 Wo ist der Markt?

Learning targets
- Asking for and giving directions
- Understanding the difference between *du* and *Sie*

Key framework objectives
5.6 Strategies – reading aloud

Grammar
- Use of *du* and *Sie*
- Introduction to the imperative

Key language
Wo ist … ?
der Markt / Park
die Kirche / Post
das Rathaus / Schwimmbad / Verkehrsamt
Geh / Gehen Sie …
links
rechts
geradeaus
Nimm / Nehmen Sie …
die erste / zweite / dritte Straße
bitte
danke

High-frequency words
wo?
geh / gehen Sie
nimm / nehmen Sie
Sie
erste / zweite / dritte
bitte
danke

Resources
CD 3, tracks 26–29
Workbooks A and B, p.55
Arbeitsblatt 6.3, p.103
Echo Elektro 1 TPP, Mod 6 4.1–4.7

Starter 1 4.2/Y7

Aim

To introduce and practise basic vocabulary for giving directions.

Blindfold directions game: tell the class that they are going to learn how to give and understand directions in German. Write the three key words *links, rechts, geradeaus* and briefly introduce them by means of pointing and repetition. Ask for a volunteer who does not mind being blindfolded, and get another pupil to tie a scarf around his/her eyes. Choose reliable members of the class to direct the volunteer safely around furniture to the opposite corner of the room, by calling out the relevant direction word whenever a change of direction is needed. Involve as many pupils as possible by frequently changing the 'caller'.

1 Hör zu. Finde die Paare. (1–6) (AT1/1) 1.1/Y7

Listening. Pupils listen to the recording and match the words they hear to the correct directions icon.

26

1 links
2 die erste Straße links
3 geradeaus
4 die zweite Straße links
5 rechts
6 die dritte Straße rechts

Answers
1 b 2 d 3 a 4 e 5 c 6 f

2 Hör zu. Sieh dir den Plan von Echostadt an. Wo geht man hin? (1–6) (AT1/2) 1.1/Y7

Listening. Pupils listen to the directions given, follow them on the map and work out which place they are being directed to.

1 – Wo ist [beep], bitte?
– Geh geradeaus und nimm die erste Straße links.
– Danke.
– Bitte.

2 – Guten Tag. Wo ist hier [beep], bitte?
– Also. Gehen sie geradeaus und nehmen Sie die dritte Straße links.
– Danke schön.
– Bitte sehr.

3 – Entschuldigen Sie, bitte. Wo ist [beep], bitte?
– Gehen Sie geradeaus und nehmen Sie die zweite Straße rechts.
– Danke.
– Bitte.

4 – Hallo. Wo ist [beep], bitte?
– Geh geradeaus und nimm die zweite Straße links.
– Danke schön.
– Bitte sehr.

5 – Wo ist [beep], bitte?
– Geh geradeaus und nimm die dritte Straße rechts.
– Danke.
– Bitte.

6 – *Wo ist [beep], bitte?*
– *Geh geradeaus und nimm die erste Straße rechts.*
– *Danke.*
– *Bitte.*

Answers
1 a **2** c **3** e **4** b **5** f **6** d

3 Partnerarbeit. (AT2/2) 1.4b/Y7

Speaking. Pupils follow the model dialogue given in order to ask for and give directions to four different places on the map, as indicated by the picture cues.

Suggestion

Quick finishers could create further dialogues for the remaining places on the map. They could then write out complete dialogues, perhaps including greetings or other extra language.

Starter 2 4.2/Y7

Aim

To reinforce the language learnt in the previous lesson for asking for and giving simple directions.

Information-gap speaking task: give out copies of **Arbeitsblatt 6.3.** Pupils each fold their sheet (or a single copy could be cut in two) so that one partner is looking at role A and the other at role B. Before starting, elicit the key language of asking for and giving directions, writing this on the board as necessary for support. Pairs work through the necessary dialogues, and label the 'missing' places on their maps.

4 Hör zu: „du" oder „Sie"? (1–6) (AT1/1) 1.1/Y7

Listening. Pupils listen again to the recording from exercise 2, and identify whether *geh* – for somebody being addressed as *du* – or *gehen Sie,* is used. Before playing the recording, look at the **ECHO-Tipp** panel with the class. After checking answers, draw pupils' attention to the imperative forms in the **ECHO-Detektiv** before starting exercise 5.

28

1 – *Wo ist der Markt, bitte?*
– *Geh geradeaus und nimm die erste Straße links.*
– *Danke.*
– *Bitte.*

2 – *Guten Tag. Wo ist hier das Rathaus, bitte?*
– *Also. Gehen Sie geradeaus und nehmen Sie die dritte Straße links.*
– *Danke schön.*
– *Bitte sehr.*

3 – *Entschuldigen Sie, bitte. Wo ist die Kirche, bitte?*
– *Gehen Sie geradeaus und nehmen Sie die zweite Straße rechts.*
– *Danke.*
– *Bitte.*

4 – *Hallo. Wo ist die Post, bitte?*
– *Geh geradeaus und nimm die zweite Straße links.*
– *Danke schön.*
– *Bitte sehr.*

5 – *Hallo. Wo ist das Verkehrsamt, bitte?*
– *Geh geradeaus und nimm die dritte Straße rechts.*
– *Danke.*
– *Bitte.*

6 – *Wo ist der Park, bitte?*
– *Geh geradeaus und nimm die erste Straße rechts.*
– *Danke.*
– *Bitte.*

Answers
1 du **2** Sie **3** Sie **4** du **5** du

ECHO-Detektiv: Giving instructions

5.1

This formalises for pupils the imperative of *gehen* and *nehmen*, in the *du* and *Sie* forms.

5 Wo ist das in Echostadt? Schreib Dialoge. „Du" oder „Sie"? (AT4/3) 5.1

Writing. Pupils write directions for each of the unknown people shown, taking into account their evident age in order to decide whether to use the *du* or *Sie* form.

Answers
1 Geh geradeaus und nimm die zweite Straße rechts.
2 Gehen Sie geradeaus und nehmen Sie die dritte Straße rechts.

\+ Pupils who finish quickly could write further directions to places on the map, using the *du* or *Sie* form. Partners could then work out the destinations.

6 Hör zu und sing mit. 5.6

Listening. Pupils listen, then have a go at singing. For authenticity, divide them into two groups to sing the questions and directions. For further ideas on how to use this exercise, see Exploiting the songs on page 9.

29

Wo ist bitte der Marktplatz?
Geh hier geradeaus.
Nimm die erste Straße links.
Das ist fünf Minuten vom Haus!

Danke, danke, danke.
Bitte, bitte, bitte.

Ich fahre in die Stadt.
Gibt es hier ein Schloss?
Ja, geh geradeaus.
Das Schloss ist neben der Post!

Danke, danke, danke.
Bitte, bitte, bitte.

Ich gehe heute schwimmen.
Gibt es hier ein Schwimmbad?
Ja, nimm die dritte Straße links.
Das geht schnell mit dem Rad!

Danke, danke, danke.
Bitte, bitte, bitte.

Plenary

4.2/Y7

Aim

To encourage pupils to reflect on what they have learnt in this unit.

Discuss with pupils the usefulness for tourists of knowing how to ask for and understand directions. Tell them to imagine they have to teach these useful phrases to a friend or relative who is going to a German-speaking country for work or on holiday. What would they need to explain, and which would be the most important words? Elicit a few ideas (key words, polite words, question form), then get pupils to work in pairs for a few minutes – one 'teaching' the other the language needed. The 'learners' should ask their 'teacher' relevant questions if all is not clear. Finally, ask for nominations of a good 'teacher' to demonstrate to the class.

Alternatively, you may wish to use the song as your plenary.

5 An der Imbissbude

Learning targets

- Buying food and drink at a snack stand using euros
- Using *ich möchte* to say what you would like

Key framework objectives

3.2/Y7 Culture – (b) challenging stereotypes

5.3 Strategies – English/other languages

Grammar

- *ich möchte* + direct object
- *sie sind* (receptive)
- Identifying nouns, verbs, adjectives
- Nouns written with capital letter (revision)

Key language

ich möchte
einmal / zweimal / dreimal
Bratwurst
Hamburger
Pizza
Pommes
Schaschlik
Ketchup
Mayonnaise
Senf
Kaffee
Tee
mit Milch / Zitrone
Cola
Limonade
Das macht …
Euro
Cent

High-frequency words

Cardinal numbers 1–100
Guten Tag
danke
bitte
Auf Wiedersehen
ich möchte
einmal / zweimal / dreimal
mit
sie sind
das macht

Mathematics

Calculating prices

Resources

CD 3, tracks 30–31
Workbooks A and B, p.56
Arbeitsblatt 6.4, p.104
Flashcards 89–96
Echo Elektro 1 TPP, Mod 6 5.1–5.6

Starter 1 5.3

Aim

To look at words for food and drink which are used in more than one language.

Give pupils 30 seconds to look for any food and drink words that they recognise from other languages, using the snack list on page 104 of their books. Discuss their findings (they do not need to write them down at this stage), and which language they think each comes from (see answers for exercise 1). You could then ask them why this might be, e.g. international food trends, adopting popular foods from other countries. Point out that although the words look the same, they may be pronounced differently.

1 Essen ist international! Welche Wörter erkennst du schon? (AT3/1) 5.3

Reading. Pupils read through the list of snack items, and write down any they recognise from other languages. They could then look up the meanings of any remaining words and make a note of them.

Answers

Hamburger = used in English ('Hamburger steak', i.e. steak in Hamburg style)
Cola = used in English
Ketchup = used in English (Chinese origin)
Limonade = French
Mayonnaise = used in English (French)
Pizza = used in English (Italian)
Pommes (frites) = French
Schaschlik = Turkish, via Russian

ECHO-Tipp 3.2b/Y7

Ask if any pupils have seen such a snack stand in other countries, and whether they drink tea with lemon or eat chips with mayonnaise. You could point out that Germans think it strange to put salt and vinegar on chips.

2 Hör zu. Was möchten sie? (1–6) (AT1/4) 1.1/Y7

Listening. Pupils listen to the dialogues at a snack stand, and work out which items, and how many of them, each customer wants. Play each dialogue twice, and suggest to pupils that they firstly listen for the items, and secondly for the quantity. Weaker pupils could listen solely for the items.

1 – *Bitte schön?*
– *Ich möchte einmal Bratwurst und einmal Kaffee, bitte.*

2 – *Bitte schön?*
– *Ich möchte einmal Schaschlik, einmal Pommes und einmal Senf, bitte.*

3 – *Guten Tag. Bitte schön?*
– *Ich möchte einmal Pizza und zweimal Limonade, bitte.*

4 – *Guten Tag. Bitte schön?*
– *Guten Tag. Ich möchte dreimal Pommes, zweimal Ketchup und eine Portion Mayonnaise, bitte.*
– *Sonst noch etwas?*
– *Ja, dreimal Cola, bitte.*

5 – *Guten Tag.*
– *Ich möchte zweimal Hamburger und eine Tasse Tee mit Zitrone, bitte.*

6 – *Guten Tag, kann ich dir helfen?*
– *Ja, bitte. Ich möchte viermal Bratwurst, viermal Pommes und achtmal Mayonnaise.*

Answers

1 b × 1, i × 1	**4** e × 3, k × 2, l × 1, g × 3
2 d × 1, e × 1, m × 1	**5** a × 2, j × 1
3 c × 1, f × 2	**6** b × 4, e × 4, l × 8

Suggestion

Refer pupils to the Key Language box, and practise the pronunciation of *ich möchte*. Then practise the use of *einmal*, etc. with food words: hold up one of the flashcards for snack items, and write the number '1' on the board (or indicate with one finger). Get a confident volunteer to ask for that item, using *ich möchte einmal …, bitte*. Repeat, getting the whole class to chorus the answers, and using different numbers and items, perhaps progressing on to pairs of items.

3 Was isst und trinkt Friedrich jeden Tag? Schreib eine Liste. (AT4/3) 5.1

Writing. Pupils use the information in the picture to write a long sentence about what Friedrich eats every day.

Answers

(Accept any order and suitable wording.)

Friedrich isst fünfmal Bratwurst, dreimal Pommes, dreimal Mayonnaise, viermal Hamburger, zweimal Pizza und trinkt achtmal Cola.

Starter 2 3.1/Y7 4.2/Y7

Aims

To revise numbers 1–100.
To practise saying prices in euros and cents.

If you have not already done so, discuss euros and cents with the class, referring pupils to the panel in their books. Explain that they are going to be learning more about buying snacks, so will need to practise saying and understanding prices. Write an example price in figures on the board and elicit how it would be said in German.

Mental arithmetic: read out a short list of single food and drink items and their prices from the price list in the Pupil's Book. Pupils listen, with books closed, and work out the total cost – writing it in figures on paper or a mini-whiteboard and holding it up as soon as they have finished. Confirm the correct answer by writing it on the board.

4 Hör zu. Was möchten sie? Was kostet das? (1–6) (AT1/4) 1.2/Y7

Listening. Pupils listen to dialogues at a snack stand, and note the food and drink items bought and their total cost. Suggest to weaker pupils that they should firstly listen for the food and drink, and then, on second hearing, for the price. Remind them that the spellings and prices are in the price list on page 104. After discussing the answers, you might wish to elicit useful extra phrases heard, and their meanings (e.g. *Was darf es sein? Sonst noch etwas? Das ist alles. Das macht …*) and to mention the use of *danke schön* and *bitte schön*. More confident pupils can then include these in their dialogues in the speaking task which follows.

1 – *Guten Tag. Ich möchte zweimal Pommes und zweimal Cola, bitte.*
– *Zweimal Pommes und zweimal Cola. … Bitte schön. Das macht acht Euro, bitte.*
– *Acht Euro, bitte schön.*
– *Danke schön, auf Wiedersehen.*

2 – *Guten Tag. Was darf's sein?*
– *Ich möchte einmal Pizza, bitte.*
– *Sonst noch etwas?*
– *Nein, danke, das ist alles.*
– *Das macht zwei Euro fünfzig, bitte.*
– *Zwei Euro fünfzig, bitte schön.*
– *Danke schön, auf Wiedersehen.*

3 – Guten Tag. Ich möchte einmal Bratwurst, bitte.
– Einmal Bratwurst. Mit Senf?
– Nein, mit Ketchup bitte.
– Also, einmal Bratwurst und einmal Ketchup, das macht zwei Euro siebzig, bitte.
– Zwei Euro siebzig, bitte schön.
– Danke schön, auf Wiedersehen.

4 – Guten Tag. Bitte schön?
– Ich möchte dreimal Hamburger, bitte.
– Und zu trinken?
– Zweimal Cola und einmal Limonade bitte.
– Dreimal Hamburger, zweimal Cola, und eine Limonade ... Das macht zwölf Euro sechzig, bitte.
– Zwölf Euro sechzig, bitte schön.
– Danke schön, auf Wiedersehen.

5 – Guten Tag. Ich möchte einmal Schaschlik und zweimal Bratwurst, bitte.
– Einmal Schaschlik und zweimal Bratwurst. Sonst noch etwas?
– Ja, dreimal Mineralwasser bitte.
– Also ... Das macht vierzehn Euro, bitte.
– Vierzehn Euro, bitte schön.
– Danke schön, auf Wiedersehen.

6 – Guten Tag. Ich möchte viermal Kaffee und einmal Tee, bitte.
– Ist der Tee mit Milch oder Zitrone?
– Tee mit Zitrone, bitte.
– Sonst noch etwas?
– Nein, danke.
– Also ... Das macht zehn Euro, bitte.
– Zehn Euro, bitte schön.
– Danke schön, auf Wiedersehen.

Answers

1	2x Pommes, 2x Cola	8,00 Euro
2	1x Pizza	2,50 Euro
3	1x Bratwurst, 1x Ketchup	2,70 Euro
4	3x Hamburger, 2x Cola, 1x Limonade	12,60 Euro
5	1x Schaschlik, 2x Bratwurst, 3x Mineralwassser	14,00 Euro
6	4x Kaffee, 1x Tee mit Zitrone	10,00 Euro

5 Partnerarbeit: Mach Dialoge an der Imbissbude. (AT2/4) 1.4b/Y7

Speaking. Pupils work with a partner, taking it in turns to be the customer at a snack stand and to ask for the items pictured. A sample dialogue is given. The vendor will need to refer to the price list at the start of the unit. Quick finishers could go on to make up their own dialogues, or write out a dialogue.

+ When pupils have completed the dialogues for pictures a–e, show them how to use *Sonst noch etwas?* to create their own extended dialogues, adding up the total price at the end.

6 Was essen und trinken sie gern oder nicht gern? (AT3/ 3) 2.1/Y7

Reading. Pupils read the three texts and complete a simple grid in English for each person, to show what they do and do not like eating and drinking. You may wish to elicit the meaning of *sie sind*, and to direct pupils to page 131 for further practice of conjugating the verb *sein*.

Answers

	✓	✗
Nina	hamburger chips lemonade	cola
Viktor	chips mayonnaise cola	tea coffee
Stefanie	kebab ketchup coffee	chips cola lemonade

+ More able pupils could translate one or more of the texts into English.

7 Lies die Texte noch mal. Finde fünf Substantive, fünf Verben und fünf Adjektive. (AT3/3) 2.1/Y7

Reading/Writing. Pupils reread the three texts from exercise 5 in order to identify nouns, verbs and adjectives. Start by reminding them that all nouns are written with capital letters, and that verbs are the second idea in the sentence. Support weaker pupils by writing a few examples on the board. For further exploitation of this activity, see the Treasure hunt activities on page 10.

Suggestion

This could lead into **Arbeitsblatt 6.4** – identifying and using information about words in a dictionary.

8 Was isst du gern oder nicht gern? Schreib einen Text. (AT4/3–4) 2.4a/Y7

Writing. Pupils use the texts from exercise 5 as models for their own writing about what they do and don't like eating. Before starting the task, encourage them to read through the texts and pick out useful phrases that they would like to re-use, drawing particular attention to adding details about opinions and using *gern* and *nicht gern* correctly. You could also discuss with them how they would like to structure the ideas in their writing.

Plenary 5.2

Aim

To focus on selecting useful vocabulary and techniques for learning it.

Top Ten vocab learning: tell the class they must decide on the Top Ten most useful new words or phrases in this unit. Elicit ideas and collate a list of ten on the board, voting on any about which there is disagreement. All pupils copy the list down. Give them a fixed time to work in small groups, helping each other to learn the ten words (decide whether they should learn meanings only, or also correct spelling, depending on the group's level of ability). You could finish with a vocabulary test, or set homework to consolidate learning for a test on these words next lesson.

6 In den Sommerferien

Learning targets

- Talking about your plans for the summer holidays
- Talking about the future (using the present tense)

Key framework objectives

1.2/Y7 Listening – unfamiliar language
2.5/Y7 Writing – different text types
4.5/Y7 Language – (a) future using present tense

Grammar

- Using the present tense to talk about the future

Key language

Was machst du in den Sommerferien?
Für wie lange?
Wie fährst du dahin?
Ich fahre / Wir fahren …
nach Schottland / Wales / Devon / Spanien / Österreich.
für … Tage / Wochen.
mit dem Auto / Bus / Flugzeug / Zug.
Ich bleibe zu Hause.
in den Sommerferien
am Montag / Dienstag / Mittwoch, etc.

High-frequency words

was?
wie?
bleiben
fahren
machen
für
mit
nach
in
zu

ICT

Word-process texts about holiday plans

Resources

CD 3, tracks 32–33
Workbooks A and B, p.57
Arbeitsblatt 6.5, p.105
Arbeitsblatt 6.6, p.106
Echo Elektro 1 TPP, Mod 6 6.1–6.7

Starter 1 4.2/Y7

Aim

To introduce the idea of holiday plans, revise country names, and give pupils the names of other countries they may need for holiday destinations.

Write the following 'word halves' of German names for countries on the board or an OHT, scattered randomly – beginnings on the left-hand side, endings on the right. Some are already known to the class; others will be new. Working in pairs, pupils write down what they think are the correct words, and their English meanings. When most have finished, link up the correct pairings and elicit meanings.

Schott	*land*
Spa	*nien*
Griechen	*land*
Öst	*erreich*
Eng	*land*
Ita	*lien*
Frank	*reich*
Amer	*ika*

1 Was passt zusammen? (AT3/2) 5.4

Reading. Pupils read the statements about plans for the summer holidays, and match each one to the correct picture postcard.

Answers
1 c **2** d **3** b **4** a

Suggestion

At this point, you could ask pupils where they are going in the next summer holidays. Start by giving your own answer, then choose confident members of the class to demonstrate. Elicit the meanings of *ich fahre nach …* and *ich bleibe.*

2 Hör zu. Was sagen sie noch? (1–3) (AT1/3) 1.1/Y7 1.2/Y7

Listening. Pupils listen to the interviews and pick out the extra information given. Before playing the recording, draw attention to the items given for support, and elicit what type of details pupils think will be heard (length of stay and mode of travel). With a less confident class, play the recording twice: encourage pupils to make brief notes on the first hearing and then write out the answers in full on the second hearing.

1 – *Peter, was machst du in den Sommerferien?*
– *Ich fahre nach Österreich.*
– *Für wie lange?*
– *Für zehn Tage.*
– *Wie fährst du dahin?*
– *Wir fahren mit dem Auto.*

2 – *Nina, was machst du in den Sommerferien?*
– *Ich fahre nach Schottland.*
– *Für wie lange?*
– *Für zwei Wochen.*
– *Wie fährst du dahin?*
– *Ich fliege mit dem Flugzeug, und fahre mit dem Auto.*

3 – *Julia, was machst du in den Sommerferien?*
– *Stefanie und ich fahren im August nach Spanien.*
– *Für wie lange?*
– *Für eine Woche.*
– *Wie fahrt ihr dahin?*
– *Wir fahren mit dem Bus.*

Answers
Peter: 10 Tage, Auto
Nina: zwei Wochen, Flugzeug + Auto
Julia und Stefanie: eine Woche, Bus

3 Partnerarbeit. (AT2/4–5) 1.4a/Y7

Speaking. Pairs interview each other about plans for the next summer holidays. Encourage more able pupils to add opinions to their replies. Before starting, make sure the words needed for different countries are known. Explain to more able learners that *nach* is used with named places.

Suggestion

The speaking task could be extended to become a class survey, or to become questions and answers about an imaginary ideal holiday.

Starter 2 4.5a/Y7

Aim

To revise verbs already familiar in the *ich* form, and to practise using them in the *wir* form, in preparation for the next tasks.

Ask the class to stand up, well spaced apart from each other. Tell them to mime any 'holiday' verb you say, to show they understand its meaning. Call out these verbs repeatedly (initially miming as well yourself, to give pupils ideas). If you prefer, make a sentence using each verb. Pupils who mime incorrectly or too slowly must sit down, until only a few remain standing (the winners of round 1). To make it more difficult, you could play the game as *Simon sagt.*

ich fahre (suggest pupils make it clear they are using some form of transport)
ich bleibe
ich spiele
ich gehe (suggest that pupils mime walking)
ich esse
ich trinke
(possible extras: *ich sehe, ich lese, ich besuche, ich höre*)

For round 2, pupils move to stand in groups of four or five. Elicit the meaning of *wir.* Call out the same verbs, but this time using the *wir* form. If any group member mimes incorrectly or too slowly, the whole group has to sit down, until only one winning group is left.

ECHO-Detektiv: Talking about the future 4.5a/Y7

Reinforce the fact that the present tense can be used to talk about the future by asking pupils to tell you one thing they are going to do this weekend or in the summer holidays. This could simply be a sentence with *ich fahre nach …* , or could include other verbs (*ich esse, ich spiele, ich besuche, ich sehe,* etc.). More able pupils could use the *wir* form or make compound sentences. You could also use **Arbeitsblatt 6.6**. For further practice, see **Grammatik** page 131.

4 Füll die Lücken (1–6) mit dem richtigen Verb aus. (AT3/5) 2.1/Y7 2.2a/Y7

Reading. Pupils focus on the first two paragraphs of the text, paying attention to details in order to select the correct verb and its form from the panel, for insertion into each gap. More able pupils should try this task without looking at the panel, using it only to check their answers. Before starting the task, give pupils one minute to skim the whole text. Ask them to tell you how difficult they find it, what it is about, and to outline the content of each of the three paragraphs.

Answers
1 fahre **2** fahren **3** haben **4** ist **5** gibt **6** kann

5 Was machen sie am Montag, Dienstag, usw.? (AT3/5) 2.1/Y7

Reading. Pupils now read the final paragraph of the text and work out what Julia's plans are for each day of the holiday, matching pictures to days.

Answers

Mo.	a, d	Do.	a, b, g
Di.	a, h	Fr.	a, e
Mi.	a, f	Sa.	a, c

ECHO-Detektiv: Time phrases for talking about the future 4.5a/Y7

This highlights a number of time phrases for talking about the future with the present tense. Here, you could ask pupils what phrases they use in English and show that there are equivalent phrases that they will both see and use in German. Highlight the point that these are the main clue that someone is talking about the future when they use the present tense, so pupils should learn them carefully.

6 Hör zu und füll die Tabelle aus. (1–3) (AT1/5) 1.1/Y7 1.2/Y7

Listening. Pupils listen to three longer passages about holiday plans, and note the required details in a copy of the grid. Weaker pupils could concentrate on filling in just the first two or three columns, perhaps listening for one item each time they hear the recording. Alternatively, groups of pupils could each listen for a different item.

33

1 *Hallo. Also, meine Pläne für die Sommerferien. Naja, wir fahren nach Toulouse in Frankreich. Ich war auch letztes Jahr dort. Wir fahren mit dem Auto und wir bleiben zwei Wochen im August. Was wir dort machen … ? Also, wir besuchen Freunde und .. ah ja … wir gehen wandern. Das ist alles ein bisschen langweilig. Ich mag das Essen in Frankreich, aber mein Französisch ist nicht sehr gut!*

2 *Was ich in den Sommerferien mache? Nicht sehr viel, aber ich fahre nach München zu meiner Großmutter. Ich fahre mit dem Zug dorthin und ich bleibe drei Tage. Meine Großmutter ist sehr lustig! Wir gehen in die Stadt, wir sehen fern und wir faulenzen auf dem Balkon. Es ist immer super in München und nie langweilig!*

3 *In den Sommerferien fahre ich mit meinem Vater nach London. Wir fliegen mit dem Flugzeug und bleiben eine Woche dort. Wir gehen in die Stadt und ins Kino. Man kann auch im Hotel schwimmen gehen oder Squash spielen. Und was noch? Ach ja … Ich möchte den Buckingham Palast sehen. Das ist wirklich toll!*

Answers

	Where?	How travelling?	How long for?	Plans	Opinion
1	France	car	2 weeks	visit friends, hiking	boring, good food, bad French
2	Munich (Grandmother)	train	3 days	go into town, watch TV, laze on balcony	super, never boring, Grandmother is funny
3	London	plane	1 week	go into town, cinema, swim/ squash, Buckingham Palace	great

7 Schreib über deine Phantasieferien mit einem Freund / einer Freundin. (AT4/4–5) 2.5/Y7

Writing. Pupils write a few sentences, or a more extended text, about an imaginary plan for a holiday with a friend. They should model their writing on the text about Julia in exercise 3. A writing frame is provided for additional support and you may wish to use **Arbeitsblatt 6.5** to guide pupils through improving their written accuracy. Encourage more confident pupils to include opinions and extra details. The finished texts will be of interest to others in the class, and can be used for the plenary below.

Suggestion

Pupils could word-process their texts and add visuals to enhance their work.

ECHO-Tipp 5.1

This reminds pupils how to order their sentences with the verb as the second idea, when including time expressions.

Plenary 4.1/Y7

Aims

To consolidate the language of this unit.
To practise authentic pronunciation and intonation.

Select pupils who have completed exercise 7 to read aloud their text about an imaginary holiday. The rest of the class listen and try to remember three facts from what they have heard – elicit these afterwards (in English, or in German using the third person singular, depending on the abilities of the group). Finally, pupils vote on their favourite text from those heard.

Lernzieltest

This is a checklist of language covered in Chapter 6. Pupils can work with the checklist in pairs to check what they have learned. Points which directly address grammar and structures are marked with a G. There is a **Lernzieltest** sheet in the Resource and Assessment File (page 108). Encourage pupils to look back at the chapter and to use the grammar section to revise what they are unclear about.

You can also use the **Lernzieltest** as an end-of-chapter plenary.

Wiederholung

This is a revision page to prepare pupils for the **Kontrolle** at the end of the chapter.

Resources

CD 3, track 34

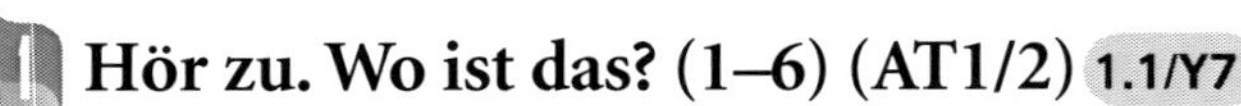

1 Hör zu. Wo ist das? (1–6) (AT1/2) 1.1/Y7

Listening. Referring to the map, pupils listen and work out which place on the map they are being directed to.

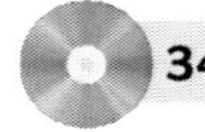

34

1 – *Guten Tag. Wo ist hier die Post, bitte?*
– *Also. Gehen Sie geradeaus und nehmen Sie die erste Straße rechts.*
– *Danke schön.*
– *Bitte sehr.*

2 – *Hallo. Wo ist das Schwimmbad, bitte?*
– *Geh geradeaus und nimm die zweite Straße links.*
– *Danke.*
– *Bitte.*

3 – *Entschuldigen Sie, bitte. Wo ist das Verkehrsamt?*
– *Gehen Sie geradeaus und nehmen Sie die erste Straße links.*
– *Danke schön.*
– *Bitte sehr.*

4 – *Guten Tag. Wo ist der Bahnhof, bitte?*
– *Geh geradeaus und nimm die dritte Straße rechts.*
– *Danke.*
– *Bitte.*

5 – *Wo ist der Park, bitte?*
– *Geh geradeaus und nimm die dritte Straße links.*
– *Danke.*
– *Bitte.*

6 – *Guten Tag, wo ist die Kirche?*
– *Gehen Sie geradeaus und nehmen Sie die zweite Straße rechts.*

Answers

1 d die Post
2 b das Schwimmbad
3 a das Verkehrsamt
4 f der Bahnhof
5 c der Park
6 e die Kirche

2 Partnerarbeit. (AT2/3) 1.4b/Y7

Speaking. Working in pairs, pupils create four dialogues, following the model and illustrations given, between customer and vendor at a snack stand.

3 Wie ist die richtige Reihenfolge? (AT3/4) 2.1/Y7

Reading. Pupils read the leaflet about Leipzig, and arrange the illustrations in the order that they are mentioned in the text.

Answers

c, g, e, l, k, b, i, d, a, j, h, f

4 Was machst du in den Sommerferien? Schreib acht Sätze. (AT4/3–5) 4.4/Y7

Writing. Pupils write sentences about their real or imaginary plans for the summer holidays. These could simply be leisure phrases for activities they do at home. Some pupils may be able to form compound sentences or include opinions.

SELF-ACCESS READING AND WRITING AT TWO LEVELS

A Reinforcement

 1 Wo geht man hin? (AT3/2 AT4/1) 2.1/Y7

Reading. Pupils read the speech bubbles giving directions, refer to the map, and copy the correct word from those provided, to show where they are being directed to.

Answers
1 das Verkehrsamt
2 der Bahnhof
3 das Schwimmbad
4 das Rathaus
5 die Kirche

2 Ordne das Gespräch. (AT3/3) 2.1/Y7

Reading. Pupils work out the correct order for the lines of a conversation at a snack bar. They could then write the conversation out.

Answers
b, e, a, d, f, c

3 Schreib die Tabelle ab und ordne die Wörter der richtigen Kategorie zu. (AT3/1 AT4/1) 4.2/Y7

Reading/Writing. Pupils make a copy of the grid, and write each item of vocabulary in the correct column.

Answers

In der Stadt:	Markt, Schwimmbad
Transport:	Auto, Zug
Wo?:	links, Straße
Essen:	Senf, Wurst
Trinken:	Bier, Tee
Land:	Irland, die Schweiz
Großstadt:	Berlin, Bern

4 Schreib noch drei Wörter für jede Kategorie. (AT4/1) 4.2/Y7

Writing. Pupils write three more ideas of their own in each column, referring back through the chapter for ideas if necessary.

B Extension

 1 Ist das Osnabrück oder Quakenbrück? (AT3/4) 2.1/Y7 2.2a/Y7

Reading. Pupils scan the texts about two places in North Germany, and decide whether each picture represents what is said about Osnabrück or Quakenbrück. Some pictures apply to both places. They record the answers in a simple grid.

Answers
Osnabrück: c, d, e, g, i, k
Quakenbrück: a, b, d, f, g, h, j, k

2 Richtig (R), falsch (F) oder nicht im Text (N)? (AT3/4) 2.1/Y7

Reading. Pupils read the texts in greater detail, and decide whether each statement is true, false, or not mentioned. Pupils could re-write the false sentences correctly.

Answers
1 falsch (Großstadt)
2 richtig
3 nicht im Text
4 falsch (jeden Freitag)
5 richtig
6 nicht im Text

3 Schreib Pläne für einen Tag in Quakenbrück. (AT4/5) 2.4a+b/Y7

Writing. Pupils write imaginary plans for a day in Quakenbrück. Remind them that the present tense can be used to talk about the future, and that they should take ideas for activities from the text. Encourage them to use *wir* as well as *ich*. Some pupils may be able to include clock times, and to form compound sentences.

Übungsheft A, Seite 52

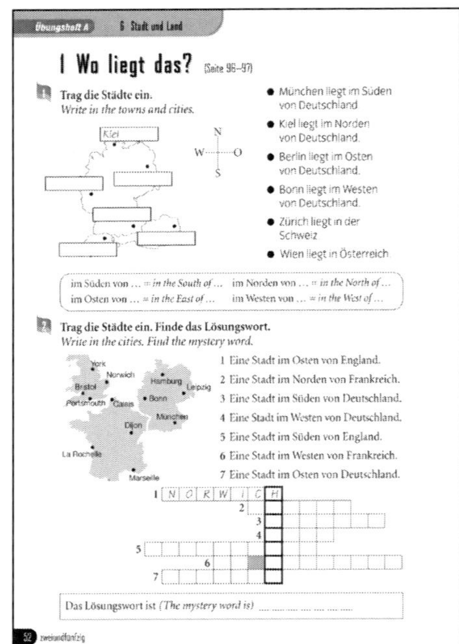
Übungsheft A 6 Stadt und Land

1 Wo liegt das? (Seite 96–97)

1 Trag die Städte ein. *Write in the towns and cities.*

- München liegt im Süden von Deutschland
- Kiel liegt im Norden von Deutschland
- Berlin liegt im Osten von Deutschland
- Bonn liegt im Westen von Deutschland
- Zürich liegt in der Schweiz
- Wien liegt in Österreich

im Süden von … = *in the South of …* im Norden von … = *in the North of …*
im Osten von … = *in the East of …* im Westen von … = *in the West of …*

2 Trag die Städte ein. Finde das Lösungswort. *Write in the cities. Find the mystery word.*

1 Eine Stadt im Osten von England.
2 Eine Stadt im Norden von Frankreich.
3 Eine Stadt im Süden von Deutschland.
4 Eine Stadt im Westen von Deutschland.
5 Eine Stadt im Süden von England.
6 Eine Stadt im Westen von Frankreich.
7 Eine Stadt im Osten von Deutschland.

1 N O R W I C H

Das Lösungswort ist (*The mystery word is*) …

52 zweiundfünfzig

1 (AT3 Level 2, AT4 Level 1)

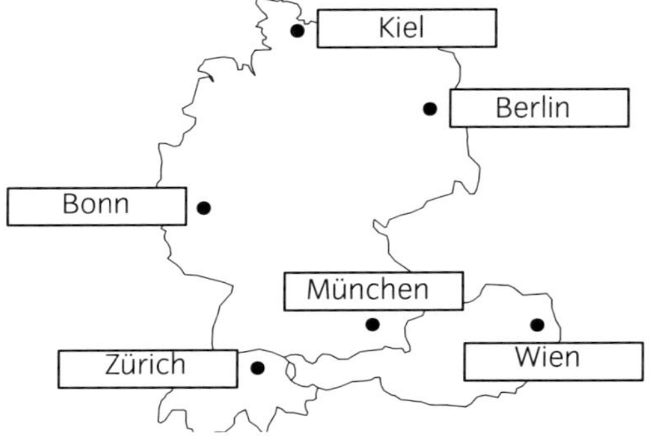

2 (AT3 Level 2) 1 Norwich **2** Calais **3** München **4** Bonn **5** Portsmouth **6** La Rochelle **7** Leipzig

Das Lösungswort ist Hamburg.

Übungsheft B, Seite 52

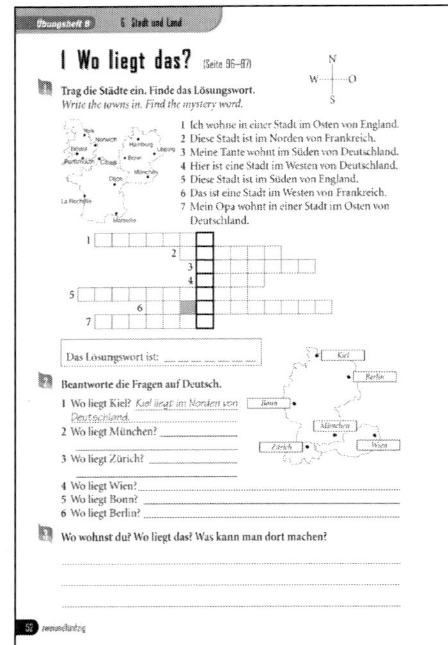
Übungsheft B 6 Stadt und Land

1 Wo liegt das? (Seite 96–97)

1 Trag die Städte ein. Finde das Lösungswort. *Write the towns in. Find the mystery word.*

1 Ich wohne in einer Stadt im Osten von England.
2 Diese Stadt ist im Norden von Frankreich.
3 Meine Tante wohnt im Süden von Deutschland.
4 Hier ist eine Stadt im Westen von Deutschland.
5 Diese Stadt ist im Süden von England.
6 Das ist eine Stadt im Westen von Frankreich.
7 Mein Opa wohnt in einer Stadt im Osten von Deutschland.

Das Lösungswort ist: ______

2 Beantworte die Fragen auf Deutsch.

1 Wo liegt Kiel? *Kiel liegt im Norden von Deutschland.*
2 Wo liegt München?
3 Wo liegt Zürich?
4 Wo liegt Wien?
5 Wo liegt Bonn?
6 Wo liegt Berlin?

3 Wo wohnst du? Wo liegt das? Was kann man dort machen?

52 zweiundfünfzig

1 (AT3 Level 2) 1 Norwich **2** Calais **3** München **4** Bonn **5** Portsmouth **6** La Rochelle **7** Leipzig

Das Lösungswort ist Hamburg.

2 (AT3 Level 2, AT4 Level 2) 1 Kiel liegt im Norden von Deutschland. **2** München liegt im Süden von Deutschland. **3** Zürich liegt in der Schweiz. **4** Wien liegt in Österreich. **5** Bonn liegt im Westen von Deutschland. **6** Berlin liegt im Osten von Deutschland.

3 (AT4 Level 3–4)

Übungsheft A, Seite 53

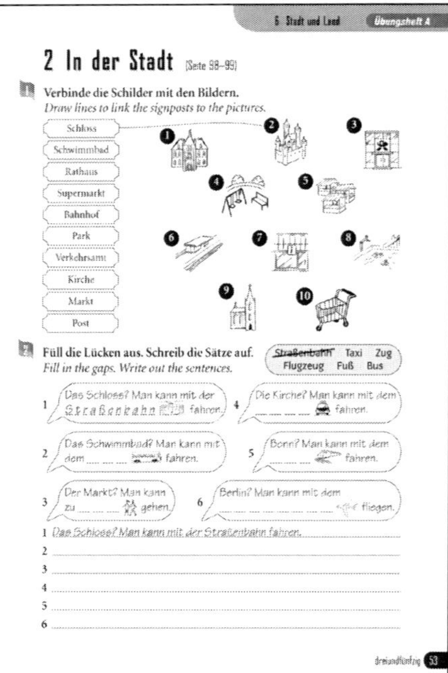
6 Stadt und Land Übungsheft A

2 In der Stadt (Seite 98–99)

1 Verbinde die Schilder mit den Bildern. *Draw lines to link the signposts to the pictures.*

Schloss, Schwimmbad, Rathaus, Supermarkt, Bahnhof, Park, Verkehrsamt, Kirche, Markt, Post

2 Füll die Lücken aus. Schreib die Sätze auf. *Fill in the gaps. Write out the sentences.*

~~Straßenbahn~~ Taxi Zug Flugzeug Fuß Bus

1 Das Schloss? Man kann mit der Straßenbahn fahren.
2 Das Schwimmbad? Man kann mit dem ___ fahren.
3 Der Markt? Man kann zu ___ gehen.
4 Die Kirche? Man kann mit dem ___ fahren.
5 Bonn? Man kann mit dem ___ fahren.
6 Berlin? Man kann mit dem ___ fliegen.

1 *Das Schloss? Man kann mit der Straßenbahn fahren.*

dreiundfünfzig 53

1 (AT3 Level 1) Schloss 2; Schwimmbad 8; Rathaus 1; Supermarkt 10; Bahnhof 6; Park 4; Verkehrsamt 7; Kirche 9; Markt 5; Post 3

2 (AT3 Level 2, AT4 Level 2) **1** Das Schloss? Man kann mit der **Straßenbahn** fahren. **2** Das Schwimmbad? Man kann mit dem **Bus** fahren. **3** Der Markt? Man kann zu **Fuß** gehen. **4** Die Kirche? Man kann mit dem **Taxi** fahren. **5** Bonn? Man kann mit dem **Zug** fahren. **6** Berlin? Man kann mit dem **Flugzeug** fliegen.

Übungsheft B, Seite 53

1 (AT3 Level 4)
1 ✓ **2** ✗ **3** ✗ **4** ✓ **5** ✓ **6** ✗ **7** ✗ **8** ✓

2 (AT4 Level 3)
Liebe Katrin, in meiner Stadt gibt es einen **Bahnhof** und drei **Supermärkte**. Wir haben auch ein **Schloss** und ein **Rathaus**. Es gibt auch drei **Kirchen** und einen **Markt**. Schreib bald, Mani

3 (AT3 Level 2, AT4 Level 3)
1 Das Schloss? Man kann mit dem Taxi fahren. **2** Das Schwimmbad? Man kann mit der Straßenbahn fahren.**3** Nach Bonn? Man kann mit dem Flugzeug fliegen.**4** Nach Berlin? Man kann mit dem Zug fahren.**5** Der Markt? Man kann zu Fuß gehen. **6** Die Kirche? Man kann mit dem Bus fahren.

Übungsheft A, Seite 54

Übungsheft A 6 Stadt und Land

3 Das Leipzigspiel (Seite 100–101)

1 Entziffere die Wörter und schreib die Sätze auf. *Unjumble the words and write out the sentences.*

1 *My turn* = Ich bin **arnd**. *Ich bin dran.*
2 *You start* = Du **nibsteng**. ___
3 *Miss one turn* = **naliEm** aussetzen. ___
4 *Go back two spaces* = Zwei Felder **krüzu**. ___
5 *I've got a three* = Ich **ebah** eine **rieD**. ___

Drei Einmal zurück ~~dran~~ beginnst habe

2 Füll die Lücken aus. *Fill in the gaps.*

Fünf dran ~~beginnst~~ Schwarz habe zurück

54 vierundfünfzig

1 (AT3 Level 2) 1 Ich bin **dran**. **2** Du **beginnst**. **3 Einmal** aussetzen. **4** Zwei Felder **zurück**. **5** Ich **habe** eine **Drei**.

2 (AT3 Level 3, AT4 Level 1) 1 Du **beginnst**. – Danke. **2** Ich habe eine **Fünf**. – Das ist **Schwarz**. **3** Zwei Felder **zurück**! – Ach, nein! **4** Ich bin **dran**.

Übungsheft B, Seite 54

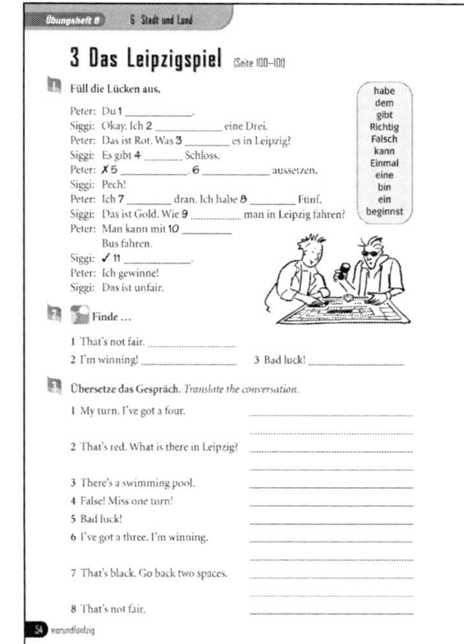
Übungsheft B 6 Stadt und Land

3 Das Leipzigspiel (Seite 100–101)

1 Füll die Lücken aus.

Peter: Du 1 ___.
Siggi: Okay. Ich 2 ___ eine Drei.
Peter: Das ist Rot. Was 3 ___ es in Leipzig?
Siggi: Es gibt 4 ___ Schloss.
Peter: ✗ 5 ___. 6 ___ aussetzen.
Siggi: Pech!
Peter: Ich 7 ___ dran. Ich habe 8 ___ Fünf.
Siggi: Das ist Gold. Wie 9 ___ man in Leipzig fahren?
Peter: Man kann mit 10 ___ Bus fahren.
Siggi: ✓ 11 ___.
Peter: Ich gewinne!
Siggi: Das ist unfair.

habe dem gibt Richtig Falsch kann Einmal eine bin ein beginnst

2 Finde …

1 That's not fair. ___
2 I'm winning! ___ 3 Bad luck! ___

3 Übersetze das Gespräch. *Translate the conversation.*

1 My turn. I've got a four.
2 That's red. What is there in Leipzig?
3 There's a swimming pool.
4 False! Miss one turn!
5 Bad luck!
6 I've got a three. I'm winning.
7 That's black. Go back two spaces.
8 That's not fair.

54 vierundfünfzig

1 (AT3 Level 3, AT4 Level 1) Peter: Du **1 beginnst**. Siggi: Okay. Ich **2 habe** eine Drei. Peter: Das ist Rot. Was **3 gibt** es in Leipzig? Siggi: Es gibt **4 ein** Schloss. Peter: **5 Falsch**. **6 Einmal** aussetzen. Siggi: Pech! Peter: Ich **7 bin** dran. Ich habe **8 eine** Fünf. Siggi: Das ist Gold. Wie **9 kann** man in Leipzig fahren? Peter: Man kann mit **10 dem** Bus fahren. Siggi: **11 Richtig**. Peter: Ich gewinne! Siggi: Das ist unfair.

2 (AT3 Level 2, AT4 Level 2) 1 Das ist unfair. **2** Ich gewinne! **3** Pech!

3 (AT4 Level 4) 1 Ich bin dran. Ich habe eine Vier. **2** Das ist Rot. Was gibt es in Leipzig? **3** Es gibt ein Schwimmbad. **4** Falsch! Einmal aussetzen. **5** Pech! **6** Ich habe eine Drei. Ich gewinne. **7** Das ist Schwarz. Zwei Felder zurück. **8** Das ist unfair.

Übungsheft A, Seite 55

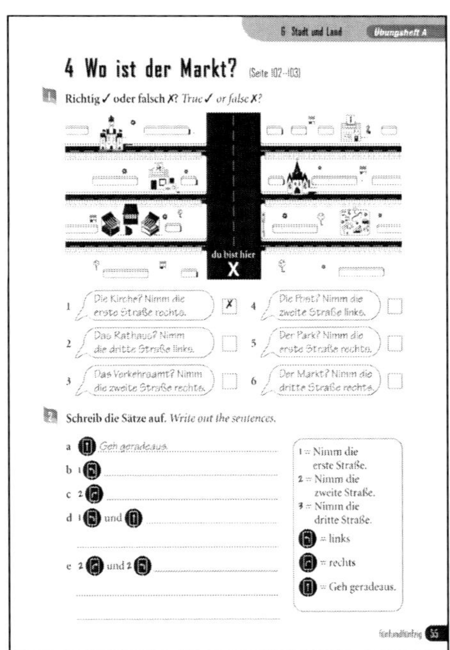
6 Stadt und Land Übungsheft A

4 Wo ist der Markt? (Seite 102–103)

1 Richtig ✓ oder falsch ✗? *True ✓ or false ✗?*

1 Die Kirche? Nimm die erste Straße rechts. ✗
2 Das Rathaus? Nimm die dritte Straße links.
3 Das Verkehrsamt? Nimm die zweite Straße rechts.
4 Die Post? Nimm die zweite Straße links.
5 Der Park? Nimm die erste Straße rechts.
6 Der Markt? Nimm die dritte Straße rechts.

2 Schreib die Sätze auf. *Write out the sentences.*

a *Geh geradeaus.*
b 1 ___
c 2 ___
d 1 und ___
e 2 und 2 ___

1 = Nimm die erste Straße.
2 = Nimm die zweite Straße.
3 = Nimm die dritte Straße.
= links
= rechts
= Geh geradeaus.

fünfundfünfzig 55

1 (AT3 Level 2) 1✗ 2✓ 3✗ 4✓ 5✓ 6✗

2 (AT4 Level 2/3) 1 Geh geradeaus. **2** Nimm die erste Straße links. **3** Nimm die zweite Straße rechts. **4** Nimm die erste Straße links und geh geradeaus. **5** Nimm die zweite Straße rechts und die zweite Straße links.

Übungsheft B, Seite 55

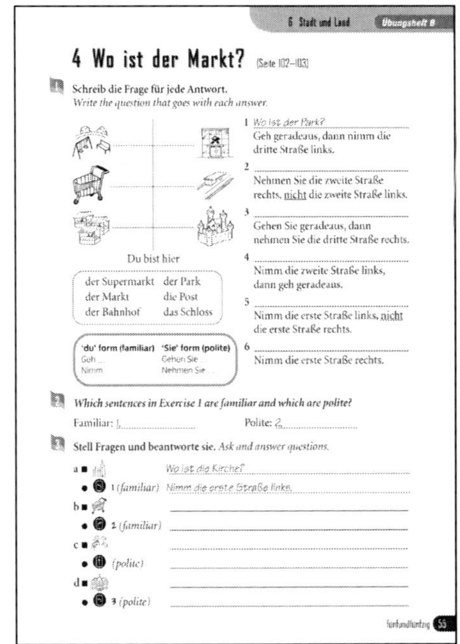
6 Stadt und Land Übungsheft B

4 Wo ist der Markt? (Seite 102–103)

1 Schreib die Frage für jede Antwort. *Write the question that goes with each answer.*

1 *Wo ist der Park?* Geh geradeaus, dann nimm die dritte Straße links.
2 ___ Nehmen Sie die zweite Straße rechts, nicht die zweite Straße links.
3 ___ Gehen Sie geradeaus, dann nehmen Sie die dritte Straße rechts.
4 ___ Nimm die zweite Straße links, dann geh geradeaus.
5 ___ Nimm die erste Straße links, nicht die erste Straße rechts.
6 ___ Nimm die erste Straße rechts.

Du bist hier

der Supermarkt der Park
der Markt die Post
der Bahnhof das Schloss

'du' form (familiar): Geh … Nimm …
'Sie' form (polite): Gehen Sie … Nehmen Sie …

2 *Which sentences in Exercise 1 are familiar and which are polite?*

Familiar: 1, ___ Polite: 2, ___

3 Stell Fragen und beantworte sie. *Ask and answer questions.*

a ■ *Wo ist die Kirche?*
● 1 (familiar) *Nimm die erste Straße links.*
b ■ ___
● 2 (familiar) ___
c ■ ___
● (polite) ___
d ■ ___
● 3 (polite) ___

fünfundfünfzig 55

1 (AT3 Level 3, AT4 Level 2) 1 Wo ist der Park? **2** Wo ist der Bahnhof? **3** Wo ist die Post? **4** Wo ist der Supermarkt? **5** Wo ist der Markt? **6** Wo ist das Schloss?

2 Familiar: 1, 4, 5, 6; Polite: 2, 3

3 (AT3 Level 1, AT4 Level 3) a r Wo ist die Kirche? ● Nimm die erste Straße links. **b** r Wo ist der Supermarkt? ● Nimm die zweite Straße rechts **c** r Wo ist der Park? ● Gehen Sie geradeaus. **d** r Wo ist das Rathaus? ● Nehmen Sie die dritte Straße links.

6 Workbooks

Übungsheft A, Seite 56

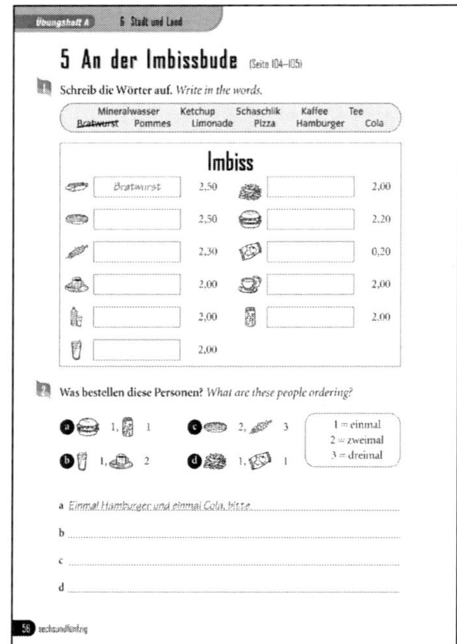
Übungsheft A 6 Stadt und Land

5 An der Imbissbude (Seite 104–105)

1 Schreib die Wörter auf. *Write in the words.*

Mineralwasser Ketchup Schaschlik Kaffee Tee
~~Bratwurst~~ Pommes Limonade Pizza Hamburger Cola

Imbiss

Bratwurst 2,50		2,00
2,50		2,20
2,30		0,20
2,00		2,00
2,00		2,00
2,00		

2 Was bestellen diese Personen? *What are these people ordering?*

a 1, 1 c 2, 3
b 1, 2 d 1, 1

1 = einmal
2 = zweimal
3 = dreimal

a *Einmal Hamburger und einmal Cola, bitte.*
b
c
d

56 sechsundfünfzig

1 (AT3 Level 1, AT4 Level 1)

Imbiss
Bratwurst, Pommes, Pizza, Hamburger, Schaschlik, Ketchup, Kaffee, Tee, Mineralwasser, Cola, Limonade

2 (AT4 Level 2) a Einmal Hamburger und einmal Cola, bitte. **b** Einmal Limonade und zweimal Kaffee, bitte. **c** Zweimal Pizza und dreimal Schaschlik, bitte. **d** Einmal Pommes mit Ketchup, bitte.

Übungsheft A, Seite 57

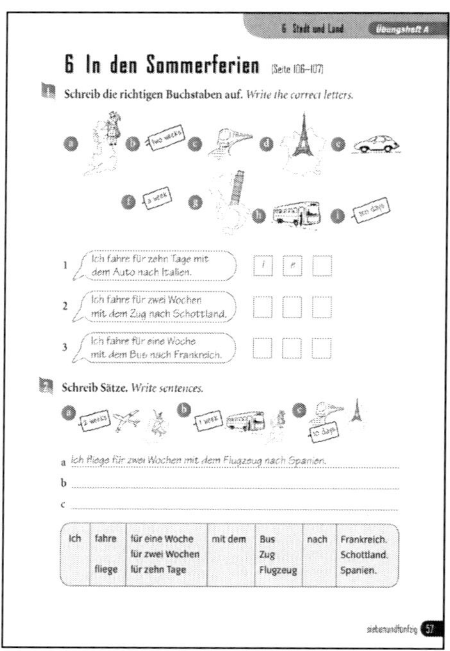
6 Stadt und Land Übungsheft A

6 In den Sommerferien (Seite 106–107)

1 Schreib die richtigen Buchstaben auf. *Write the correct letters.*

1 Ich fahre für zehn Tage mit dem Auto nach Italien. *i* *e*
2 Ich fahre für zwei Wochen mit dem Zug nach Schottland.
3 Ich fahre für eine Woche mit dem Bus nach Frankreich.

2 Schreib Sätze. *Write sentences.*

a *Ich fliege für zwei Wochen mit dem Flugzeug nach Spanien.*
b
c

Ich	fahre fliege	für eine Woche für zwei Wochen für zehn Tage	mit dem	Bus Zug Flugzeug	nach	Frankreich. Schottland. Spanien.

siebenundfünfzig 57

1 (AT 3 Level 2) 1 i, e, g **2** b, c, a **3** f, h, d

2 (AT4 Level 3) 1 Ich fliege für zwei Wochen mit dem Flugzeug nach Spanien. **2** Ich fahre für eine Woche mit dem Bus nach Schottland. **3** Ich fahre für zehn Tage mit dem Zug nach Frankreich.

Übungsheft B, Seite 56

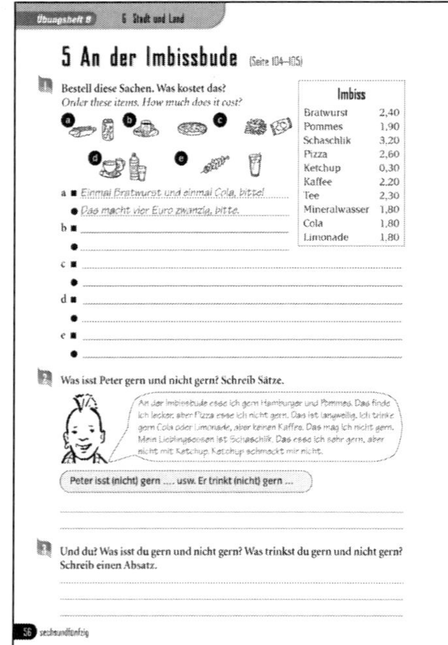
Übungsheft B 6 Stadt und Land

5 An der Imbissbude (Seite 104–105)

1 Bestell diese Sachen. Was kostet das?
Order these items. How much does it cost?

Imbiss	
Bratwurst	2,40
Pommes	1,90
Schaschlik	3,20
Pizza	2,60
Ketchup	0,30
Kaffee	2,20
Tee	2,30
Mineralwasser	1,80
Cola	1,80
Limonade	1,80

a ■ *Einmal Bratwurst und einmal Cola, bitte!*
● *Das macht vier Euro zwanzig, bitte.*
b ■
●
c ■
●
d ■
●
e ■
●

2 Was isst Peter gern und nicht gern? Schreib Sätze.

Peter isst (nicht) gern .... usw. Er trinkt (nicht) gern ...

3 Und du? Was isst du gern und nicht gern? Was trinkst du gern und nicht gern? Schreib einen Absatz.

56 sechsundfünfzig

1 (AT4 Level 2/3)
a r Einmal Bratwurst und einmal Cola, bitte. ● Das macht vier Euro zwanzig, bitte. **b** r Einmal Kaffee und zweimal Pizza, bitte. ● Das macht sieben Euro vierzig, bitte. **c** r Zweimal Pommes mit Ketchup, bitte. ● Das macht vier Euro zehn, bitte. **d** r Einmal Tee und einmal Mineralwasser, bitte. ● Das macht vier Euro zehn, bitte. **e** r Zweimal Schaschlik und dreimal Limonade, bitte. ● Das macht elf Euro achtzig, bitte.

2 (AT3 Level 3, AT 4 Level 3) Peter isst gern Hamburger, Pommes und Schaschlik. Er isst nicht gern Pizza und Ketchup. Er trinkt gern Cola und Limonade. Er trinkt nicht gern Kaffee.

3 (AT4 Level 4)

Übungsheft B, Seite 57

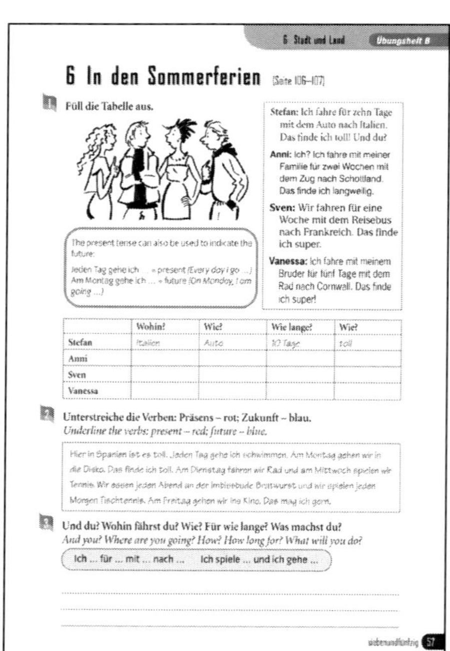
6 Stadt und Land Übungsheft B

6 In den Sommerferien (Seite 106–107)

1 Füll die Tabelle aus.

Stefan: Ich fahre für zehn Tage mit dem Auto nach Italien. Das finde ich toll! Und du?

Anni: Ich? Ich fahre mit meiner Familie für zwei Wochen mit dem Zug nach Schottland. Das finde ich langweilig.

Sven: Wir fahren für eine Woche mit dem Reisebus nach Frankreich. Das finde ich super.

Vanessa: Ich fahre mit meinem Bruder für fünf Tage mit dem Rad nach Cornwall. Das finde ich super!

The present tense can also be used to indicate the future:
Jeden Tag gehe ich … = present (*Every day I go …*)
Am Montag gehe ich … = future (*On Monday, I am going …*)

	Wohin?	Wie?	Wie lange?	Wie?
Stefan	*Italien*	*Auto*	*10 Tage*	*toll*
Anni				
Sven				
Vanessa				

2 Unterstreiche die Verben: Präsens – rot; Zukunft – blau.
Underline the verbs: present – red; future – blue.

Hier in Spanien ist es toll. Jeden Tag gehe ich schwimmen. Am Montag gehen wir in die Disko. Das finde ich toll. Am Dienstag fahren wir Rad und am Mittwoch spielen wir Tennis. Wir essen jeden Abend an der Imbissbude Bratwurst und wir spielen jeden Morgen Tischtennis. Am Freitag gehen wir ins Kino. Das mag ich gern.

3 Und du? Wohin fährst du? Wie? Für wie lange? Was machst du?
And you? Where are you going? How? How long for? What will you do?

Ich ... für ... mit ... nach ... Ich spiele ... und ich gehe ...

siebenundfünfzig 57

1 (AT 3 Level 3, AT4 Level 1) Stefan: Italien, Auto, 10 Tage, toll **Anni**: Schottland, Zug, zwei Wochen, langweilig **Sven**: Frankreich, Bus, eine Woche, super **Vanessa**: Cornwall, Rad, 5 Tage, super

2 (AT3 Level 5) *Underlined in red:* ist, gehe, finde, essen, spielen, mag.

Underlined in blue: gehen, fahren, spielen, gehen.

3 (AT4 Level 4–5)

Übungsheft A, Seite 58

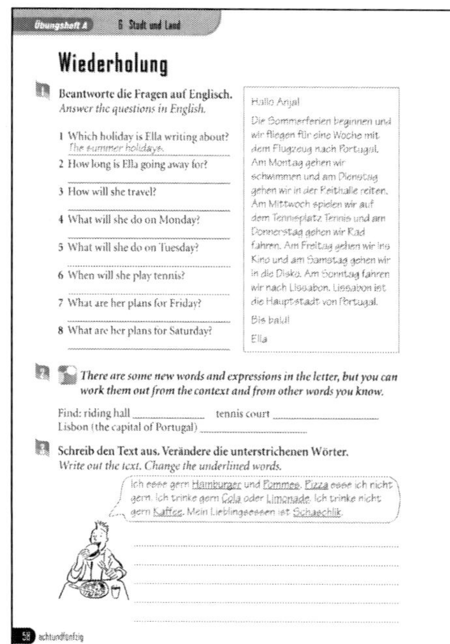

Übungsheft A 6 Stadt und Land

Wiederholung

1 **Beantworte die Fragen auf Englisch.**
Answer the questions in English.

1 Which holiday is Ella writing about? *The summer holidays.*
2 How long is Ella going away for? ______
3 How will she travel? ______
4 What will she do on Monday? ______
5 What will she do on Tuesday? ______
6 When will she play tennis? ______
7 What are her plans for Friday? ______
8 What are her plans for Saturday? ______

Hallo Anja!

Die Sommerferien beginnen und wir fliegen für eine Woche mit dem Flugzeug nach Portugal. Am Montag gehen wir schwimmen und am Dienstag gehen wir in der Reithalle reiten. Am Mittwoch spielen wir auf dem Tennisplatz Tennis und am Donnerstag gehen wir Rad fahren. Am Freitag gehen wir ins Kino und am Samstag gehen wir in die Disko. Am Sonntag fahren wir nach Lissabon. Lissabon ist die Hauptstadt von Portugal.

Bis bald!

Ella

2 *There are some new words and expressions in the letter, but you can work them out from the context and from other words you know.*

Find: riding hall ______ tennis court ______
Lisbon (the capital of Portugal) ______

3 **Schreib den Text aus. Verändere die unterstrichenen Wörter.**
Write out the text. Change the underlined words.

58 achtundfünfzig

1 (AT3 Level 3) 1 The summer holidays. **2** 1 week. **3** By plane. **4** Go swimming. **5** Go riding. **6** On Wednesday. **7** Go to the cinema. **8** Go to the disco.

2 Reithalle, Tennisplatz, Lissabon

3 (AT3 Level 3, AT4 Level 3)

Übungsheft B, Seite 58

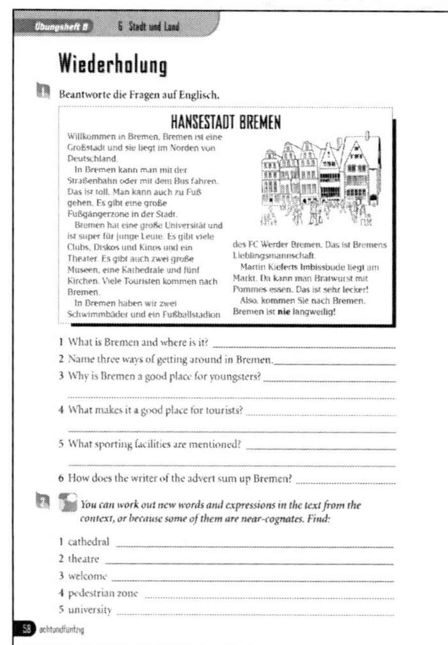

Übungsheft B 6 Stadt und Land

Wiederholung

1 **Beantworte die Fragen auf Englisch.**

HANSESTADT BREMEN

Willkommen in Bremen. Bremen ist eine Großstadt und sie liegt im Norden von Deutschland.

In Bremen kann man mit der Straßenbahn oder mit dem Bus fahren. Das ist toll. Man kann auch zu Fuß gehen. Es gibt eine große Fußgängerzone in der Stadt.

Bremen hat eine große Universität und ist super für junge Leute. Es gibt viele Clubs, Diskos und Kinos und ein Theater. Es gibt auch zwei große Museen, eine Kathedrale und fünf Kirchen. Viele Touristen kommen nach Bremen.

In Bremen haben wir zwei Schwimmbäder und ein Fußballstadion des FC Werder Bremen. Das ist Bremens Lieblingsmannschaft.

Martin Kieferts Imbissbude liegt am Markt. Da kann man Bratwurst mit Pommes essen. Das ist sehr lecker!

Also, kommen Sie nach Bremen. Bremen ist **nie** langweilig!

1 What is Bremen and where is it? ______
2 Name three ways of getting around in Bremen. ______
3 Why is Bremen a good place for youngsters? ______
4 What makes it a good place for tourists? ______
5 What sporting facilities are mentioned? ______
6 How does the writer of the advert sum up Bremen? ______

2 *You can work out new words and expressions in the text from the context, or because some of them are near-cognates. Find:*

1 cathedral ______
2 theatre ______
3 welcome ______
4 pedestrian zone ______
5 university ______

58 achtundfünfzig

1 (AT3 Level 4) 1 It's a city in north Germany. **2** By tram, by bus, on foot. **3** Big university, lots of clubs, discos, cinemas and a theatre. **4** Two large museums, a cathedral and five churches. **5** Two swimming pools and a football stadium. **6** It's never boring!

2 1 Kathedrale **2** Theater **3** Willkommen **4** Fußgängerzone **5** Universität

3 (AT4 Level 5)

Arbeitsblatt 6.1

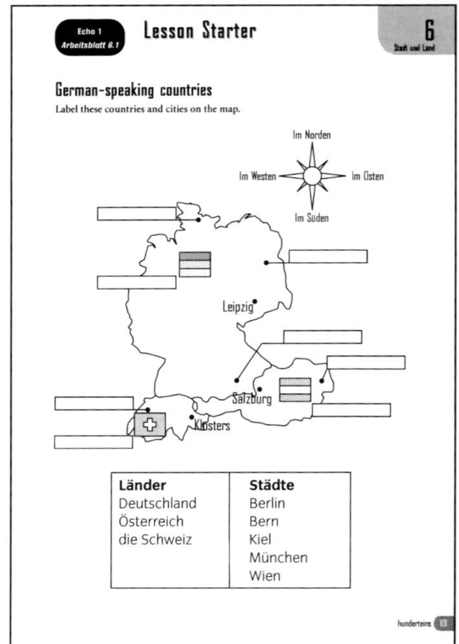

Echo 1 Arbeitsblatt 6.1

Lesson Starter

6 Stadt und Land

German-speaking countries

Label these countries and cities on the map.

Länder	Städte
Deutschland	Berlin
Österreich	Bern
die Schweiz	Kiel
	München
	Wien

hunderteins 101

Deutschland, Österreich, die Schweiz, Kiel, Berlin, München, Wien, Bern

Arbeitsblatt 6.2

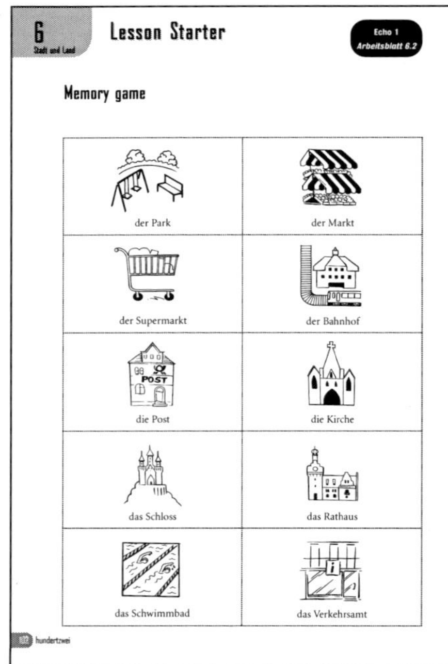

6 Stadt und Land

Lesson Starter

Echo 1 Arbeitsblatt 6.2

Memory game

102 hundertzwei

Arbeitsblatt 6.3

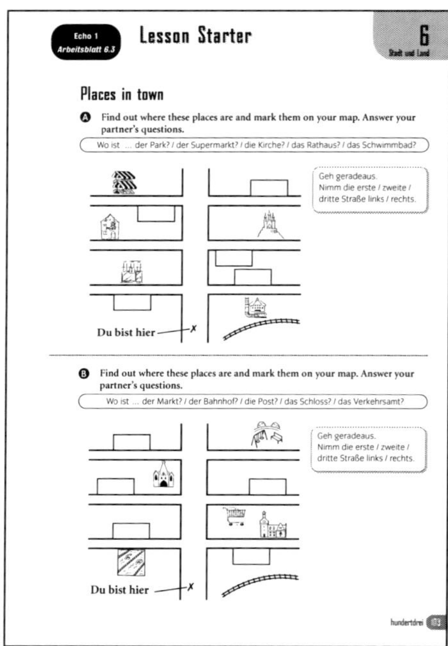

Echo 1 Arbeitsblatt 6.3

Lesson Starter

6 Stadt und Land

Places in town

A Find out where these places are and mark them on your map. Answer your partner's questions.

Wo ist … der Park? / der Supermarkt? / die Kirche? / das Rathaus? / das Schwimmbad?

B Find out where these places are and mark them on your map. Answer your partner's questions.

Wo ist … der Markt? / der Bahnhof? / die Post? / das Schloss? / das Verkehrsamt?

hundertdrei 103

Arbeitsblatt 6.4

6 Stadt und Land

Learning Skills

Echo 1 Arbeitsblatt 6.4

Name: ______________________

Using a dictionary

Beware! The dictionary will give you more information than you actually need. Train yourself to focus on the bit you want.

A Write the correct letters in the boxes.

a – **river** [rivə(r)] *n* Fluss m – b, c, d, e

1 How to pronounce the English word. ☐
2 The German word. ☐
3 The English word. ☐
4 It is masculine (*der*). ☐
5 It is a noun. ☐

B Use a dictionary to find the German for these nouns. Write them out with *der* (m), *die* (f) or *das* (n).

Beispiel: *exhibition* die Ausstellung

1 museum ________ 3 bakery ________
2 car park ________ 4 airport ________

You can recognise **verbs** in the dictionary, by looking for **v**, **vi** or **vt**. The German infinitive will be given (usually ending in **–en**).
You can recognise **adjectives** by looking for **adj**. Some English words can be a verb or an adjective, e.g. 'clean / to clean'. Look carefully for **v** or **adj** to make sure you choose the correct German word.

C Find the German for these verbs and adjectives.

Verbs	Adjectives
1 to juggle ________	6 ugly ________
2 to chew ________	7 fashionable ________
3 to knit ________	8 exciting ________
4 to speak ________	9 tired ________
5 to clean ________	10 clean ________

104 hundertvier

A

1 b **2** d **3** a **4** e **5** c

B

1 das Museum **2** der Parkplatz **3** die Bäckerei **4** der Flughafen

C

1 jonglieren **2** kauen **3** stricken **4** sprechen **5** putzen / sauber machen **6** hässlich **7** modisch **8** spannend **9** müde **10** sauber

Arbeitsblatt 6.5

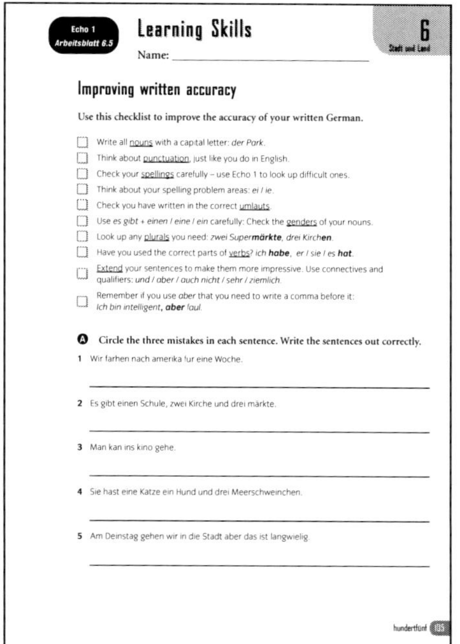

Echo 1 Arbeitsblatt 6.5

Learning Skills

6 Stadt und Land

Name: ____________________

Improving written accuracy

Use this checklist to improve the accuracy of your written German.

- ☐ Write all nouns with a capital letter: *der Park*.
- ☐ Think about punctuation, just like you do in English.
- ☐ Check your spellings carefully – use Echo 1 to look up difficult ones.
- ☐ Think about your spelling problem areas: *ei / ie*.
- ☐ Check you have written in the correct umlauts.
- ☐ Use *es gibt + einen / eine / ein* carefully: Check the genders of your nouns.
- ☐ Look up any plurals you need: *zwei Super**märkte**, drei Kirch**en***.
- ☐ Have you used the correct parts of verbs? *ich **habe**, er / sie / es **hat***.
- ☐ Extend your sentences to make them more impressive. Use connectives and qualifiers: *und / aber / auch nicht / sehr / ziemlich*.
- ☐ Remember if you use *aber* that you need to write a comma before it: *Ich bin intelligent, **aber** faul.*

A Circle the three mistakes in each sentence. Write the sentences out correctly.

1 Wir farhen nach amerika fur eine Woche.

2 Es gibt einen Schule, zwei Kirche und drei märkte.

3 Man kan ins kino gehe.

4 Sie hast eine Katze ein Hund und drei Meerschweinchen.

5 Am Deinstag gehen wir in die Stadt aber das ist langwielig.

hundertfünf 105

Arbeitsblatt 6.6

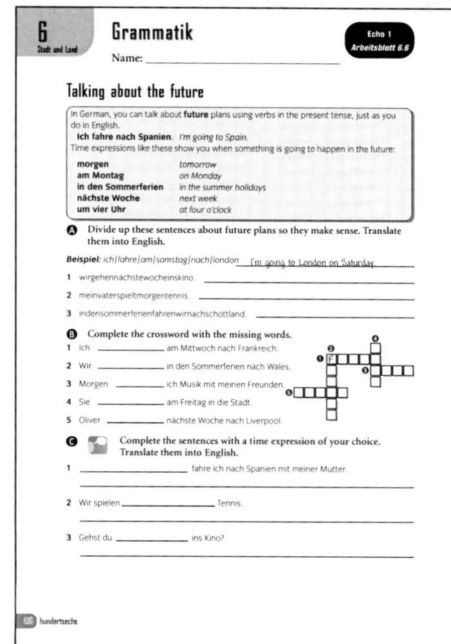

6 Stadt und Land

Grammatik

Echo 1 Arbeitsblatt 6.6

Name: ____________________

Talking about the future

In German, you can talk about **future** plans using verbs in the present tense, just as you do in English.

Ich fahre nach Spanien. *I'm going to Spain.*

Time expressions like these show you when something is going to happen in the future:

morgen	*tomorrow*
am Montag	*on Monday*
in den Sommerferien	*in the summer holidays*
nächste Woche	*next week*
um vier Uhr	*at four o'clock*

A Divide up these sentences about future plans so they make sense. Translate them into English.

Beispiel: *ich|fahre|am|samstag|nach|london* I'm going to London on Saturday.

1 wirgehennächstewocheinskino.

2 meinvaterspieltmorgentennis.

3 indensommerferienfahrenwirnachschottland.

B Complete the crossword with the missing words.

1 Ich ________ am Mittwoch nach Frankreich.

2 Wir ________ in den Sommerferien nach Wales.

3 Morgen ________ ich Musik mit meinen Freunden.

4 Sie ________ am Freitag in die Stadt.

5 Oliver ________ nächste Woche nach Liverpool.

C Complete the sentences with a time expression of your choice. Translate them into English.

1 ________ fahre ich nach Spanien mit meiner Mutter.

2 Wir spielen ________ Tennis.

3 Gehst du ________ ins Kino?

106 hundertsechs

A

1 Wir fa**hr**en nach **A**merika f**ü**r eine Woche. **2** Es gibt ein**e** Schule, zwei Kirche**n** und drei **M**ärkte. **3** Man kan**n** ins **K**ino gehe**n**. **4** Sie ha**t** eine Katze**,** ein**en** Hund und drei Meerschweinchen. **5** Am D**ie**nstag gehen wir in die Stadt**,** aber das ist langw**ei**lig.

A

1 Wir gehen nächste Woche ins Kino. *We're going to the cinema next week.*

2 Mein Vater spielt morgen Tennis. *My father is playing tennis tomorrow.*

3 In den Sommerferien fahren wir nach Schottland. *In the summer holidays we're going to Scotland.*

B

1 fahre **2** fahren **3** höre **4** geht **5** fährt